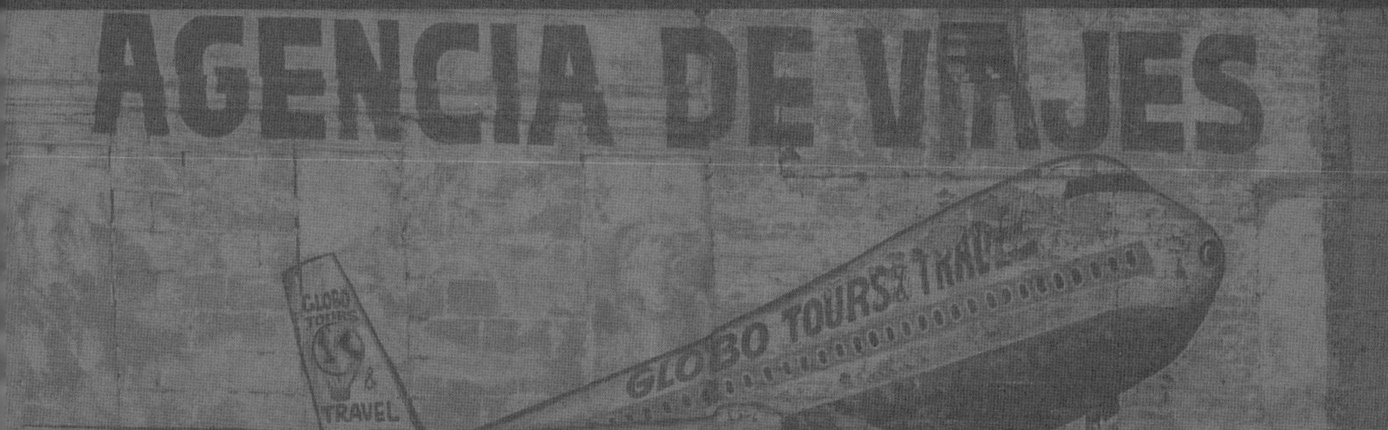
AGENCIA DE VIAJES
GLOBO TOURS & TRAVEL
GLOBO TOURS
¡COMPRE SU BOLETO!

For the Curious Traveler

Los Angeles

Andrea Richards
Giovanni Simeone

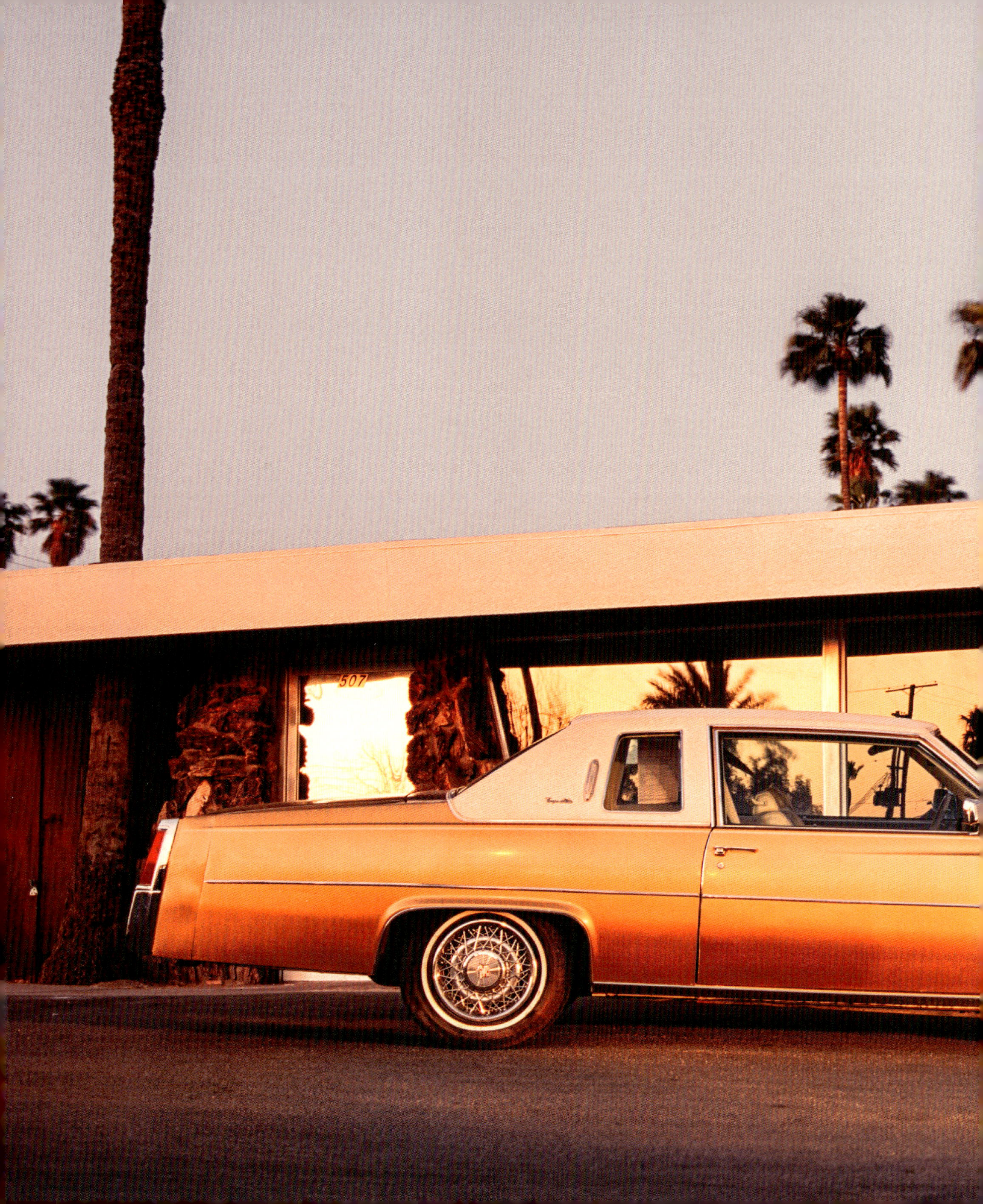
507

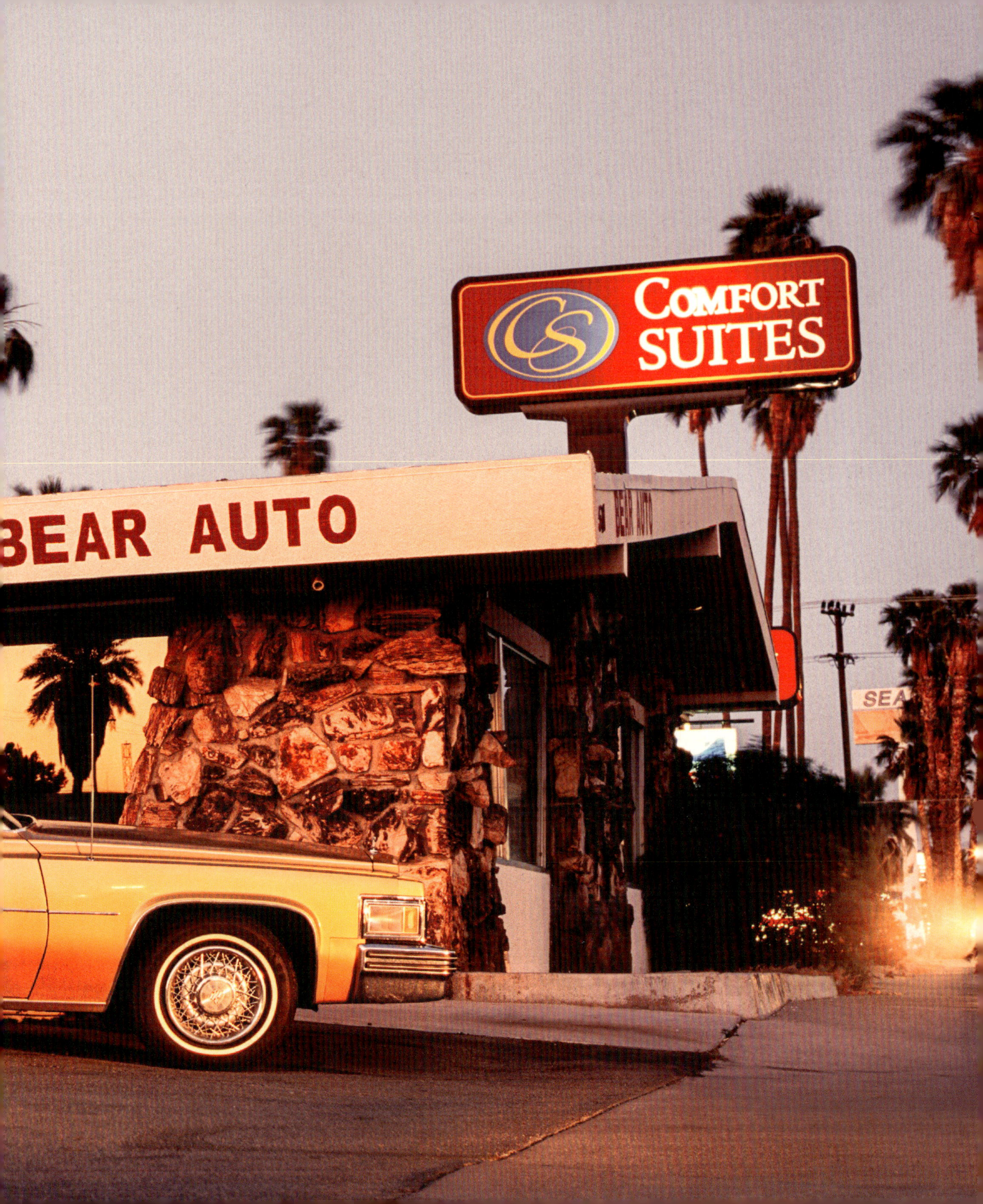
COMFORT
SUITES
BEAR AUTO

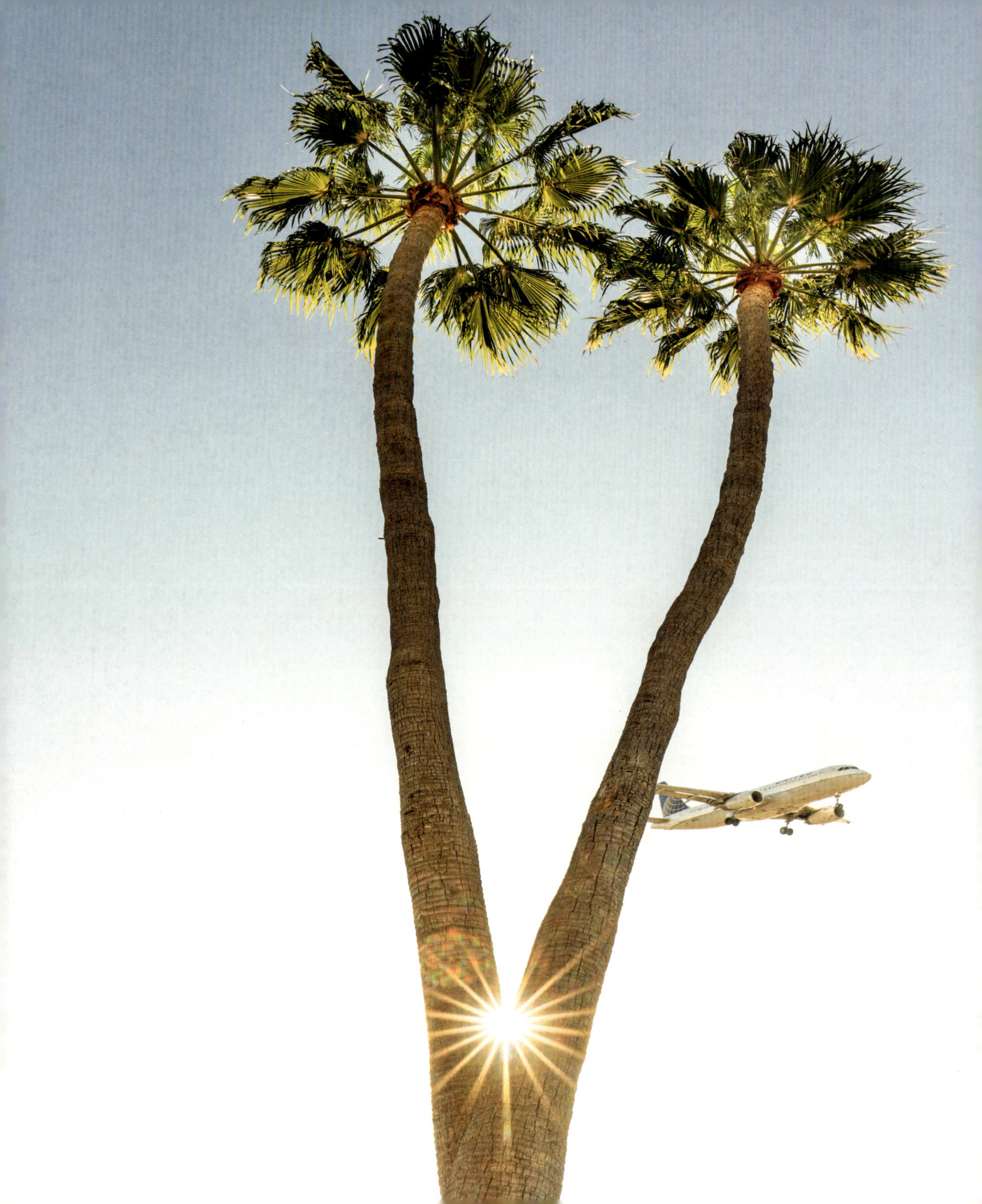

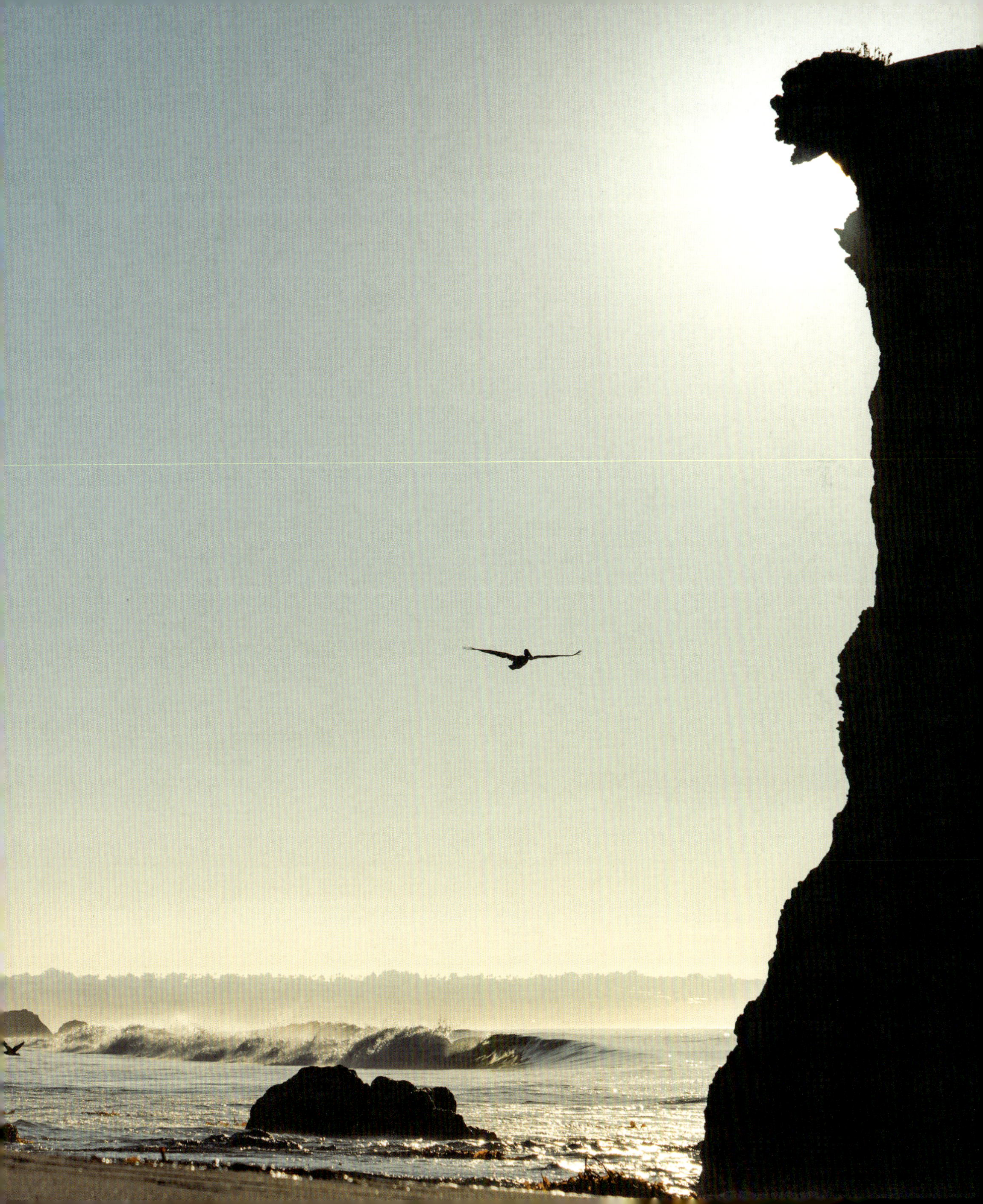

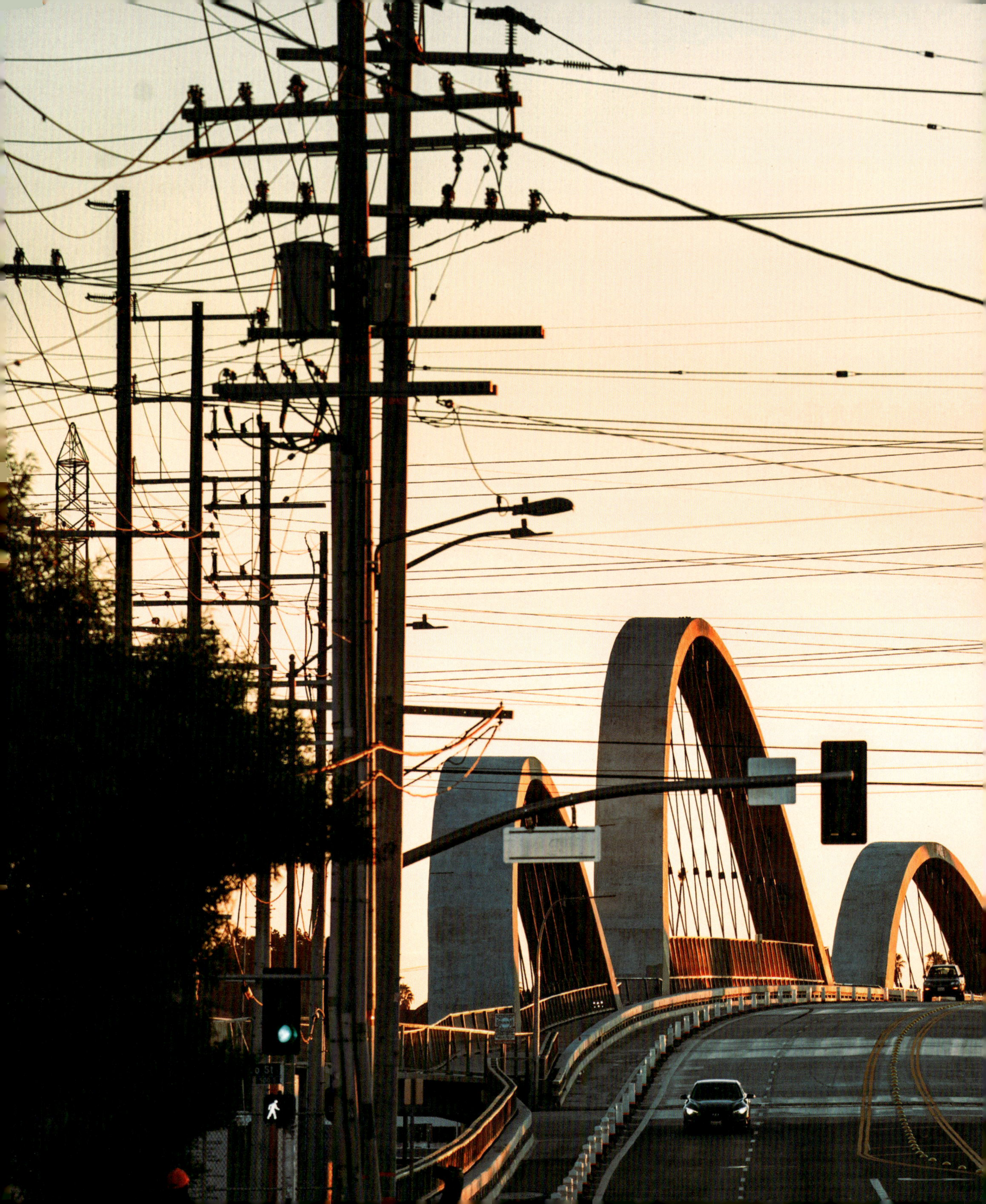

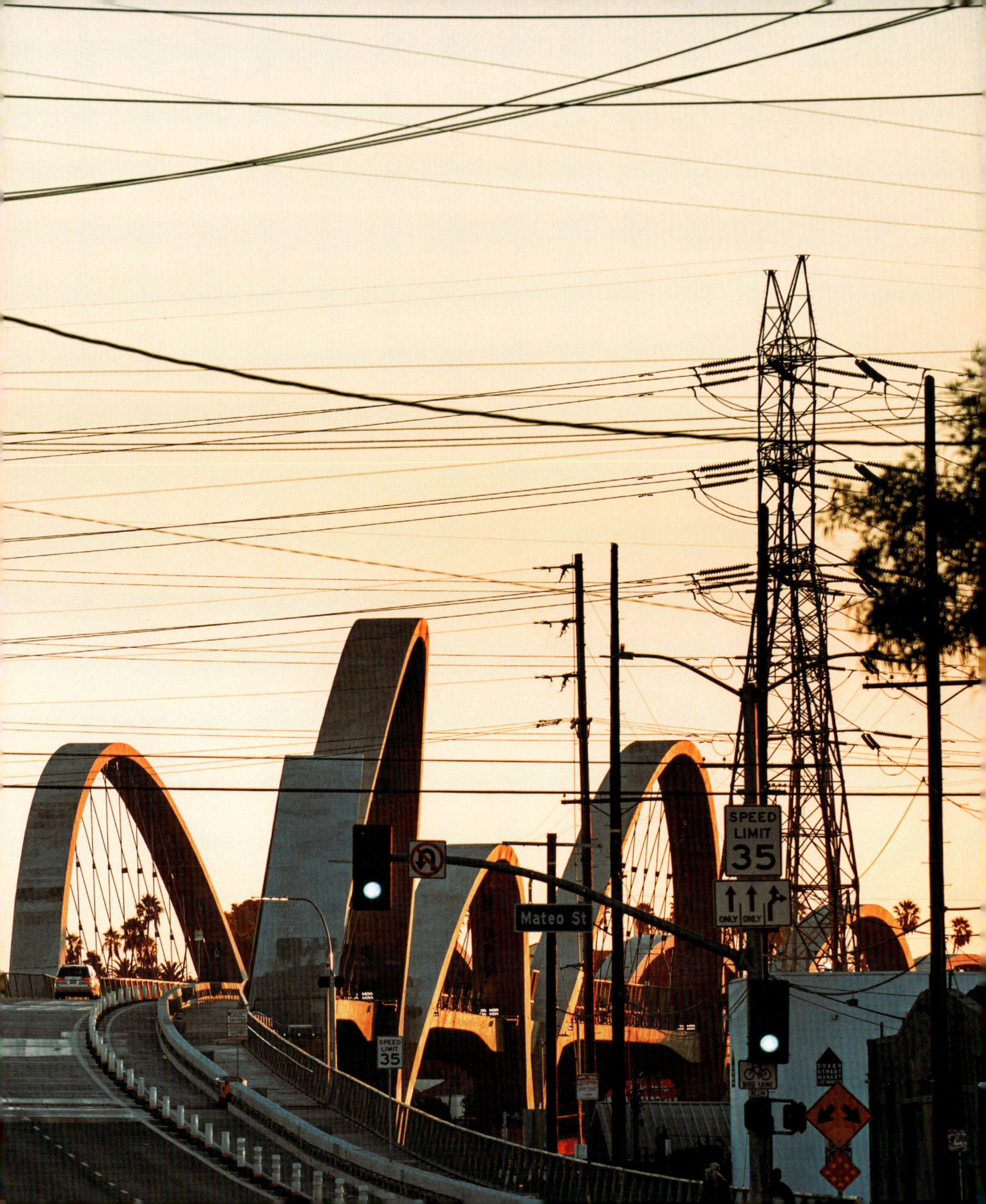
SPEED LIMIT 35
ONLY ONLY
Mateo St
SPEED LIMIT 35
BIKE LANE

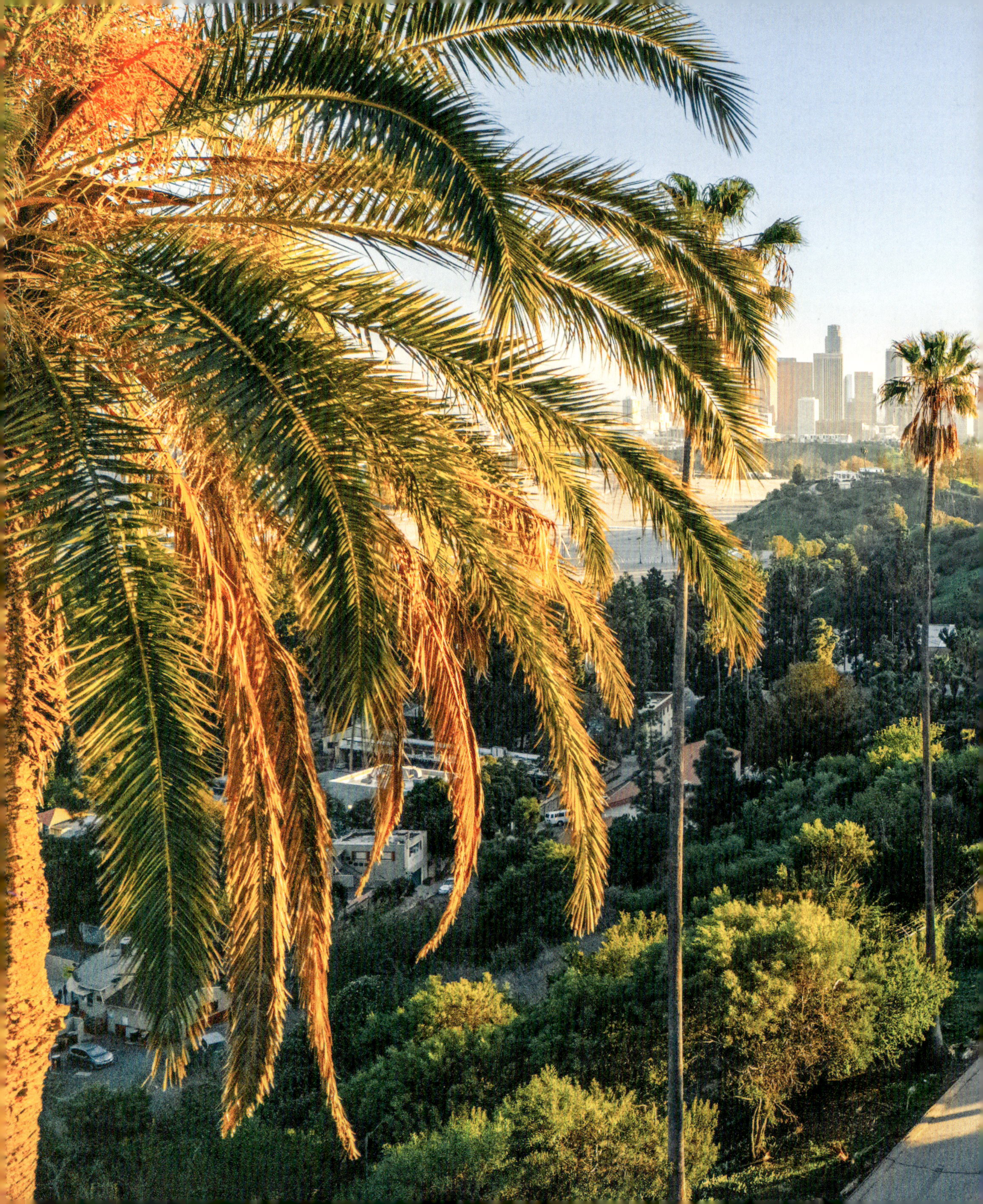

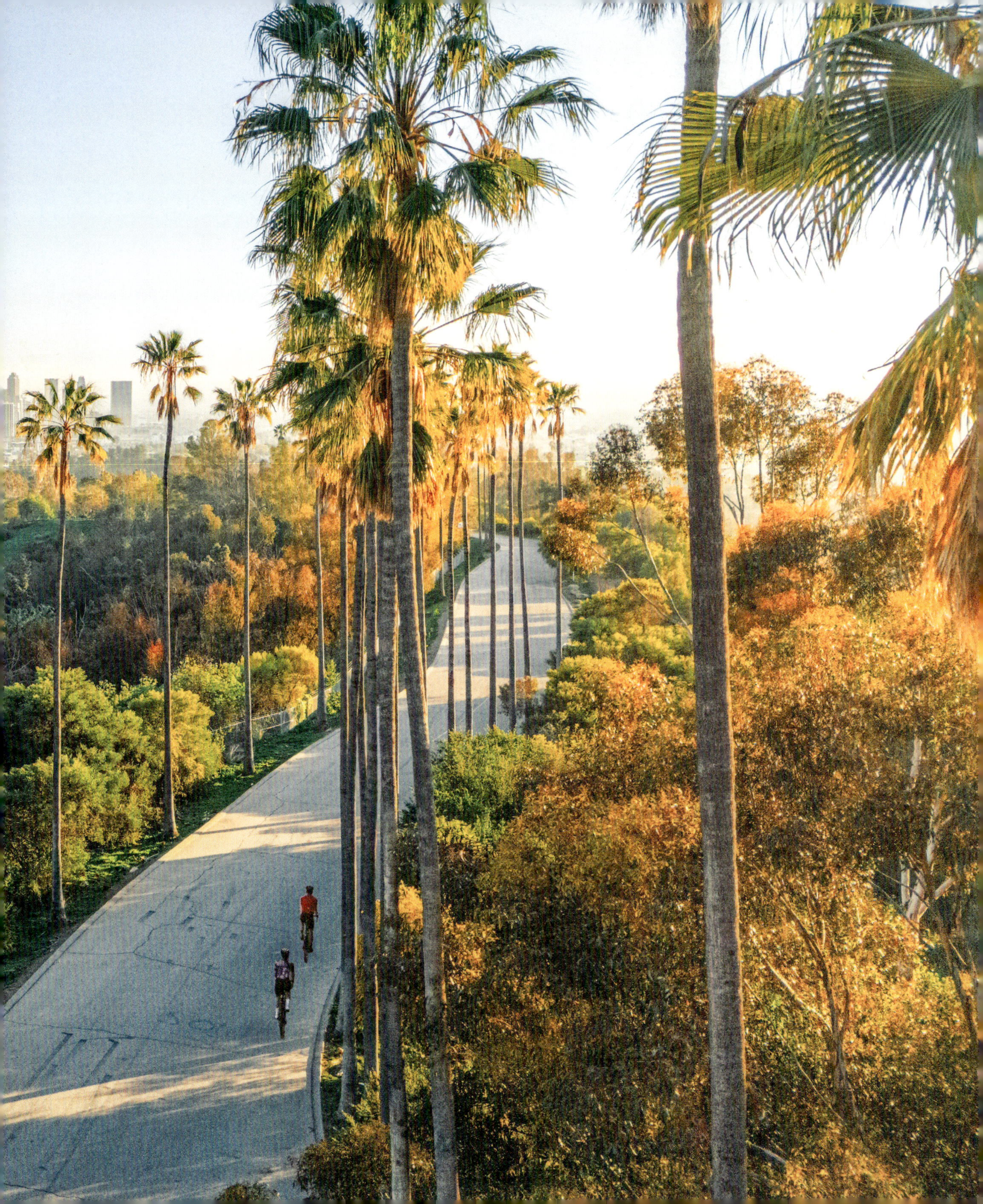

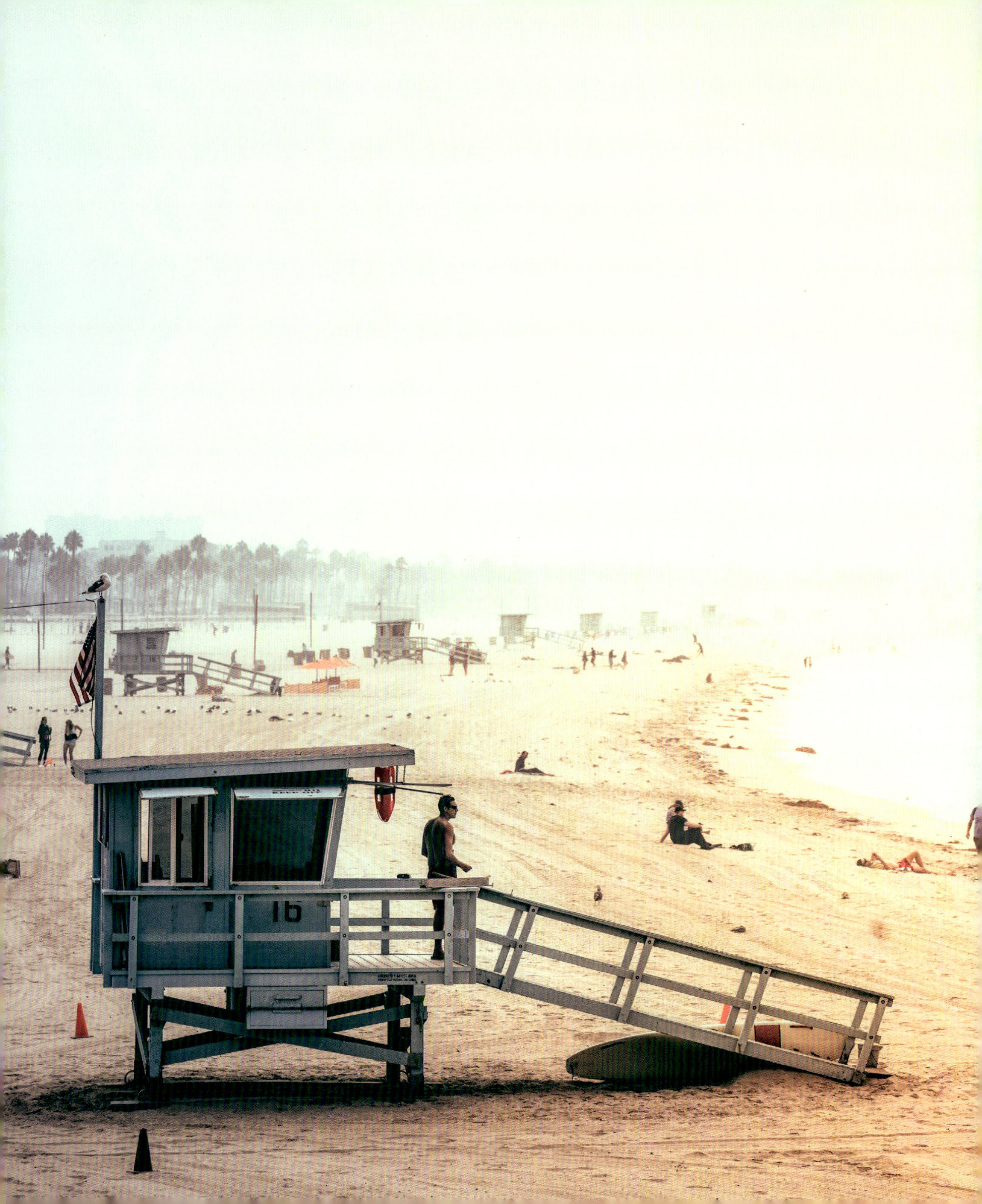

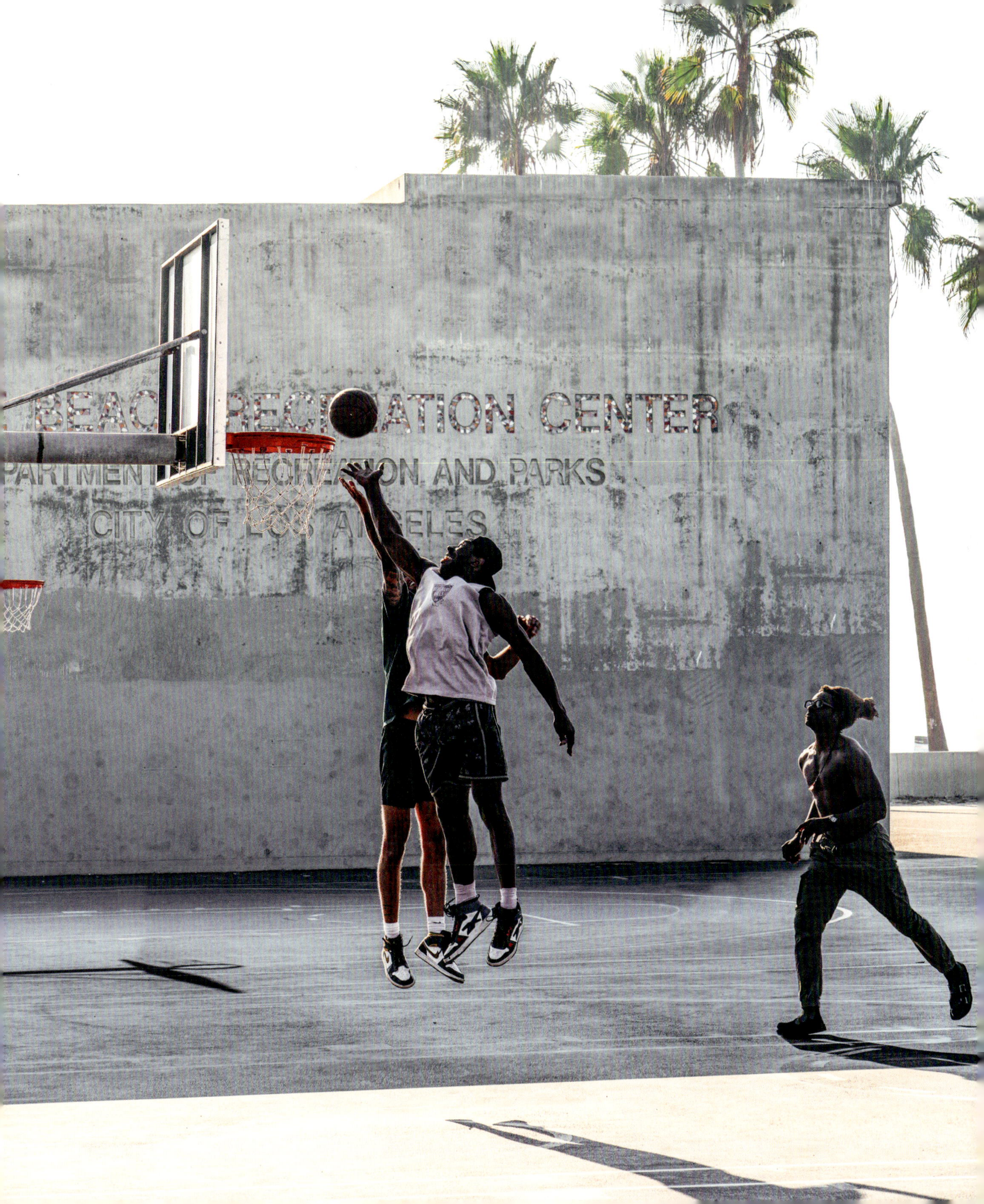
CENTER
AND PARKS

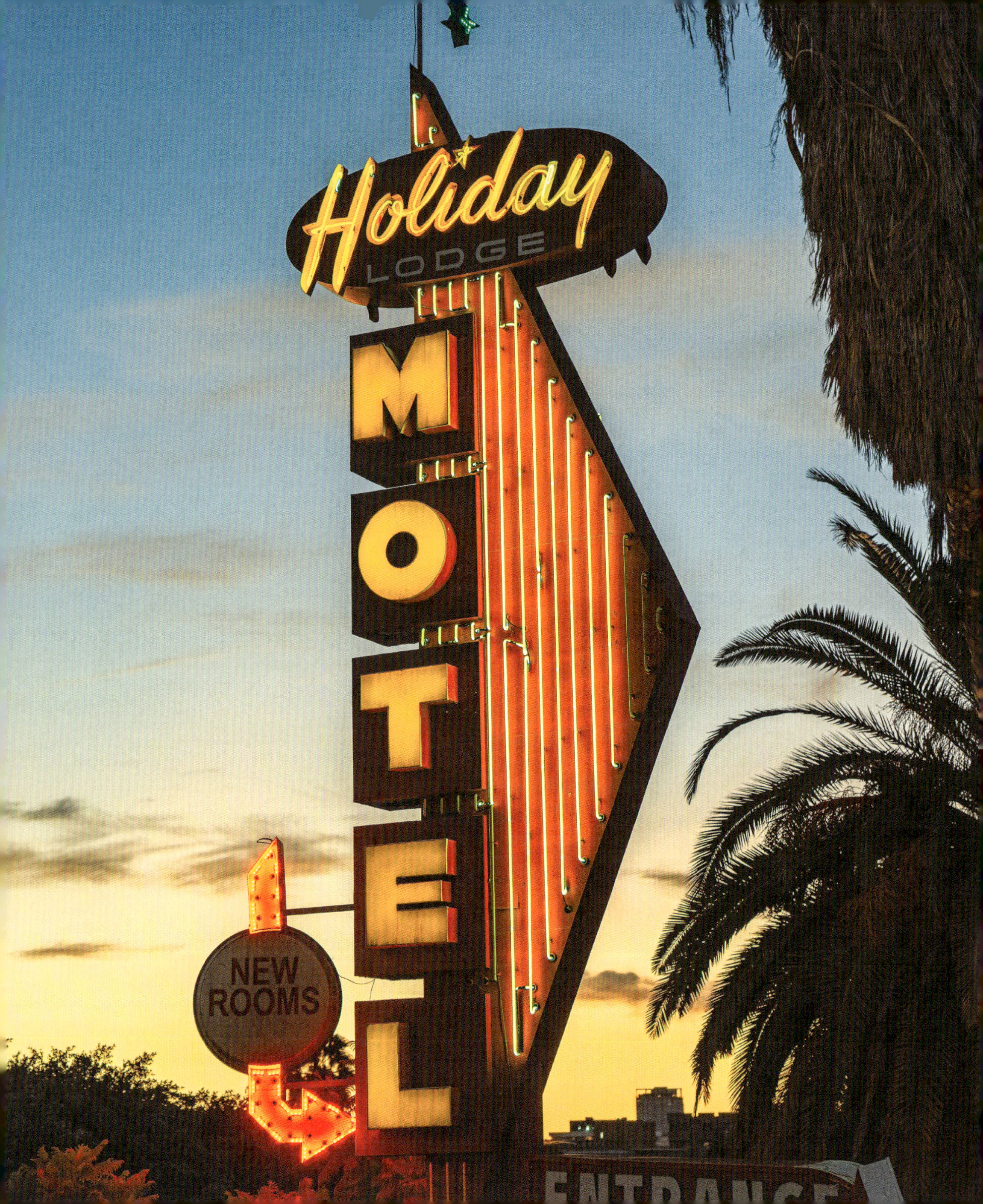
Holiday
LODGE
MOTEL
NEW ROOMS

(Page 2–3) Though known for its car culture, it is possible to get around Los Angeles using public transportation—the LA Metro offers a huge network of subways, light rails, buses, and shuttles that span the city.

(Page 4) LAX serves more than 75 million travelers a year and is the international gateway to Southern California.

(Page 5) One of the many wonders of LA is that one can visit the mountains and the sea in the same day—here, the beach is El Matador State Park in Malibu.

(Page 6–7) The Sixth Street Viaduct connects downtown LA to Boyle Heights. While the population within the city limits is around four million, the greater metro area is home to twelve million people.

(Page 8–9) A view of Elysian Park shows how unique LA's mix of urbanism and natural beauty is. It's a vibrant, sprawling city mixed in with remote beaches, canyons, and mountains.

(Page 10) Famous for its sun-soaked beaches like this one in Santa Monica, LA is also legendary for its distinctive, natural light—that bright shimmer that brought the film industry here in the first place.

(Page 11) Located on the Boardwalk, the legendary Venice Beach basketball courts are the perfect place for a pickup game.

(Page 12) Neon has a rich cultural history lighting up the city, and there are many gorgeous neon signs like this one from a hotel in the Westlake neighborhood.

(Page 14) The Art Deco El Rey theater, a beloved landmark of LA's Miracle Mile neighborhood, now hosts concerts, but it was originally a movie theater. Home to the film industry, there's no better city than LA for movie watching thanks to the plethora of beautiful, historic movie theaters.

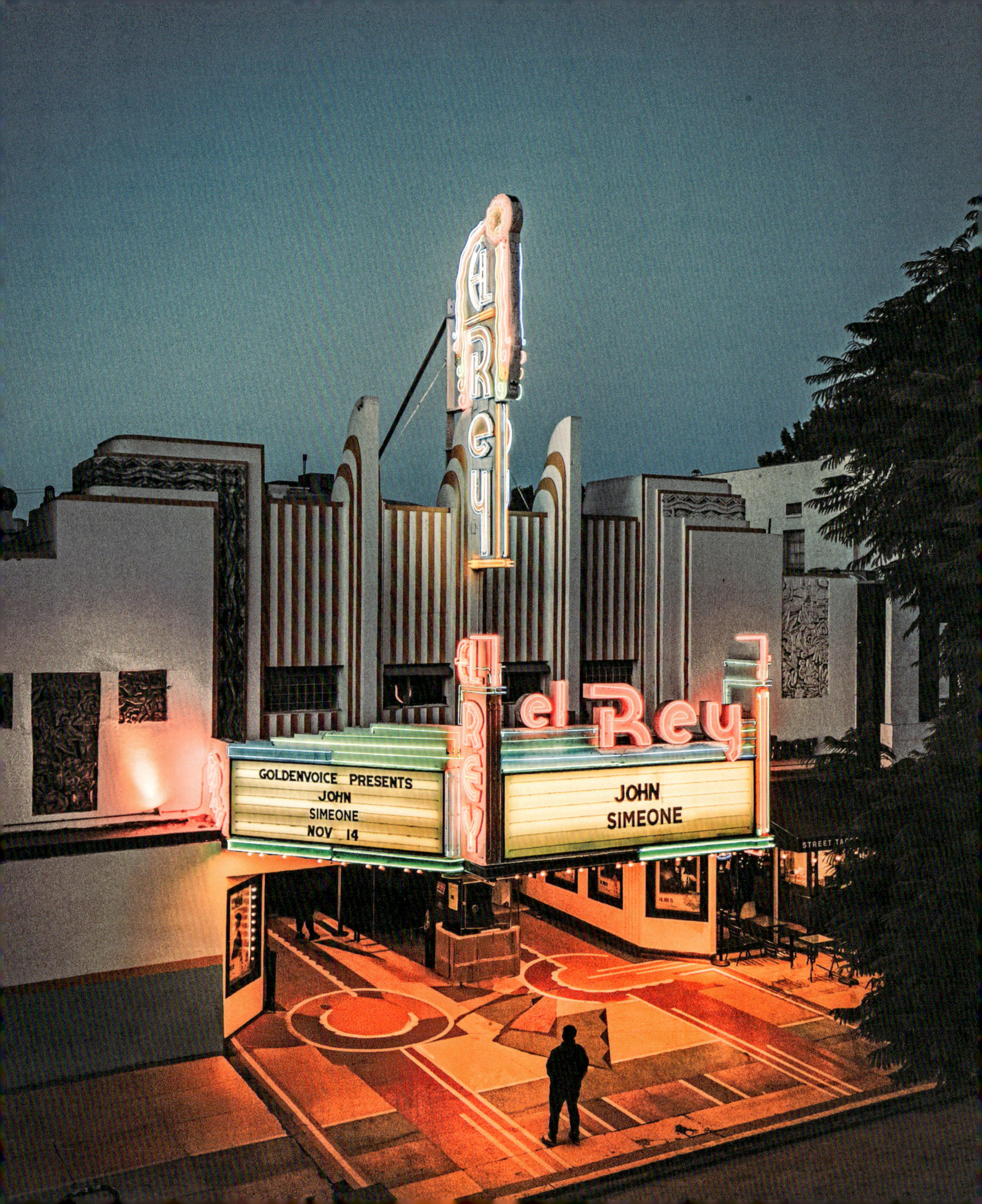
El Rey
El Rey
el Rey
GOLDENVOICE PRESENTS
JOHN
SIMEONE
NOV 14
JOHN
SIMEONE

Los Angeles is a dynamic place, and it's impossible to see it all. There's not even one way to see a single site. Every place you go in the city is full of stories, and the story changes with who is telling it. This is why we hope you visit with a curious mind, open to possibilities you didn't expect, and an even bigger heart, ready to connect and share. Vistas are places we see together: stranger or family, visitor or local, it doesn't matter—we experience a place together.

What makes Los Angeles a wonderful place to visit—and to live in—is people.

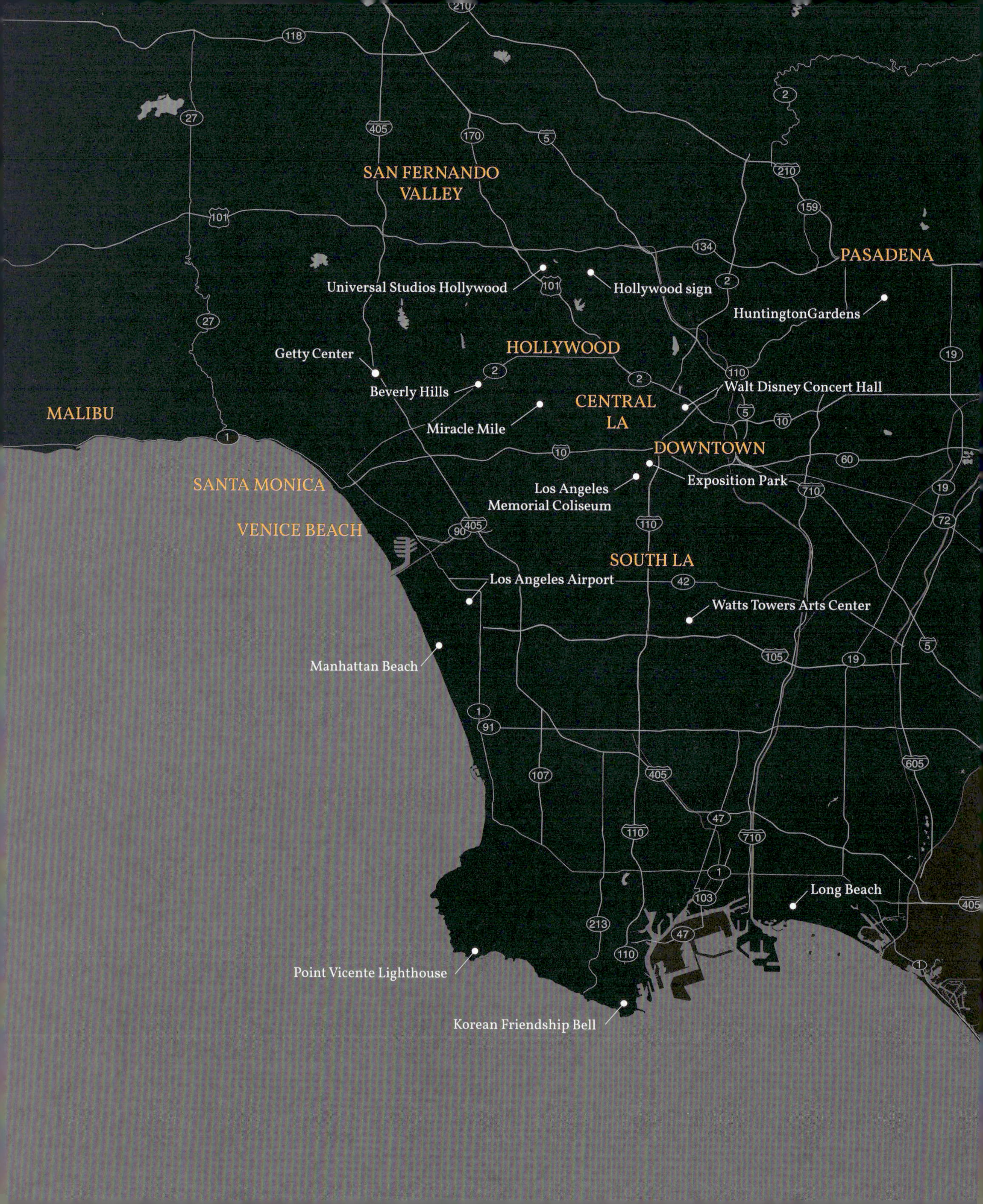
SAN FERNANDO VALLEY
PASADENA
Universal Studios Hollywood
Hollywood sign
HuntingtonGardens
Getty Center
HOLLYWOOD
Beverly Hills
CENTRAL LA
Walt Disney Concert Hall
MALIBU
Miracle Mile
DOWNTOWN
SANTA MONICA
Los Angeles Memorial Coliseum
Exposition Park
VENICE BEACH
SOUTH LA
Los Angeles Airport
Watts Towers Arts Center
Manhattan Beach
Long Beach
Point Vicente Lighthouse
Korean Friendship Bell

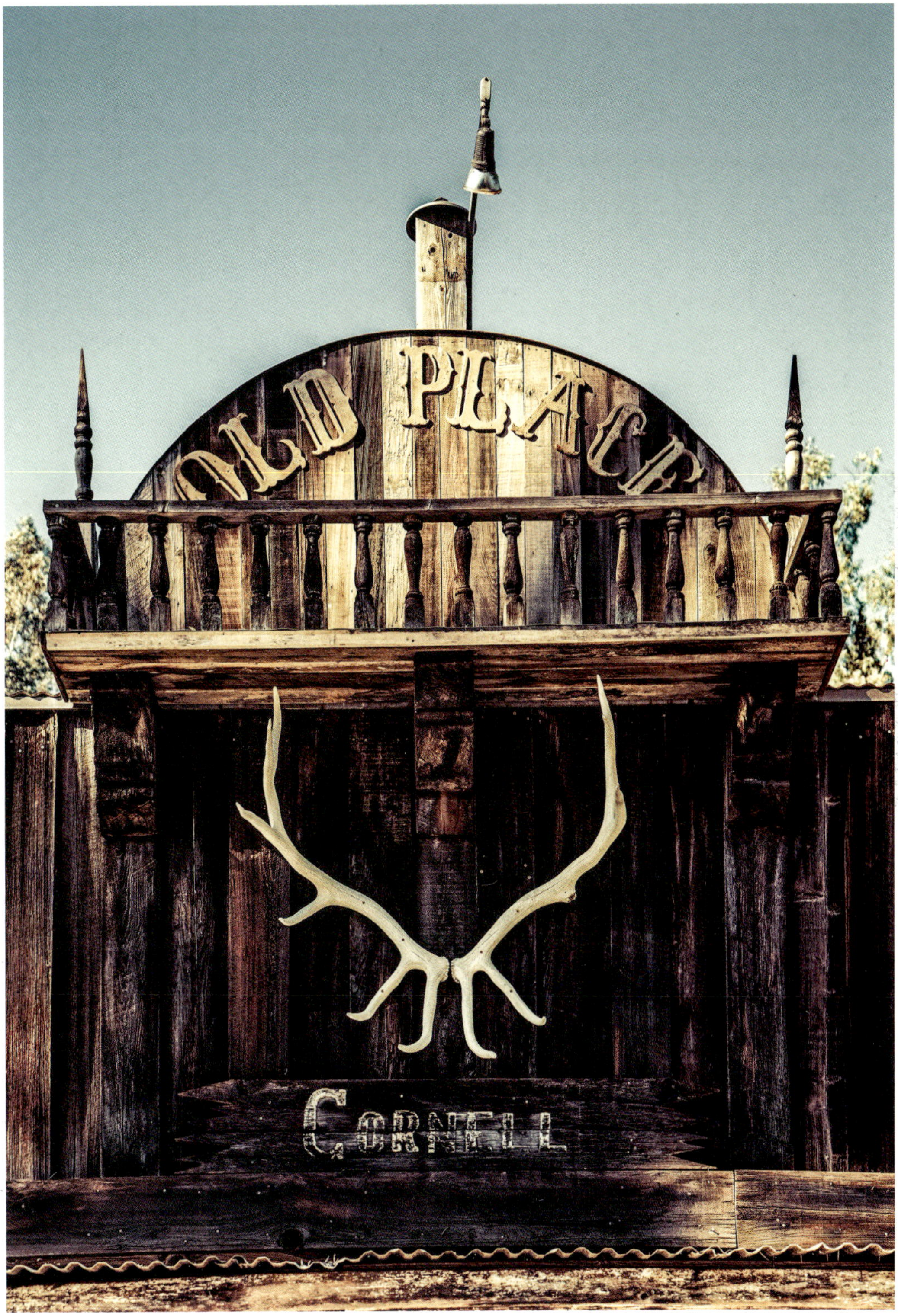

Hidden deep in the canyons of the Santa Monica Mountains, the building that houses the Old Place restaurant dates back to 1915 and miraculously survived wildfires in 2018 and 2025.

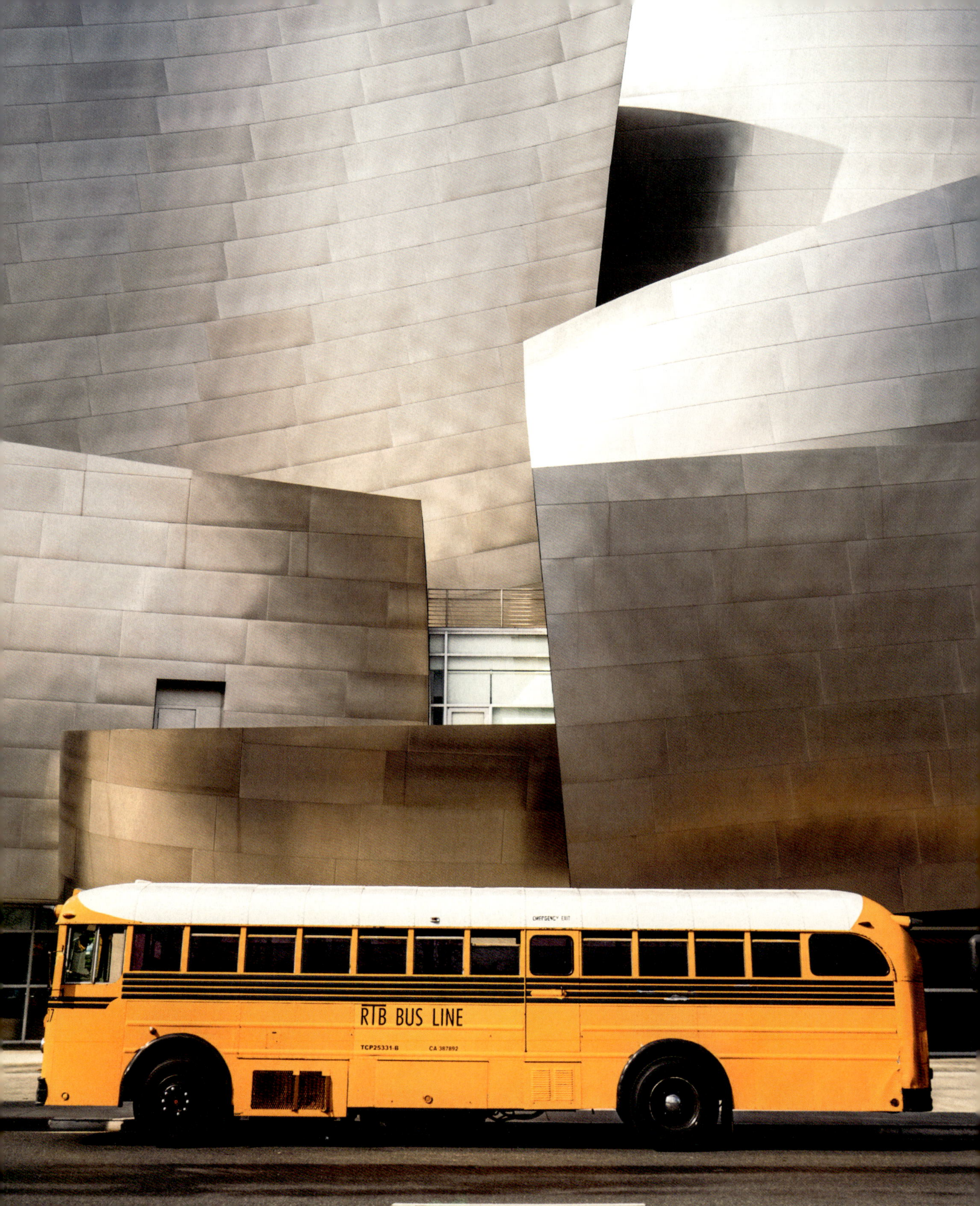
RTB BUS LINE
TCP25331-B
CA 387892

Vistas Include

A school bus in front of the Walt Disney Concert Hall. The iconic yellow color of school buses in the United States is the result of a 1939 conference focused on standardizing school bus design and safety.

(Page 20–21) A view of downtown from the Omaha Heights neighborhood shows many Mexican fan palm trees, an iconic symbol of the city that ironically, is not native to the area. In the 1930s, thousands of the trees were planted across the city, some of which have grown to be more than 100 feet high.

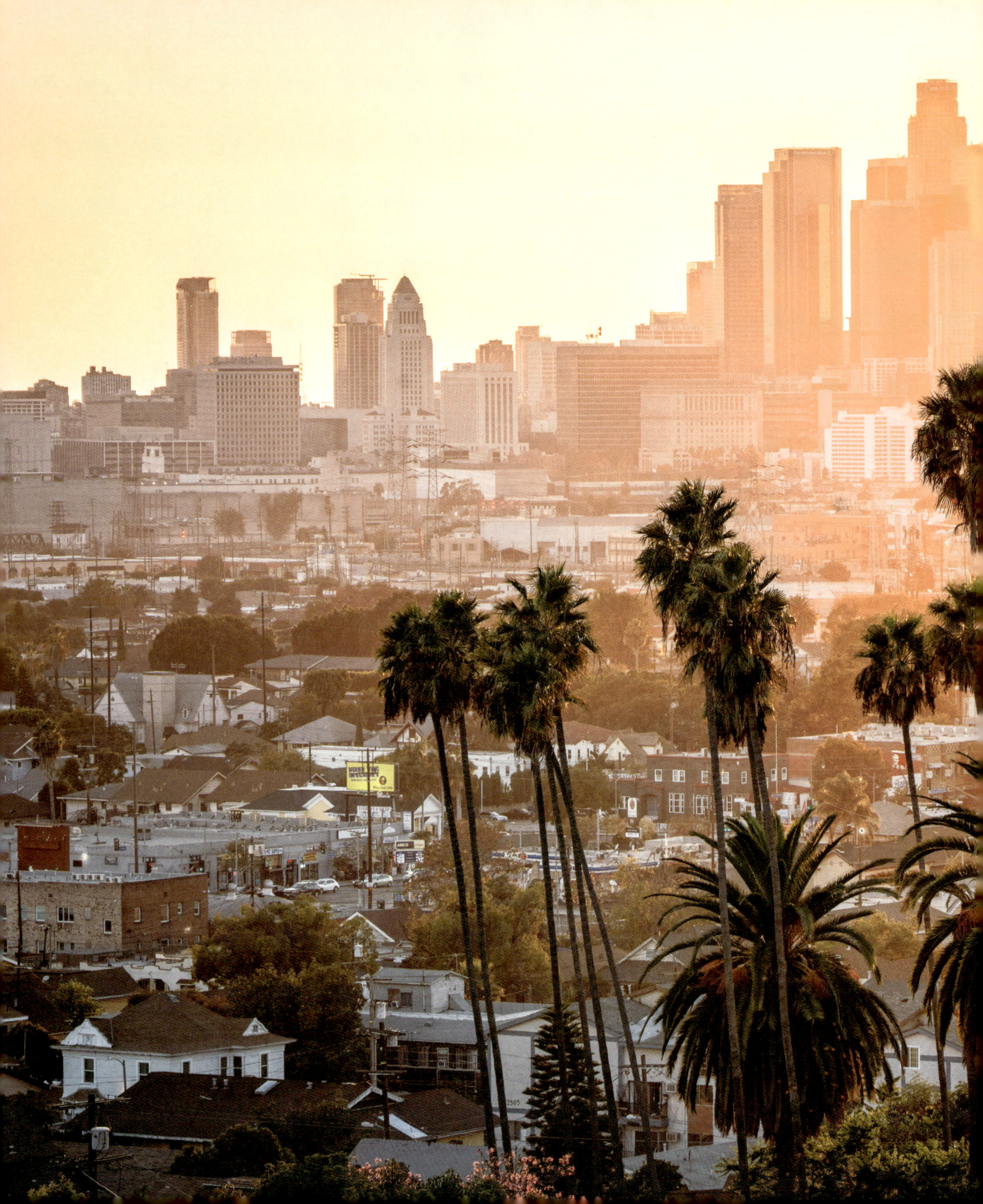

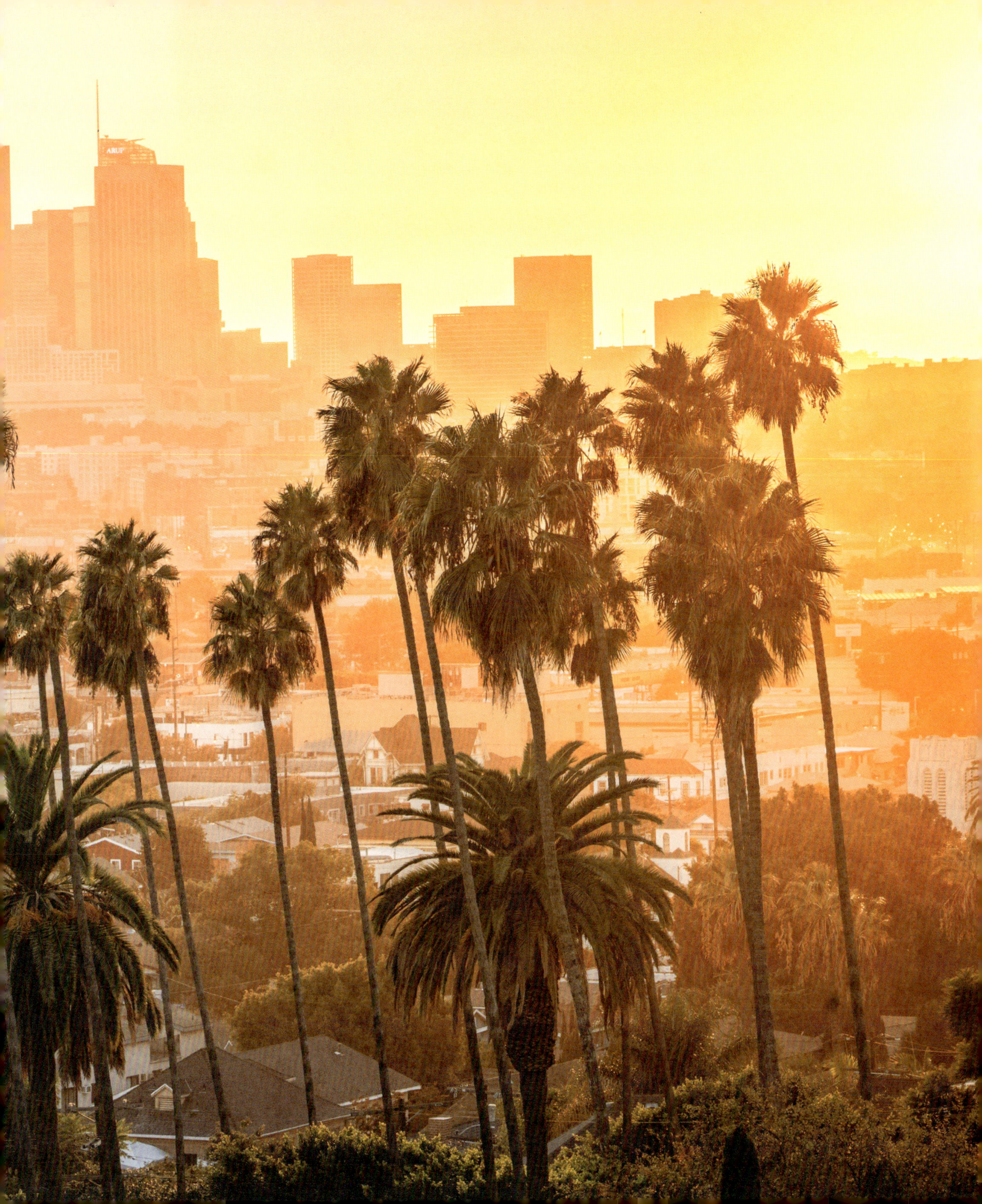

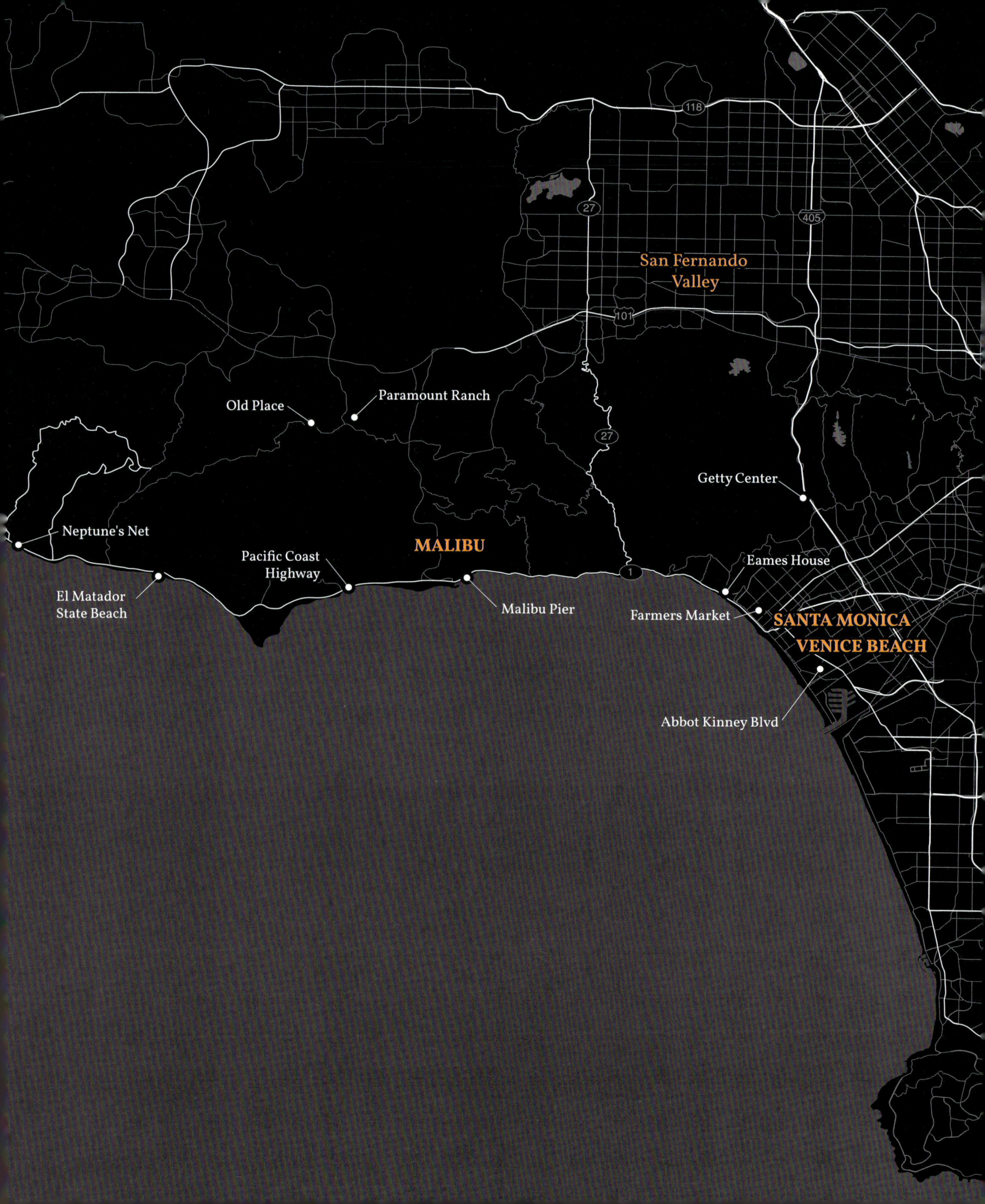
San Fernando Valley
Old Place
Paramount Ranch
Getty Center
Neptune's Net
MALIBU
Pacific Coast Highway
Eames House
El Matador State Beach
Malibu Pier
Farmers Market
SANTA MONICA
VENICE BEACH
Abbot Kinney Blvd
118
27
405
101
1

Beaches: Malibu, Santa Monica, Venice

Iconic Sites

A Sun-Soaked Pacific Paradise

What's the first place that people think of when they hear Los Angeles? Probably it's an image of sun-drenched golden sand and the tantalizing deep blue water of the Pacific Ocean. LA's beaches are some of the most recognizable and most popular in the world—more than 50 million people visit them annually. Los Angeles County has 25 miles of beaches along its 75 miles of scenic coastline, and it's worth checking out as many of these glorious beaches as possible. They are, quite simply, paradise.

From wading around in tidal pools and exploring sea caves to riding the waves or suntanning in the sand, LA's beaches hold something for everyone. Along with their natural beauty, LA's beach cities have vibrant art scenes, shopping, food, activities, and nightlife. Each of these beach communities—Malibu, Santa Monica, Venice Beach, Manhattan Beach, Redondo Beach, San Pedro, Long Beach, just to name a few—have their own unique identity. Sure, all offer sun, sand, and surf, but they also hold specific histories and stories.

LA's beaches are famous for many reasons—they are dramatic and beautiful, full of wildlife, and bring the natural world into a big, urban city. The vibe of having the Pacific next door permeates the city, no matter how far you actually are from the ocean. And it's true, for months at a time the city is under a marine layers. Locals dub this atmospheric phenomena "May Gray" and "June Gloom." For Angelenos, the ocean is always part of the city.

LA's beaches are also emblematic of a certain lifestyle that is associated with living here—that laid-back, casual attitude that blends an effortless glamour with creativity, endless possibility, and vibrant diversity. While the temperatures might be hot, LA's beaches are the epitome of cool—and what happens here has influence all over the world.

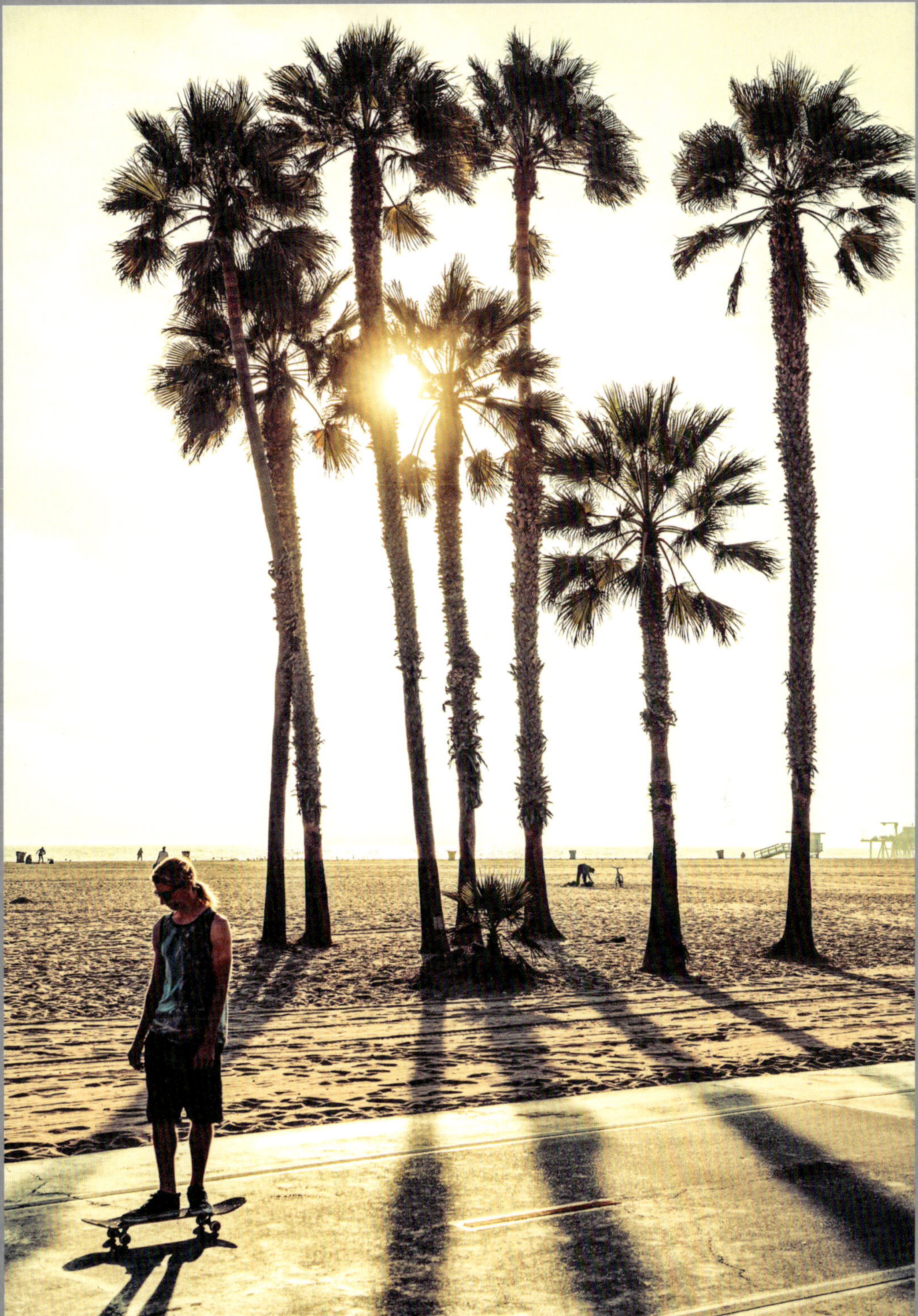

Stretching two miles along the coast since 1905, the Venice Beach Boardwalk offers a lively compendium of see-and-be-seen beach culture—street performers and vendors, bodybuilders, bike riders, skaters, and, of course, surfers on their way to the waves.

(Page 26–27) Santa Monica State Beach is one of the most iconic beaches in the world, offering almost three miles of wide, sandy beaches that jut against dramatic, mountainous cliffs.

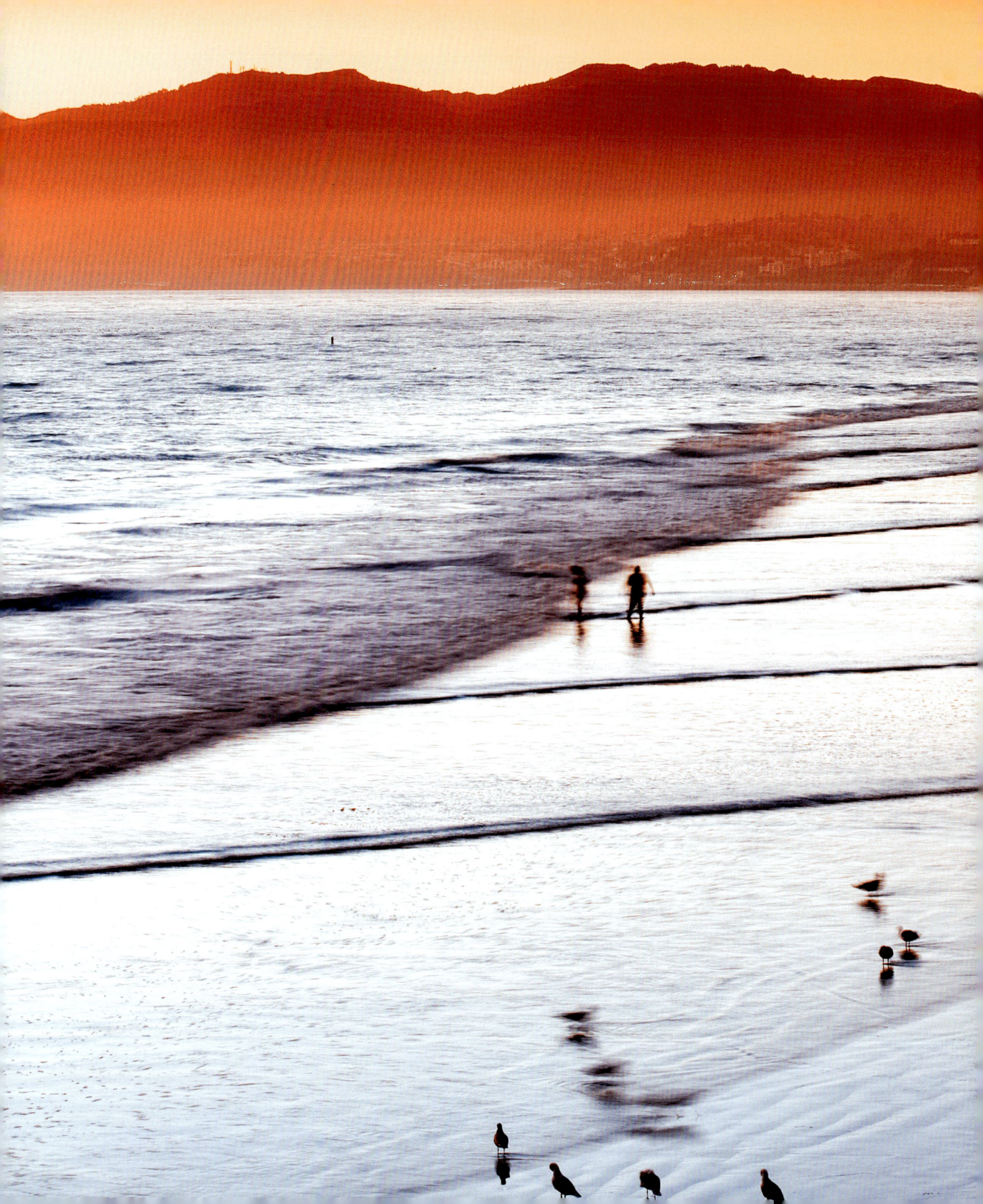

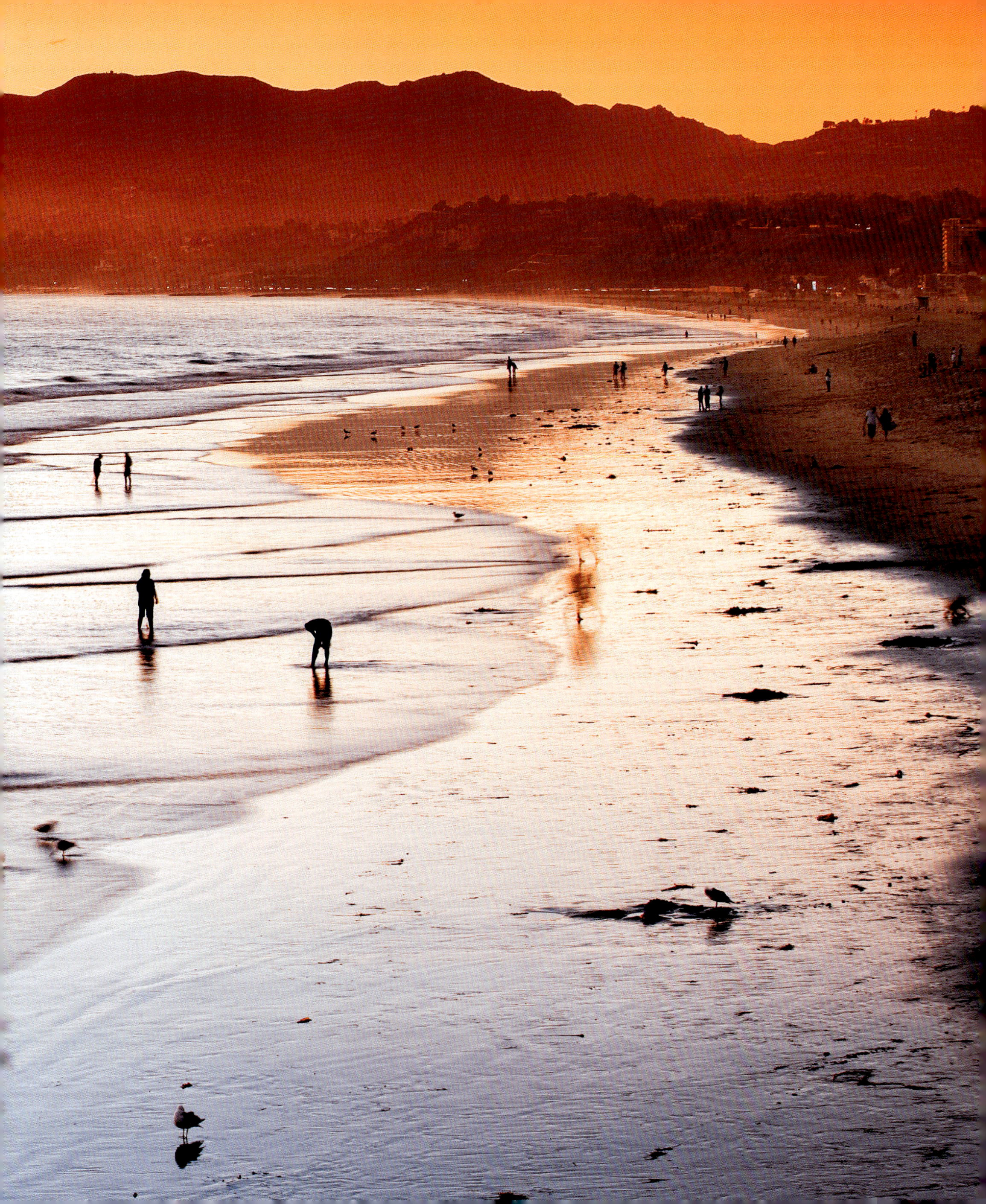

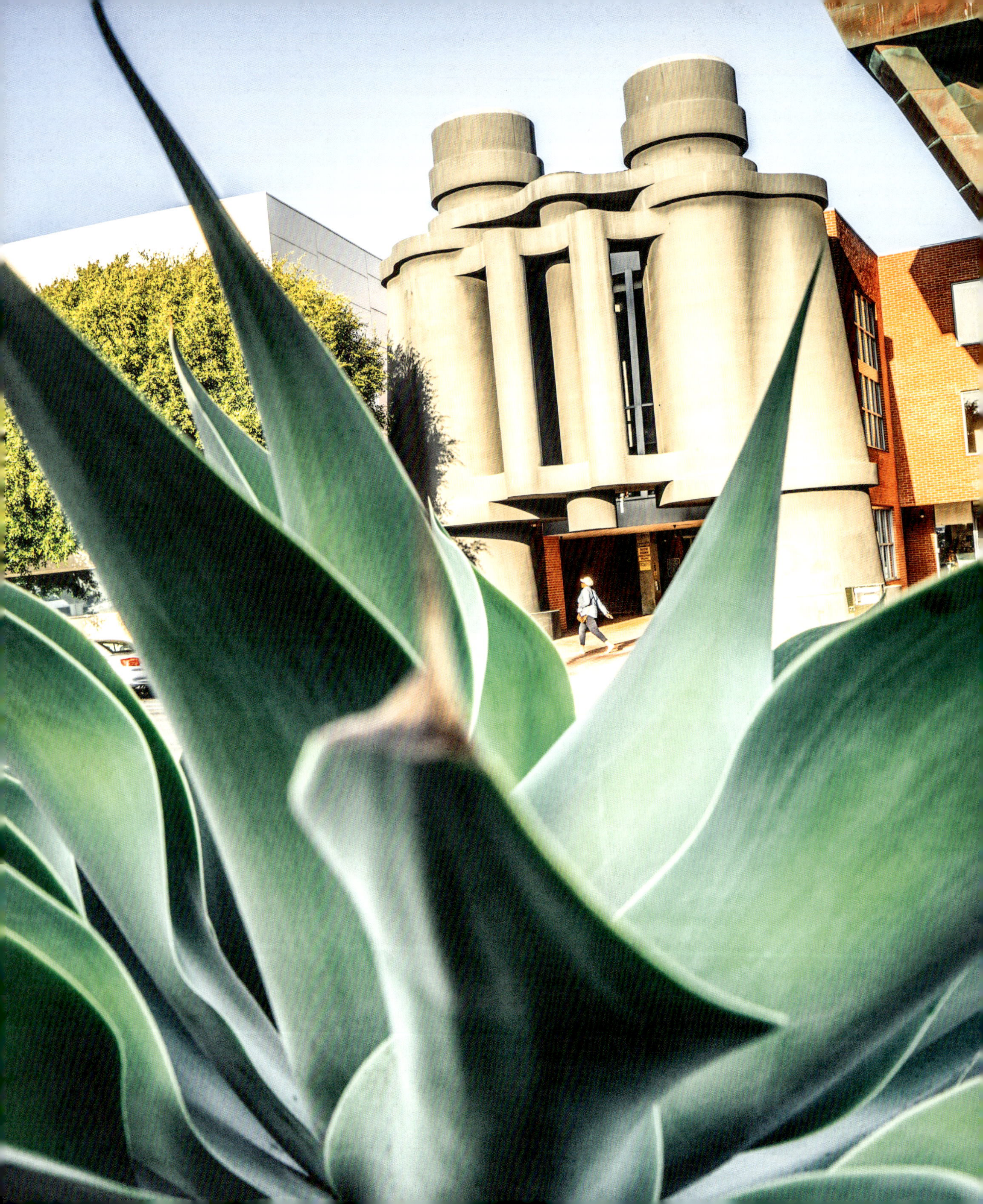

A view of architect Frank Gehry's "Binoculars Building" through an agave plant in Venice shows the sculpture designed by Claes Oldenburg and Coosje van Brugge that serves as its entrance.

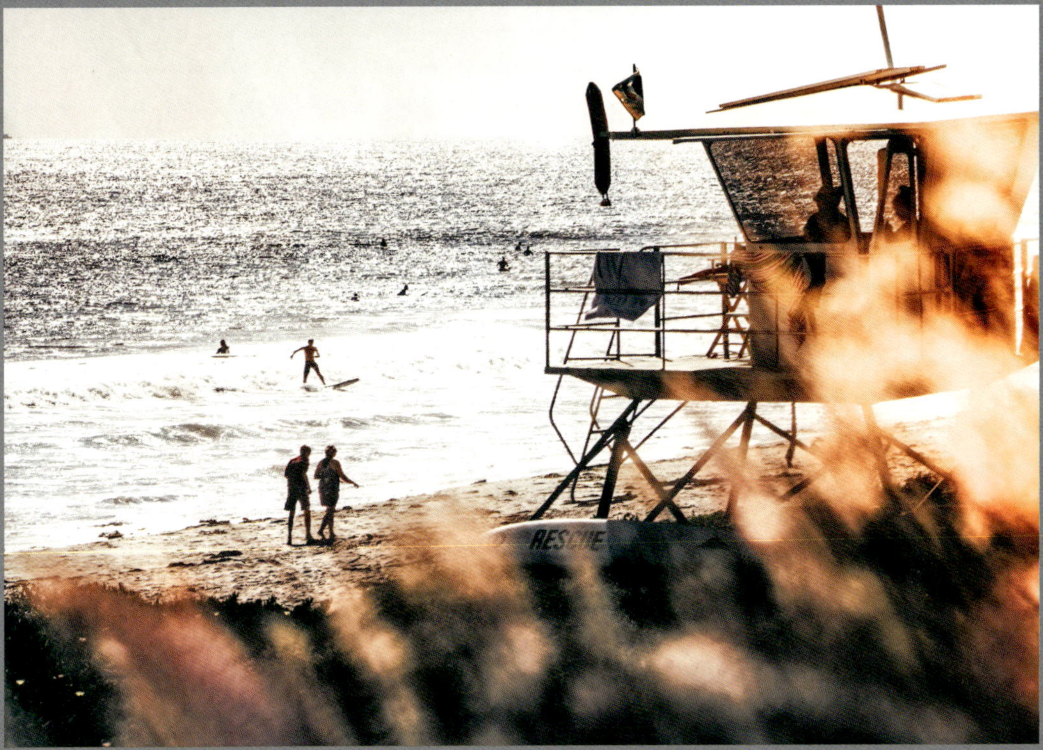

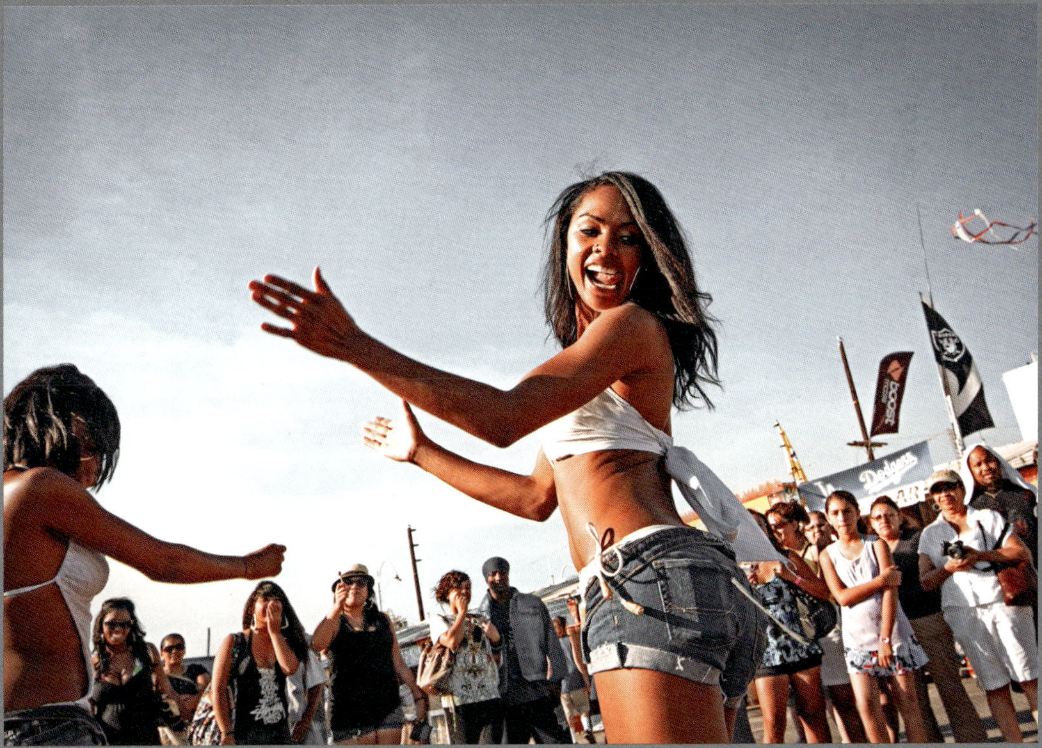

Some parts of the naturally rocky and wild coastline, like that in Santa Monica, were transformed during the 20th century to be the more accessible, flat beaches that are there today.

From the days of Frankie and Annette to now, LA's beaches, like Venice Beach, make popular party spots for young people, sparking trends that emanate from here to the rest of the world.

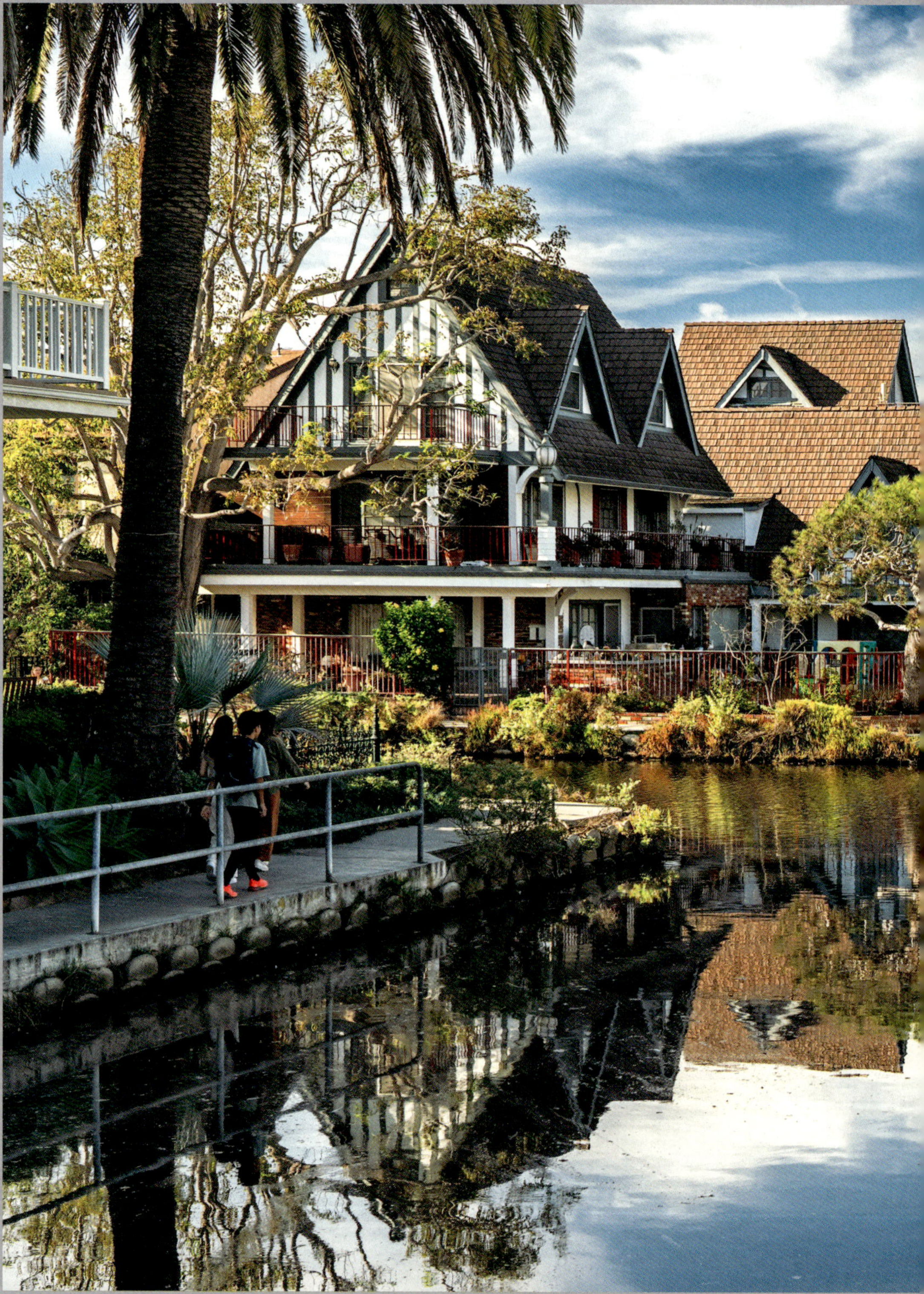

One of the last remaining remnants of Abbot Kinney's 1905 Venice of America development, the Venice Canal Historic District boasts six picturesque canals that are a perfect setting for scenic walks.

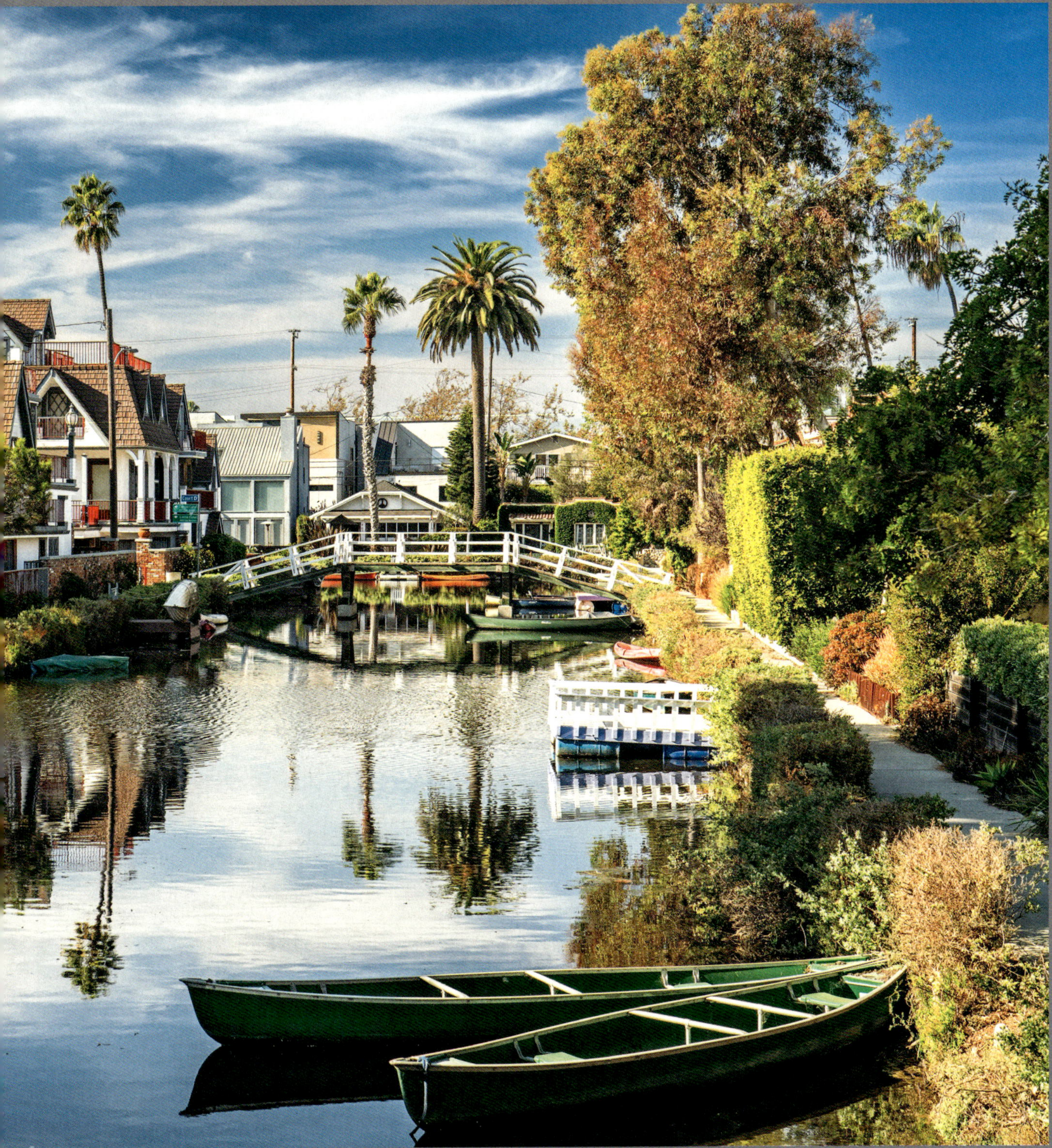

Malibu

The Sun-Kissed Celebrity Coast

Originally all of the land that makes up Malibu was home to the Chumash, the Native American people who cared for a large swath of Southern California's coastline, from San Luis Obispo to the area now known as Malibu. A village named Humaliwo, which is said to translate as "where the surf sounds loudly," was located near what is now Malibu Lagoon State Beach. Today, this area houses the historic Adamson House and the Malibu Lagoon Museum and offers views of the famed Surfrider Beach.

Malibu was a mostly rural area, full of horses and small farms, until the opening of the Pacific Coast Highway in 1929 (then called the Roosevelt Highway). Its isolation and beauty attracted Hollywood stars, who leased second homes in the Malibu Movie Colony, a collection of seaside bungalows opened in 1926. With the highway came even more movie stars—Gloria Swanson, Clara Bow, Delores del Río, Mary Pickford, and Douglas Fairbanks all had homes in the Colony in the 1920s. In the 1930s, Myrna Loy, Barbara Stanwyck, and Joan Crawford joined them. While a fresh water supply wasn't reliable in the colony (a city-run water system didn't arrive until the 1940s), apparently the gin always flowed in abundance. Now a private, gated community known as Malibu Colony, the homeowners remain an exclusive, rich bunch but they seem a lot less fun.

For all its sun-kissed glamour, Malibu has always had its bohemian side as well. Of course, it is the cradle of surf culture from its birth in the postwar years to today. Surf legends like Kathy Kohner-Zuckerman (better known by her nickname Gidget), Miki Dora, and Terry Tracy helped pioneer a new style of surfing and birthed a scene that lives on and expanded across the world. During the 1960s and '70s, bohemian artists and musicians moved in, bringing the Laurel Canyon vibe. Legendary songs, books, and films—from the Rolling Stones to Sting, *Chinatown* to *Blade Runner* were written or worked on by these sunny shores.

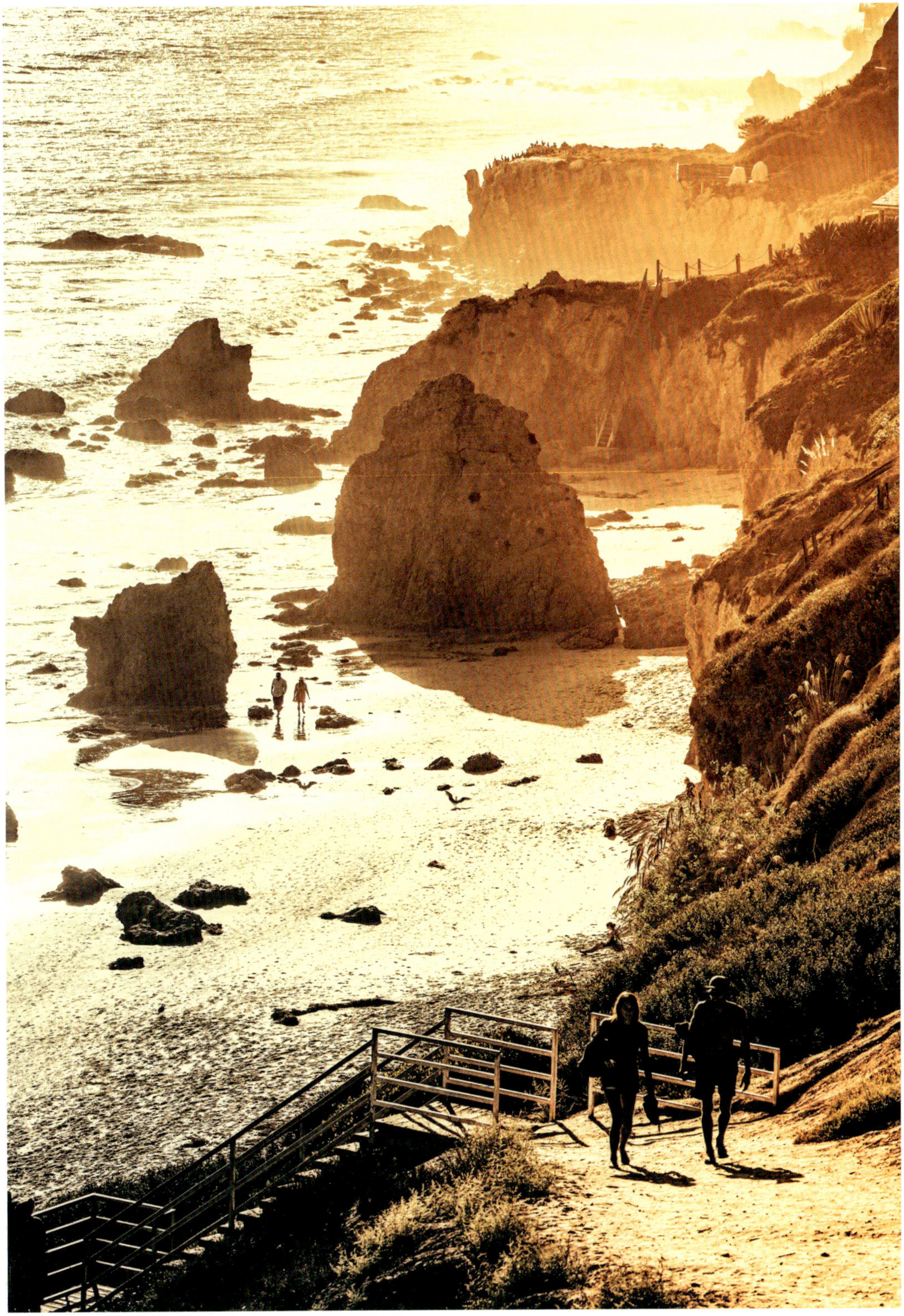

A view of El Matador State Beach in Malibu illustrates the reason for American film producer and music executive David Geffen's advice: "Move to California. Malibu is paradise."

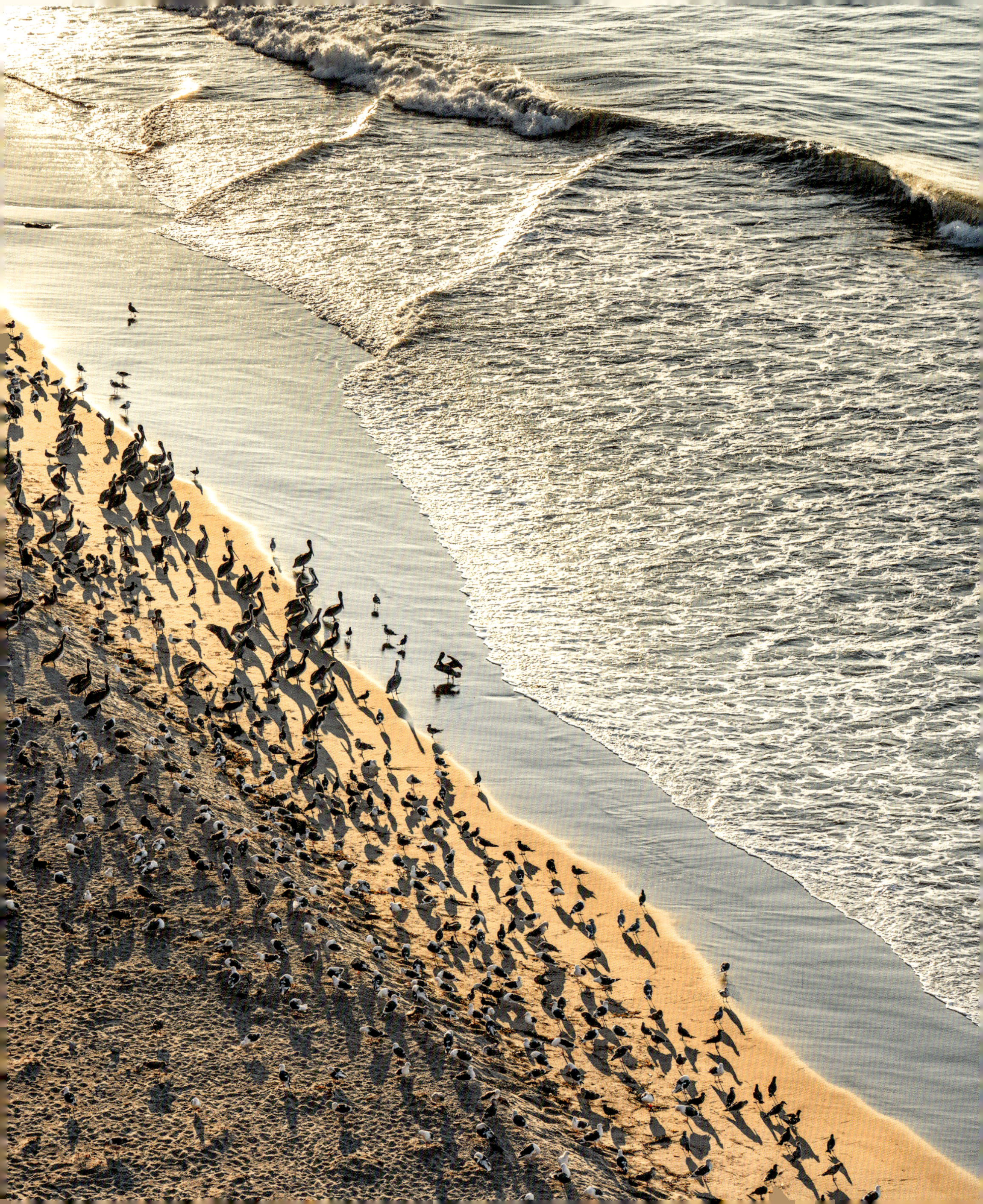

Another view of El Matador State Beach is complemented by words from writer James M. Cain: "Whatever else may be said of Malibu, the place where the movie queens grow their sunburn, there is one thing that you have to hand it: it is probably the finest beach ever created by God."

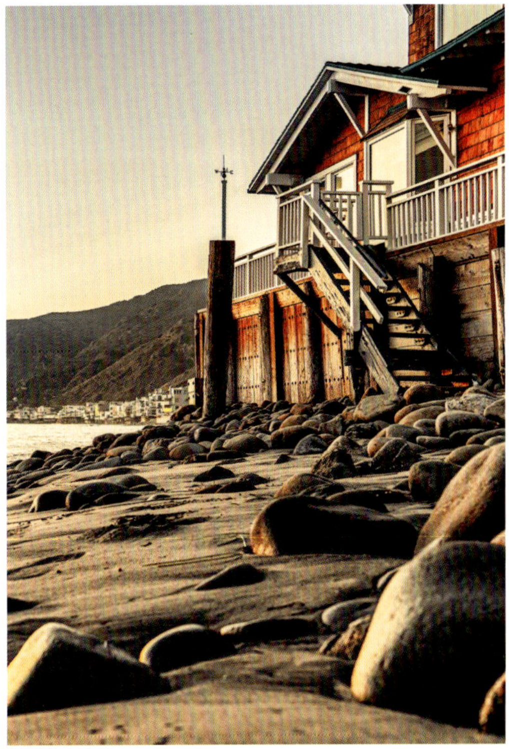

Though known for expensive real estate and exclusivity, there are no private beaches in Malibu—if the sand is wet, it's public. Topanga Beach, pictured here, is a popular surfing spot.

Large, molded fiberglass statues like this one that sits atop a local restaurant in Malibu are relics of Southern California's car culture.

There's an abundance of wildlife in Malibu, and El Matador State Beach is a great place to see it. During certain times of the year, gray whales migrate through these waters.

(Page 36–37) The Malibu Pier dates back to 1905—its sweeping views and the tasty Malibu Farm Restaurant make it the perfect place for a sundowner.

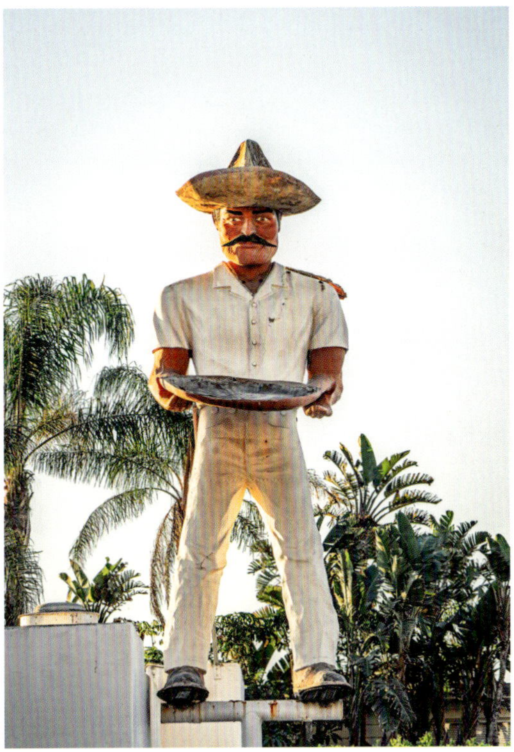

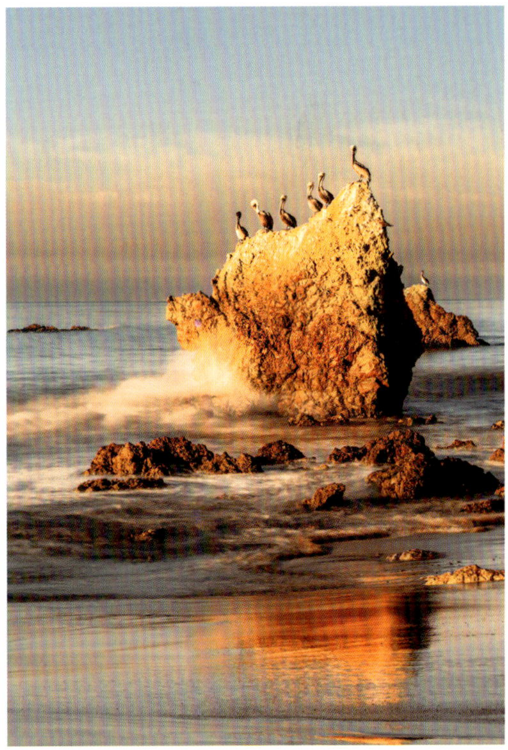

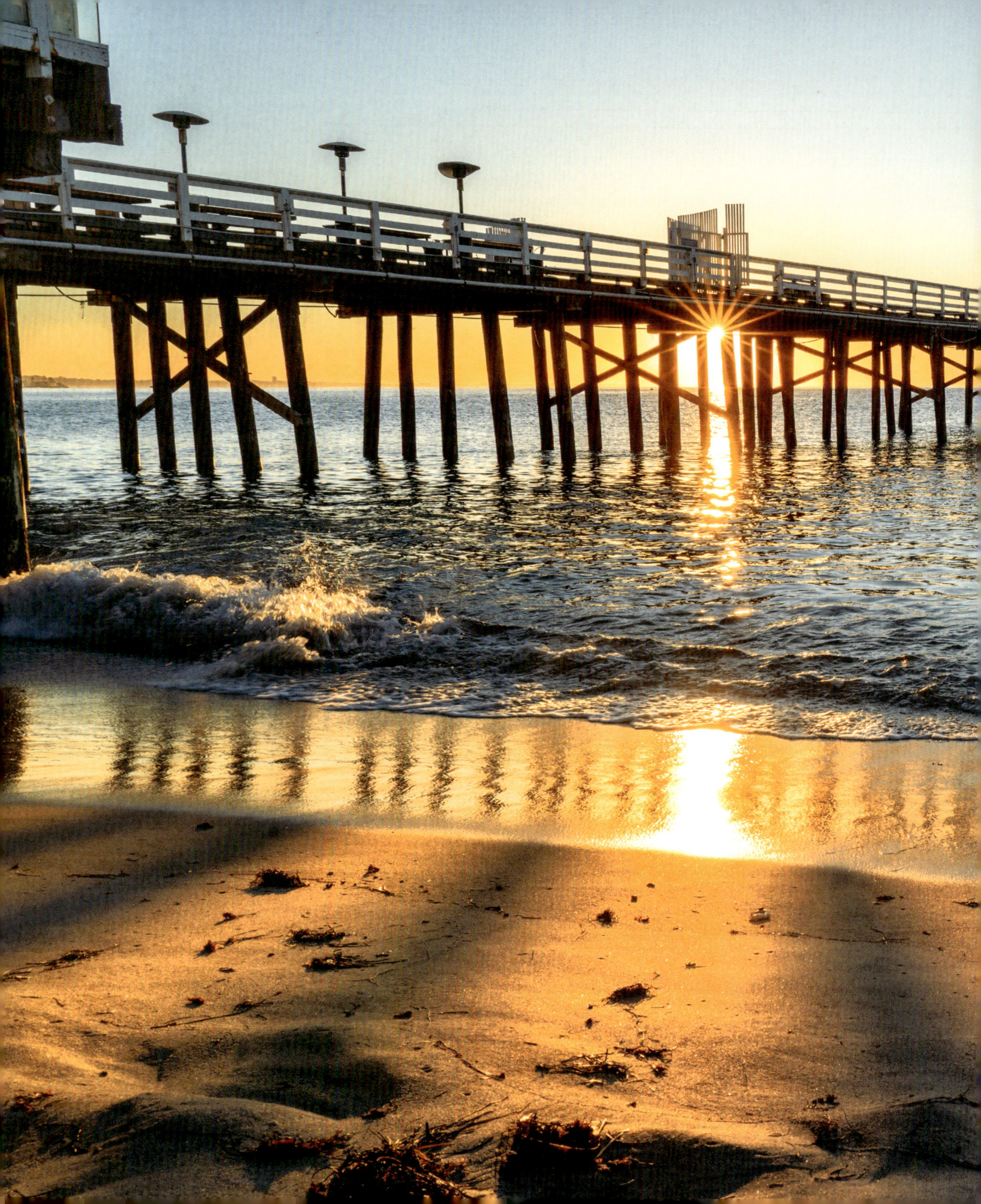

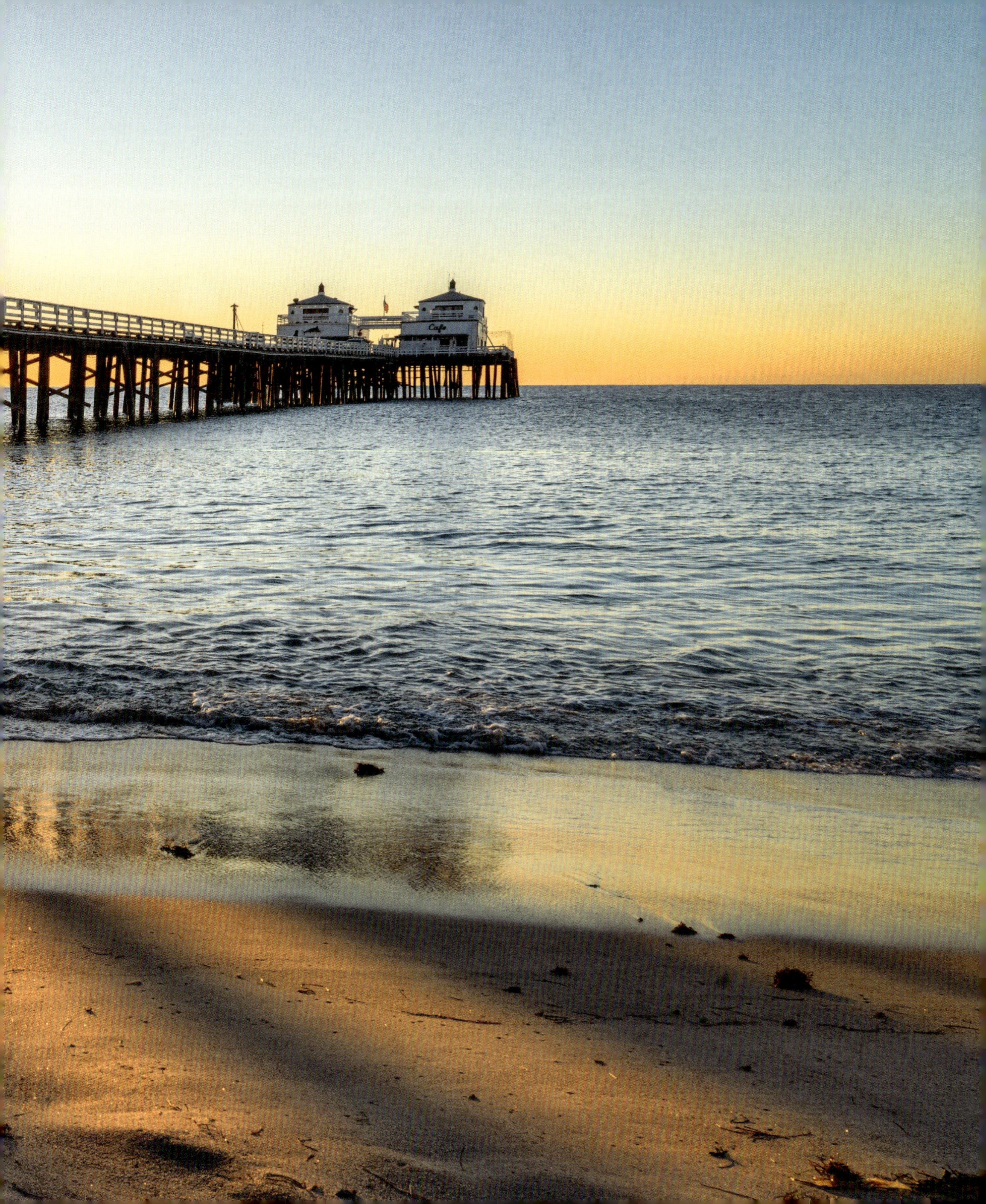
Cafe

Eames House

A Modernist Masterpiece in the Pacific Palisades

Built in 1949, this landmark of midcentury modern architecture served as the home and studio for two of the twentieth century's most important designers, Charles and Ray Eames. Commissioned by *Arts & Architecture* magazine for its experimental Case Study House program—this was house #8, and there are others in the neighborhood—the house used only inexpensive, prefabricated materials. It is a pioneering example of many of the thoughtful elements that have come to be the gold standard in LA architecture, such as integrating the outdoors and nature with the home, respecting the materials, and making life better through design.

Today, the house is a magical shrine that can be visited by reservation only—contact the Eames Foundation for tours. Perched in the bluff of the Pacific Palisades, it's an enchanting space of creativity and coziness, with light streaming through its massive windows and moveable walls. The couple lived here until their deaths, and their joyful spirit certainly lives on here.

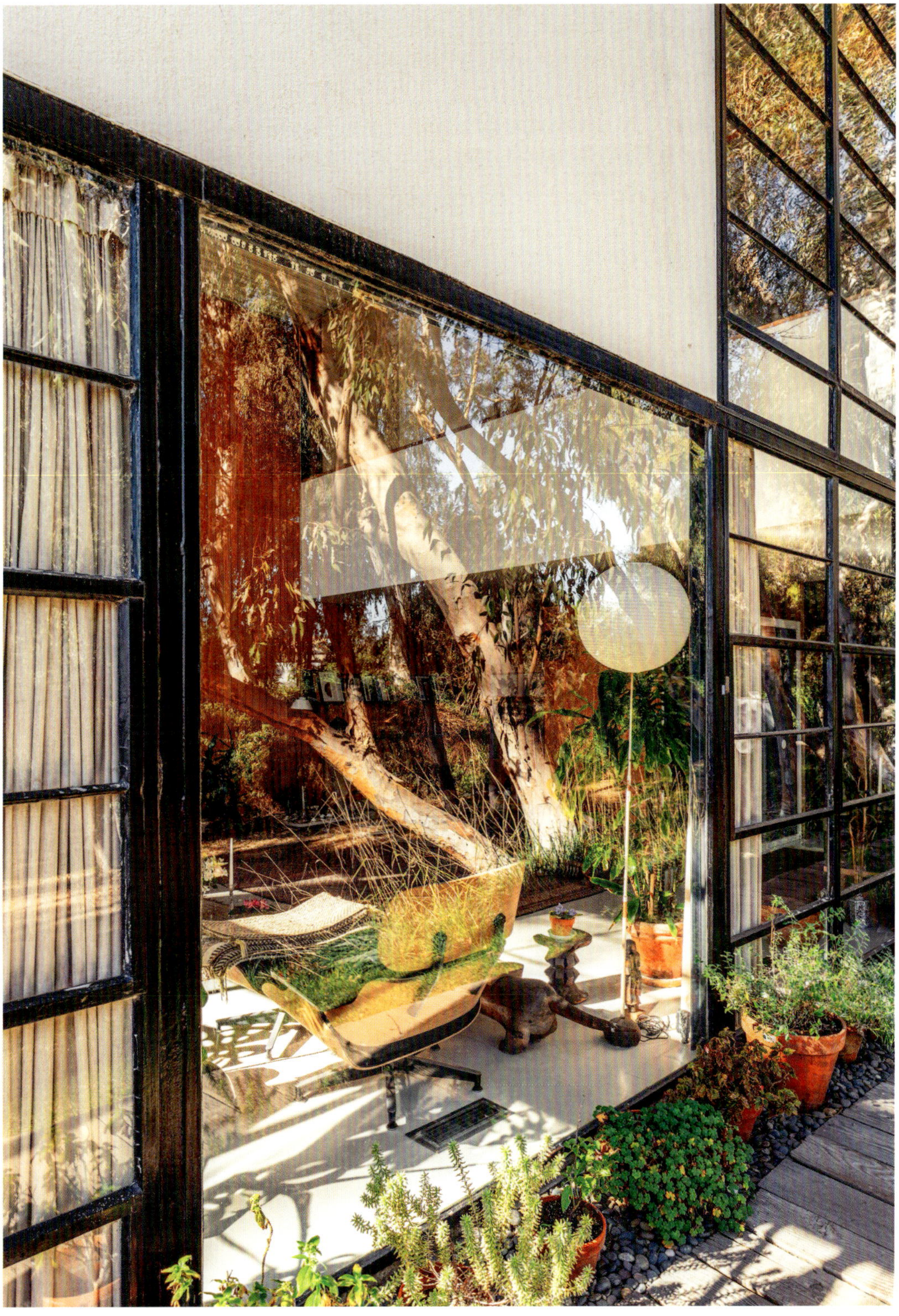

A view of the living room from outside the "living laboratory of the Eameses' ideals and creativity," as the Eames Foundation writes of the house.

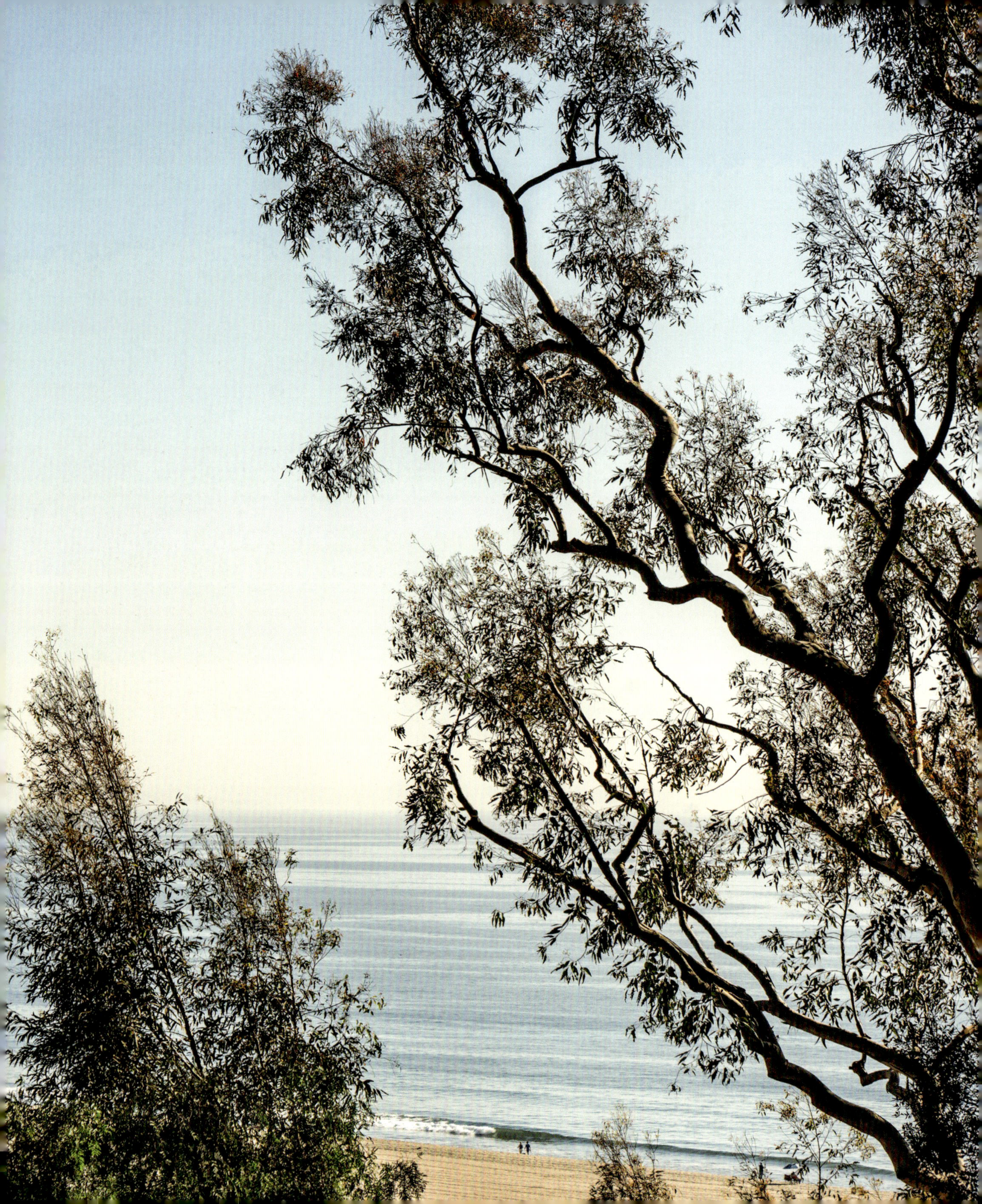

View of the beach from the garden of the Eames House in the Palisades Bluffs.

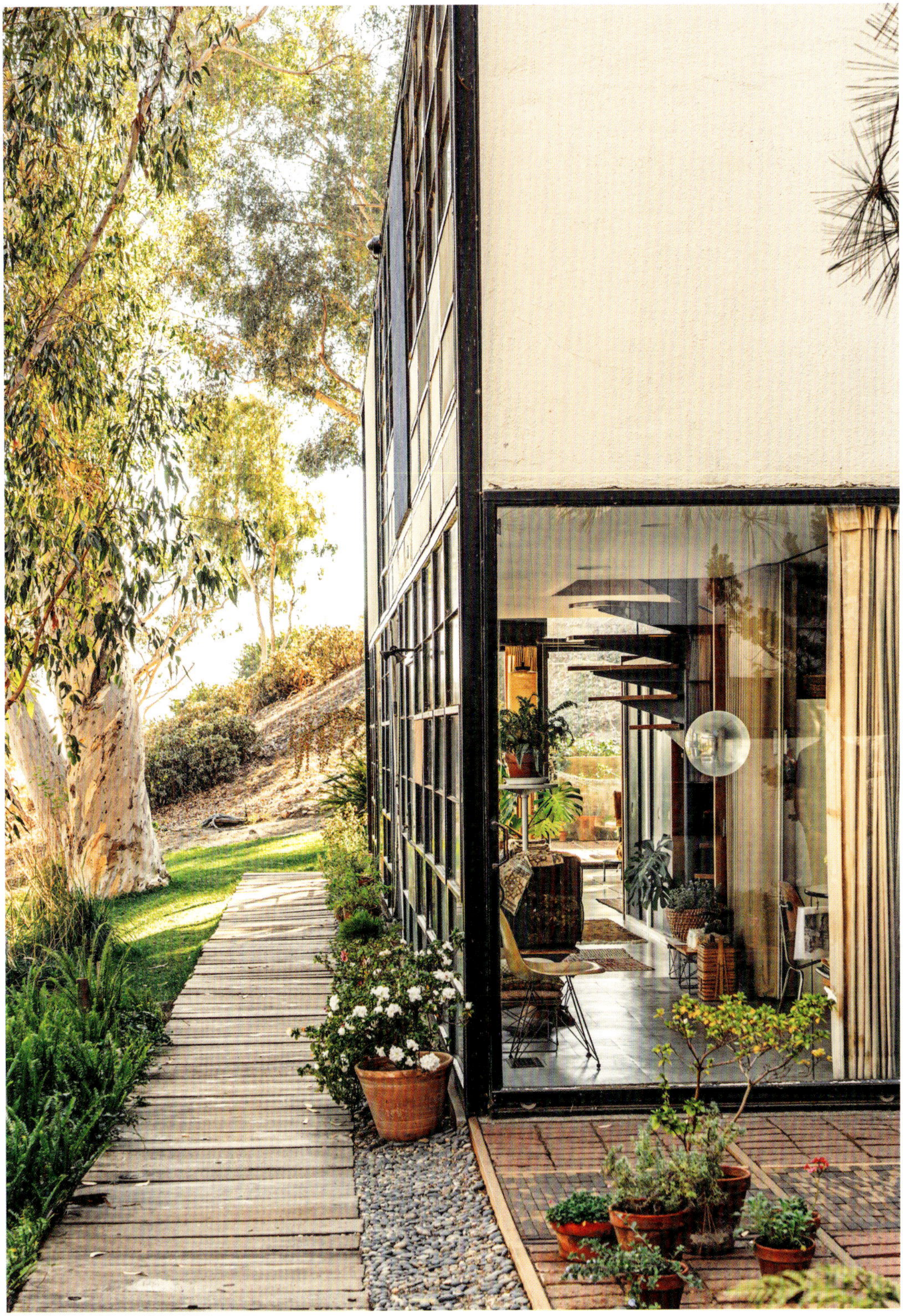

Located on a 1.6-acre site, the Eames House and its setting were declared National Historical Landmarks on Charles Eames's 100th birthday in 2007.

Santa Monica

The Beachside City We All Know

The Kuruvungna Springs, located on what is today the campus of University High School is one of the last remaining sacred sites of the Tongva, the indigenous people who inhabited and cared for the Los Angeles Basin for thousands of years. These springs, which are still cared for by Tongva descendants, are tied to the naming of the city of Santa Monica according to the Santa Monica Conservancy. When Spanish colonizer and priest Father Juan Crespí saw the springs during the Portola expedition, he was reminded of the story of Saint Monica, who cried for her wayward son.

Though famous as a beach resort, Santa Monica, the city, was initially founded in 1875 to be an industrial port for Los Angeles. That never stuck—instead, Santa Monica, linked to LA via Pacific Electric's streetcar system in 1908, became a residential and recreational area full of attractions like amusement piers, beach clubs, and even for a while, gambling ships docked in the bay. World War II brought the aviation industry to Santa Monica and with it a dramatic increase in population. Vestiges of this time can be seen today in places like the Museum of Flying and the Aero Theatre on Montana Avenue, a movie theater built specifically for workers at the nearby aircraft plant. (You can still see movies there today.)

Today, Santa Monica offers its beautiful beaches alongside unparalleled urban attractions—award-winning restaurants, historic watering holes, a plethora of shopping centers, art galleries, and museums. Many sites, especially the Santa Monica Pier, might seem familiar from seeing them on-screen. Legendary films such as T*he Sting, Fast Times at Ridgemont High, Iron Man, Forrest Gump,* and TV series like *Three's Company, Modern Family,* and *Gray's Anatomy* feature Santa Monica landmarks. A couple other iconic aspects of Santa Monica include the city's Big Blue Bus, an eye-catching system of public transport that was featured prominently in the film *Speed,* and the fact that Route 66, the mother road of American highways, ends here at the intersection of Lincoln and Olympic Boulevards.

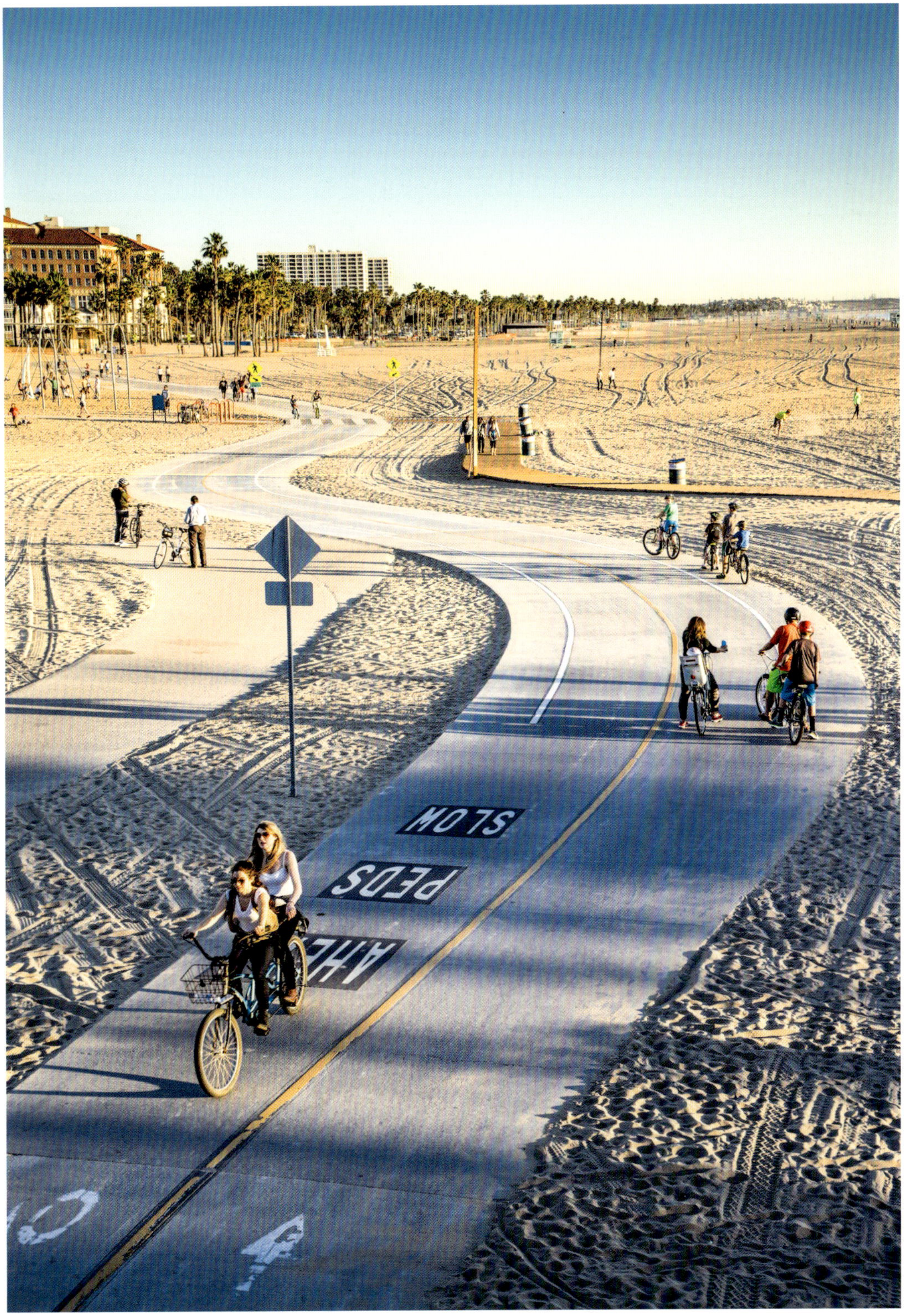

The 22-mile Marvin Braude Bike Trail stretches from Will Rogers State Beach in the Pacific Palisades south through Santa Monica and Venice Beach to Manhattan Beach, Hermosa, and Redondo Beaches, finally ending at Torrance County Beach.

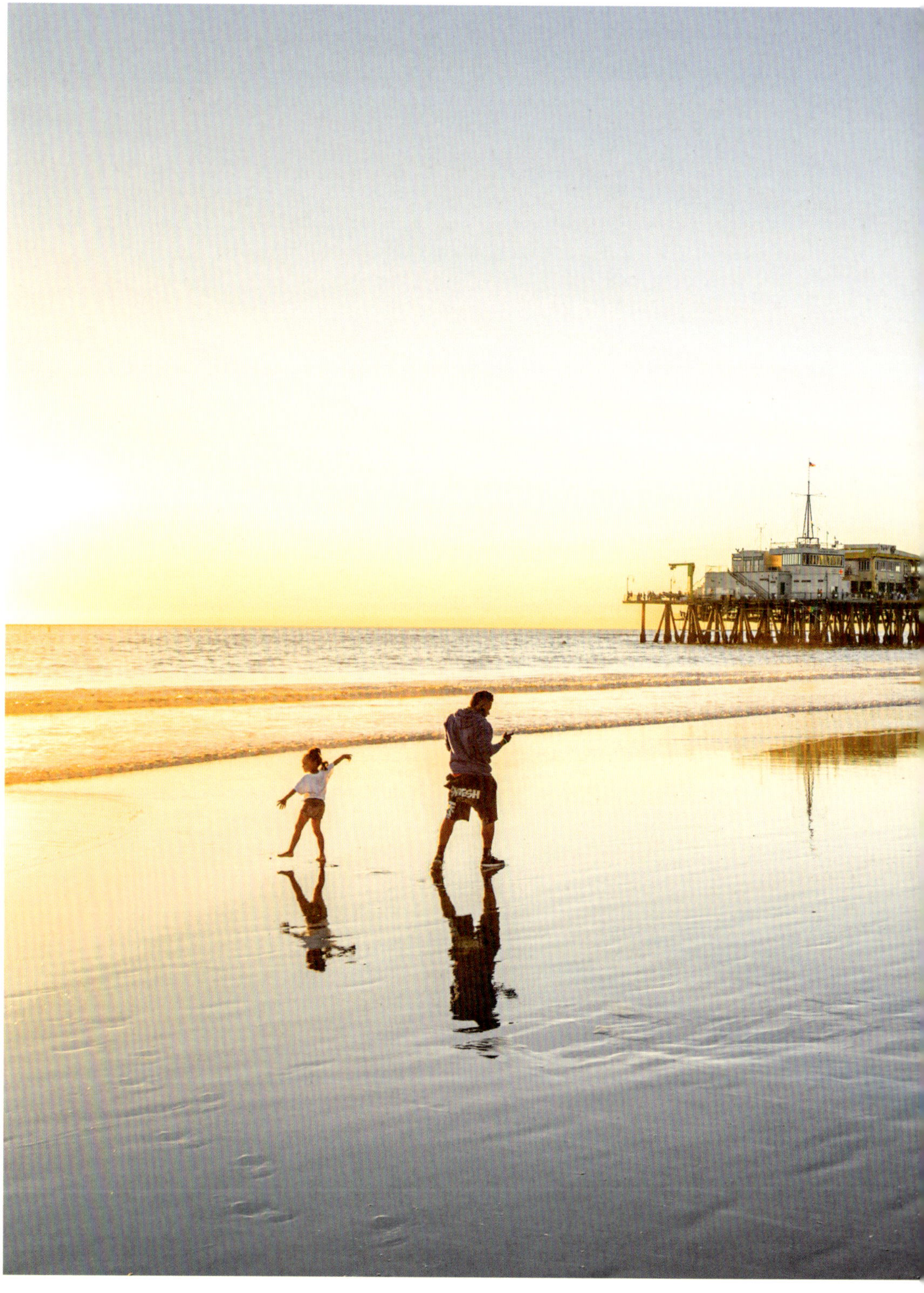

Completed in 1917, the Santa Monica Pier is comprised of two different piers that combine to form the quintessential pleasure pier, a special place that has delighted sun seekers with its amusements for more than a century.

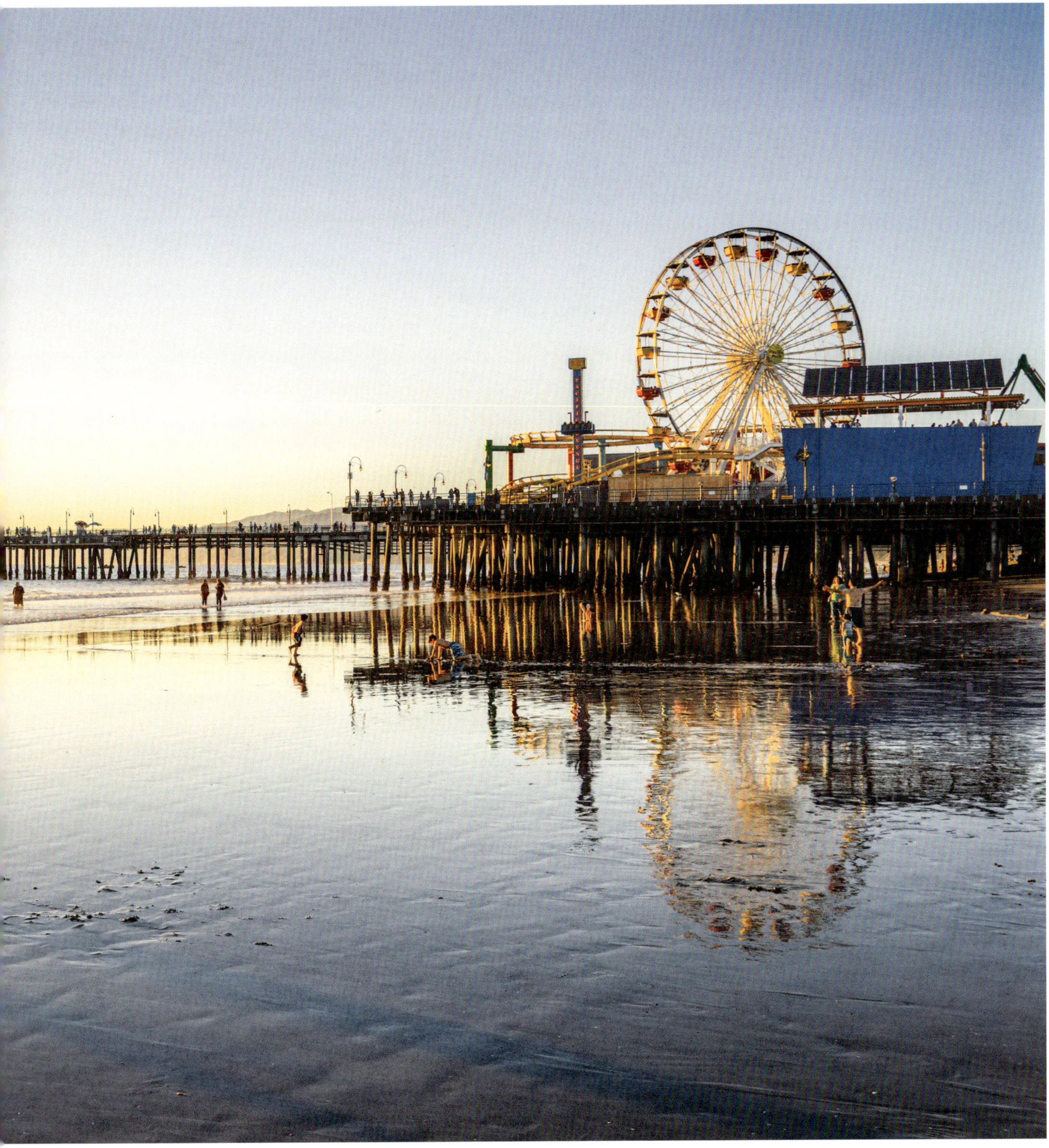

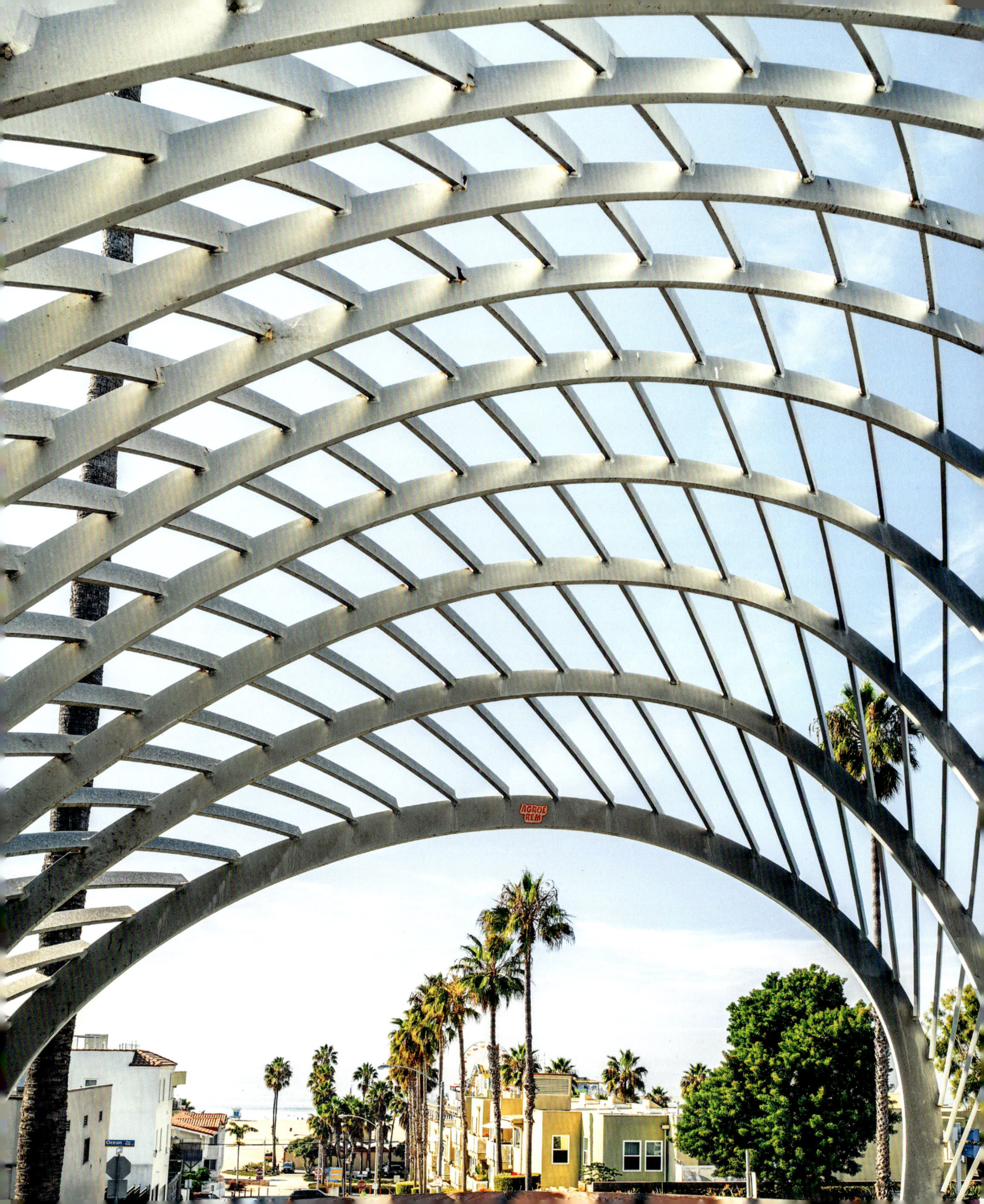
AGROE REM
Ocean

Within walking distance of the Santa Monica Pier, Tongva Park—named in honor of the city's original inhabitants, the indigenous people who have called LA home for thousands of years—offers six acres of public space for play.

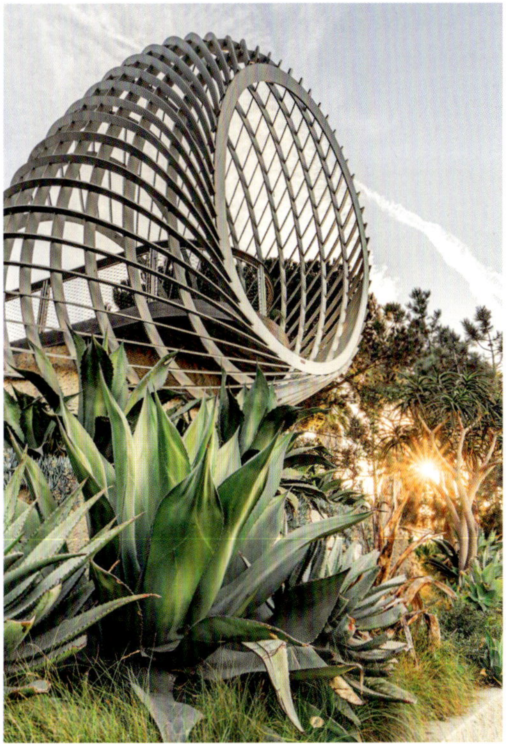

Views from the steel pavilions of Tongva Park offer incredible vistas of the beach across the street and the surrounding city of Santa Monica.

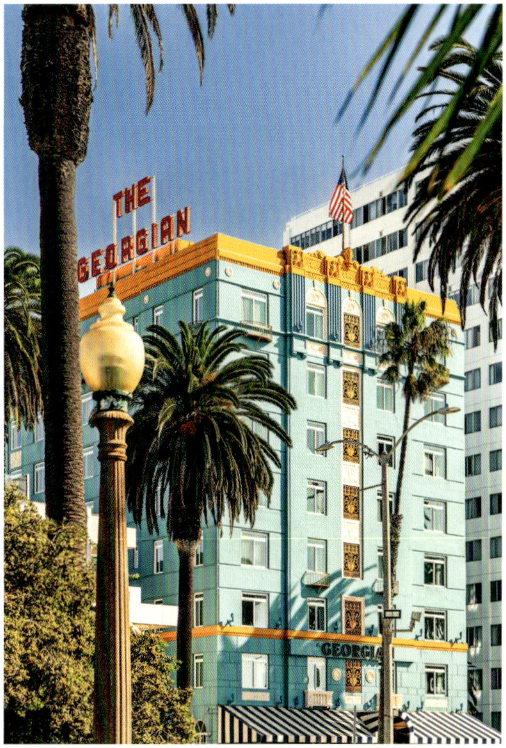

Built in 1931, the Georgian Hotel served for many years as one of the tallest buildings in Santa Monica and its Art Deco style captures the opulence of the chic seaside beach clubs of its era.

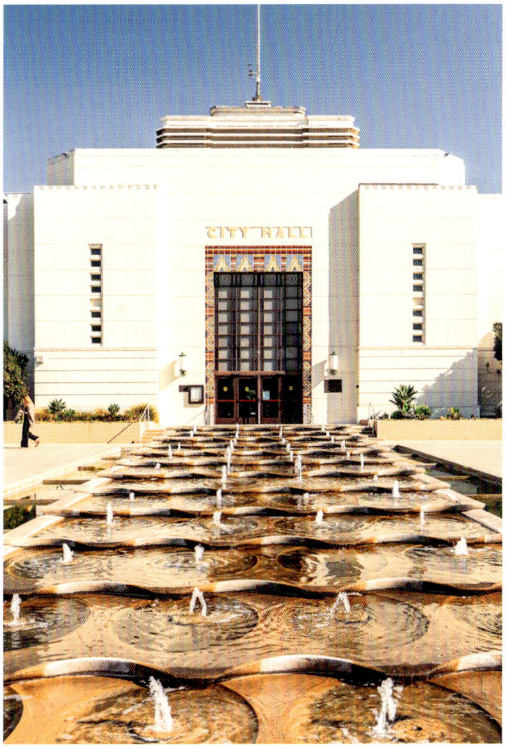

Another example of the city's love for Art Deco, Santa Monica's City Hall was built in 1939 and funded mostly by the Public Works Administration.

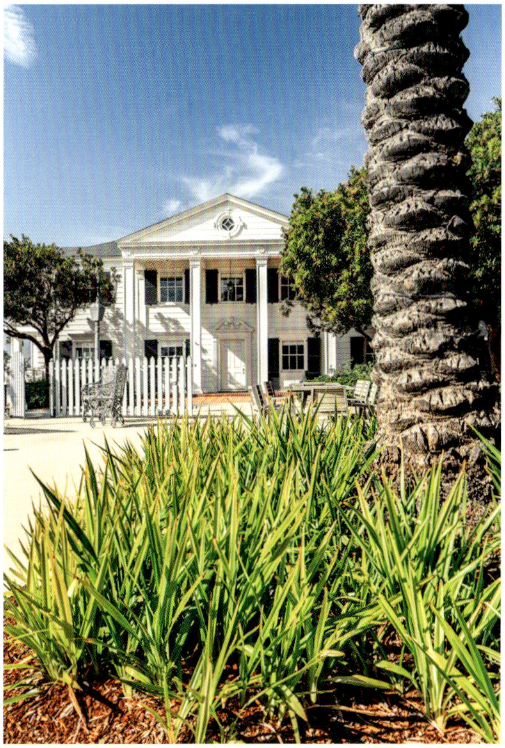

A view of the historic Marion Davies Guest House, which is part of the Annenberg Community Beach House, an oceanside community center complete with beach access, a restaurant, and a pool. Once the site of actor Marion Davies's grand mansion, the guest house is all that remains of her estate, a relic of Santa Monica's days as Hollywood's Gold Coast.

Lifeguard Towers

Symbols of the SoCal Beach

An incredibly large part of LA's public beaches are free to use and offer a host of public facilities such as restrooms, volleyball courts, concession stands, showers, and playgrounds. Plus, most are patrolled by lifeguards, ensuring the safety of swimmers, surfers, and sunbathers. In fact, Los Angeles boasts the largest professional lifeguard service in the world, securing 31 miles of beach. Those lifeguards are an iconic part of SoCal culture—as are the wooden stands or huts they work from that dot the beaches.

Though they look like tiny, homemade cabins, the midcentury style structures you'll see lining the coastline of Southern California are lifeguard towers, built to shield lifeguards from the oppressive sun. Built on stilts so the lifeguards can better see the action happening in the ocean, these wooden structures serve as stations for the lifeguards, and the buildings are usually uniformly painted light blue. Each tower is numbered, and along with its lifesaving purpose, also serves as a useful landmark when trying to find your beach friends or way back to the car.

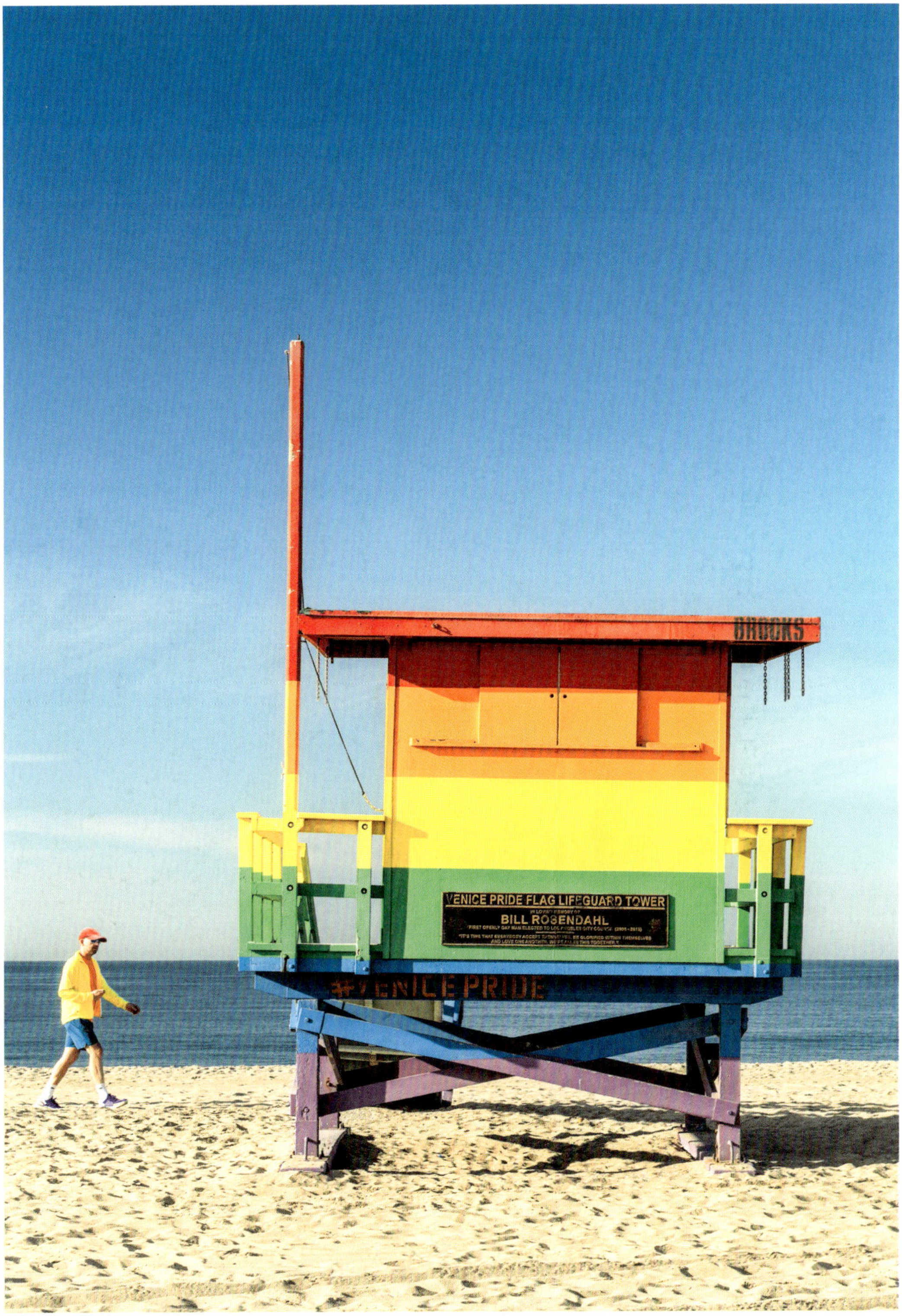

Located just north of the Venice Beach Skate Park at the end of Brooks Avenue, this lifeguard tower received a makeover in 2017 in honor of Pride Month.

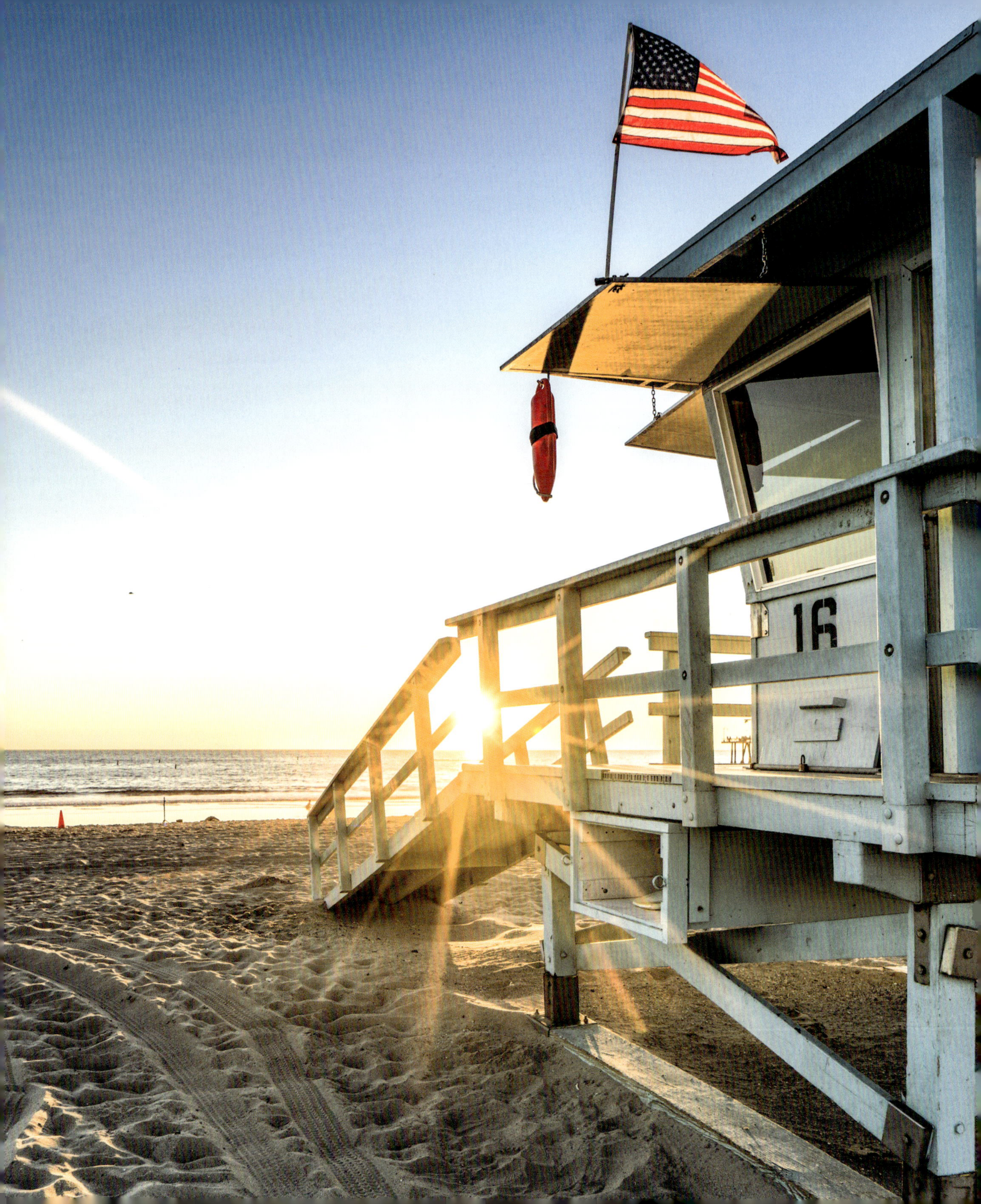
16

LA's iconic blue lifeguard towers have become symbols of the Southern California beach—and as such, they show up frequently in film and TV, including *Baywatch*, *Three's Company*, and *The O.C.*

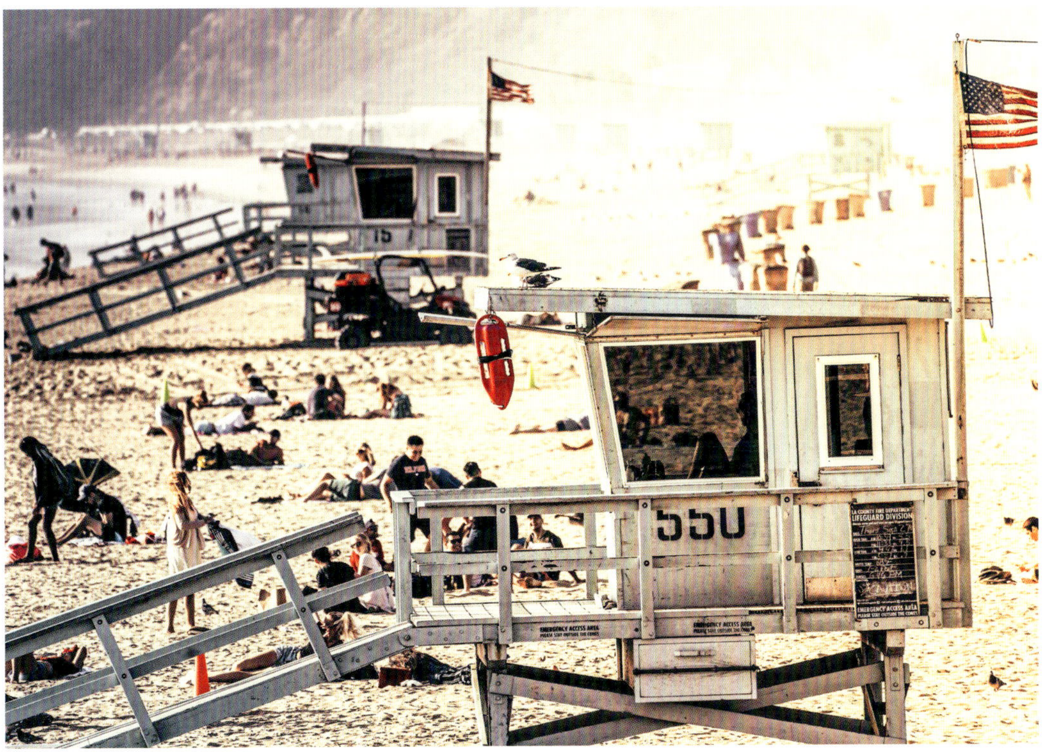

There are so many beaches in LA, and each has its own personality—some, like Santa Monica and Venice, are crowded and great for people watching; others are spots locals know for surfing or for taking their dogs (there are special dog beaches!).

The Pacific Coast Highway

The Rustic Roadway that Gives Coastal Drama

One of the most unique highways in the US, the Pacific Coast Highway—or "PCH" as it's colloquially called—provides an unforgettable driving experience along the dramatic California coastline. Officially designated as California State Route 1, this road is the stuff of car commercials—a narrow sliver of the asphalt perched on the edge of the continent, winding its way through rocky twists and turns. All the while, the cerulean blue of the Pacific Ocean glimmers beside you, beckoning. This is why tourists rent convertibles, so they can soak it all in during their limited time here.

For those of us who live in LA, the PCH might still conjure joy, but also frustration—it's congested, the traffic on weekends at a dead stop, and due to various disasters (earthquakes, mudslides, fires), often in need of repair. Still, we love our piece of State Route 1, which is California's official designation for the road that is mostly just referred to as either "the PCH" or "the One." (You've seen *Saturday Night* Live's "The Californians" skits, right?) And as far as roads go, this is absolutely the one.

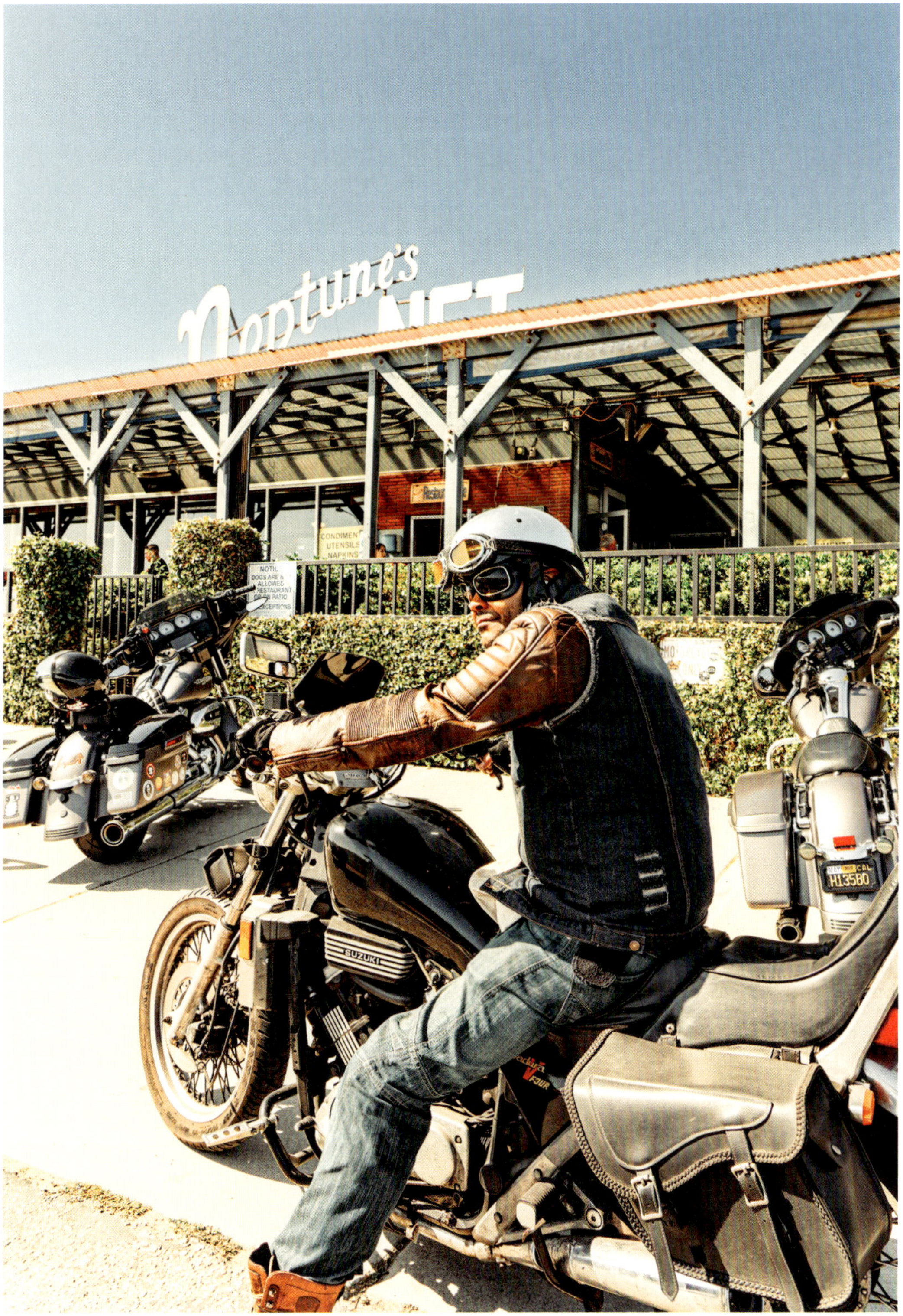

A roadside seafood shack, Neptune's Net opened in 1956 and is across the street from the County Line Beach, a popular surf spot called out by the Beach Boy's in "Surfin' USA."

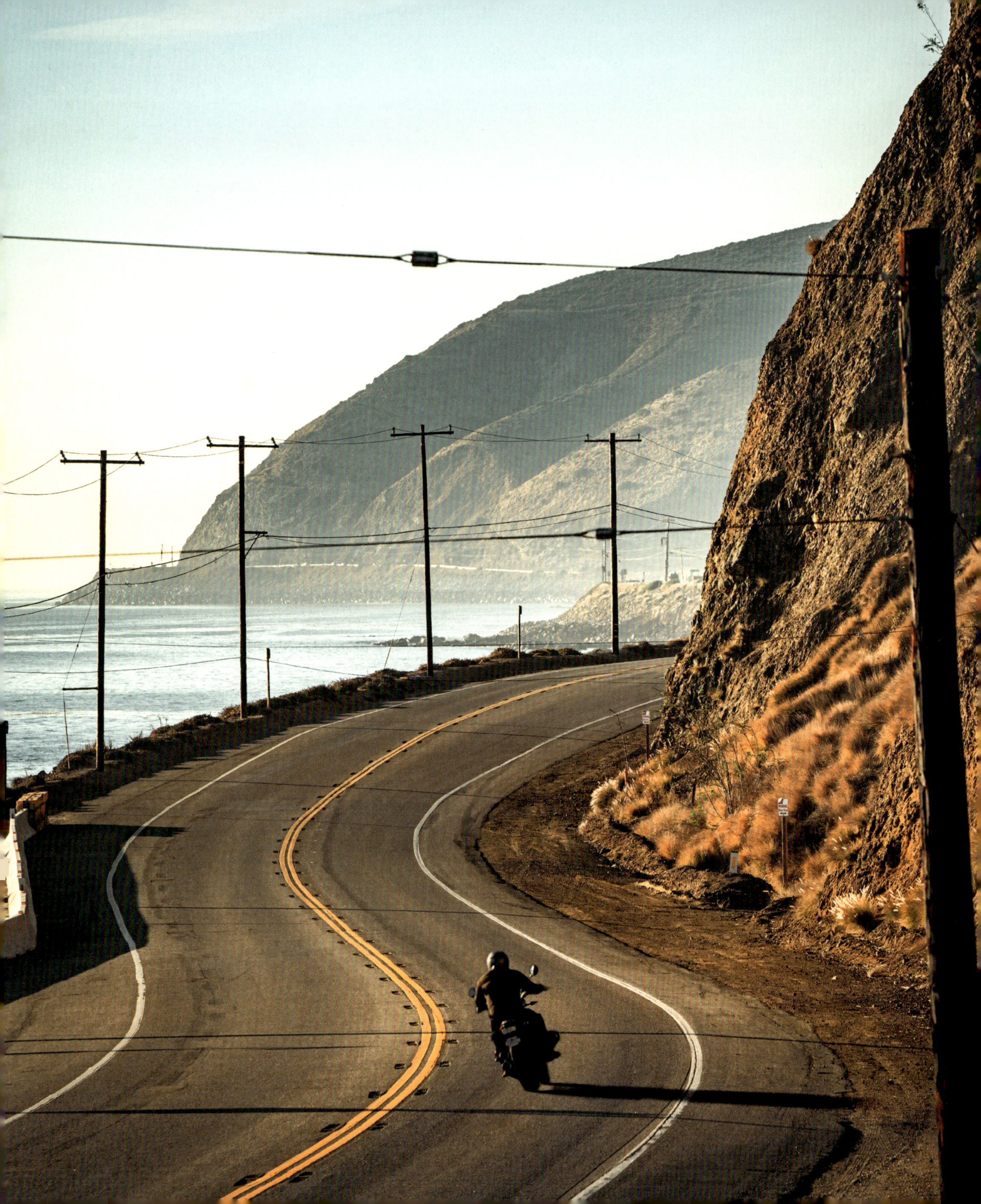

Musicians from the Beach Boys and Burt Bacharach to Courtney Love's band Hole have taken the iconic PCH as inspiration for songs, trying to capture the feeling of driving along the beautiful coastline.

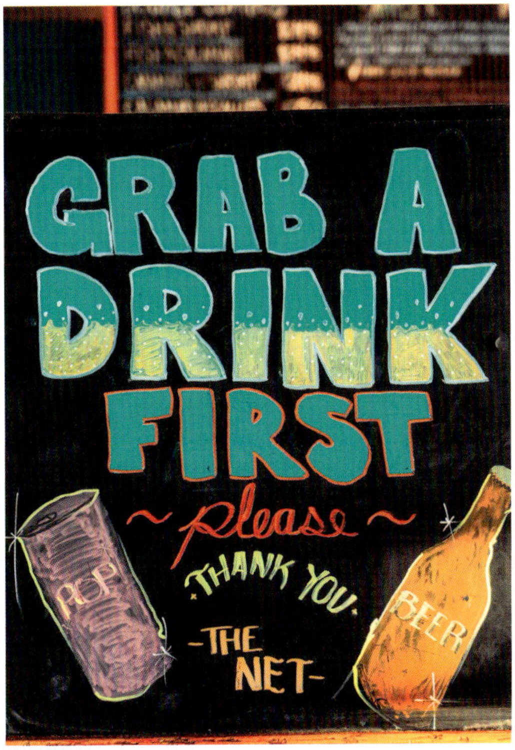

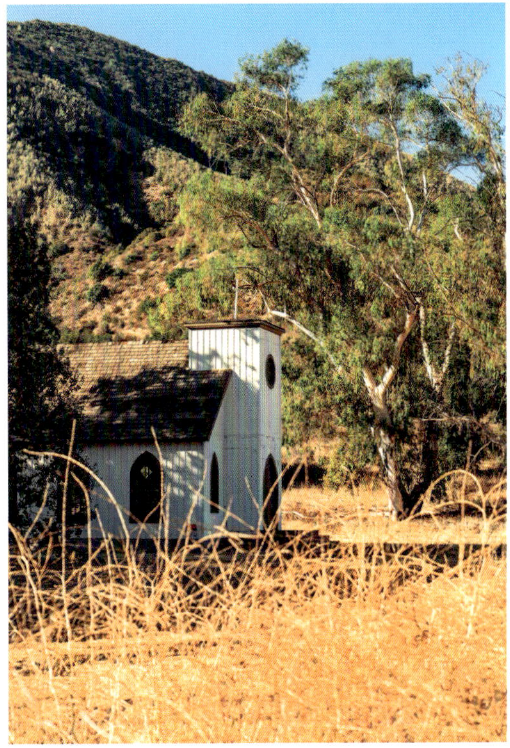

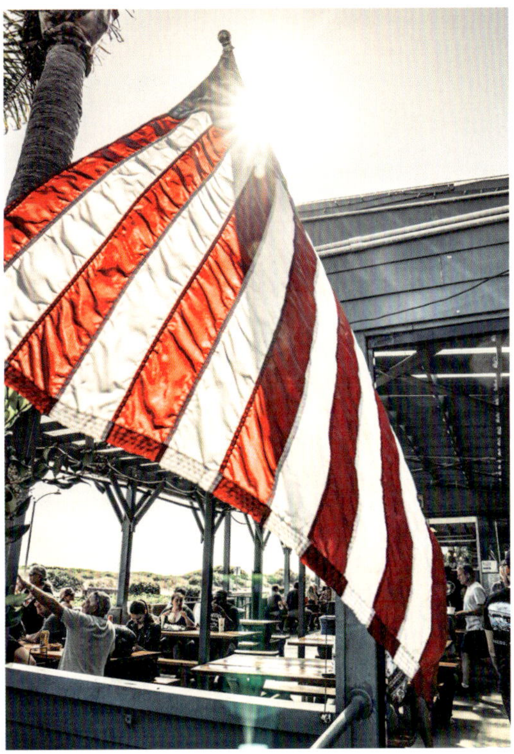

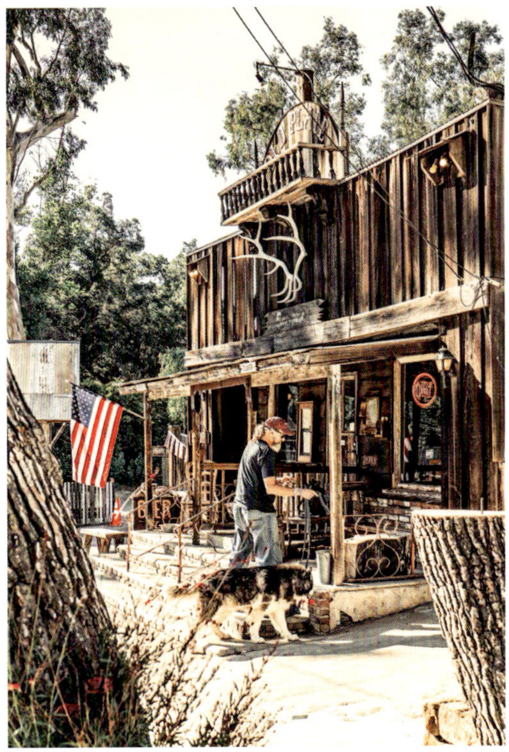

A sign at Neptune's Net on the PCH guides you to get it done.

After being badly damaged in the 2018 wildfires, Paramount Ranch, a park owned by the National Park Service that includes Paramount Pictures' old moviemaking ranch, remains open for visits, and the chapel used in the TV show *Westworld* survived the fires.

Neptune's Net shows up frequently on-screen, from *Point Break* to *The Fast and the Furious*, but it's also a place actors enjoy in their off-work hours—everyone from Liz Taylor to Bono, Bob Dylan, Cher, Drew Barrymore, and Arnold Schwarzenegger have been spotted here.

Farther inland, deep in the canyon, is another old gem of a restaurant, the Old Place, which has remarkably survived many bad wildfires to offer a singular experience of dining in the midst of the Santa Monica Mountains.

Venice Beach

A Boho Beach That Shows LA's Wacky Side

Originally named "Venice of America" to distinguish it from that *other* Venice, today's famed beach town started out in 1905 as the vision of developer Abbot Kinney, who sought to create a seaside resort inspired by Italy's Floating City. Building a system of canals with romantic footbridges, a pleasure pier, and a carnival-worthy assortment of related attractions, Kinney's Venetian fantasy came to life and brought sun and fun seekers from all over.

It's a fittingly quirky start to what has become the edgiest and most bohemian beach in Southern California. Venice Beach has a vibe, and the heartbeat of it emanates from the boardwalk, aka Ocean Front Walk, the oceanside promenade of street performers, caricature artists, and effusive vendors selling goods of all kinds. There's a reason the 2014 reality show about the area was titled *Freakshow*, and you won't find a better place for people watching maybe in all of LA.

Venice Beach is second only to Disneyland as Southern California's most popular tourist attraction, so expect crowds and a lively atmosphere. Whether you are into skateboarding or roller skating, basketball or drum circles, there's an activity for everyone here. And that eclecticism applies to food and shopping as well—there's a mix of high and low, from fancy boutiques, art galleries, and fine dining spots to delicious burger and taco stands (try Tito's, it's an institution) and the veritable swap meet of the boardwalk.

Street mime? Hot Dog on a Stick? Marijuana? You'll find it here, all in close proximity to famed spots like the health food store Erewhon and the iconic "Venice" sign that spans across Windward Avenue. As the actor Orson Bean once said, "Most municipalities grow up around commerce; there's a harbor, or the train stops there. Venice, CA, was founded for fun."

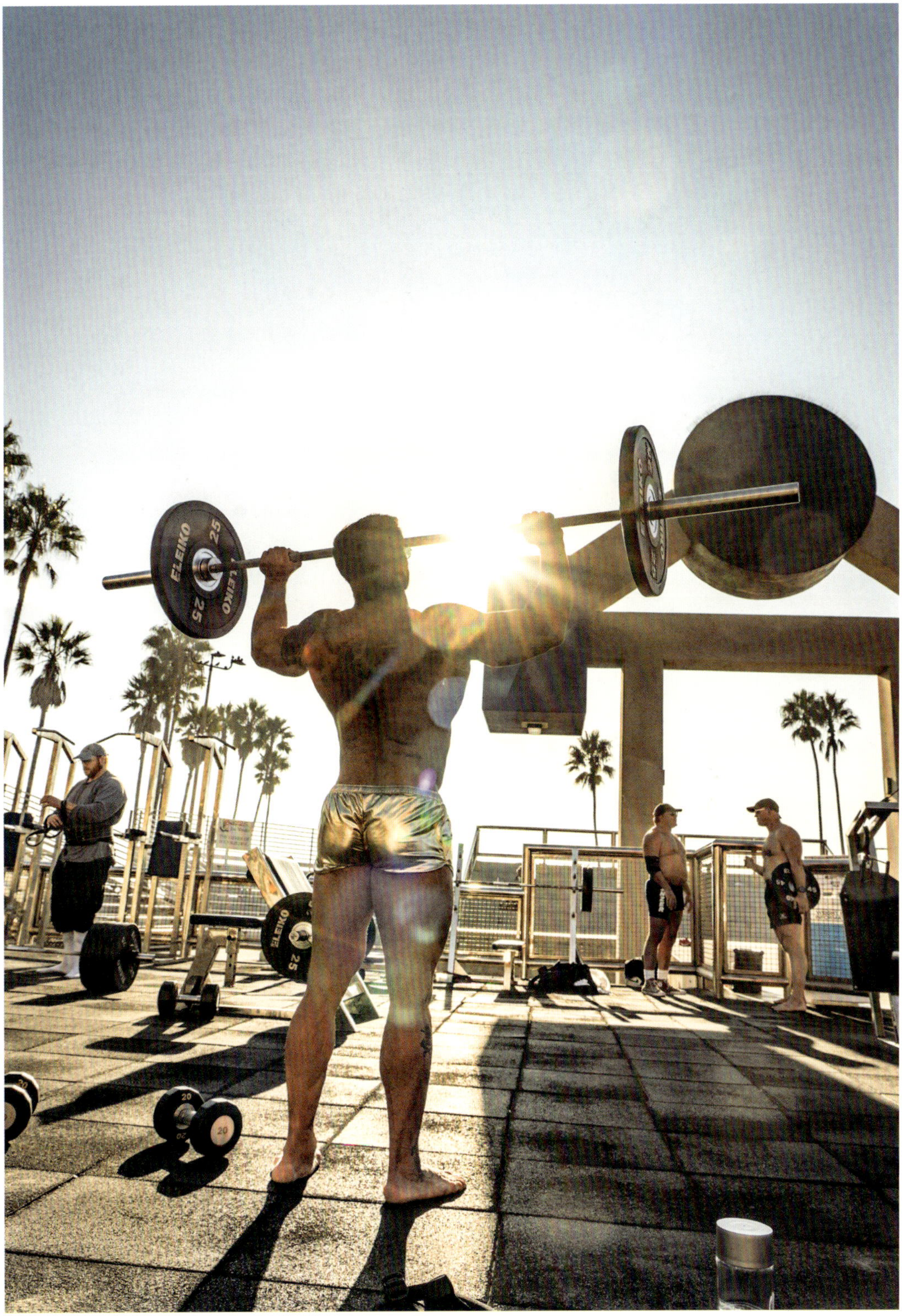

A view from Venice's Muscle Beach, a hub for displays of athletic prowess from all kinds of fitness enthusiasts.

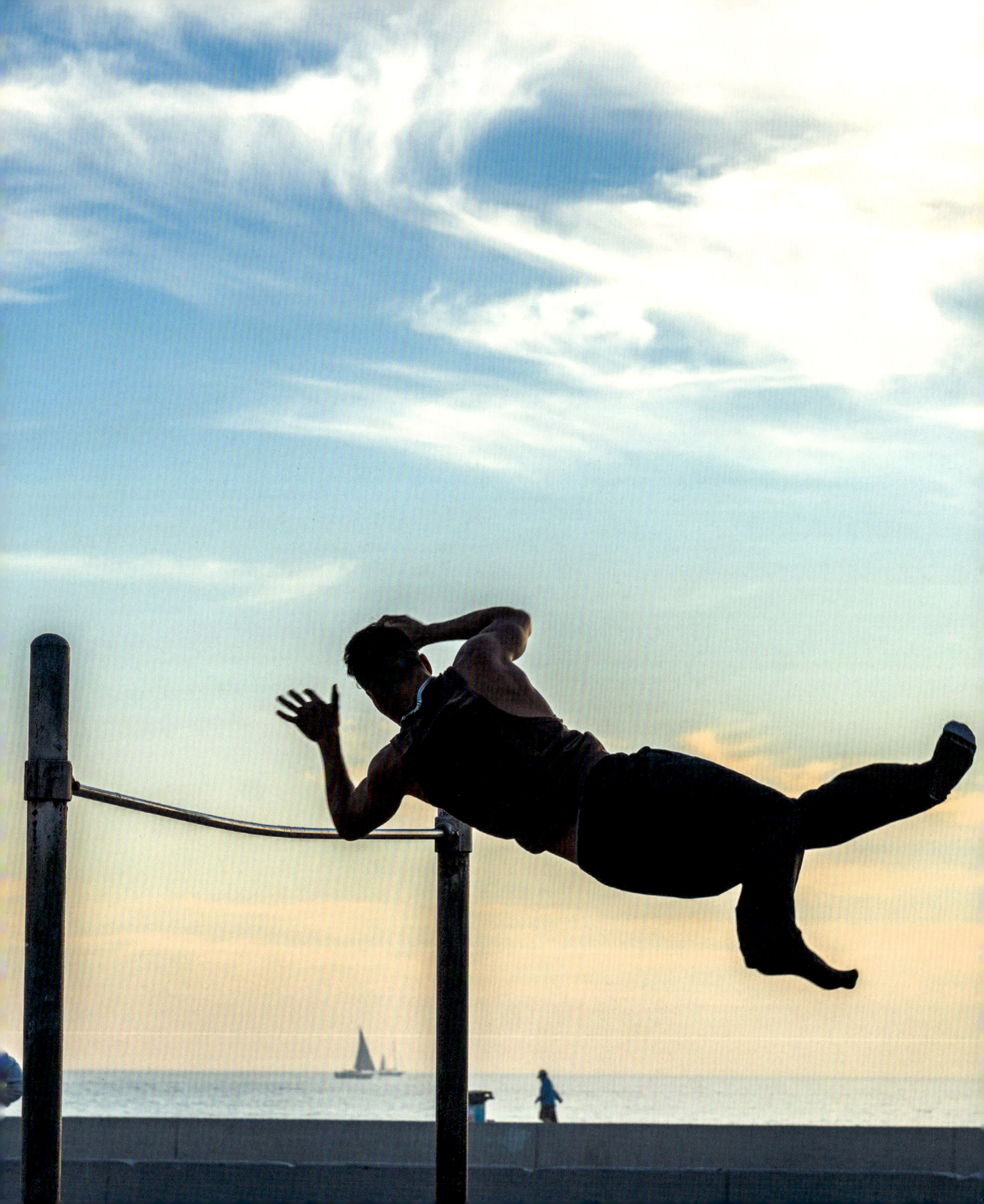

Though today's Muscle Beach is in Venice, the original Muscle Beach that launched the fitness craze for bodybuilding in the 1930s was actually located in Santa Monica.

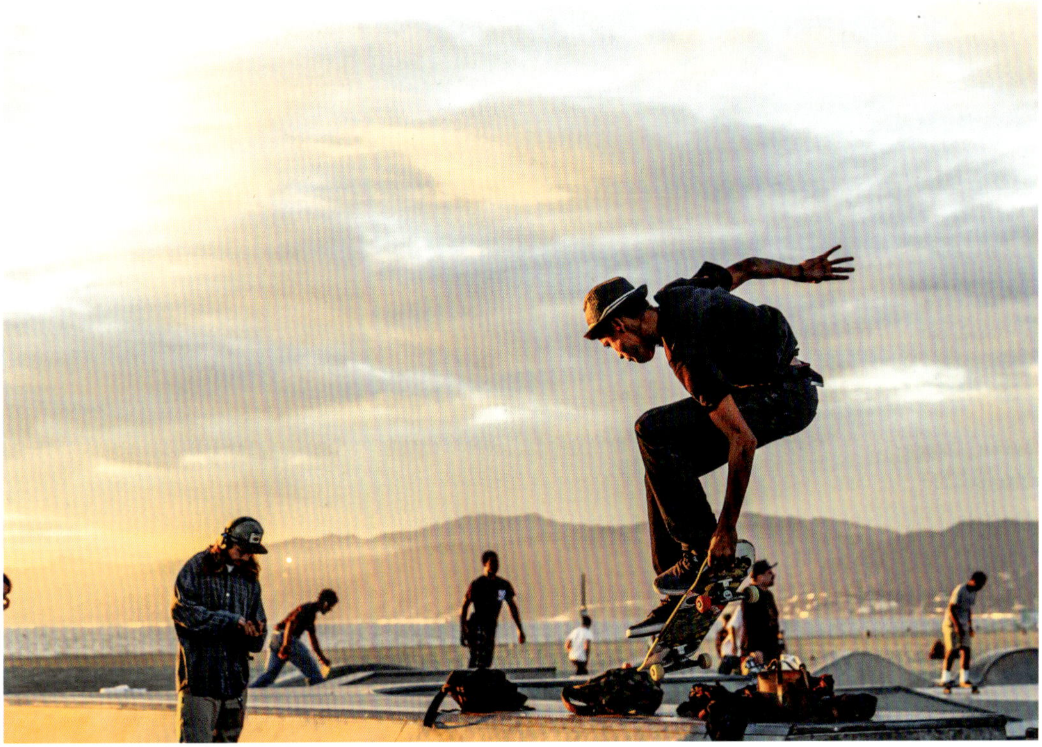

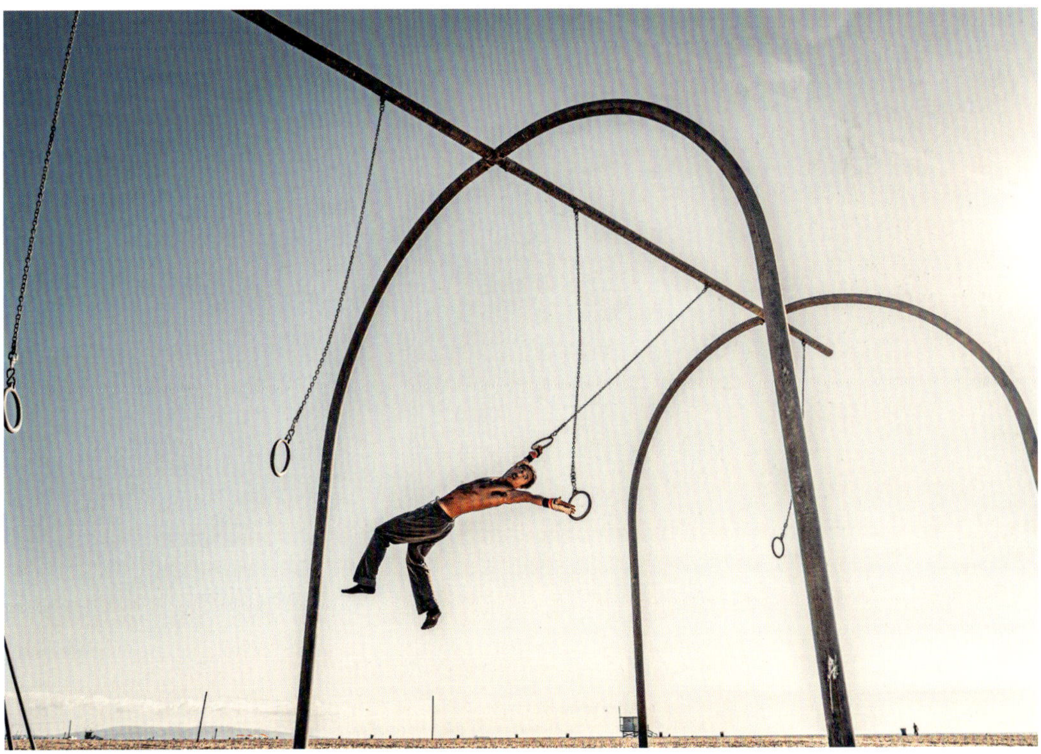

Skateboarding has long been a part of Venice culture, from the Z-Boys of the 1970s to the diverse group of folks that frequent the 16,000-square-foot Venice Beach Skate Park, which is one of the only oceanfront skate parks in the world.

Muscle Beach's famous exercise rings inspire beachside acrobatics and gymnastic feats of all kinds. It's a free playground for kids of all ages.

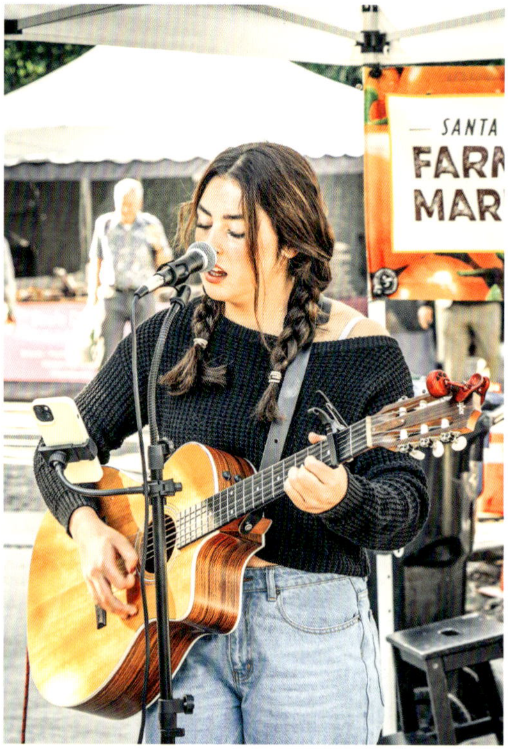

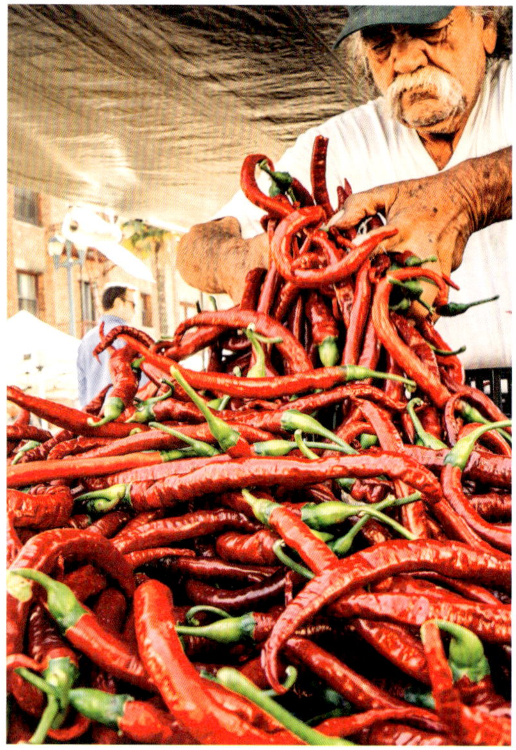

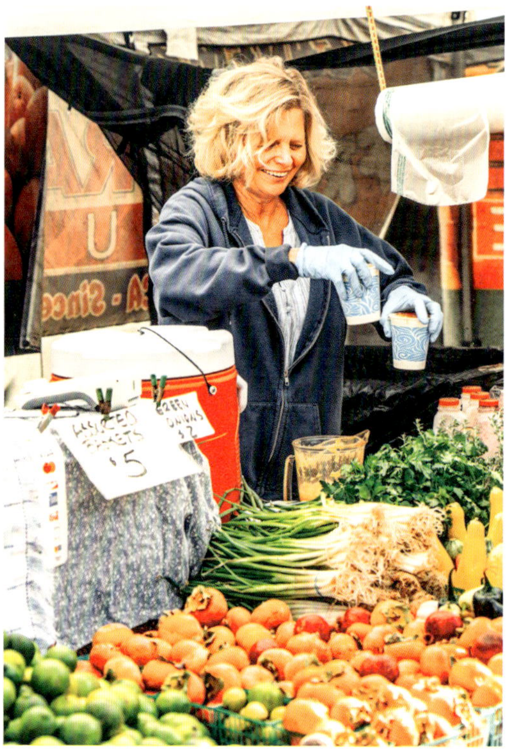

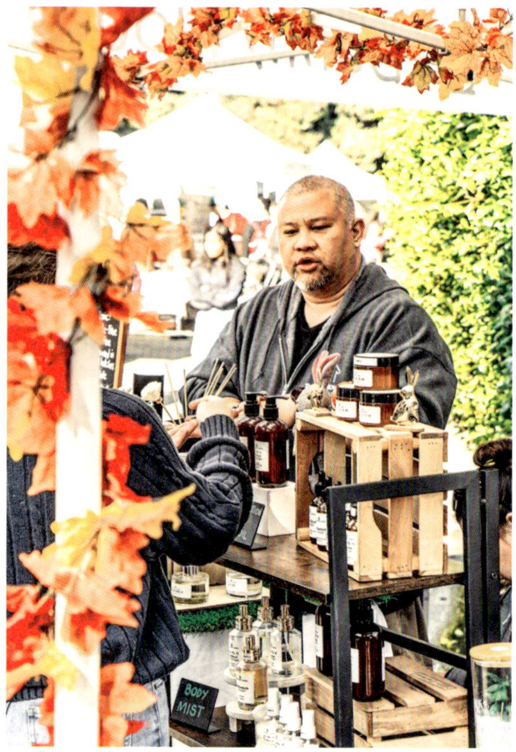

A musician performs at Santa Monica's famed downtown farmers market.

Locally grown produce—like these peppers—provide a taste of the city.

Farmers markets also provide prepared food alongside fresh produce and other goods.

To sell at the market, farmers must certify that their goods are made in California.

Farmers Markets

Where to Shop for the Best Produce and Artisanal Food

Farmers markets are a big deal in Los Angeles—bountiful, outdoor markets that pop up once a week in various places and bring the best and most beautiful produce, along with other locally made artisan foods and goods, directly to Angelenos in their own neighborhoods. Whether it's Atwater Village or Crenshaw, Mar Vista or Bunker Hill, Torrance or Silver Lake, there are dozens of options, but look online first to check which market is happening in what neighborhood. No matter what location, expect the best in seasonal produce, along with local food and craft vendors, and maybe even some local musicians performing. And don't confuse these weekly markets with the one and only Original Los Angeles Farmers Market, located at Third and Fairfax in Hollywood—it's the iconic open-air market that is open every day and has been for almost a century!

The granddaddy of all LA's weekly farmers markets, however, is the famous Downtown Santa Monica Farmers Market, which is so big it actually happens twice a week—Wednesdays and Saturdays at Arizona Avenue and 2nd Street. Wednesday's market is famous for being frequented by some of the city's most notable chefs, such as Niki Nakayama of n/naka and Suzanne Goin of A.O.C. For chef sightings, arrive when the market opens, as they like to be there early to get the very best produce the market has to offer. For the best deals, go right as the market closes, when vendors are hoping to clear out their booths. In any case, go hungry and sample as many as the offerings as possible—Los Angeles is a foodie destination for so many good reasons, and this is one of them.

Abbot Kinney Boulevard

A Shopping District of Beach Bungalows and More

Named after the nineteenth century developer who founded "Venice of America," Abbot Kinney is the chicest shopping street in Venice, offering a full mile of stores and restaurants to peruse, from big chains to decidedly local businesses. Of course, "chic" is a moving target in a city as big as LA, and almost every neighborhood has its own cool row of shops and eateries that evolve over time from trendy to tired and then back again. But in Venice, Abbot Kinney is certainly a place to check out the local culture, and it will be less crowded than the more touristic spots like the boardwalk.

Firstly, there's a branch of Erewhon, the high-priced health food store that's known worldwide for its celebrity smoothies on the street. As far as boutiques, several promote local and California-made goods, such as Ilan Dei Venice and Sofia Kaman Fine Jewels, and you'll also find the flagship stores for many brands like Aviator Nation, TOMS, and Industry of All Nations that were all born in LA. The boulevard offers no shortage of bars and restaurants, including chef Evan Funke's Felix Trattoria, and, of course, Gjelina, the quintessential Venice restaurant with its veggie-forward menu and unbeatable vibe, especially on the back patio.

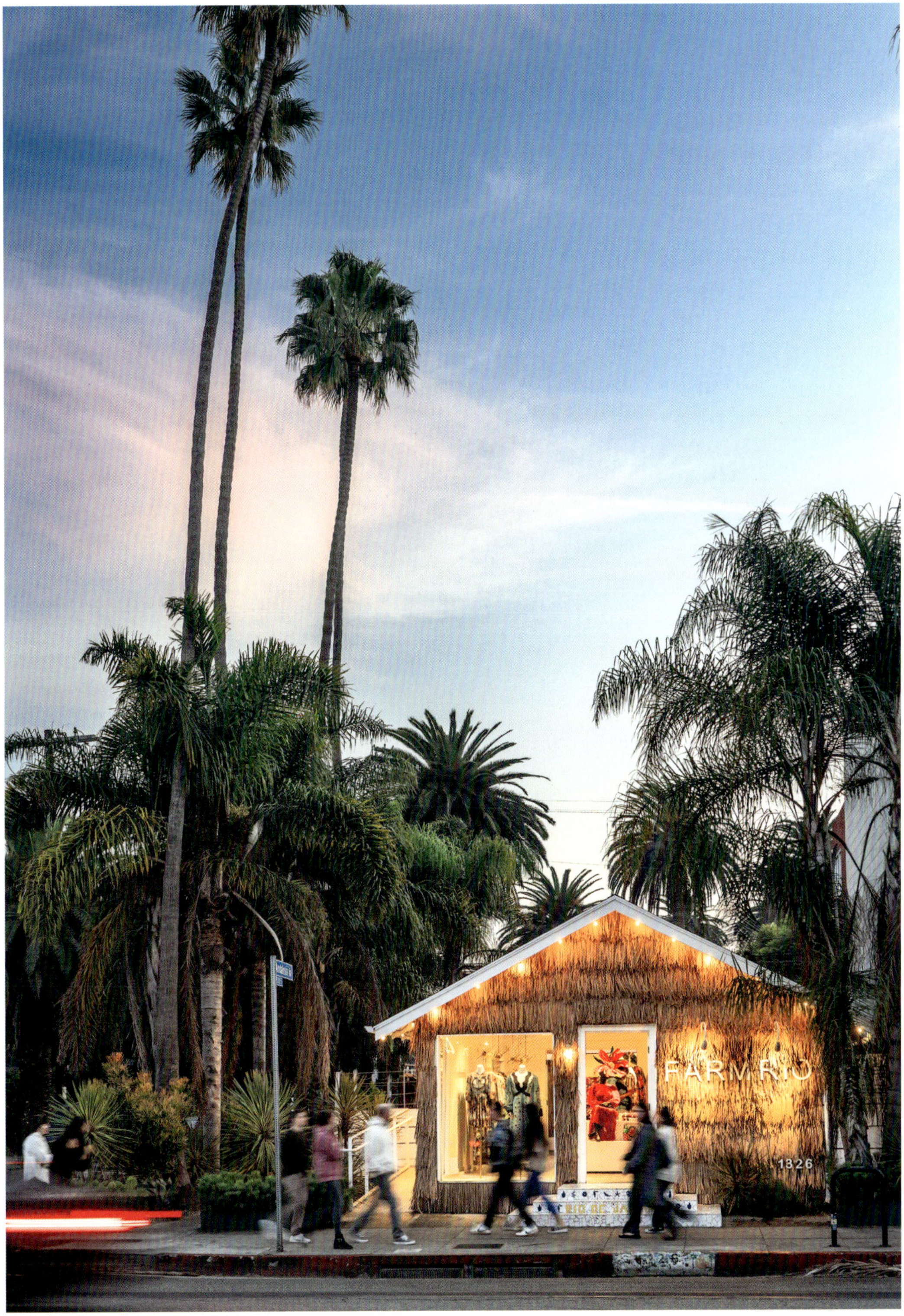

Shopping is just one part of Abbot Kinney's appeal—another is people watching with a beautiful backdrop.

(Page 64–65) A mural by artist Thunder Voice Eagle acknowledges that Abbot Kinney Boulevard and the land around it is the ancestral land of the Tongva people, who continue to live in Los Angeles.

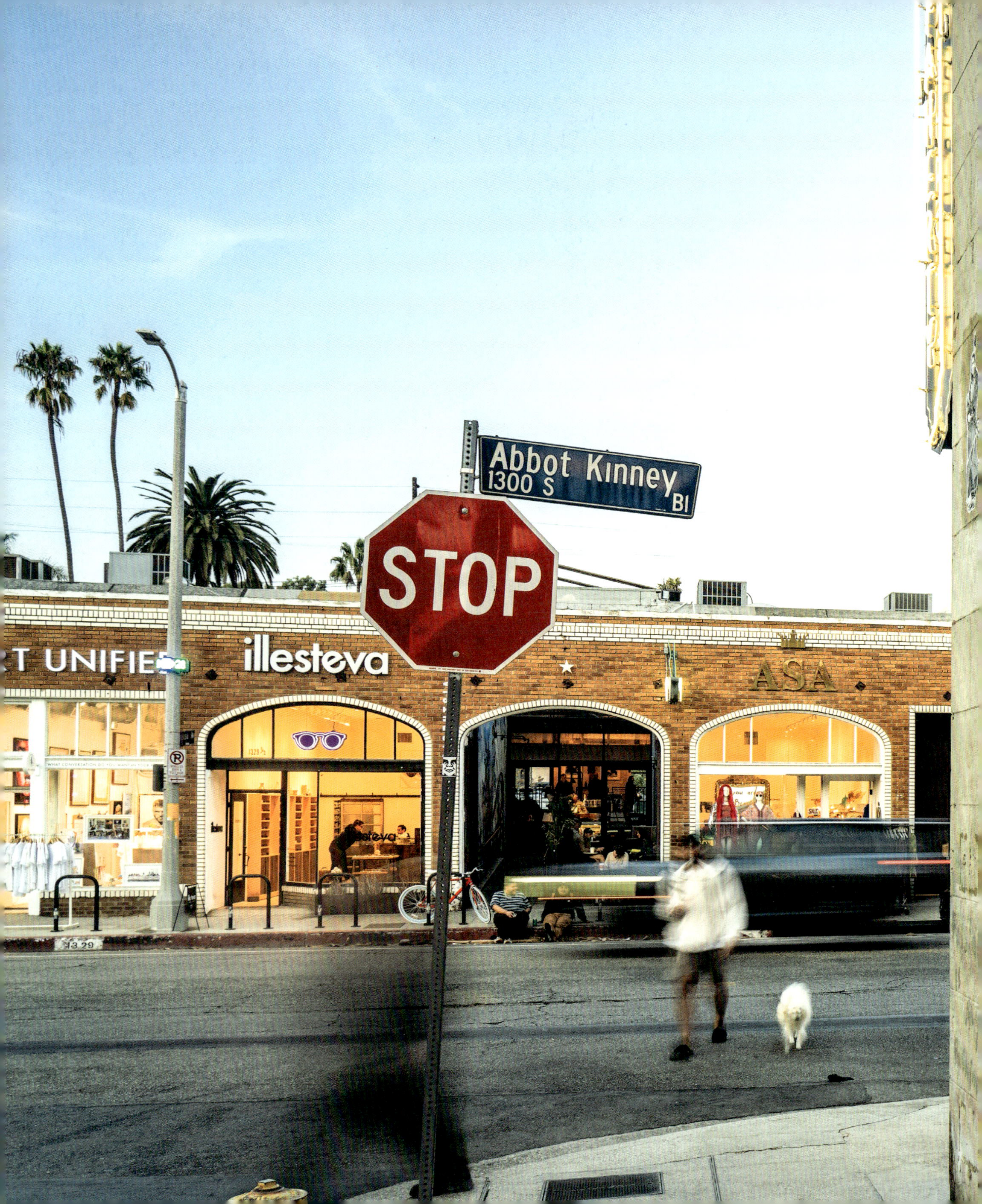
Abbot Kinney
1300 S
Bl
STOP
T UNIFIE
illesteva
ASA

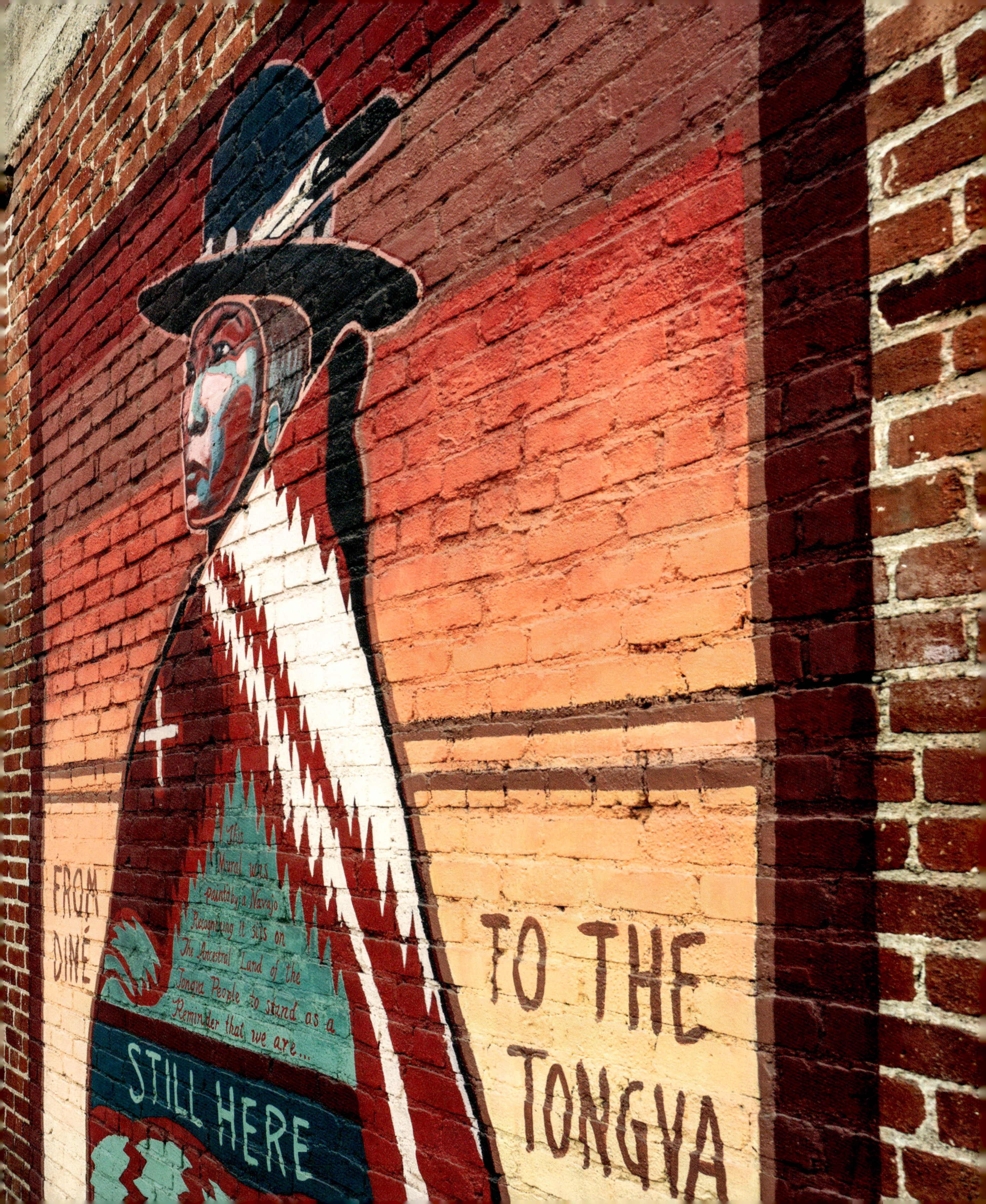
FROM
DINÉ
This
Mural was
painted by a Navajo
Recognizing it sits on
The Ancestral Land of the
Tongva People to stand as a
Reminder that we are...
STILL HERE
TO THE
TONGYA

Getty Center

World-Class Art, Architecture, and Gardens

Perched over the city in the dramatic hills above West LA is the Getty Center, a blindingly bright complex of buildings designed by famed architect Richard Meier and clad in Italian travertine. The complex includes the J. Paul Getty Museum, which houses art from the Middle Ages to the present day, as well as the Getty Research Institute and the Getty Conservation Institute. There's also more than eighty-six acres of outdoor space, including artist Robert Irwin's Central Garden. While admission is free to the Center, reservations are required, and there is a parking fee. If one Getty isn't enough, there's another in Malibu, the Getty Villa Museum, which offers a collection of Greek and Roman antiquities, with a stunning view of the ocean.

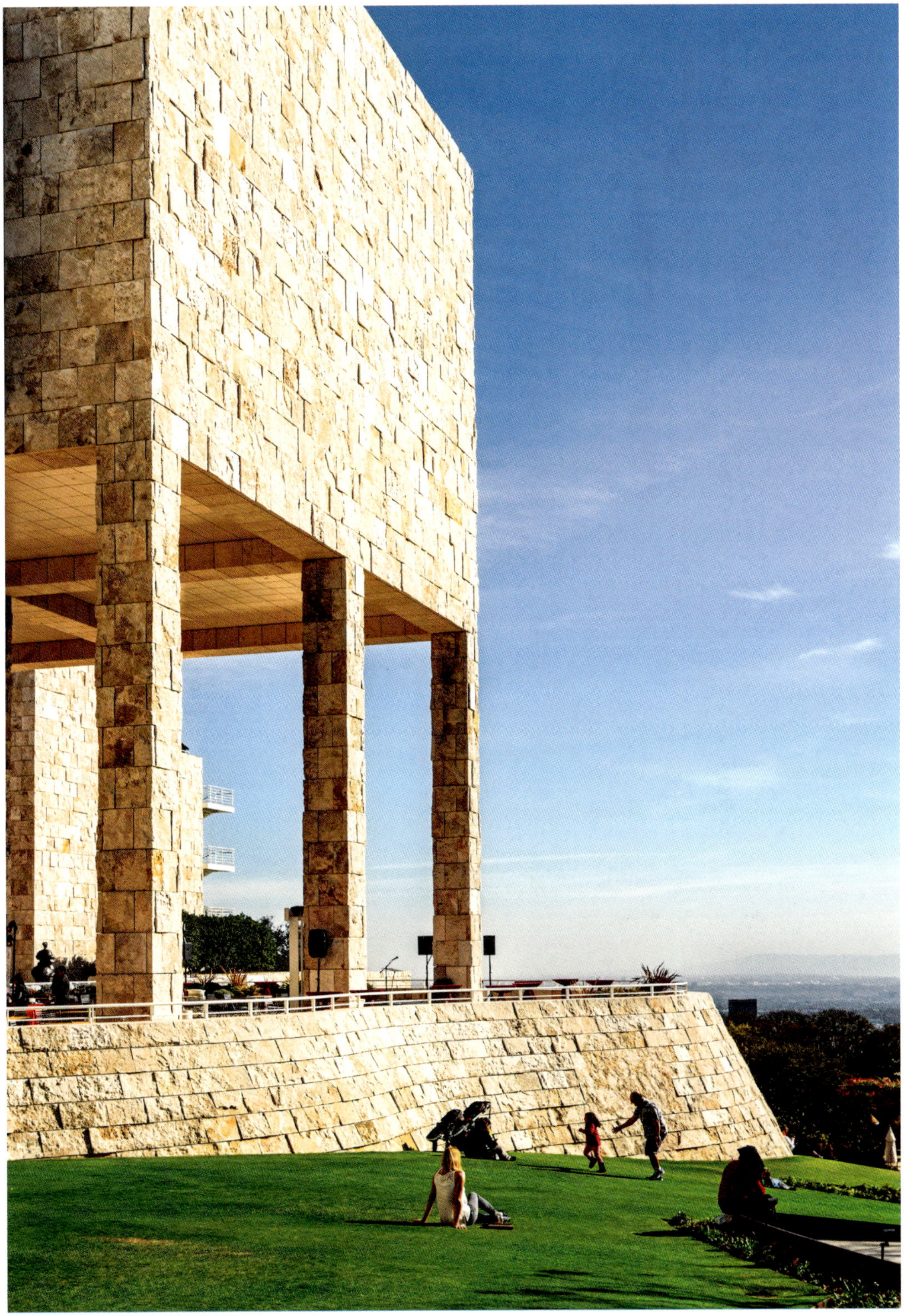

Open to the public six days a week, the Getty Center welcomes nearly a million and a half visitors each year.

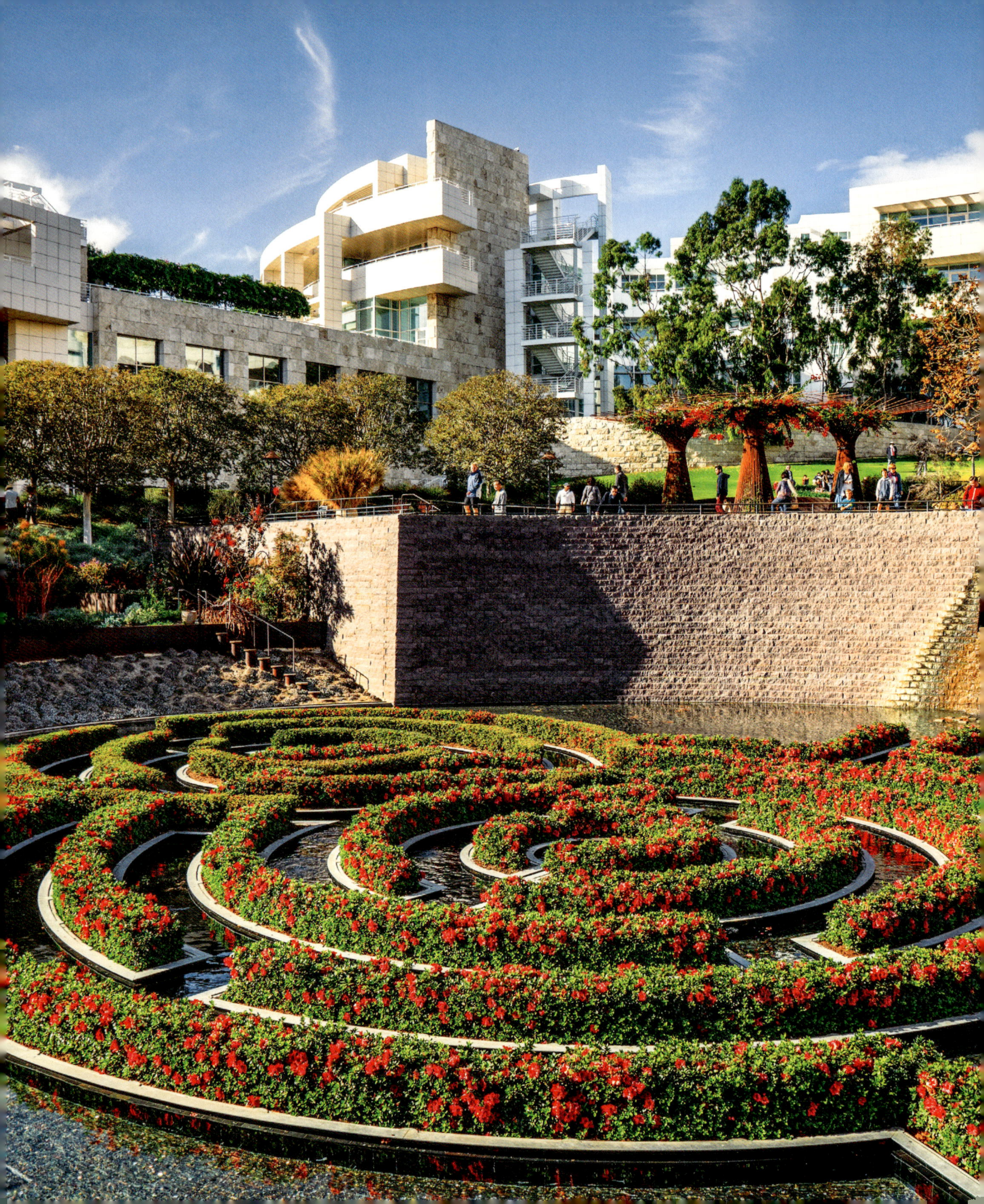

Artist Robert Irwin's design for the Central Garden incorporates more than 500 different species of plants and is a 134,000-square-foot work of art commissioned for the space.

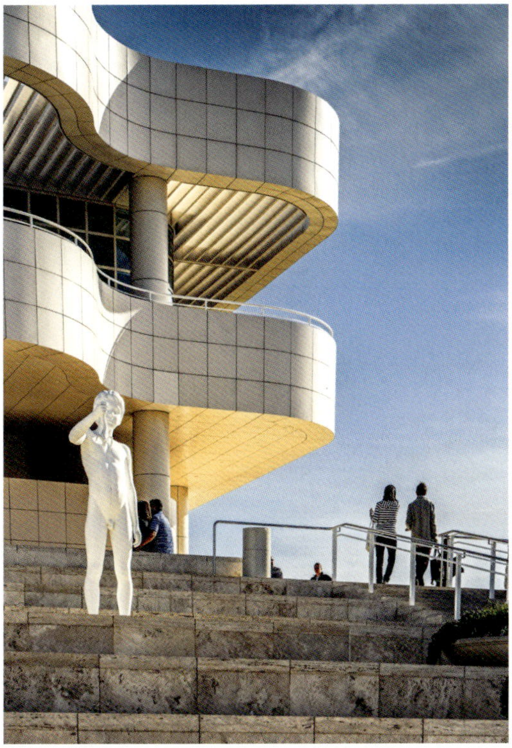

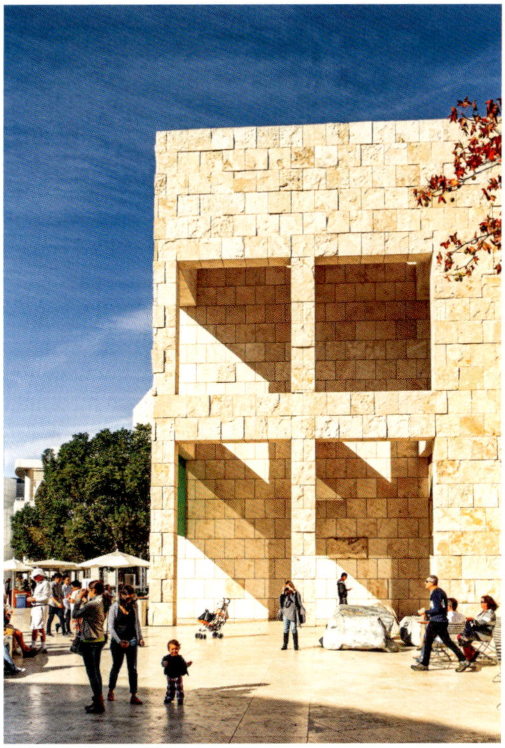

■□ The buildings' curvilinear lines are designed to harmonize with the surrounding natural landscape, and the Center complex took fourteen years to build.

□■ Set on 110 acres, the Getty Center offers stunning glimpses of the Pacific and a panoramic view of the city—and fossils can be found in the buildings' travertine.

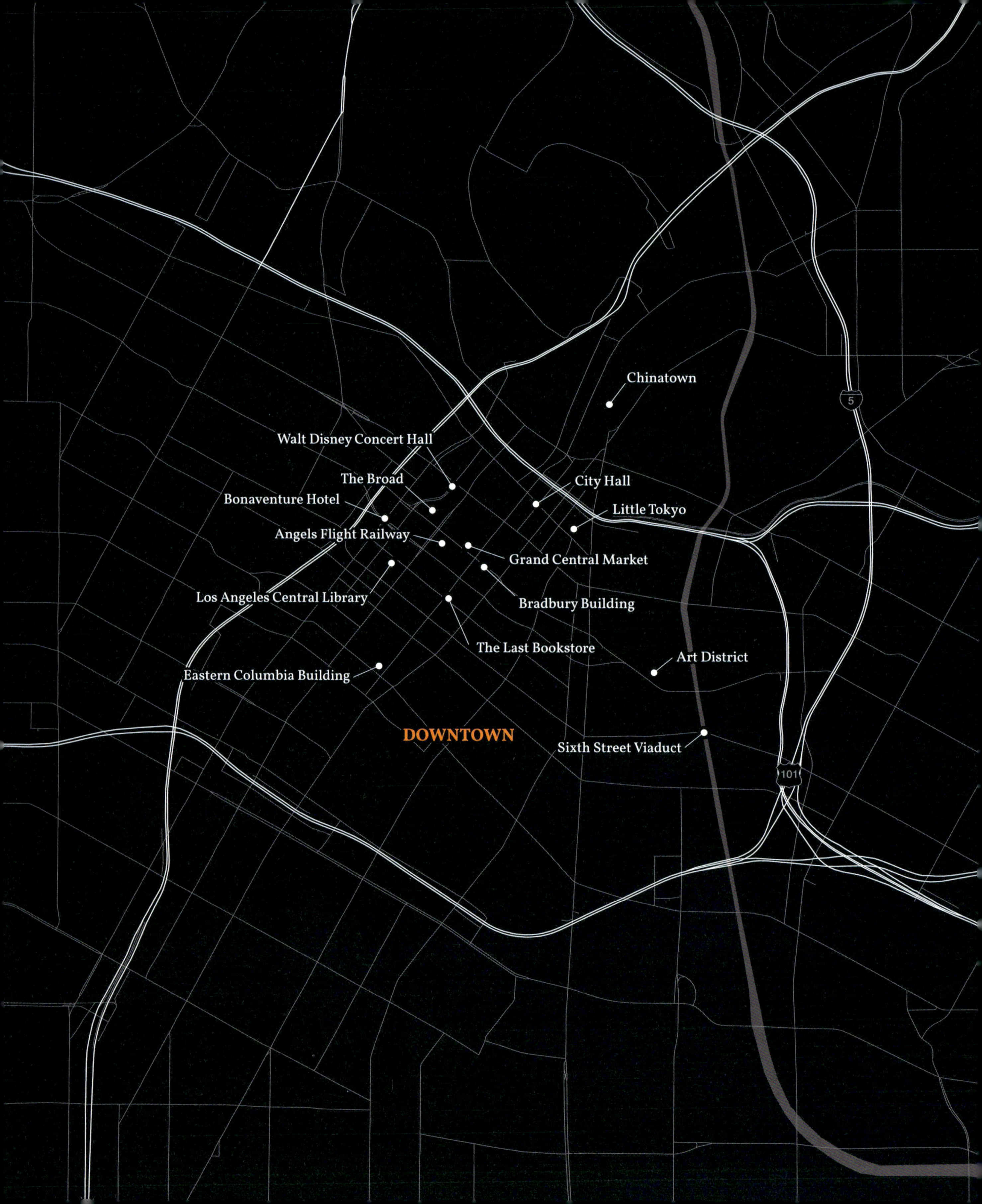

Chinatown
5
Walt Disney Concert Hall
The Broad
City Hall
Bonaventure Hotel
Little Tokyo
Angels Flight Railway
Grand Central Market
Los Angeles Central Library
Bradbury Building
The Last Bookstore
Art District
Eastern Columbia Building
DOWNTOWN
Sixth Street Viaduct
101

Downtown Los Angeles (DTLA)

Iconic Sites

An Epicenter for Creativity and Culture

For some, Los Angeles doesn't fit their idea of a conventional city because of its decentralized structure—those looking for the "city" often point to the skyscrapers concentrated downtown and say it's there. But that's not the whole story: while downtown (DTLA as it is often abbreviated) might look like the city, the city is, in fact, all around you! DTLA comprises just about six square miles of the 469 that make up the city of Los Angeles. It's not even the most densely populated area of the city—that honor goes to the nearby neighborhood of Koreatown.

So what is DTLA then? It's a vibrant, historic district that once was largely commercial but is now more residential and entertainment based. Basically, it's the heart of the big metropolis that surrounds it. It is also where the city gets its name—in 1781, a group of multiracial Mexican families established a settlement here under Spanish rule that they named El Pueblo de Nuestra Señora la Reina de Los Àngeles.

The best way to explore DTLA is by walking around—the Los Angeles Conservancy offers fantastic walking tours of downtown architecture and sites. But feel free to go your own way too, there's fun all around.

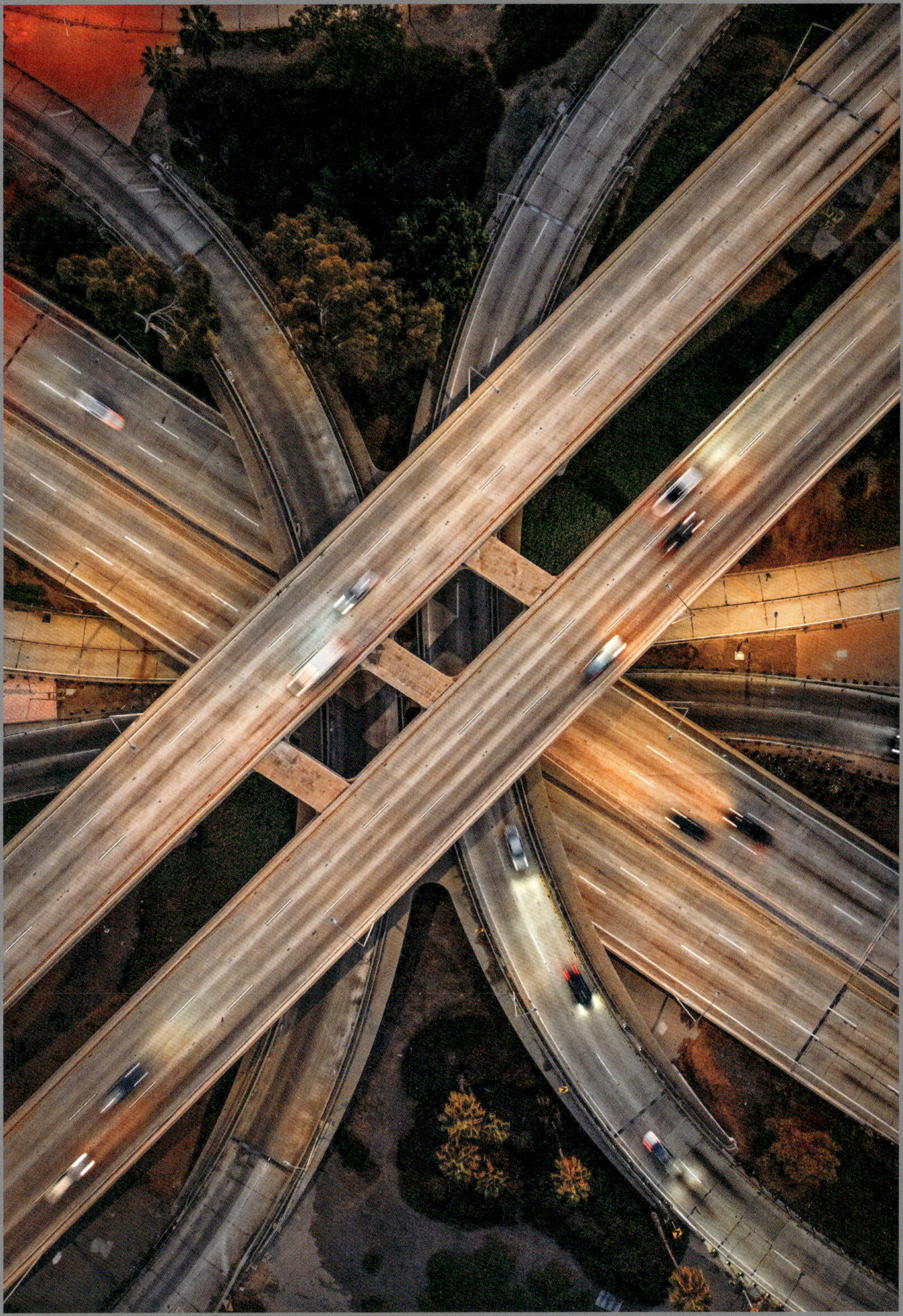

The more than 500 miles of freeways connect the city's various regions and create complicated ribbons of asphalt and concrete—engineering feats and environmental nightmares.

(Page 74–75) Home of the Los Angeles Philharmonic, the stainless-steel ship structure of Frank Gehry's landmark Walt Disney Concert Hall is one of the most acoustically sophisticated performance centers in the world.

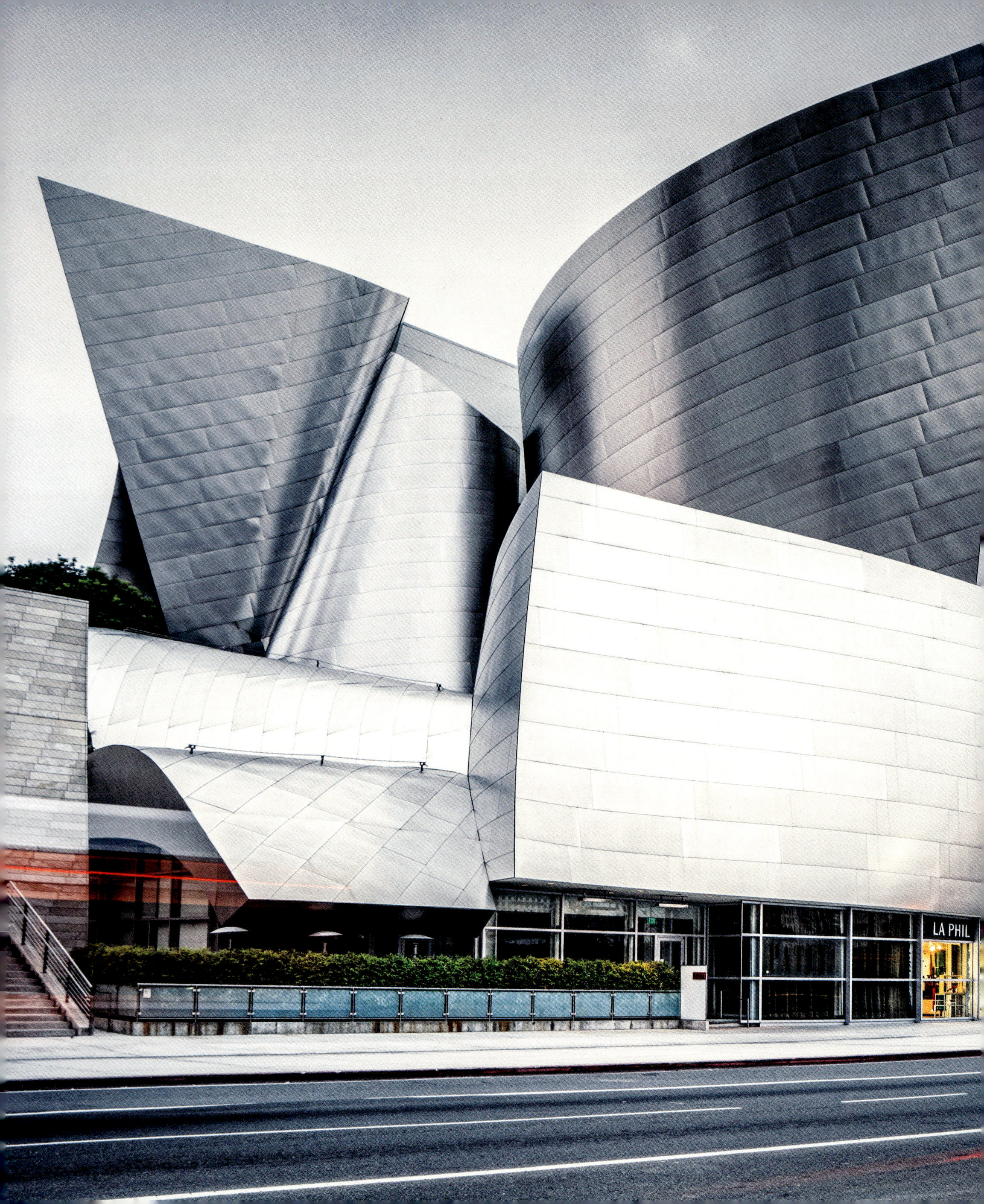
LA PHIL

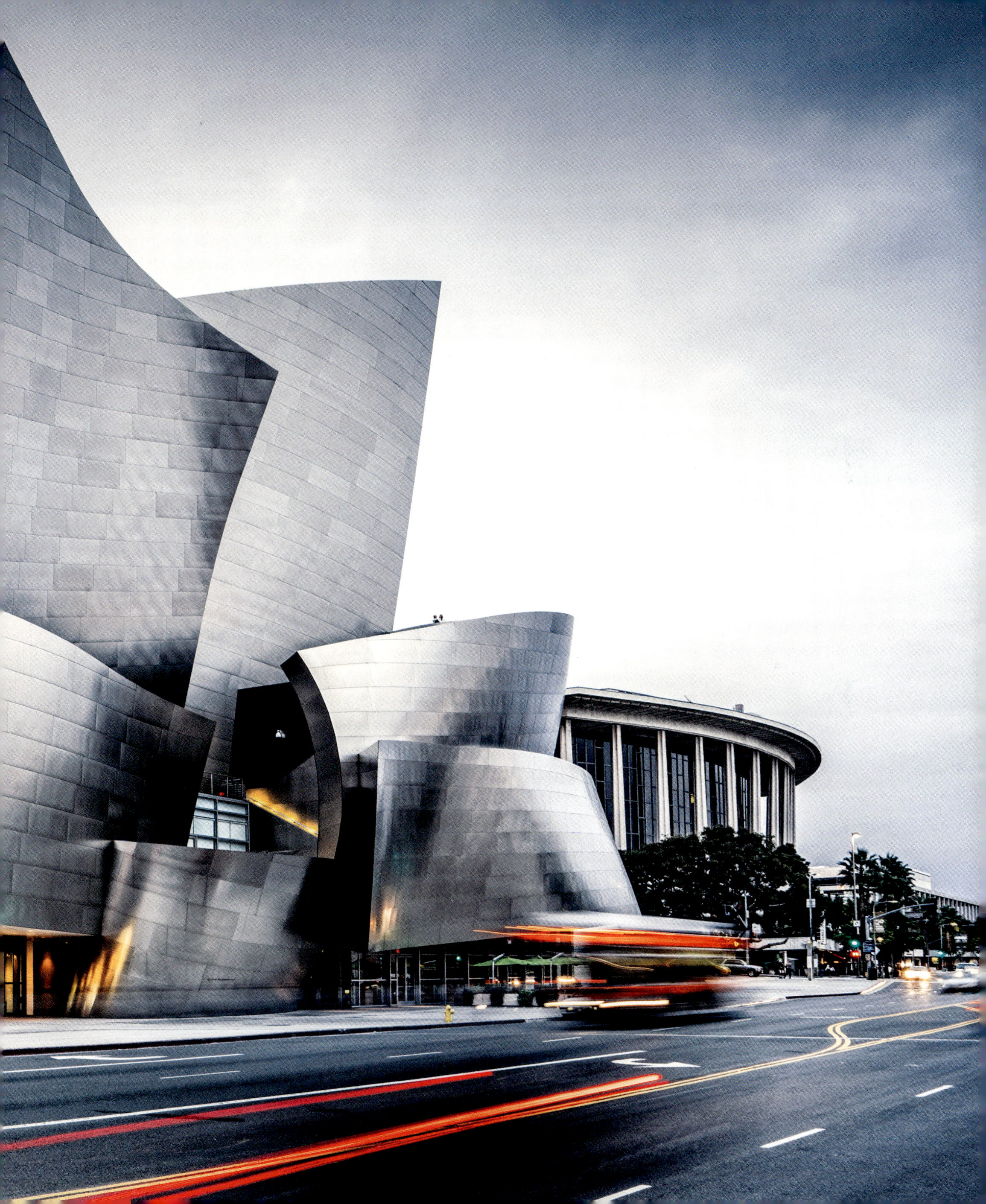

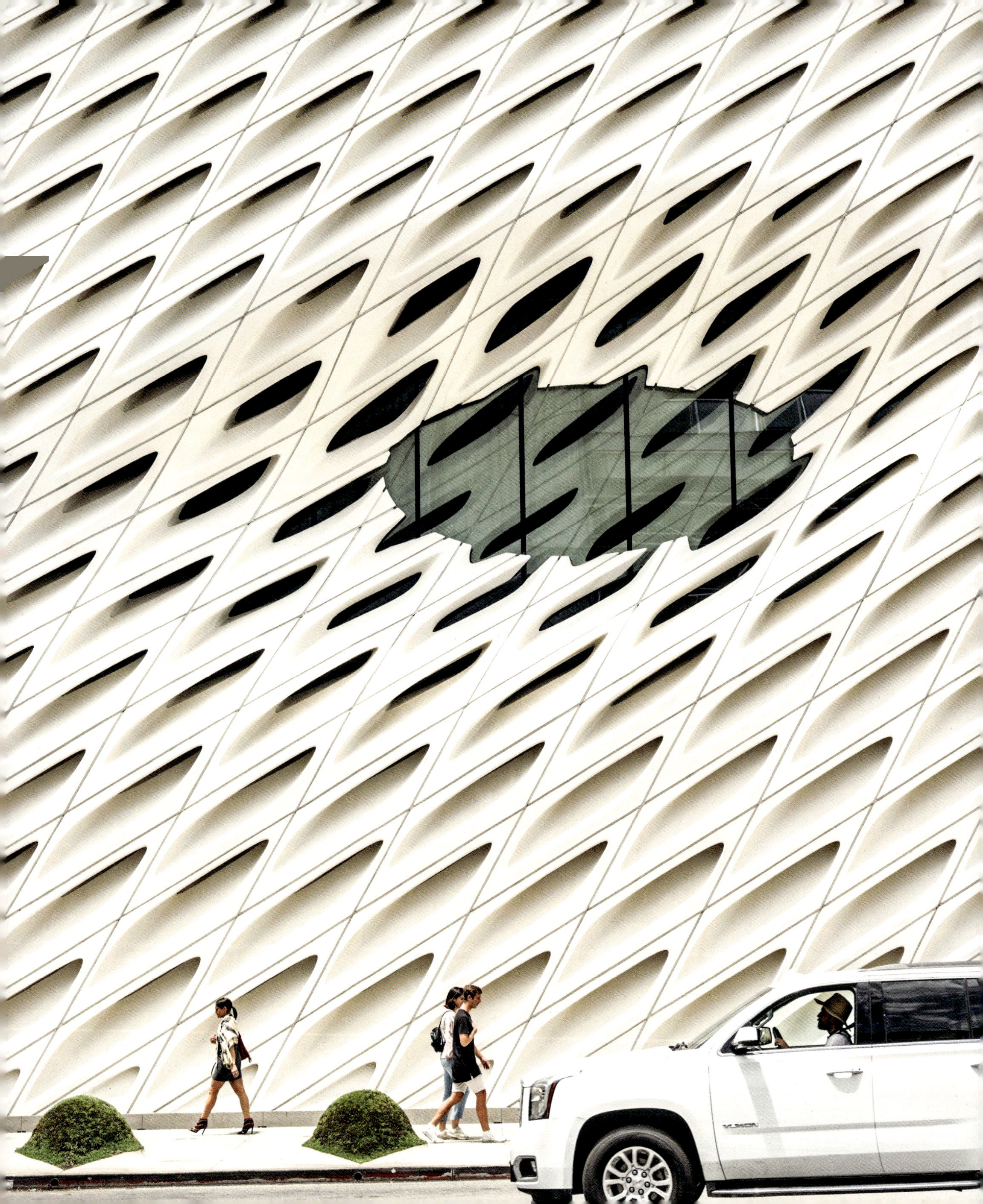

The honeycomb-like façade of the Broad—an art museum that houses two thousand contemporary works and offers free admittance—is fittingly sweet for all the goodness that awaits inside.

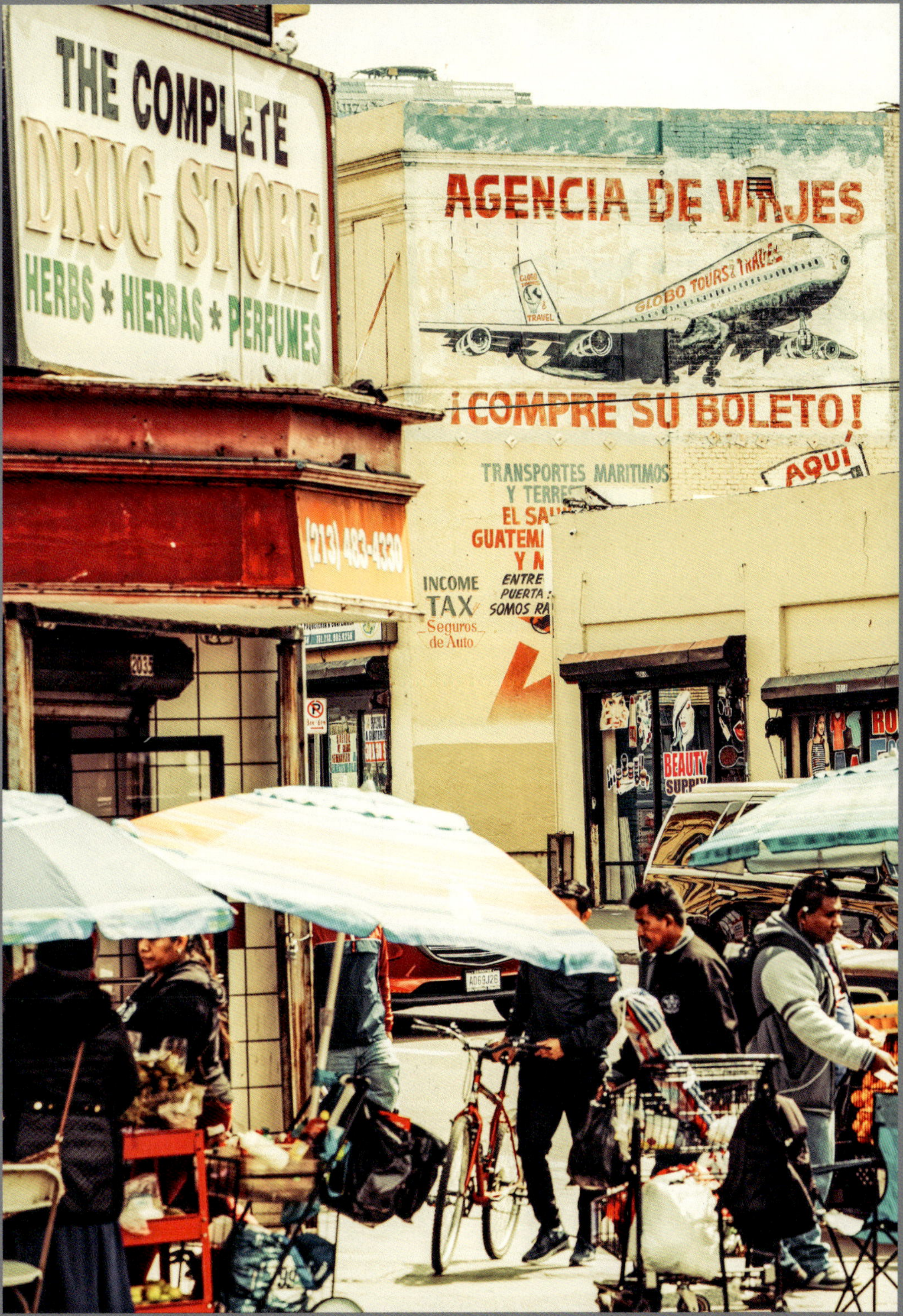

Near downtown, the Westlake neighborhood boasts sidewalks busy with street vendors by MacArthur Park.

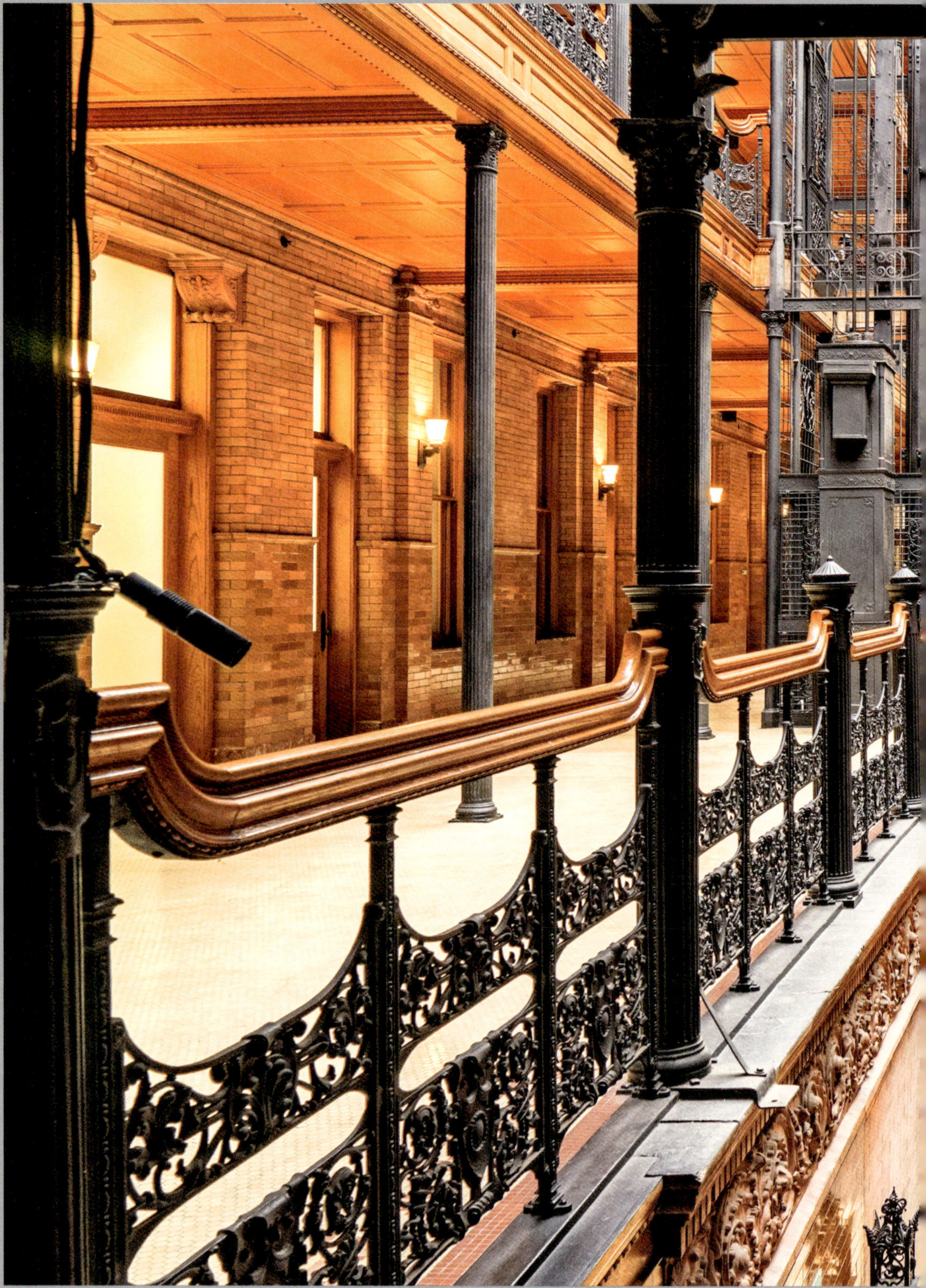

The 1893 Bradbury Building is recognizable to *Blade Runner* fans and is one of the oldest commercial buildings in DTLA.

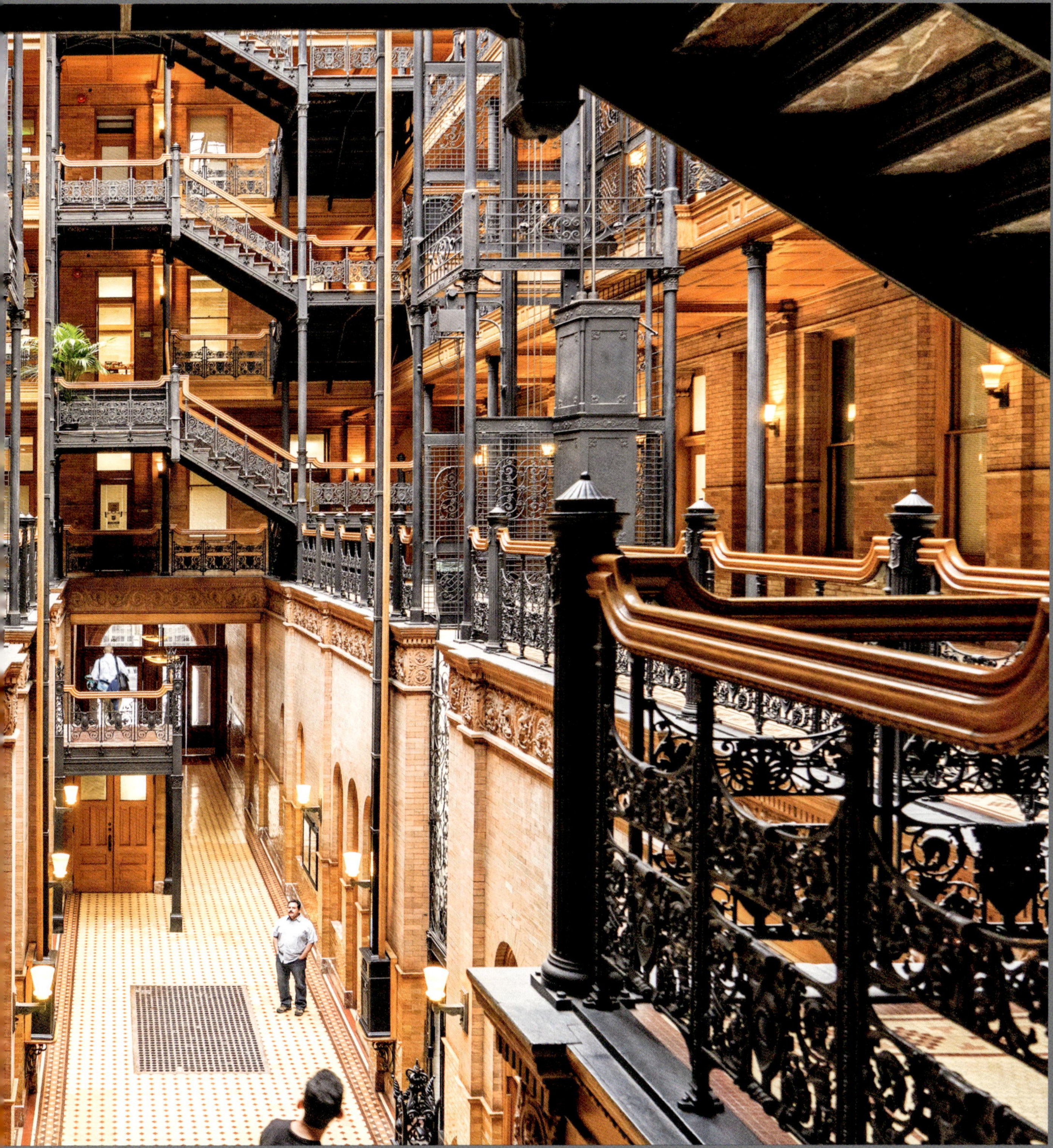

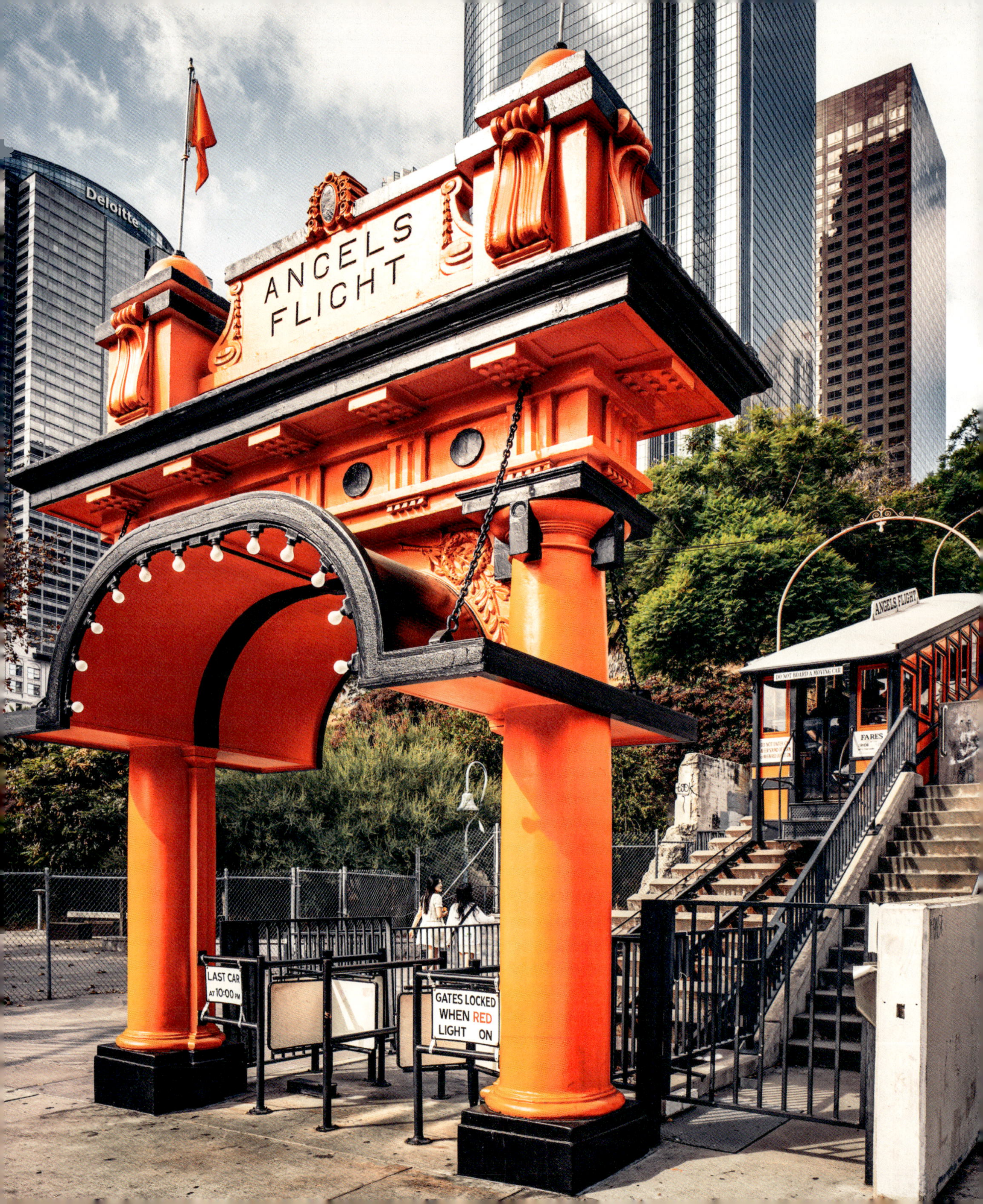
Deloitte
ANGELS
FLIGHT
ANGELS FLIGHT
DO NOT BOARD A MOVING CAR
FARES
LAST CAR
AT 10:00 PM
GATES LOCKED
WHEN RED
LIGHT ON

Opened in 1901, Angels Flight, the world's shortest railway, has two cars—named Sinai and Olivet—who just might be the biggest celebrities in town; their historic interiors have been featured in more than 100 films.

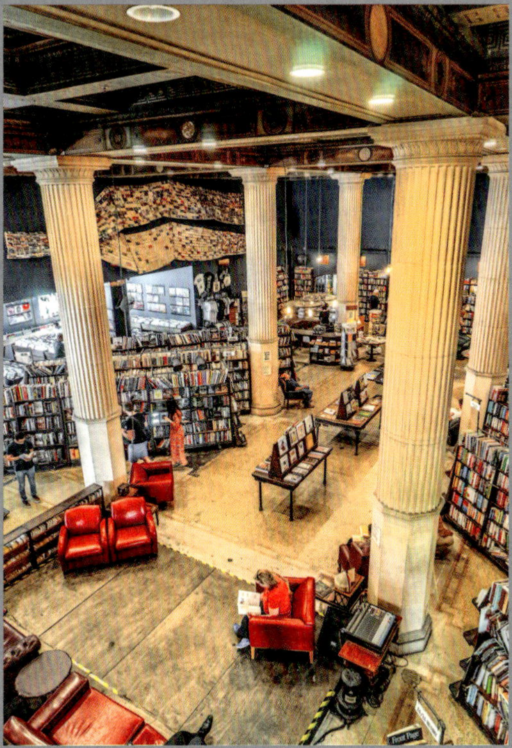

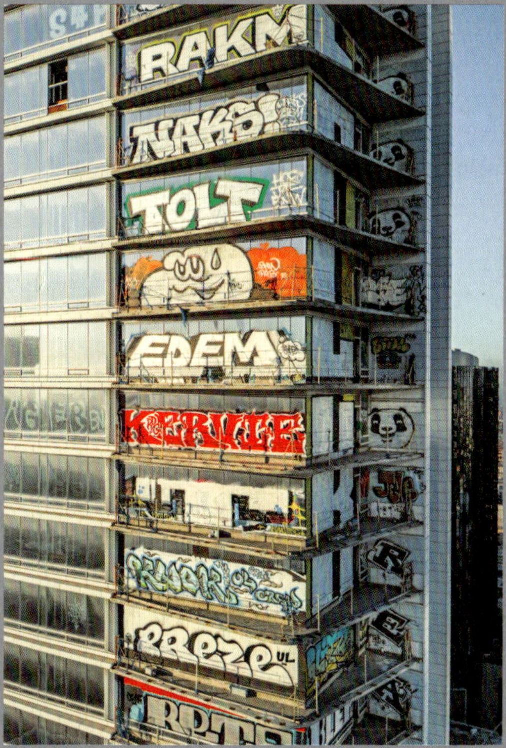

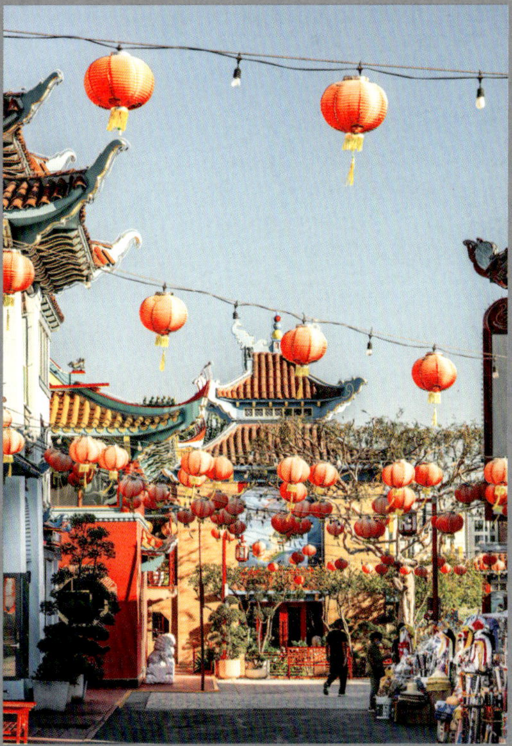

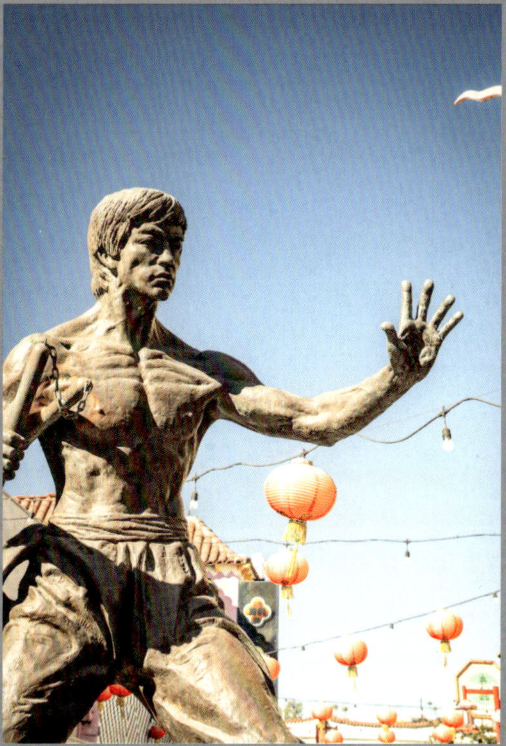

Downtown's behemoth of a book shop, the Last Bookstore, offers more than 20,000 square feet of books to browse, making it one of the largest independent bookstores in the world.

An unfinished skyscraper project whose developer ran out of money and abandoned the project is transformed into art by downtown graffiti artists.

Central Plaza is the heart of LA's Chinatown, which is actually the city's second Chinatown and dates back to 1938 (the first was located where Union Station is).

A statue of Bruce Lee, martial artist and movie star, stands in Chinatown's Central Plaza.

Sixth Street Viaduct

Cinematic Bridge Connecting Downtown and Boyle Heights

Also known as the Sixth Street Bridge, this is LA's most famous bridge. It connects downtown's Arts District to the historic neighborhood of Boyle Heights and offers incredible views of both downtown LA. and the LA River. Made of concrete, the 3,500-foot bridge opened in 2022 and spans both the river and the 101 freeway, as well as eighteen different railroad tracks. Its distinctive, sculptural arches—ten pairs of them—harken back to the historic bridge that was built on this site in 1932 and demolished in 2016 due to deterioration.

That earlier viaduct—which had only two distinctive arches—was the star of the city's beautiful Art Deco bridges that cross the river. And like any star, it frequently appeared on-screen, in films such as *Grease, Terminator 2, Repo Man, Transformers, Drive*, and *Furious 7*. Hollywood loved it as a location, as did musicians—the Beastie Boys filmed the music video for "Sabotage" here, as did Pharrell Williams for "Happy" and Kendrick Lamar for "Humble." Part of the appeal was not just the graceful sweep of the bridge but the concrete channel beneath it, the LA River's famous manmade bed built to control flooding.

Today, the new Sixth Street Viaduct hosts dedicated lanes for pedestrians and bike riders, and a twelve-acre public park beneath it, providing much needed recreational fields. The new design allows for the bridge to function not just as a road but as a public gathering space—offering to connect more than just geography.

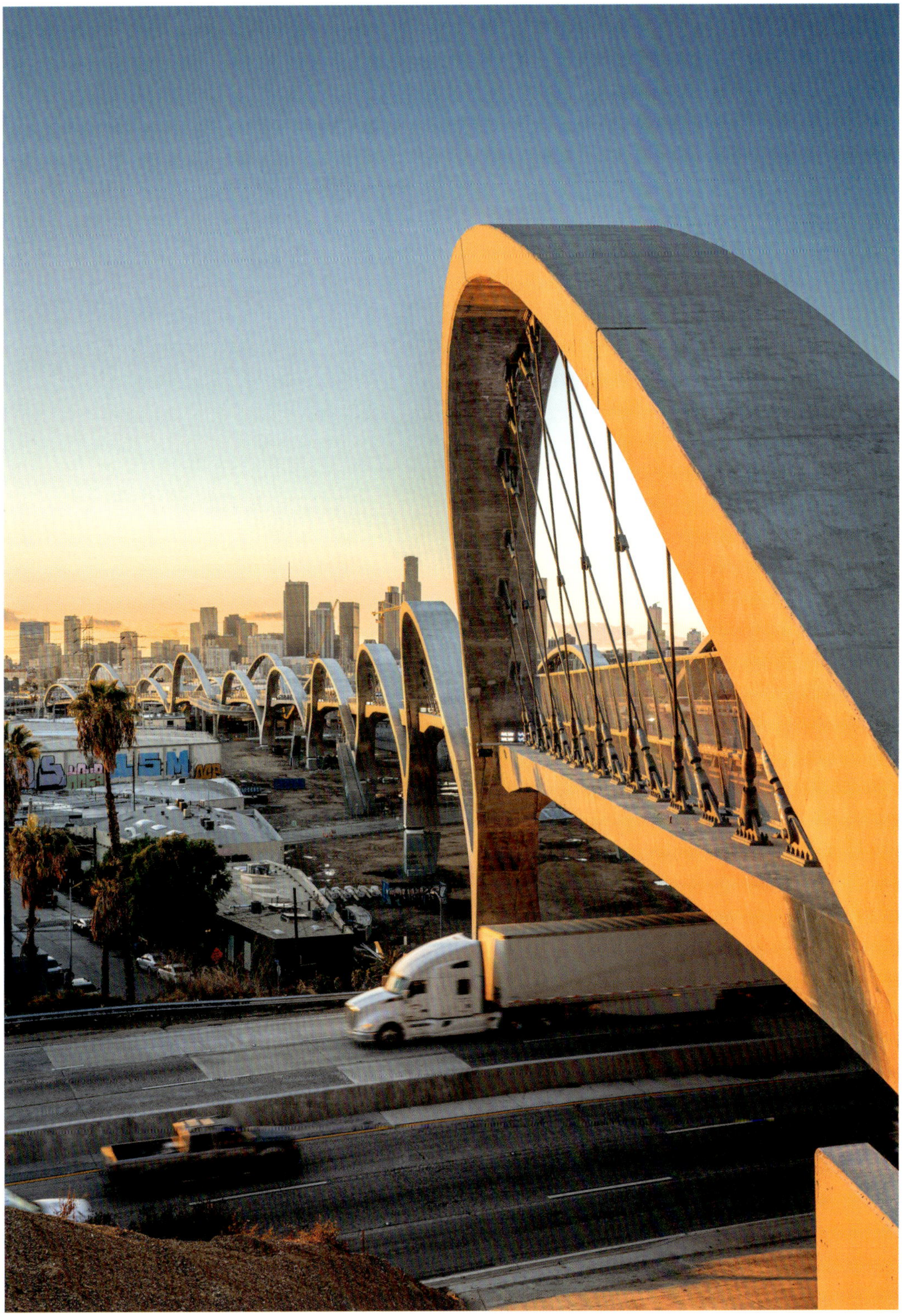

A view of the Sixth Street Viaduct shows downtown Los Angeles.

(Page 84–85) A rider twists down part of the Sixth Street Viaduct that's dubbed the Monumental Helical Bike Ramp, a spiral access ramp that connects the bridge to the park beneath it.

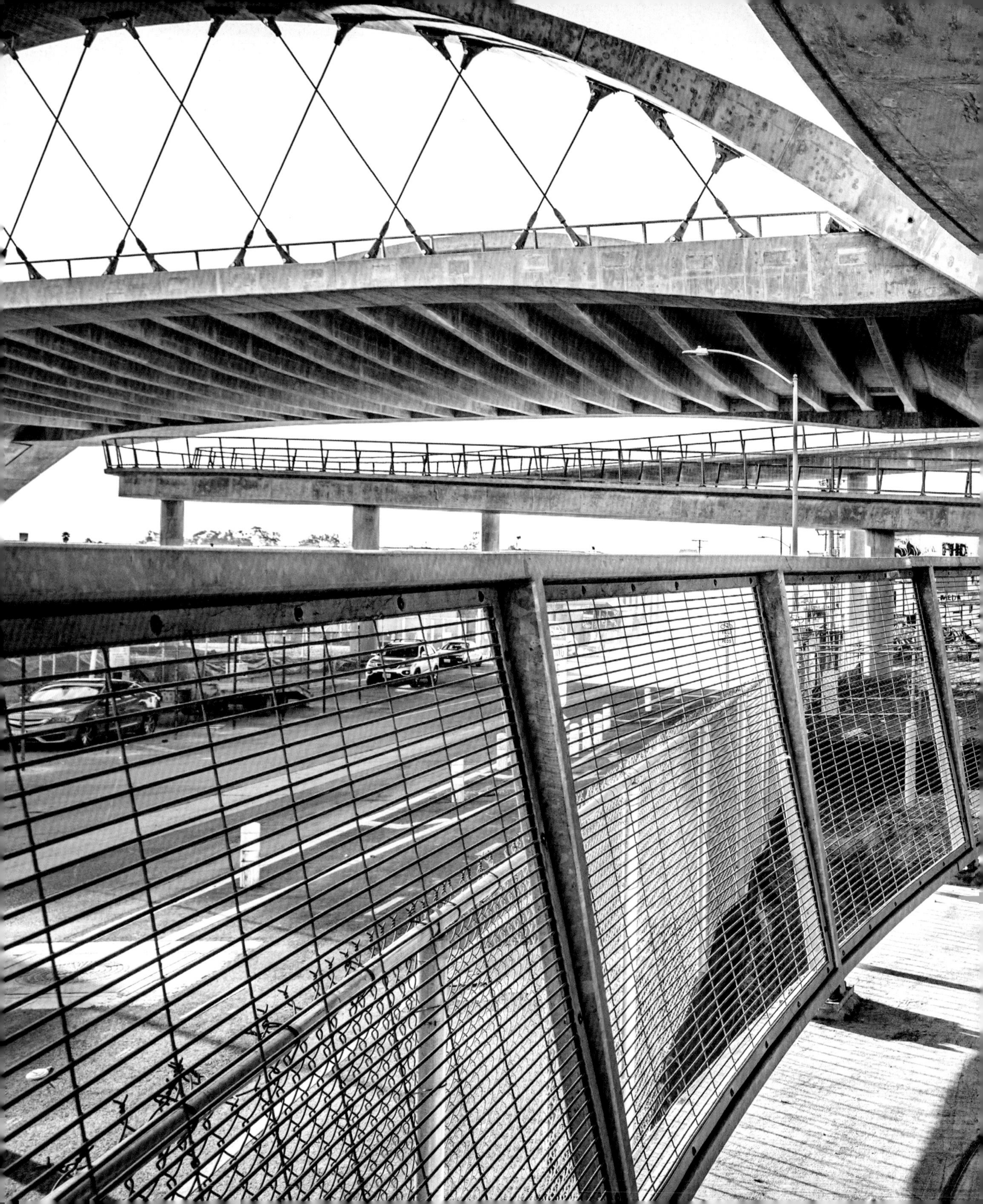

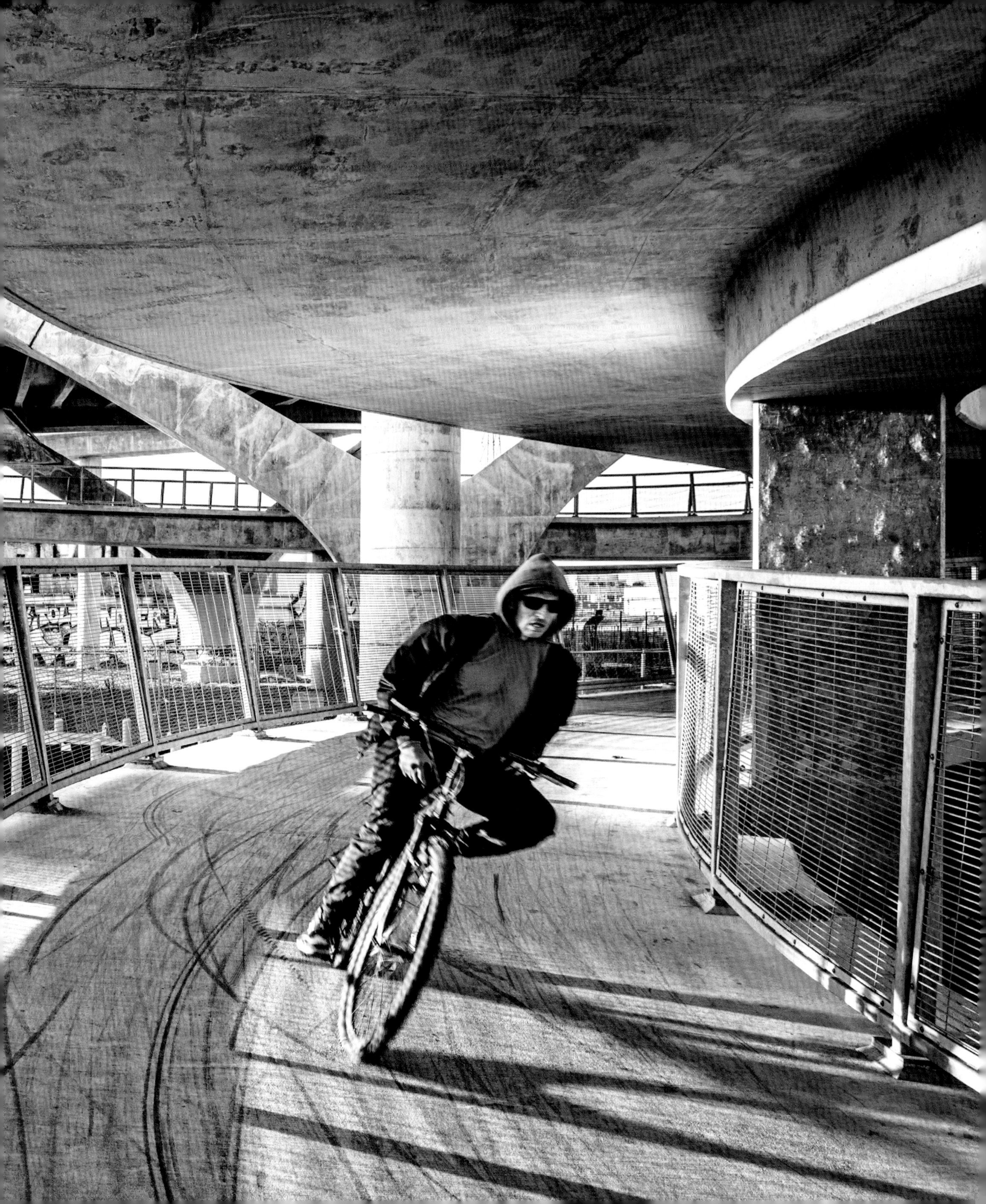

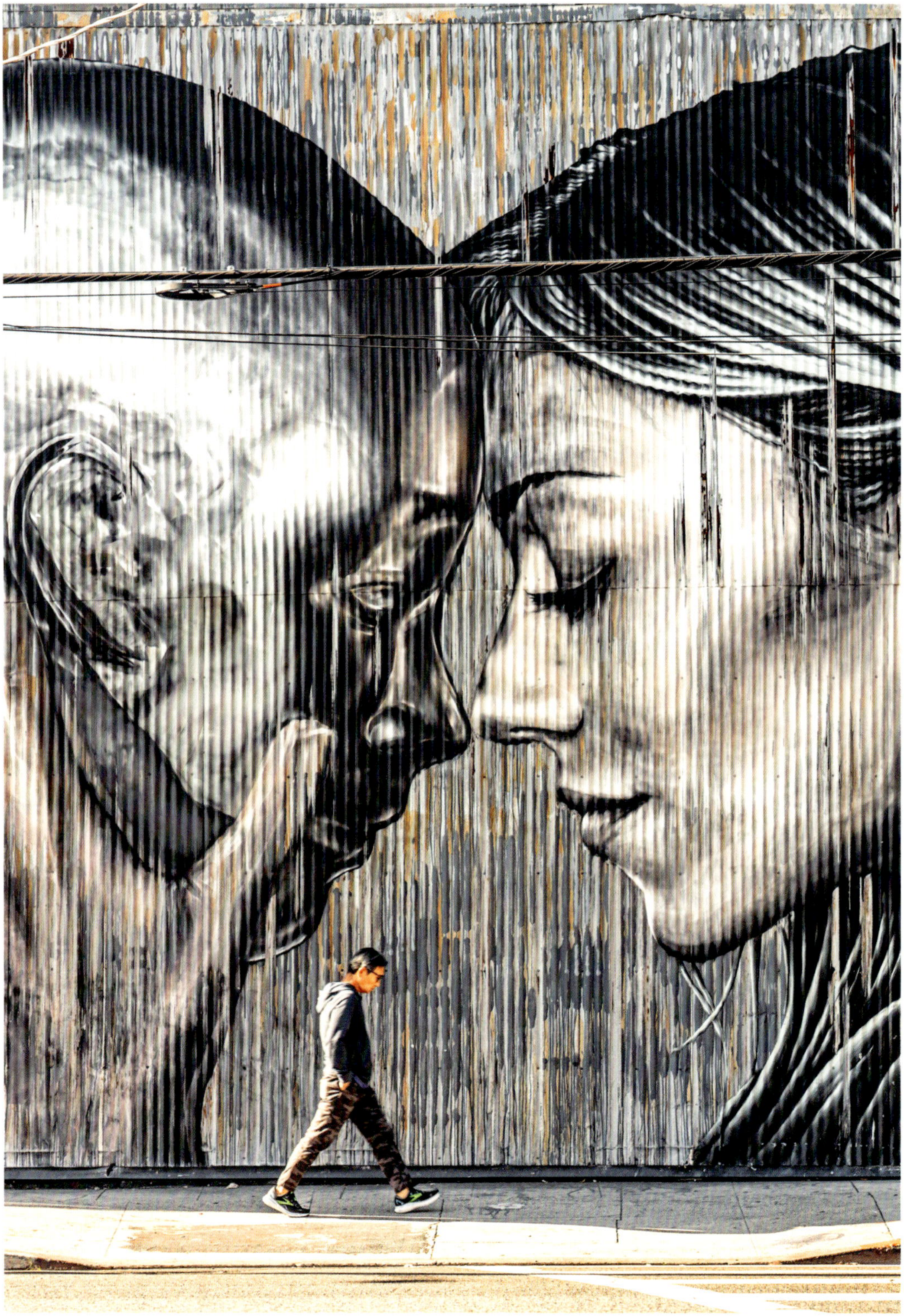

A pedestrian passes a mural on 4th Street that is a collaboration between LA-based artist Christina Angelina and Fanakapan, a London-based artist.

Murals

Streets Tell Stories

Los Angeles is a great city for street art, especially murals, which can be found across the city in almost every neighborhood, expressing the many cultures, histories, and concerns of the city's diverse communities. Some areas, like downtown's Arts District, are known for their murals. Another great neighborhood known for mural art is Pacoima's Mural Mile in the San Fernando Valley. The high concentration of murals and street art in the Arts District has everything to do with the neighborhood's name: In the 1970s, when artists couldn't afford to live in other places in the city, they began moving into old industrial buildings here. Those forgotten industrial buildings and the streets around them became canvases for their artworks.

Today, those murals and more are available for free for all to enjoy—the price of admission is simply keeping one's eyes open as you walk around. The usual amount of street sense and caution are necessary—the economically blighted area known as Skid Row borders the Arts District, which ironically has now become one of the most expensive districts downtown. That's how gentrification works—today's struggling artists don't live in the Arts District; they live next door.

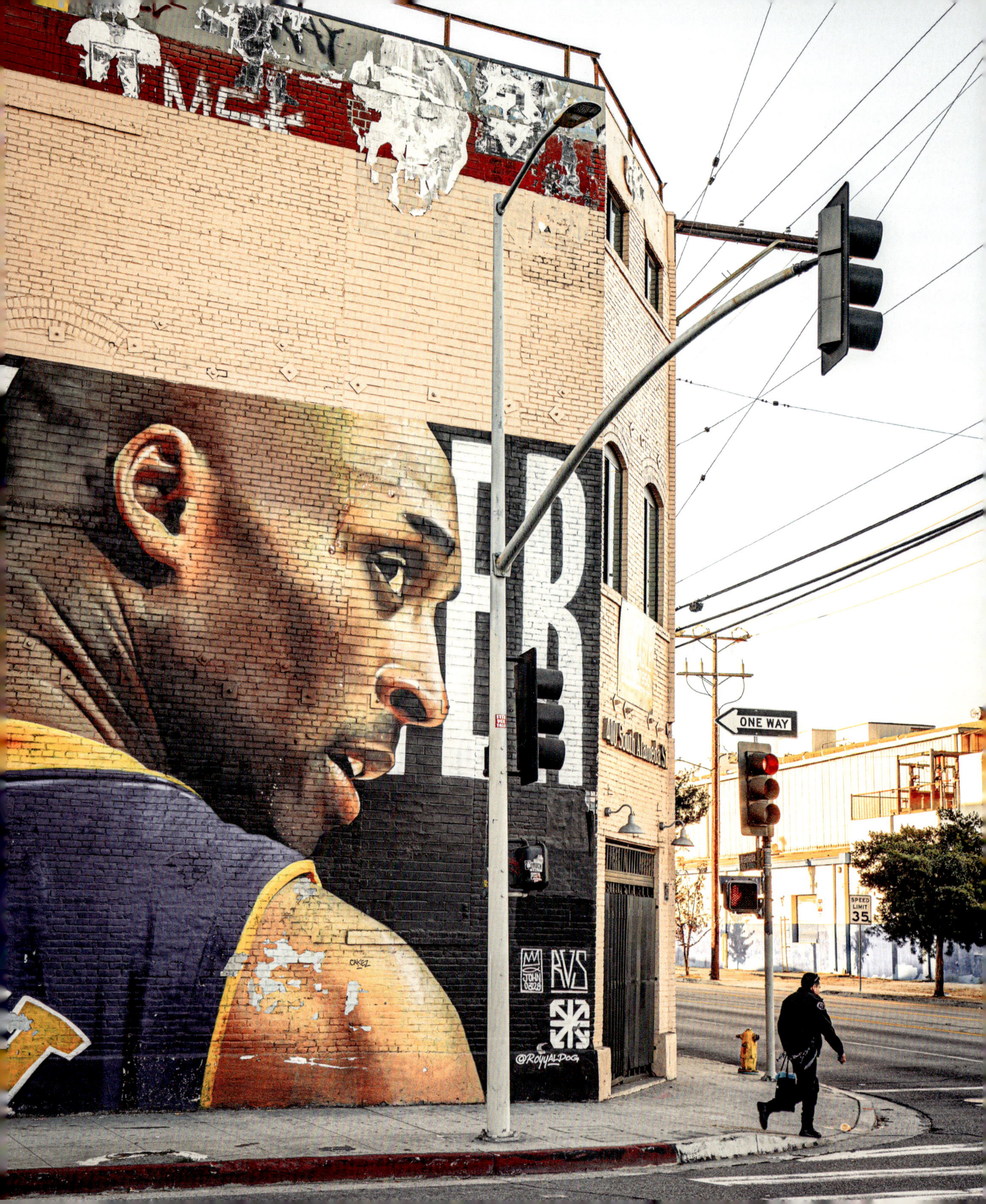
400 South Alameda St
ONE WAY
SPEED LIMIT 35
RVS
@RoyalDog

The "Legends Are Forever," mural at the Container Yard is by LA artist Royyal Dog (aka Chris Shim) and is one of the hundreds of street artworks that pay tribute to basketball legend Kobe Bryant.

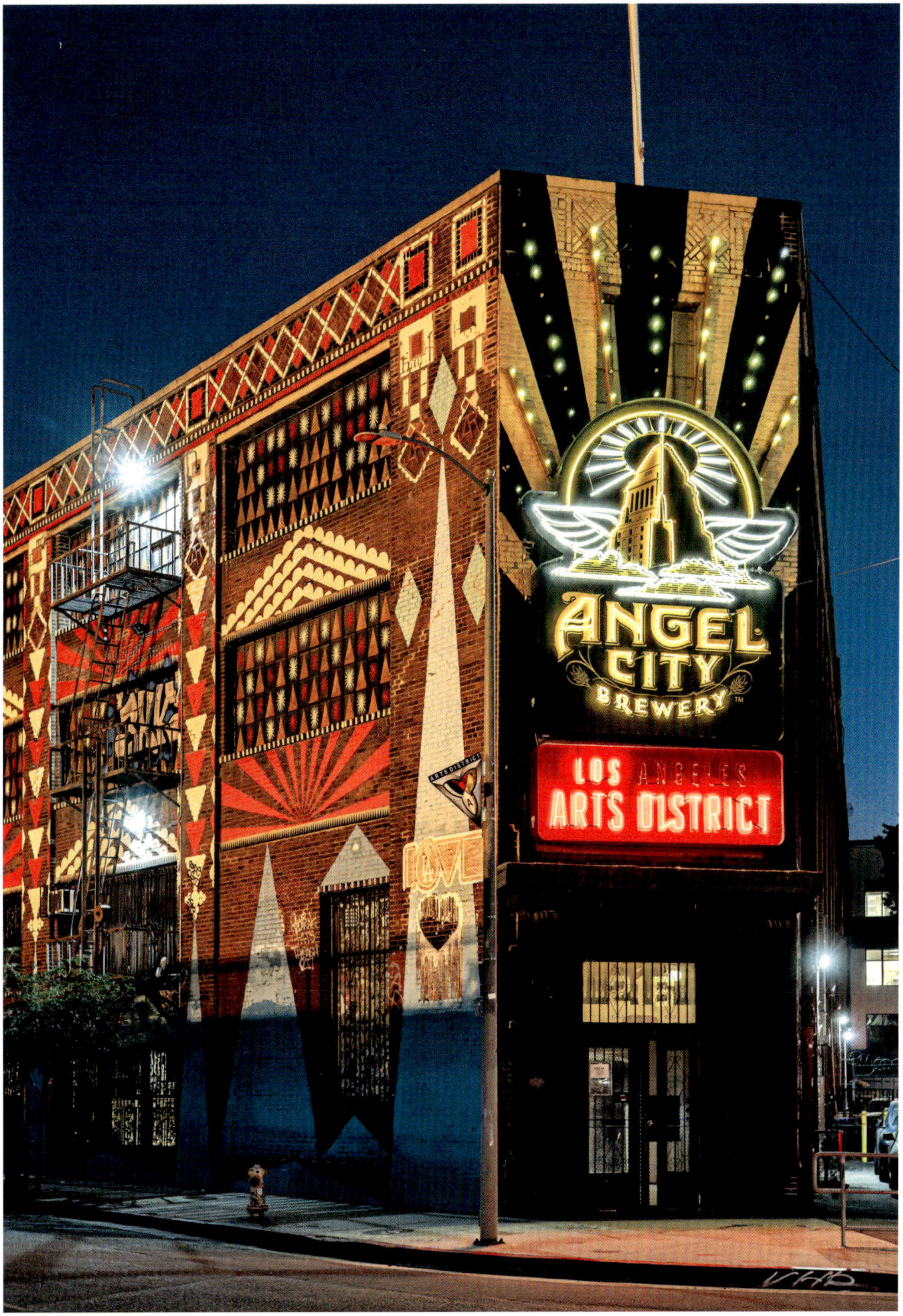

Housed in a 103-year-old building that boasts several murals, including works by Shepard Fairey, Erika Weitz, and "Untitled" by Shrine, the geometric art seen here, Angel City Brewery partners with Art Share L.A. to create projects across the district.

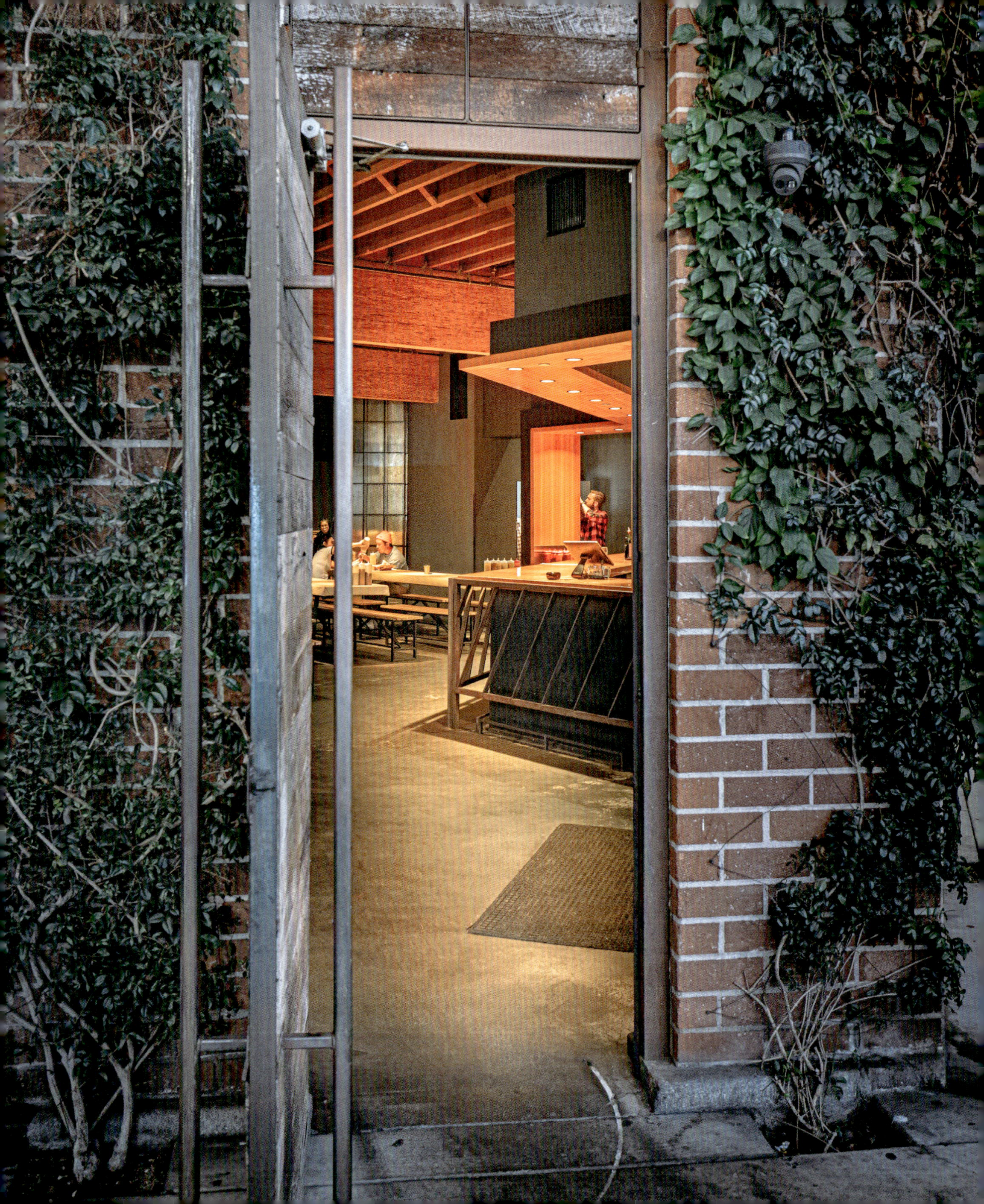

A beer hall and hot dog joint, Wurstküche offers exotic sausages and big, communal tables, capturing the spirit of the district.

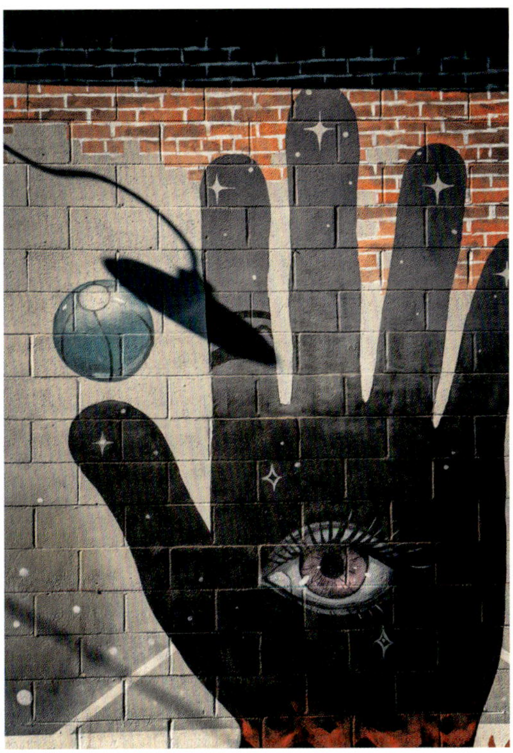

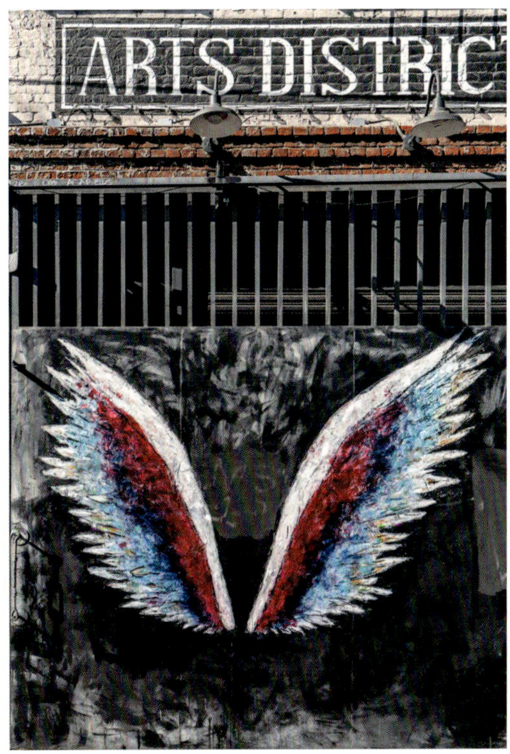

■□ An untitled mural by artist Mikolaj Wyszynski appears near the Arts District Co-Op.

□■ Little did artist Colette Miller know when she painted this mural in the Arts District in 2012 that her murals of wings people could pose in would become a global project.

Little Tokyo

A Historic Enclave of Japanese American Culture

This wonderful, walkable neighborhood is a historic landmark and hub of Japanese American culture, food, and shopping. One of the last remaining Japantowns in the US, Little Tokyo is 140 years old and has survived immeasurable odds. The cultural home of LA's Japanese community, this vibrant neighborhood was decimated by the incarceration of Japanese Americans during World War II and left a ghost town. But when the war ended, some of those displaced families returned and rebuilt—they preserved a vital link to the past and a continuance of community.

Today, the struggle to keep Little Tokyo continues, but the issue is gentrification. Rising rents make it harder for legacy businesses to remain open, although many remain—including the 112-year-old sweet shop Fugetsu-Do, which sells handmade mochi. A new community center and gymnasium, the Terasaki Budokan, recently opened, and more affordable housing is promised by planners. This special place is where the past, present, and the future of Los Angeles all come together.

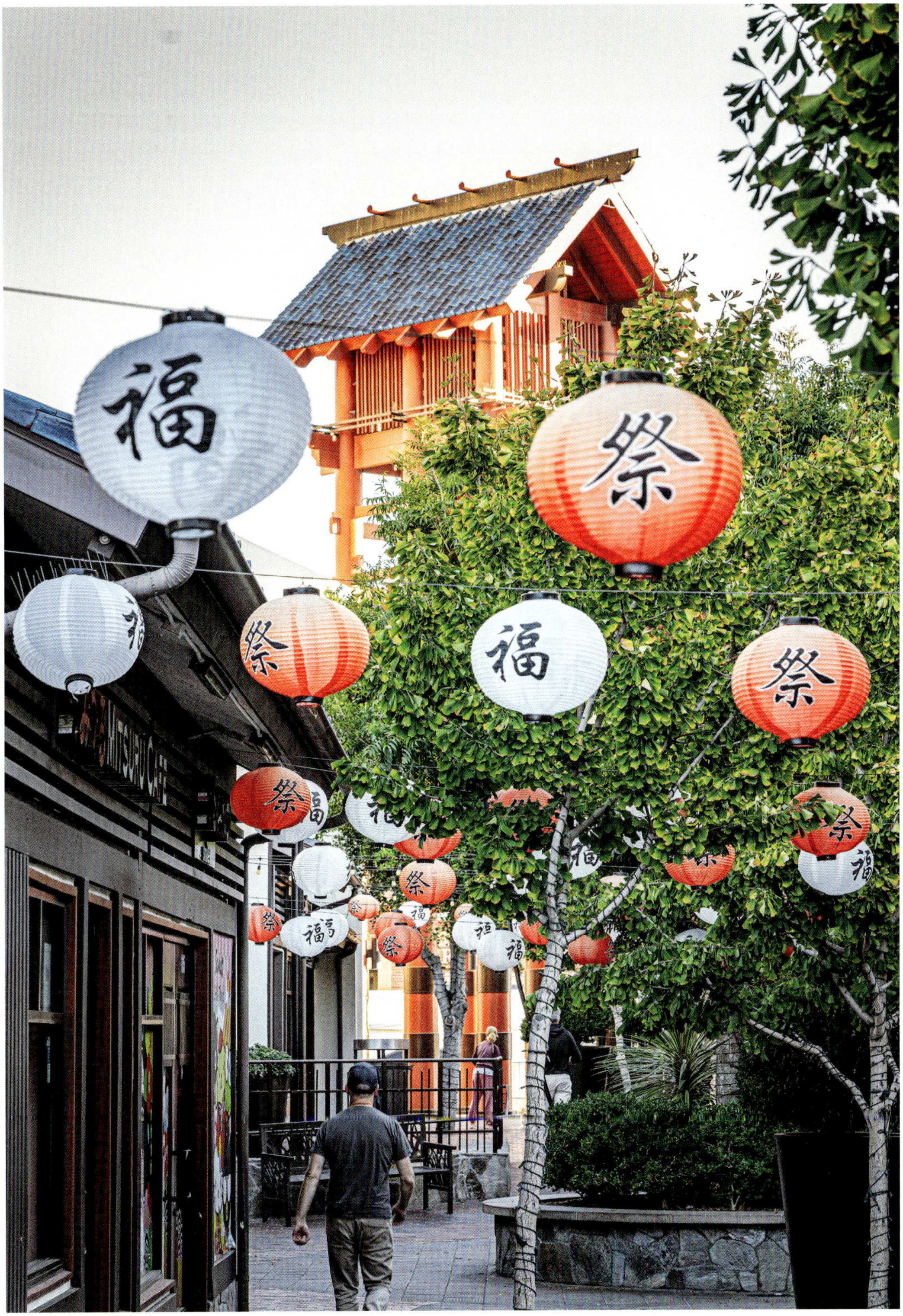

A symbol of Little Tokyo, the 55-foot Yagura Fire Tower presides over the Japanese Village Plaza, a walkable, themed shopping center that includes many independently owned businesses, cafes, and restaurants that help to preserve the neighborhood's character.

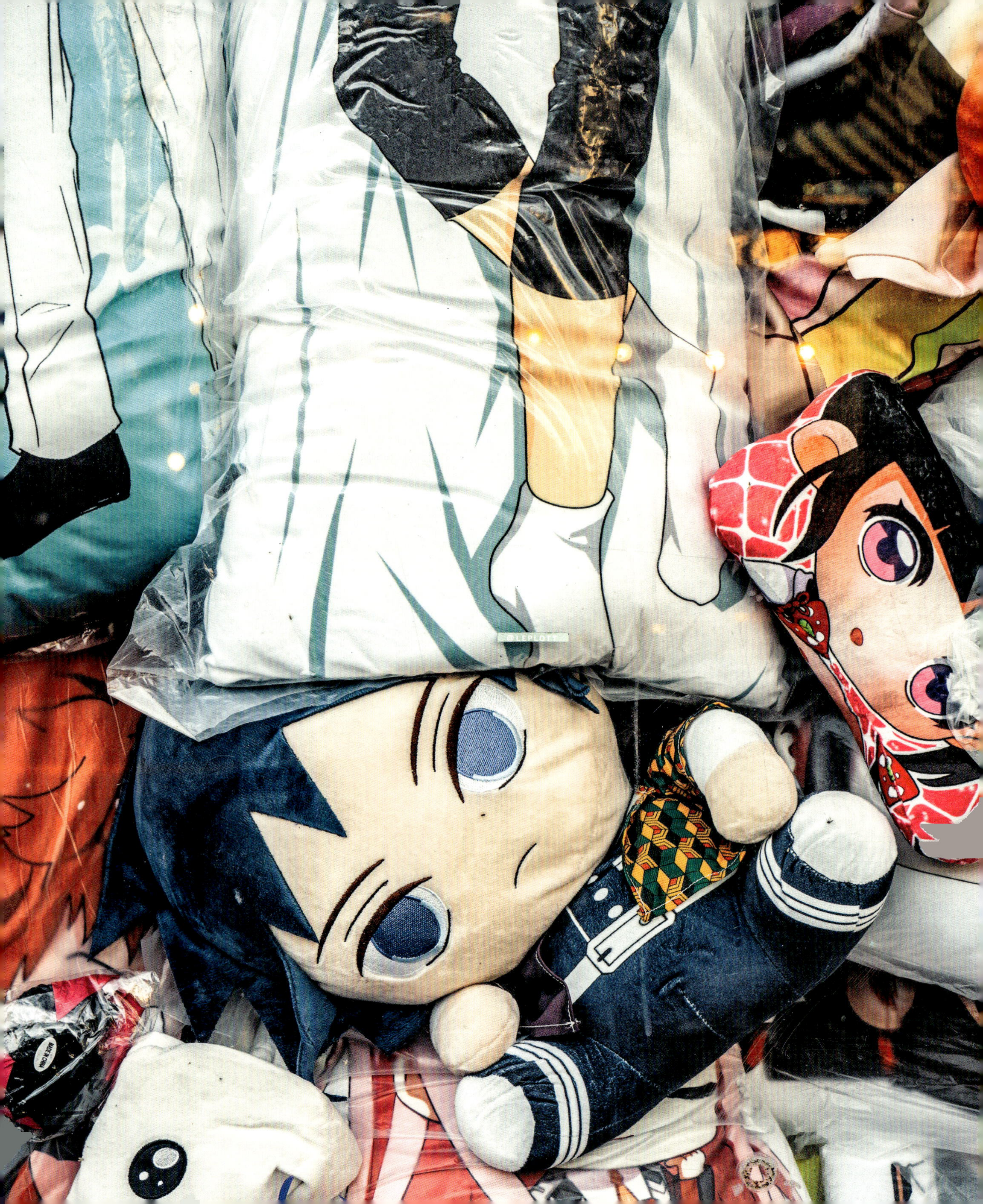

High rents and rising costs make staying in business more difficult for mom-and-pop operations. The National Trust for Historic Preservation declared Little Tokyo to be one of the US's most endangered historic places.

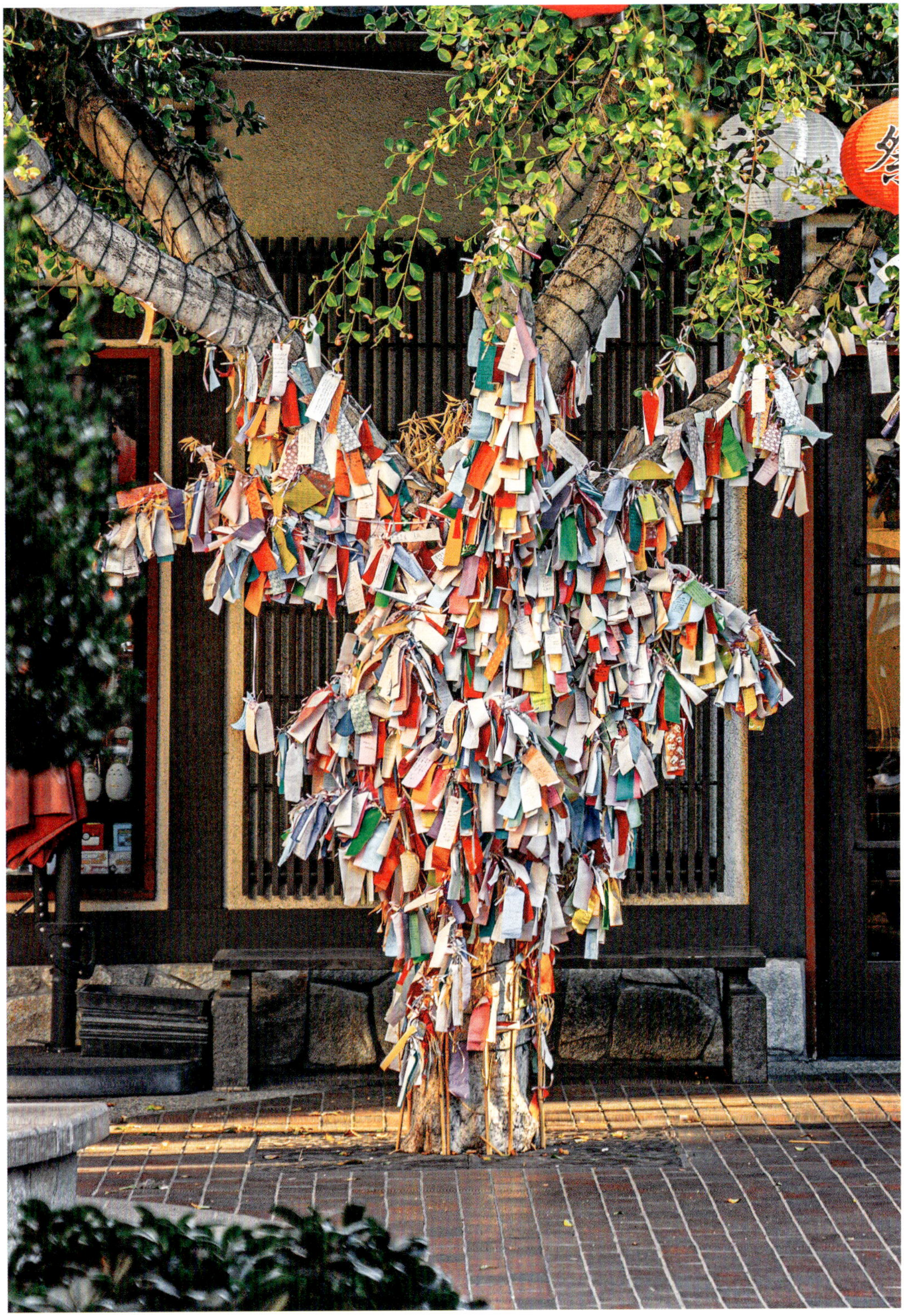

The Wishing Tree in Japanese Village Plaza was a fixture for 13 years, started by the owner of the nearby Blooming Art Gallery, who invited people to write their wishes on tanzaku paper and tie them to the tree. Sadly, she was forced to remove the wishes by property management.

Bonaventure Hotel

Sleek and Sexy Late-Modern Landmark

Now known as the Westin Bonaventure Hotel and Suites, this unforgettable structure—and the largest hotel downtown—is a masterpiece of twentieth century Century design. Designed by architect John Portman, the 1976 concrete and glass building showcases his "atrium hotel" concept, with a seven-story atrium at center amid a Brutalist-style interior of reflecting pools, curved walkways, floating lounges, dramatic staircases, and glass elevators that move up the exterior of the building. It's an incredible ride with great views—and there are four elevators to choose from, so try a few!

Some say the Bonaventure looks like a rocket ship about to take off, and writer Fiona Alison Duncan describes it as "four AA batteries united around a C and plugged into a terminal of concrete." The neo-futuristic look of the hotel has inspired many filmmakers and artists to use it as a location for movie, TV shows, and music videos. Kendrick Lamar and SZA's "Luther" music video shows some incredible, sci-fi interiors, and the high-flying elevators are the true stars of the films *True Lies, Heat,* and *Interstellar*. Plus, there's a revolving lounge on the 34th floor with a 360-degree of DTLA, provided one stays long enough.

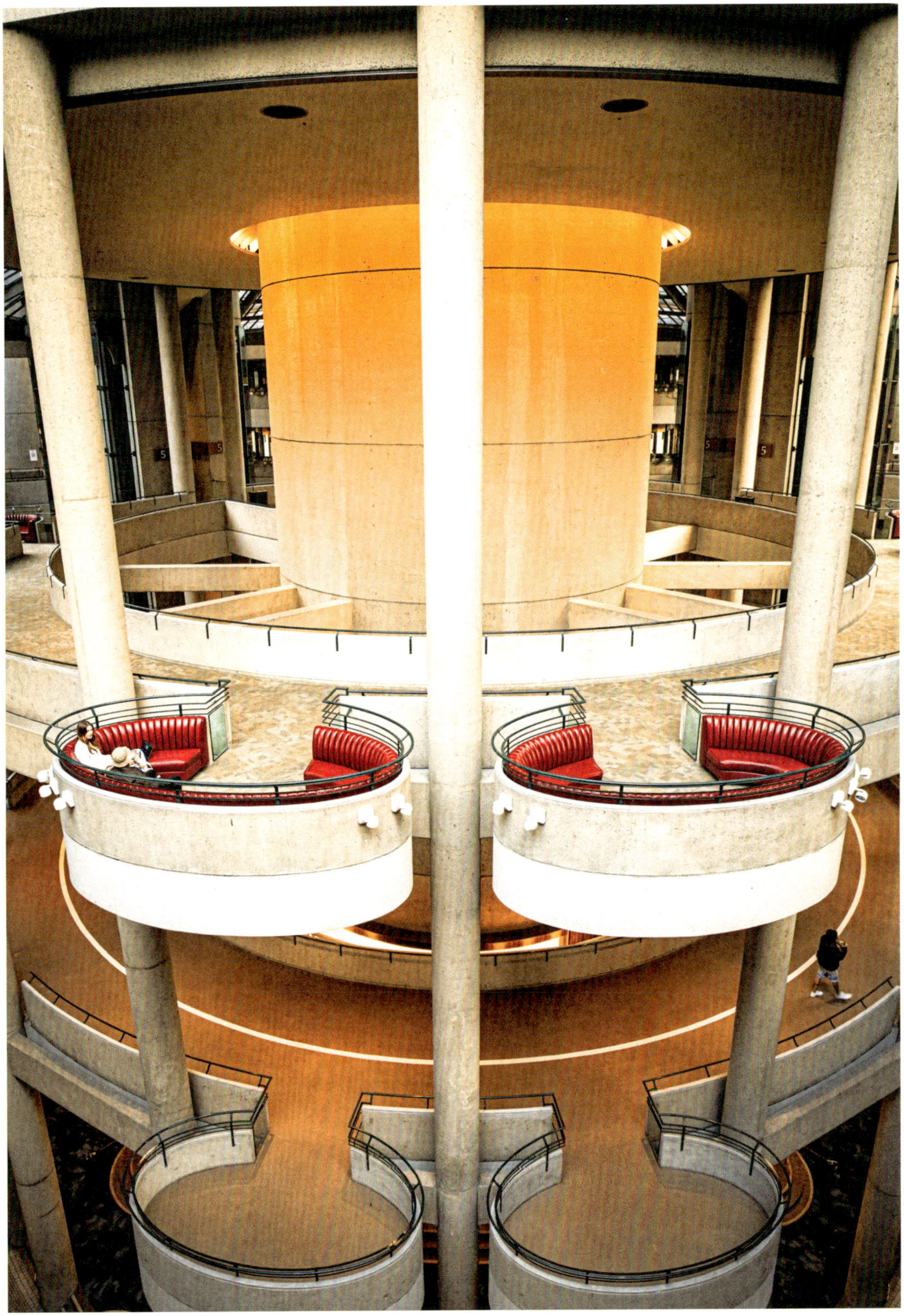

The suspended lounge areas in the hotel's atrium are pods that connect via the hotel's circular walkways. Hovering stories above the lobby, one feels how massive the space is.

(Page 98–99) "It is true that Fredric Jameson came to an academic conference at the Bonaventure, got lost in the lobby, and thus discovered post-modernism."
—filmmaker Thom Andersen

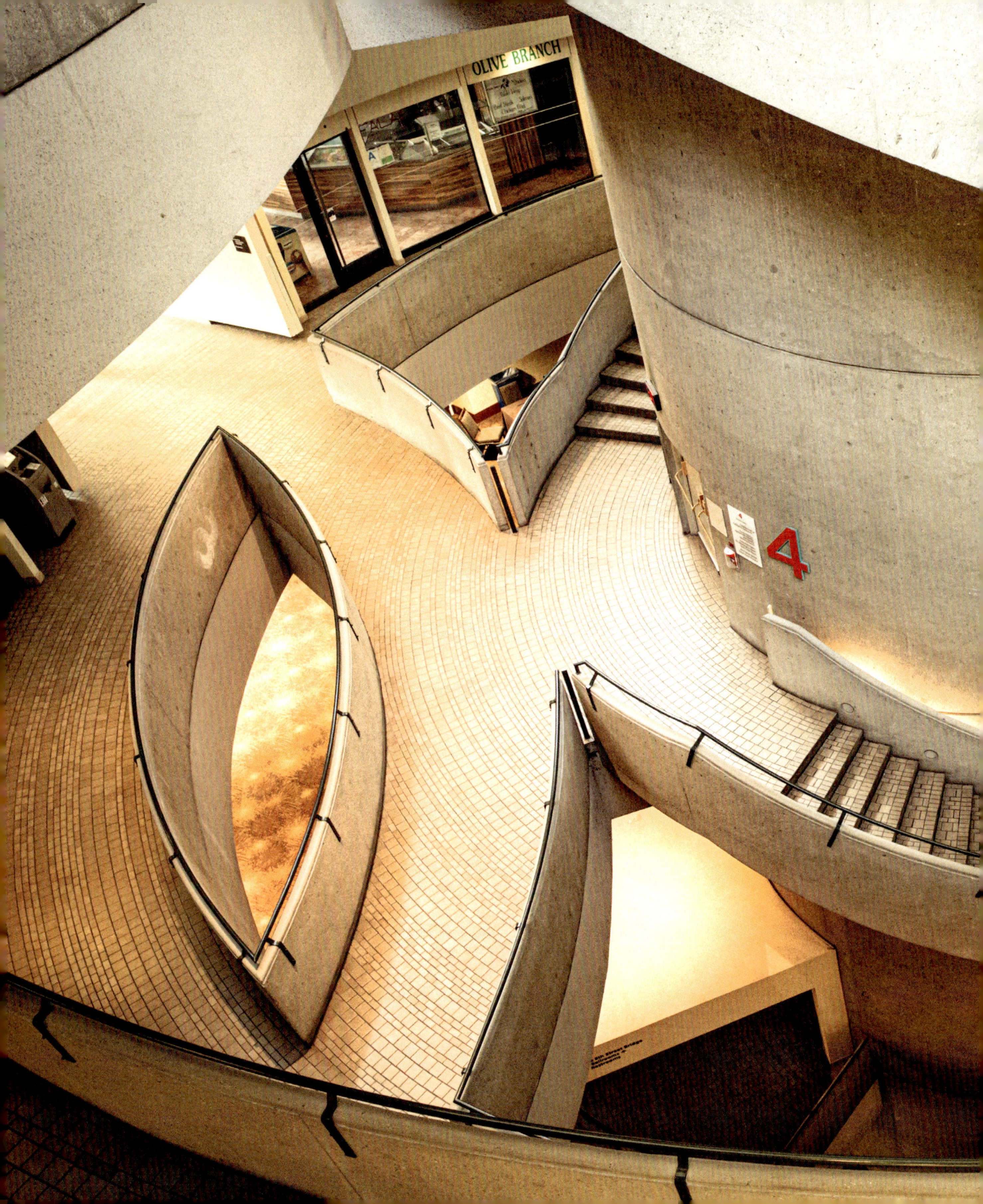
OLIVE BRANCH
4

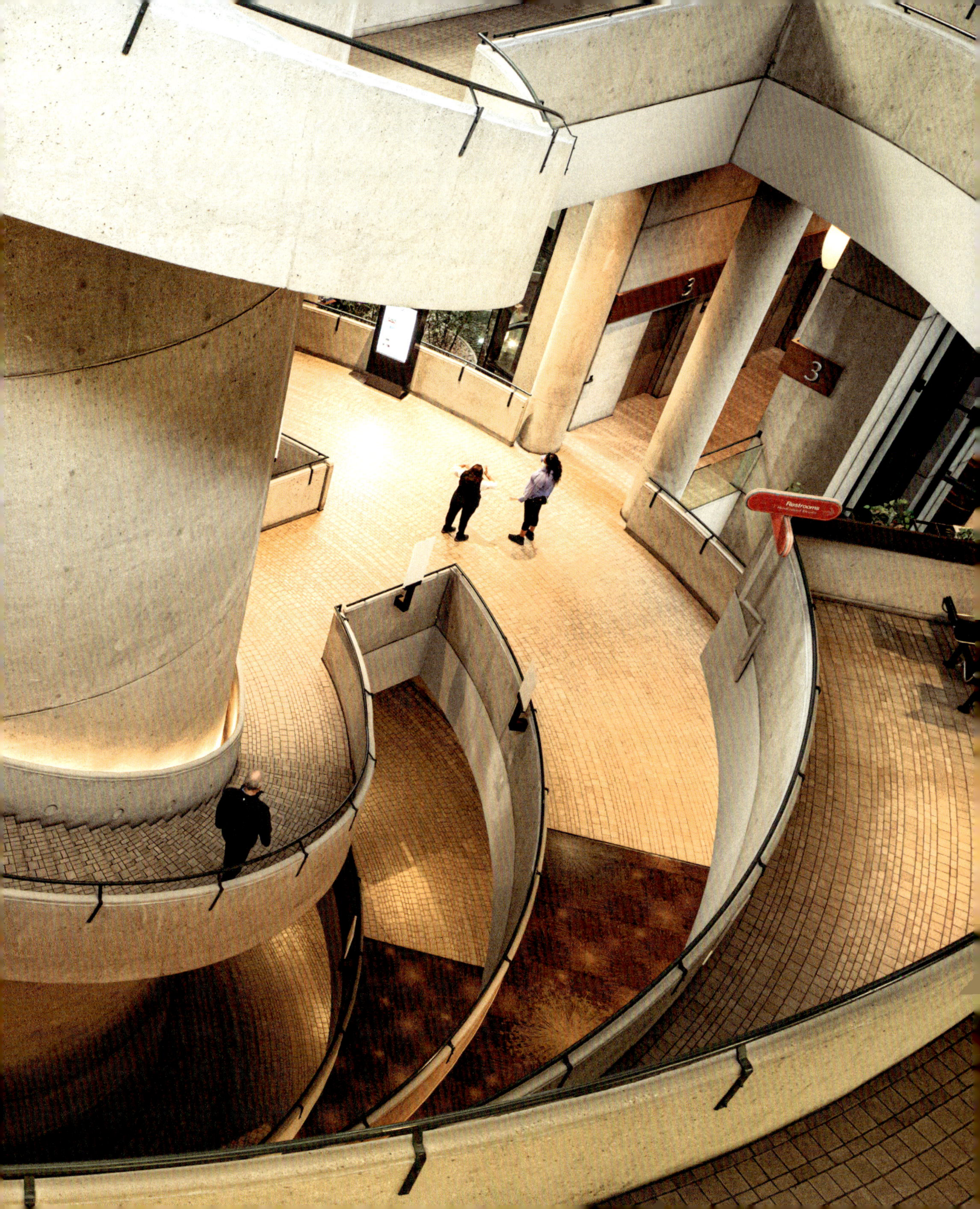
3
3
Restrooms

Cocktail Bars

A City Full of Spirits

There's a plethora of wonderful, historic watering holes in DTLA, as well as plenty of newer bars offering a wide range of atmospheres—and activities. There are hidden speakeasies and jazzy discos; places to play pool or spots to have a drink by the pool; arcade bars, karaoke joints, taprooms with Skee-Ball. From fancy cocktails to a 6 a.m. beer, you'll find it here.

Part of the resurgence of downtown in the 1990s came from cocktail bars. After the economic downturn of the 1970s and 80s, LA's downtown districts were hurting, with many streets seemingly deserted after the working hours. An adapative reuse ordinance law was passed that made it easier for developers to convert old buildings, and Angelenos like Cedd Moses (son of painter Ed Moses) revitalized old bars, like the 1905/1939 Golden Gopher, that were on the brink of closure.

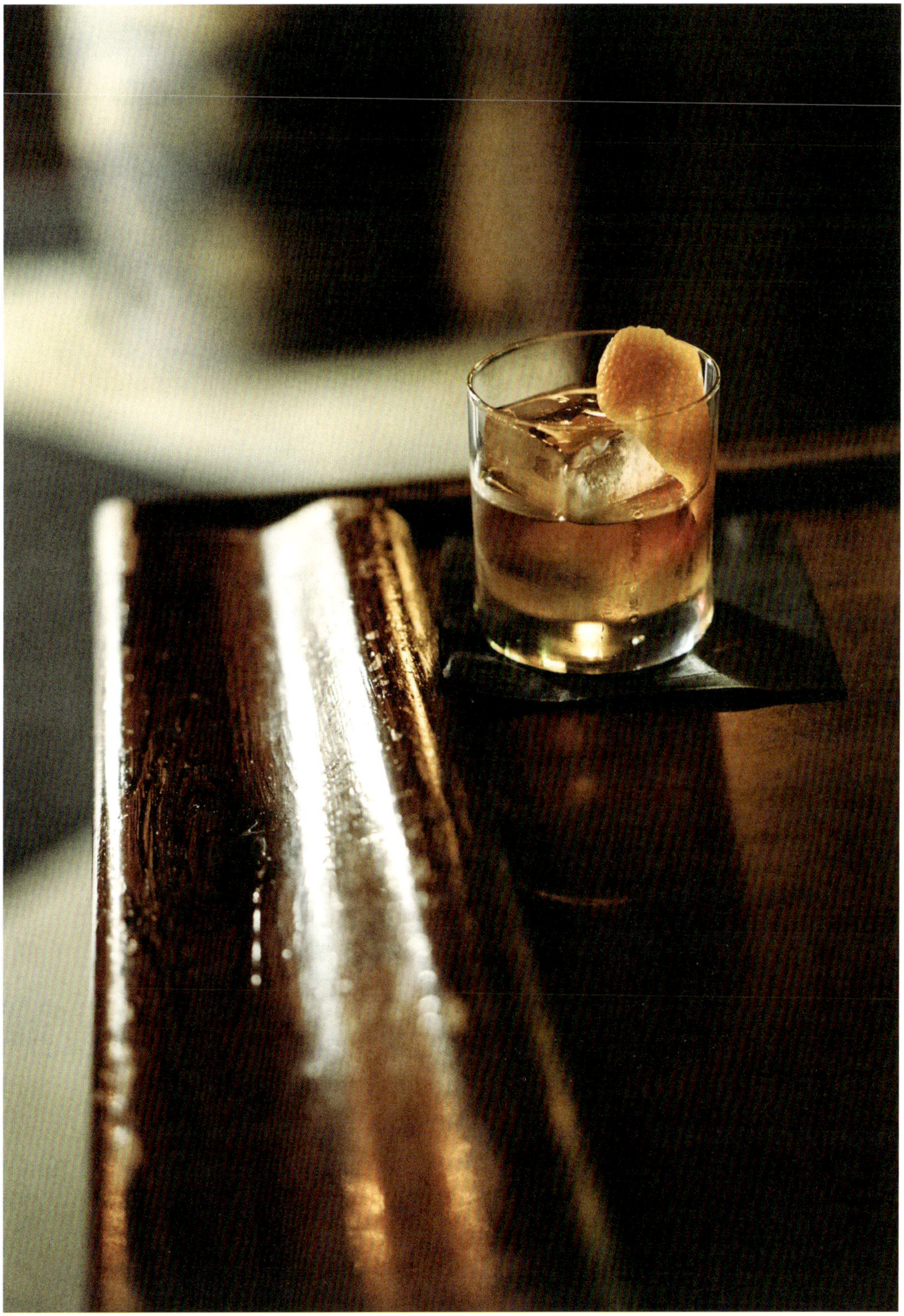

Tony's Saloon, a revamped roadside saloon in the Arts District, makes a delicious play on an Old Fashioned using rye and Amaro Nonino called Rye of the Beholder.

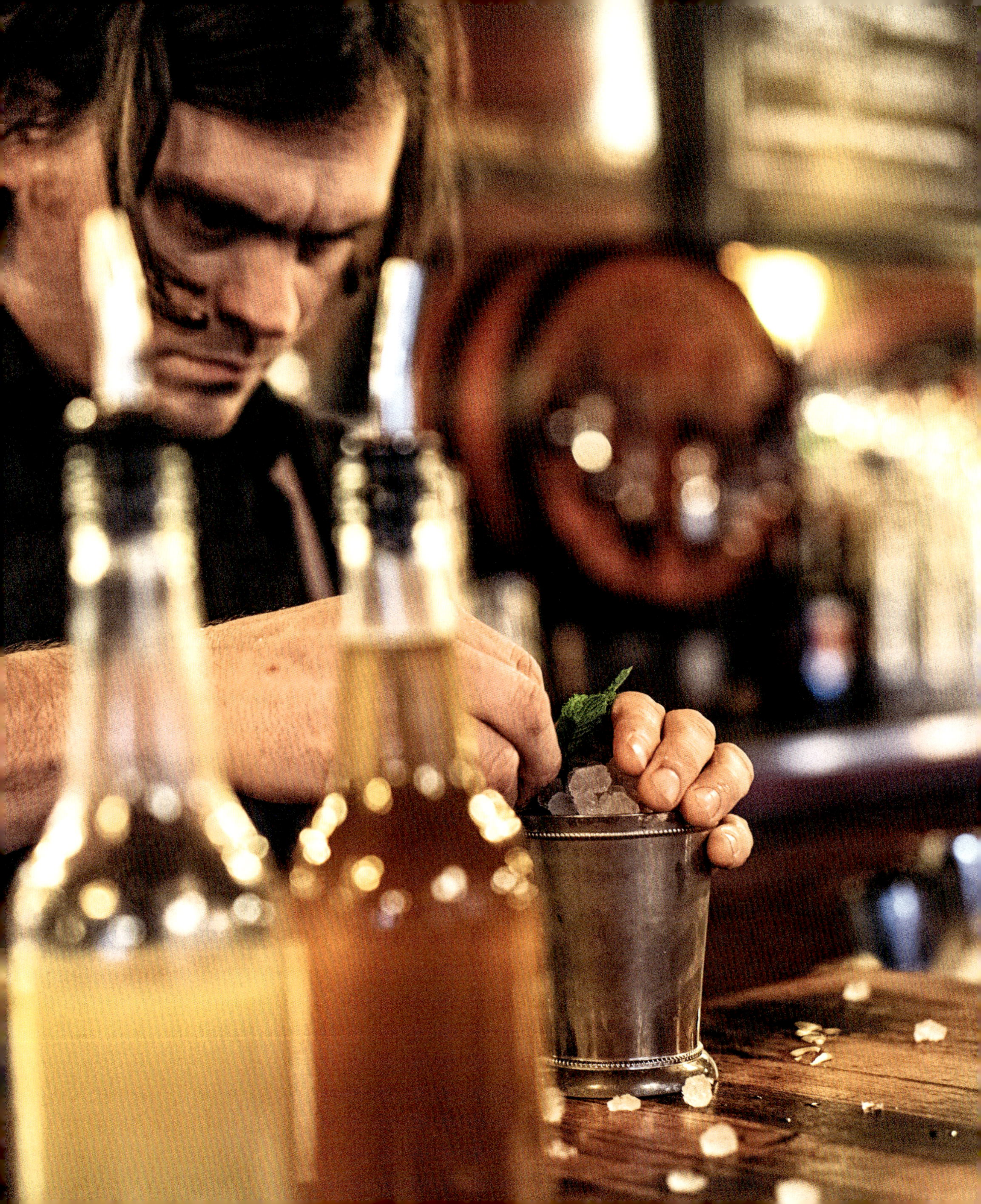

The last call for drinks occurs just before 2 a.m. at establishments that stay open “late” in Los Angeles because alcohol sales are prohibited between 2 a.m. and 6 a.m. throughout California.

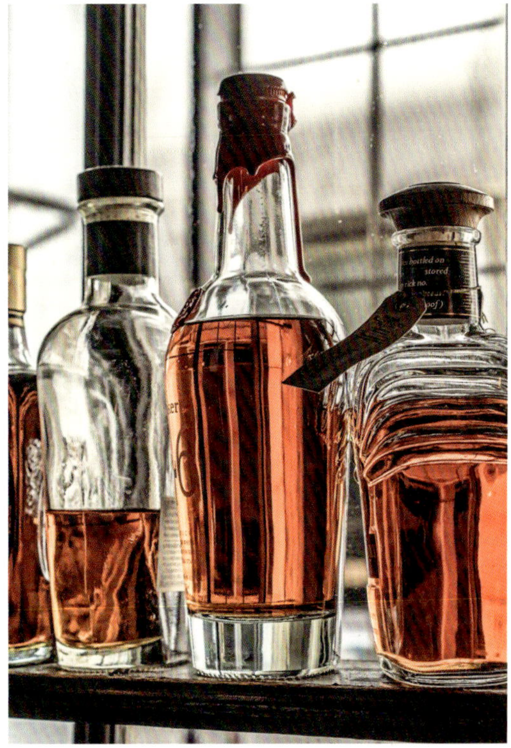

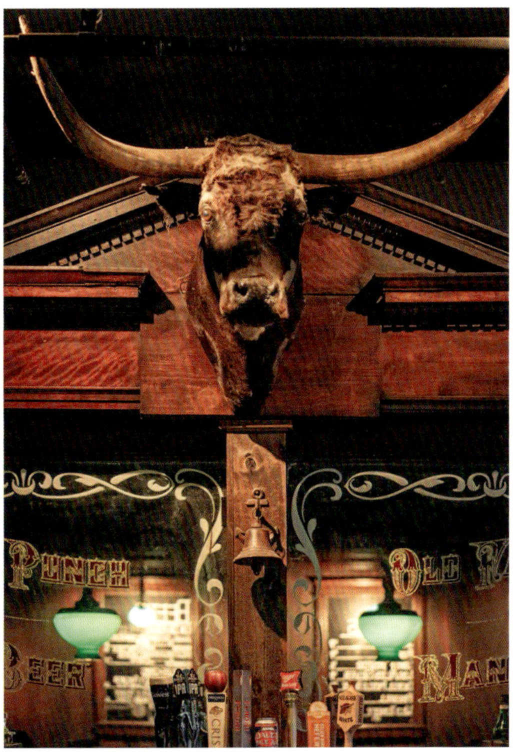

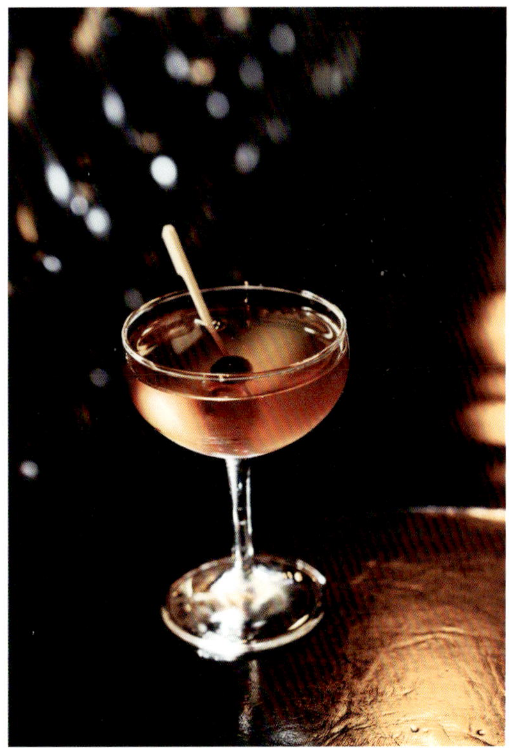

The “whiskey wall” at downtown’s Seven Grand features more than 400 bottles from all over the world.

A giant bison head oversees all at Tony’s Saloon, a neighborhood bar in the Arts District.

As a good whiskey bar should, Seven Grand serves a fantastic Manhattan, albeit in downtown Los Angeles.

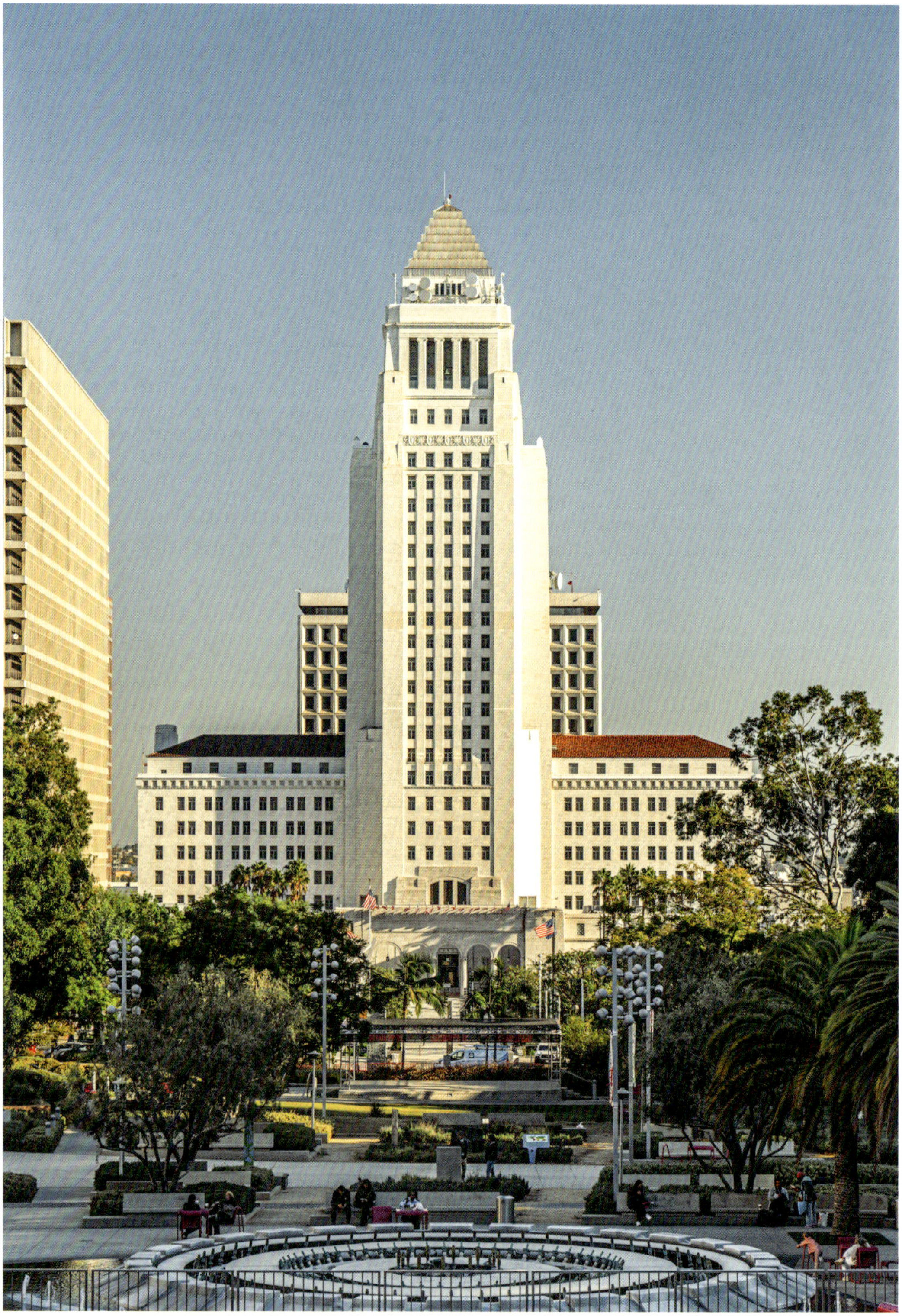

This view of City Hall from Gloria Molina Grand Park shows a view of the iconic center of LA's government with the park's Arthur J. Will Memorial Fountain in the foreground (which is curiously without water).

(Page 106–107) Gaining access to City Hall's observation deck can be tricky but the trouble is worth it—the view of downtown is amazing.

City Hall

Landmark with a View (And a Great Park Nearby)

For fans of classic TV shows, it's hard not to hear the opening lines of *Dragnet* when sighting City Hall or thinking of Superman visiting the headquarters of the *Daily Planet* (it's also featured prominently in the film *L.A. Confidential*). Built in 1928, this iconic building is the center of the city's civic life and the headquarters of its government, including the offices of the mayor and city council. Located in the heart of downtown, it was the tallest structure in Los Angeles until 1964. Today, it's certainly overshadowed in height by downtown's many skyscrapers, but few of those new behemoths offer the charm, beauty, or history of this building.

The inside of this landmark is as impressive as the exterior's Art Deco ziggurat tower, and guided tours of the building are available. Not to be missed is the observation deck on the 27th floor, which, if open to the public, provides an incredible, 360-degree view of the city. Also not to be missed: Gloria Molina Grand Park, the public park across the street that offers all kinds of fun, from an interactive splash pad to events, cultural programs, and protests.

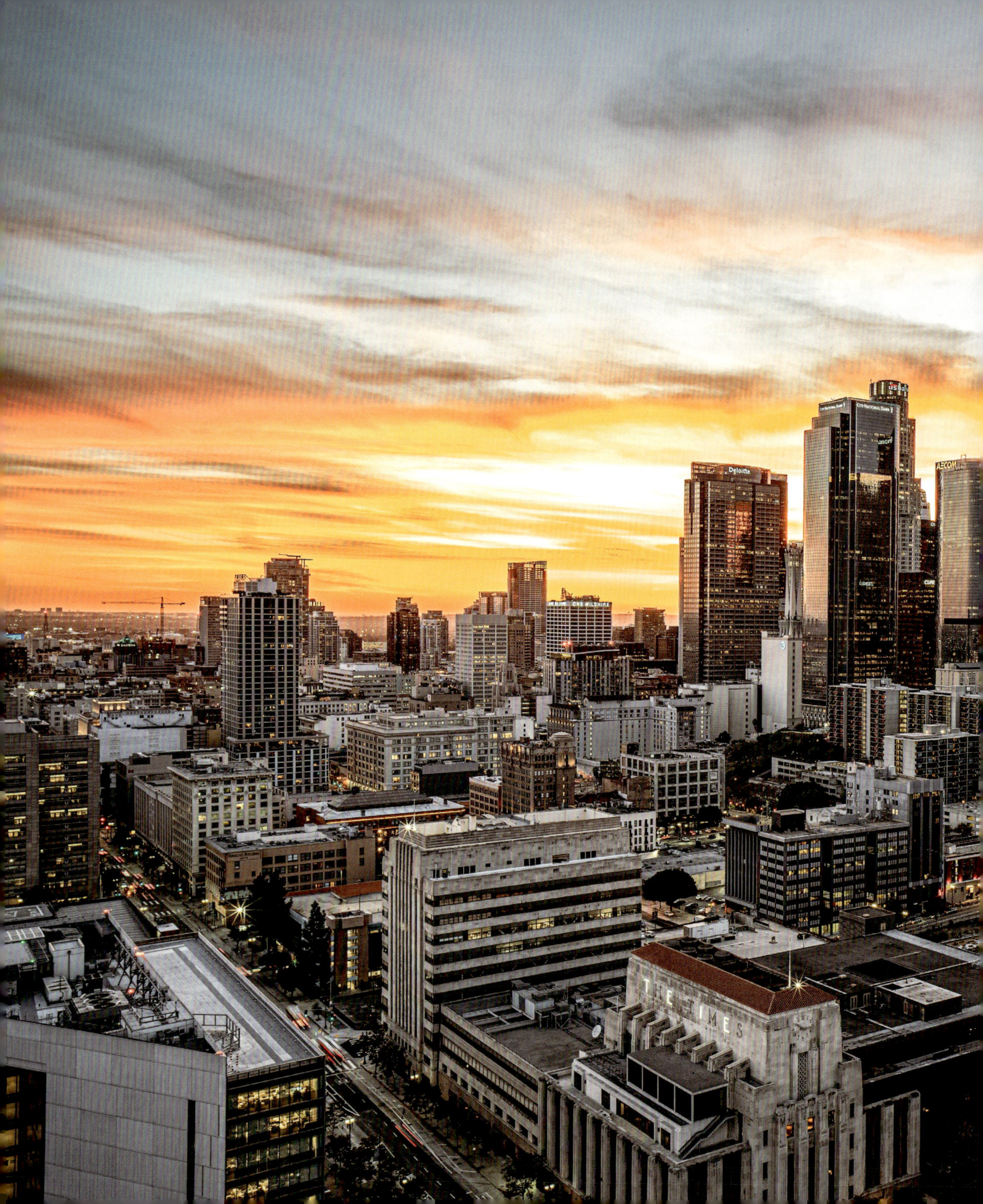
Deloitte
ONE WILSHIRE
AECOM

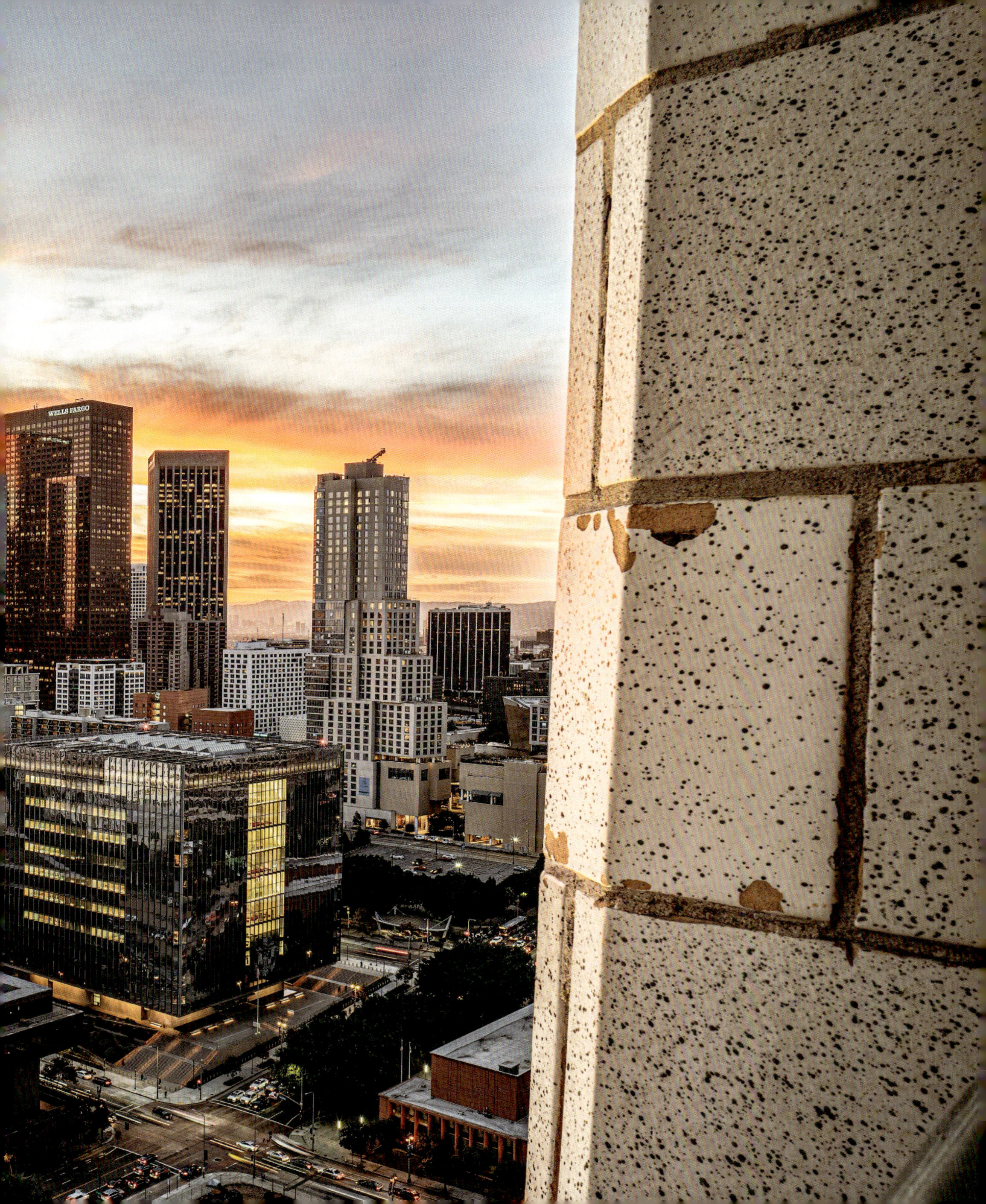
WELLS FARGO

Grand Central Market

Best Place to Get a Taste of the City

What was once a traditional market is now a food hall that is one of downtown's most popular attractions—Grand Central Market is a century-old institution that should not be missed, especially if you're hungry! Opened in 1917, this visual cacophony of food stalls with hand-painted or neon signs is full of delicious and diverse offerings. From legacy businesses like Roast to Go (1952) and China Café (1959) to the latest in hip food trends, your options for what to eat are seemingly endless.

Grand Central Market has been called a microcosm of the city's culinary scene, and that's true—so many foods are here to try, from pupusas to pizza, bento boxes to currywurst. Los Angeles is a city of immigrants from around the world who continue to create incredible cultures and cuisines.

Outside the market, there's a shrine of sorts to the city's patron saint, food critic Jonathan Gold who passed away in 2018. A plaque bears an excerpt from *City of Gold*, a documentary film about Gold, where the Pulitzer Prize-winning critic says: "The thing that people find hard to understand, I think, is sort of the magnitude of what's here, the huge number of multiple cultures that live in the city who come together in this beautiful and haphazard fashion. And the fault lines between them are sometimes where you find the most beautiful things."

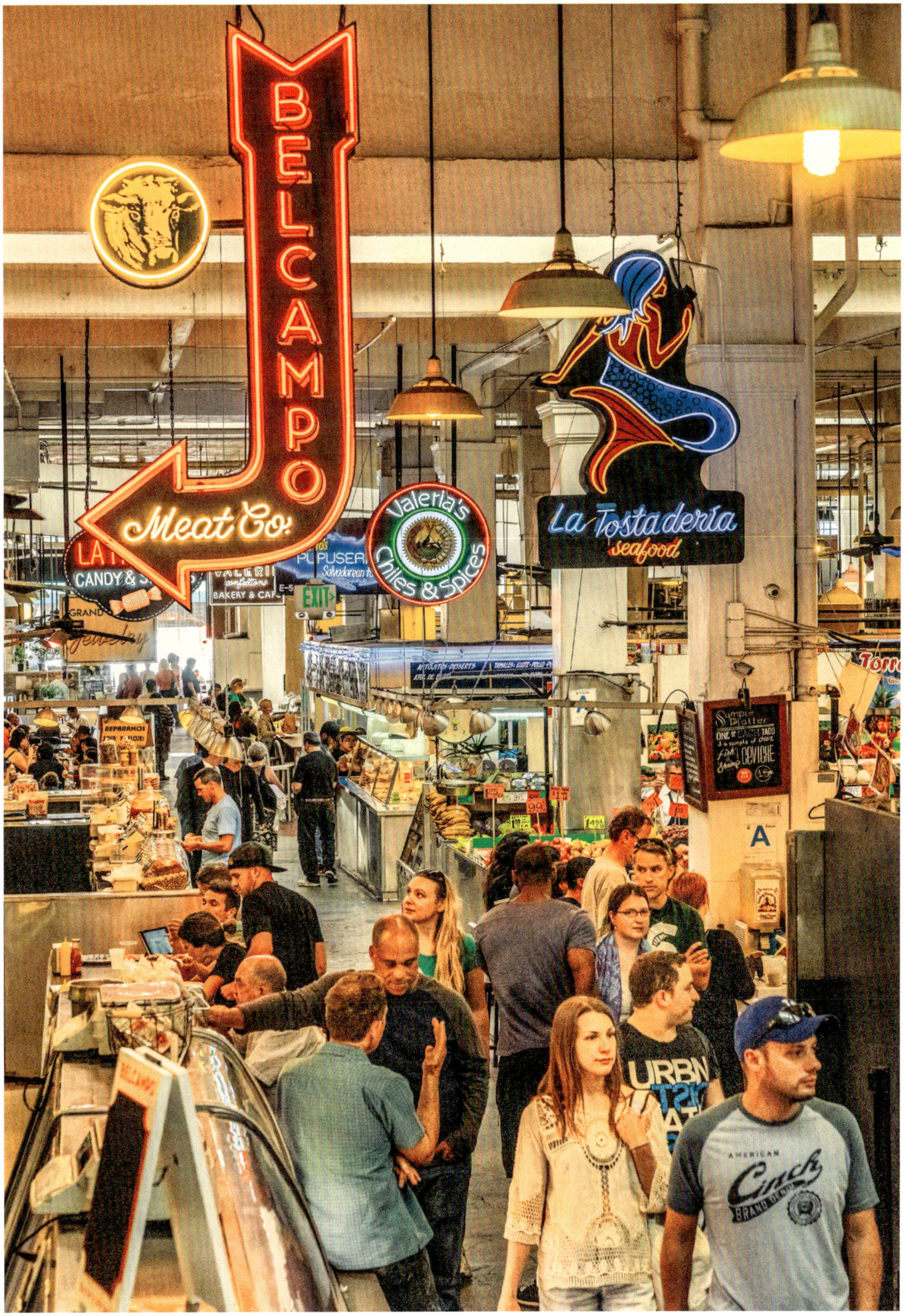

Bustling crowds fill the spaces between food stalls at Grand Central Market, which offers mostly prepared foods but still has a few shops as well.

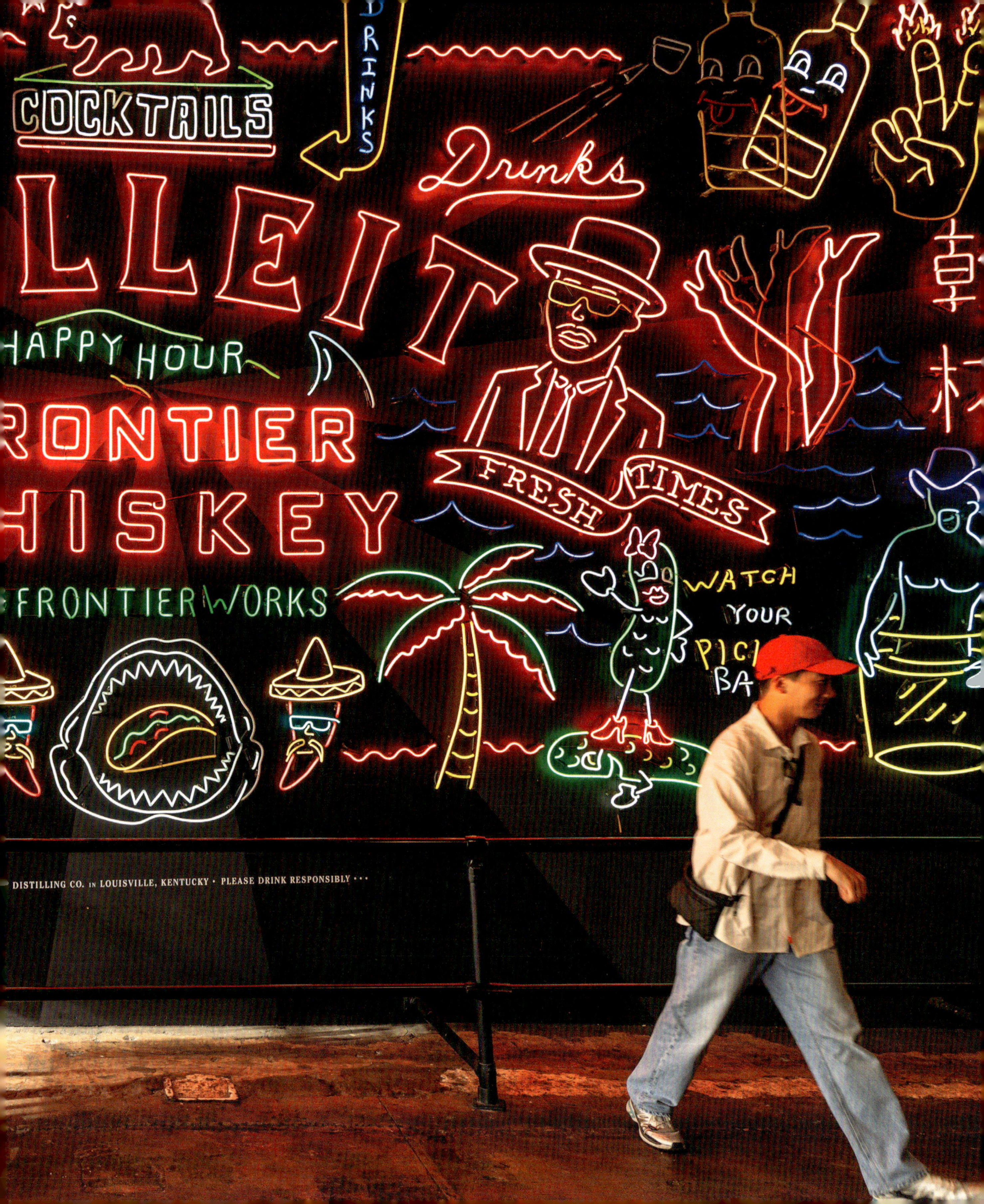
COCKTAILS
DRINKS
Drinks
LLEIT
HAPPY HOUR
RONTIER
HISKEY
FRONTIER WORKS
FRESH TIMES
WATCH
YOUR
PIC
BA
DISTILLING CO. IN LOUISVILLE, KENTUCKY · PLEASE DRINK RESPONSIBLY · · ·

The market is full of great murals, including this neon collaboration between Glendale's Museum of Neon Art and Bulleit Whiskey, which acts as a fundraiser for neon restoration (post it and tag it and the company will make a donation to the museum).

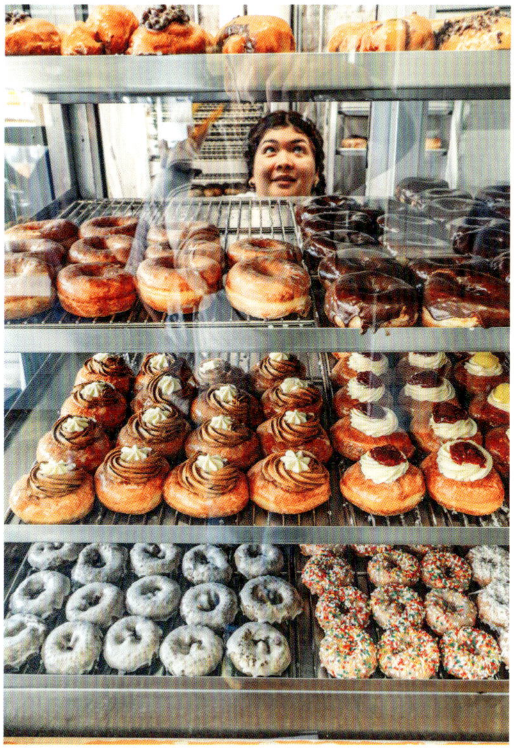

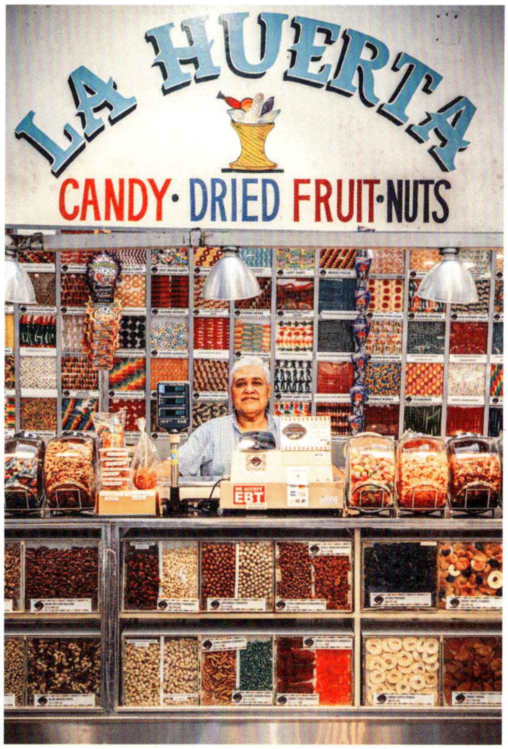

■□ A worker prepares fresh donuts at the Donut Man, the market's outpost of the 50-year-old institution on Route 66 that invented the Fresh Strawberry Donut.

□■ The beautiful La Huerta Candy sells all kinds of sweet and savory snacks since 1999.

Art Deco

Heavy On the Jazz Age Elegance

The architectural variety of Los Angeles is legendary, and the city is a showcase for almost every style—plus the birthplace for a few, like the Craftsman California bungalow court and Mid-Century Modern. Long known as an incubator for innovative architecture, knock-out buildings—commercial, civic, and residential—are all around that capture the diversity and creativity of Angelenos.

One popular style that appears throughout the city—and is especially prevalent in downtown—is Art Deco, perhaps because it, like Los Angeles, embodied a sense of modernity during its heyday of the 1920s to 1940s. During this time, more than one million people moved into Los Angeles, and the city's rapid growth meant a major building boom. The sleek and modern "streamlined" style of Art Deco, which pulled inspiration from exotic cultures (motifs like zigzags and ziggurats, Egyptian, Mayan, and Assyrian design elements) and technology (aerodynamics, ships) promised both grandeur and possibility. And dare we say, a century later, these structures still deliver.

There are many masterful examples that can be easily overlooked because they are so very functional: take Union Station, for example, the largest railroad passenger terminal in the Western US, which was completed in 1939 and fuses Spanish Colonial Revival with Art Deco into one of the most beloved landmarks of the city. Or downtown's Central Library, opened in 1926, a beacon for book lovers with its trademark tiled pyramid on the roof. And City Hall, of course, which stands as a symbol of the city and was built in the Art Deco Style, complete with its iconic tower, topped with yet another pyramid. These examples are just tips of the iceberg—or maybe it's more accurate to say pieces of limestone—the starting point of what can be a much longer exploration of how the architectural elegance of the Art Deco style has shaped not just downtown but all of the city (and especially Hollywood). For a dedicated tour, the Los Angeles Conservancy offers a weekly walking tour that highlights downtown's Art Deco delights.

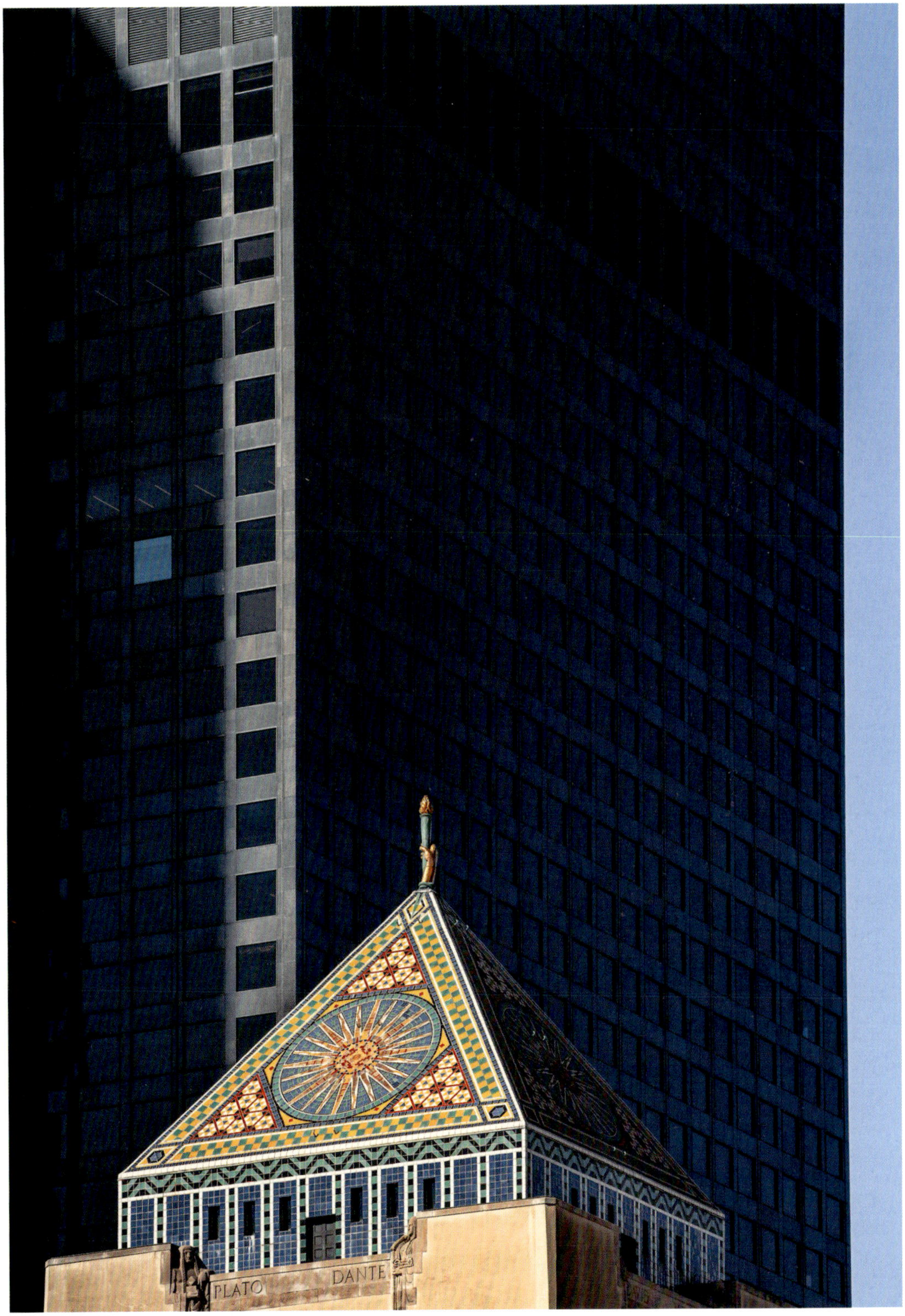

A tiled mosaic pyramid tops Los Angeles Central Library, which offers free docent-led tours of the building and its art, as well as exhibitions and events.

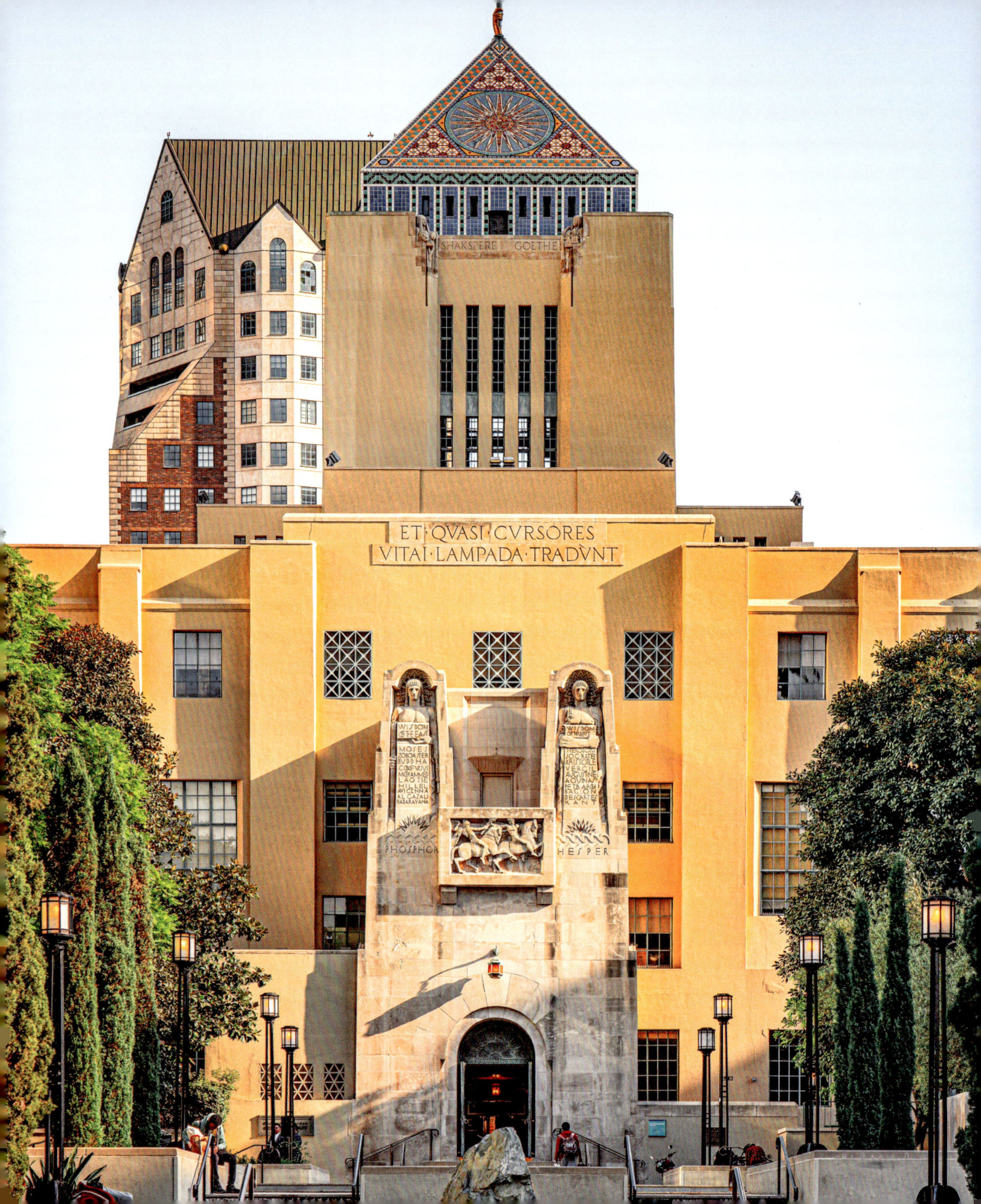
SHAKSPERE GOETHE
ET·QVASI·CVRSORES
VITAI·LAMPADA·TRADVNT
HESPER

The original building that houses Central Library was designed by architect Bertram Goodhue, and this entrance on Flower Street bears a sculpture on the façade by Lee Lawrie based on the theme "Light of Learning."

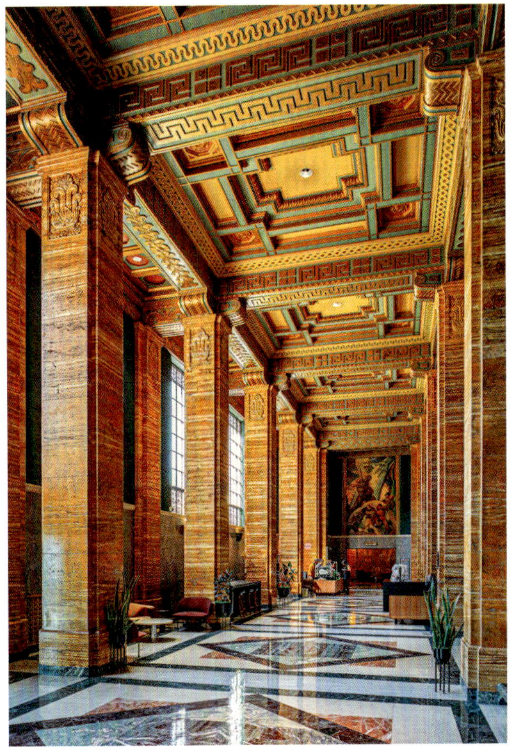

The marble lobby of the 1931 Edison (now CalEdison) Building is, like the rest of the structure, a gorgeous example of Art Deco's visual opulence.

The stunning rotunda of the library's Goodhue Building features the famed Zodiac Chandelier, also designed by Lee Lawrie.

The library's former Reference Room is now the home of the magical Children's Department and retains the original Art Deco décor, including these reproductions of the original gorgeous table lamps.

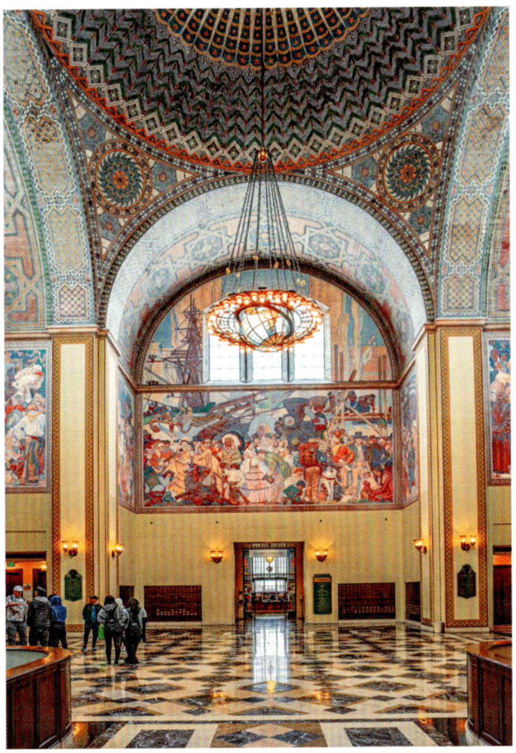

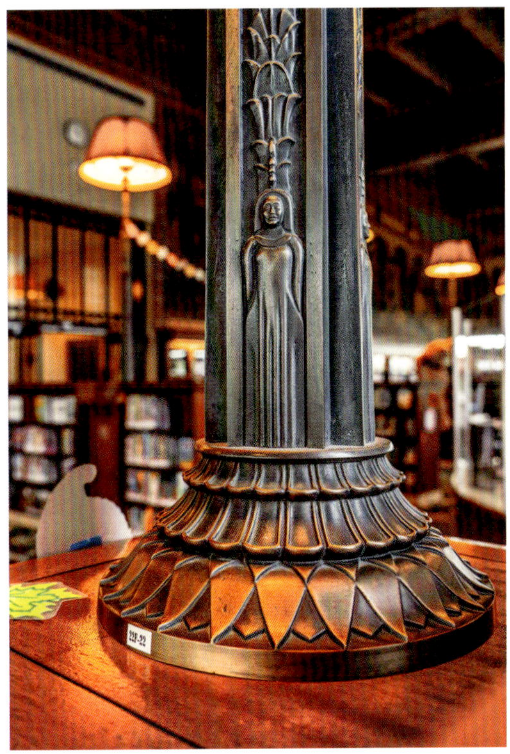

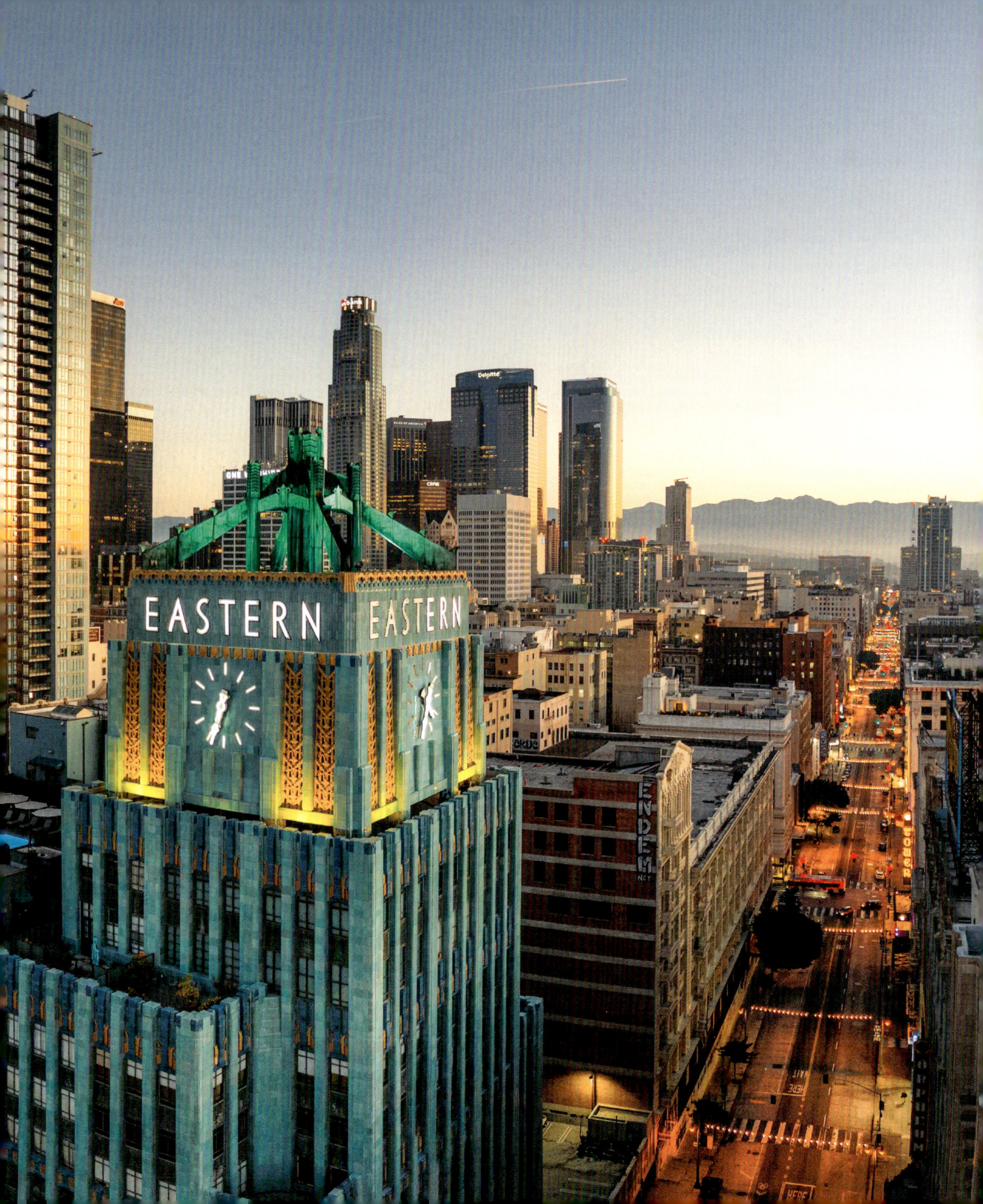
EASTERN
EASTERN
Deloitte

The majestic clock tower of the Eastern Columbia Building is forty feet high and features a neon-lit clock on each side of the building.

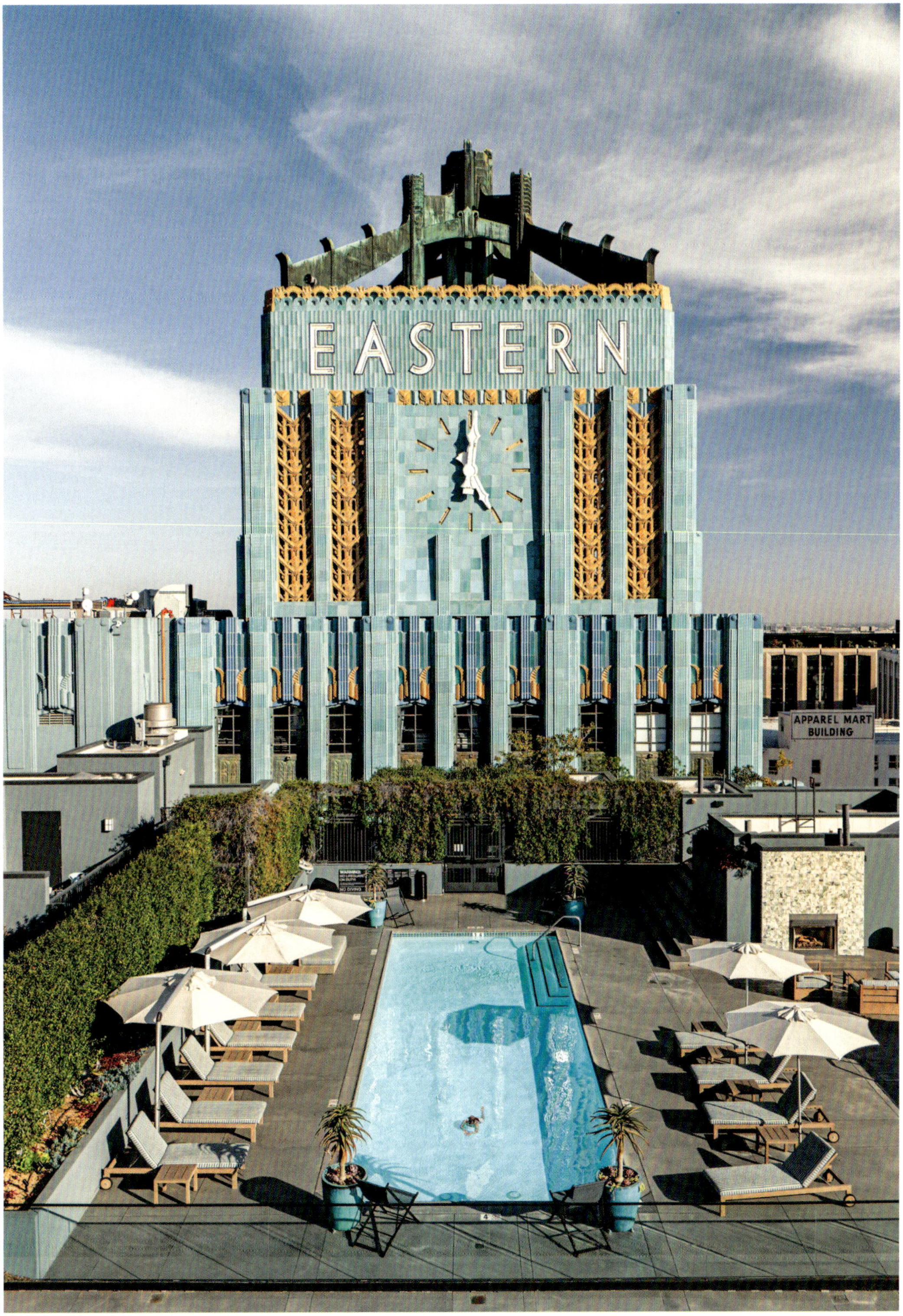

With its vibrant turquoise terracotta walls and gold leaf details, the 1930 Eastern Columbia Building (now known as Eastern Columbia Lofts) is the crown jewel of downtown's Art Deco buildings.

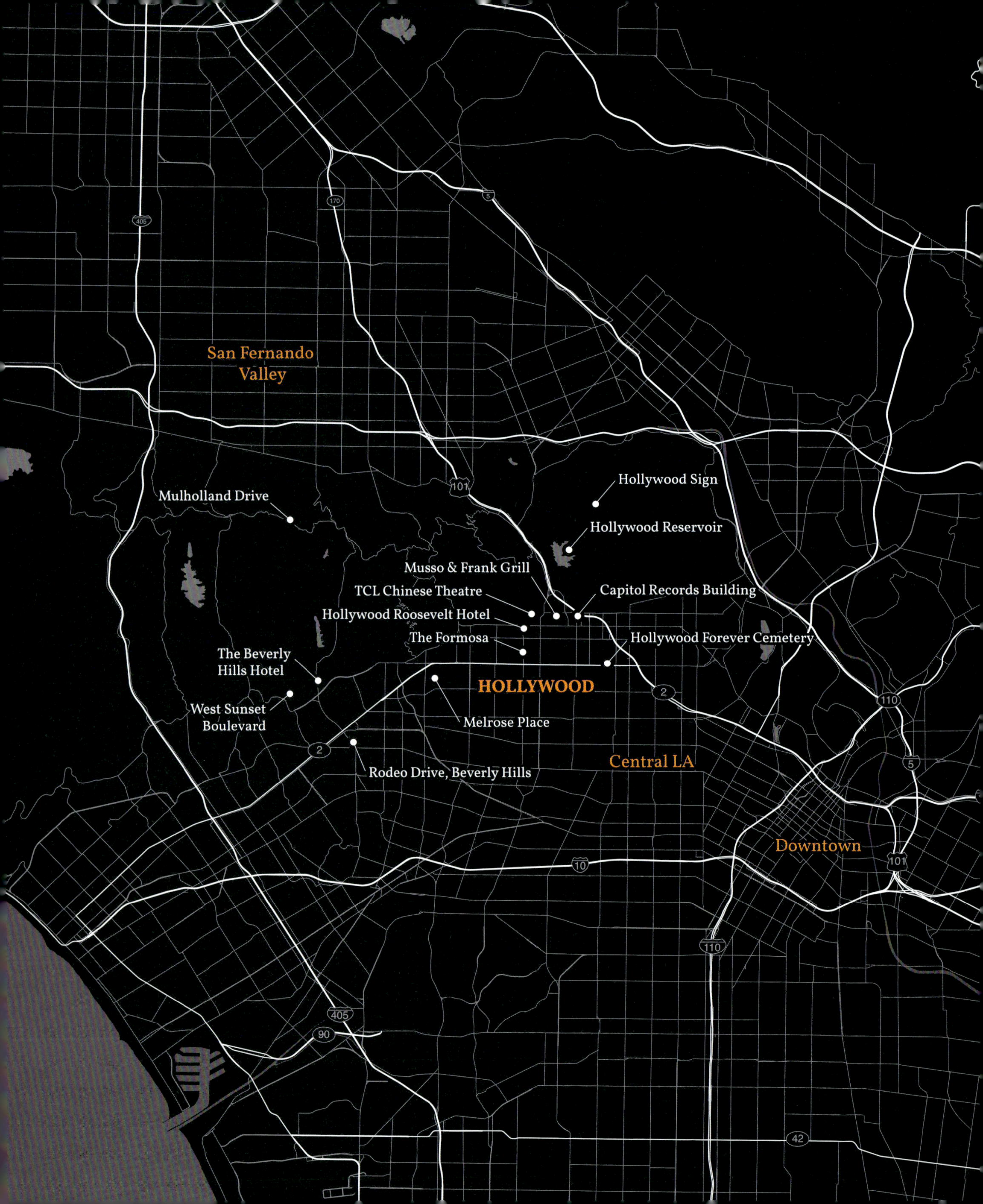
San Fernando Valley
Mulholland Drive
Hollywood Sign
Hollywood Reservoir
Musso & Frank Grill
TCL Chinese Theatre
Capitol Records Building
Hollywood Roosevelt Hotel
The Formosa
Hollywood Forever Cemetery
The Beverly Hills Hotel
HOLLYWOOD
West Sunset Boulevard
Melrose Place
Rodeo Drive, Beverly Hills
Central LA
Downtown
405
170
5
101
2
110
10
90
42

Hollywood

Iconic Sites

Where Dreams and Reality Meet

City of Dreams, Filmland, Tinseltown, the Movie Capital of the World, La La Land, Filmdom, Lotus Land, Screenland, Hollyweird—the nicknames are many, but there's only one Hollywood. Well, two actually—the name that has come to describe the US's entertainment industry *and* the actual geographic neighborhood named Hollywood. The two overlap, certainly, as the place Hollywood is where the early film pioneers came to establish their burgeoning studios in the first few decades of the twentieth century. Who would guess that before that, the town of Hollywood was founded by a prohibitionist from Kansas in 1887? Or that Hollywood only officially joined the city of Los Angeles (mostly to get access to water) in 1910?

By 1915, Hollywood was the center of motion picture production, and the name became synonymous with the film industry. As the studios grew and needed more space, they moved to other parts of Los Angeles—mostly the San Fernando Valley—and Hollywood became the center of television production as well as being an important hub of other forms of entertainment, like the recording industry. More than a century later, Hollywood is still drawing crowds of movie lovers and dream seekers, and there are still many historic sites to behold: the Lasky-DeMille Barn (home of the wonderful Hollywood Heritage Museum), the Hollywood Bowl, the iconic Hollywood Sign, the Walk of Fame and all the landmark theaters and movie palaces along Hollywood Boulevard, and the much-beloved Musso and Frank Grill. The list can go on, so the best advice is to get out there and do what people have done for years: try and make it in Hollywood.

"Hollywood is a place where they'll pay you a thousand dollars for a kiss and fifty cents for your soul. I know, because I turned down the first offer enough and held out for the fifty." —Marilyn Monroe

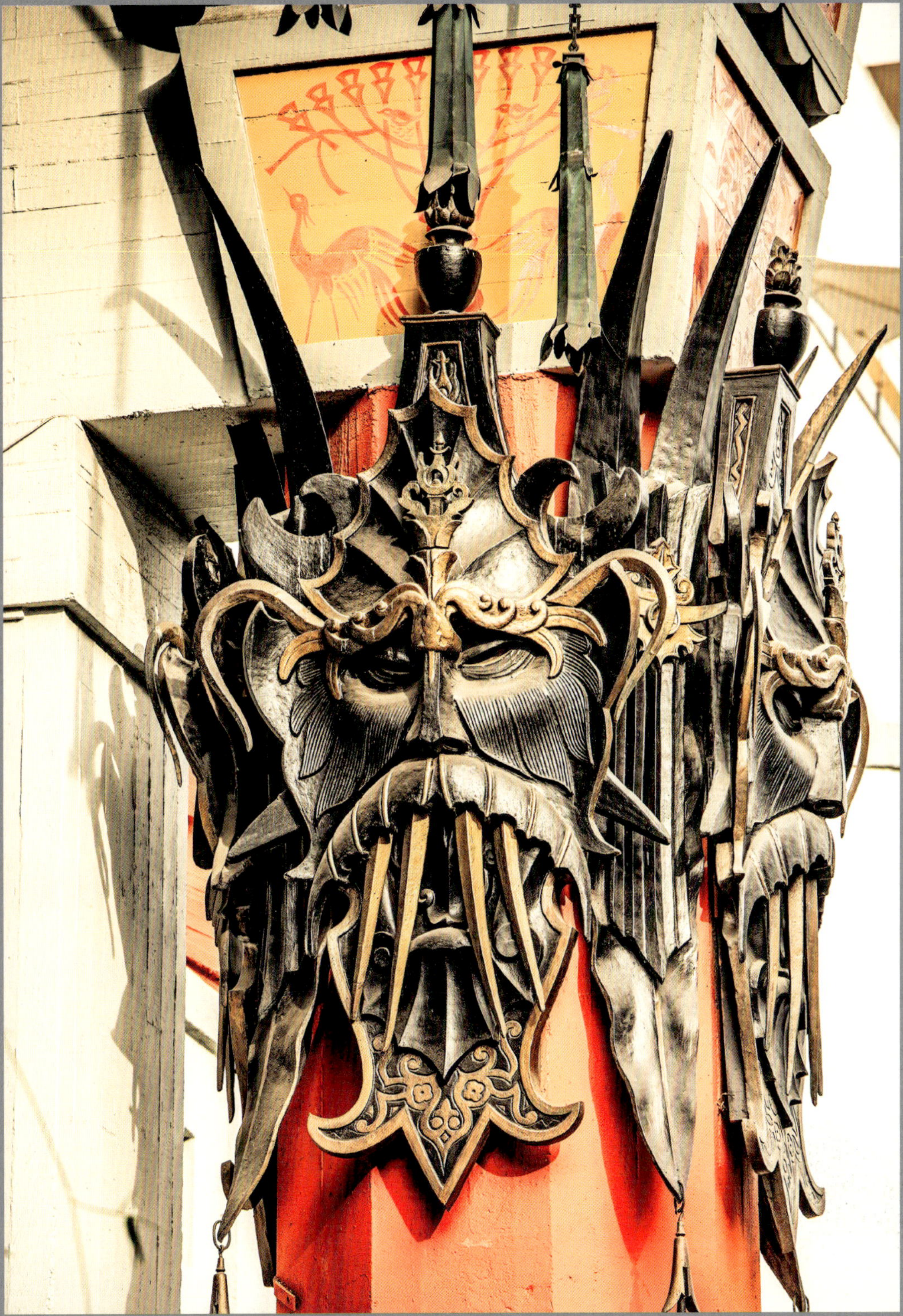

Wrought iron masks look out from the red columns that flank the entrance of the world-famous Chinese Theatre, opened by impresario Sid Grauman in 1927.

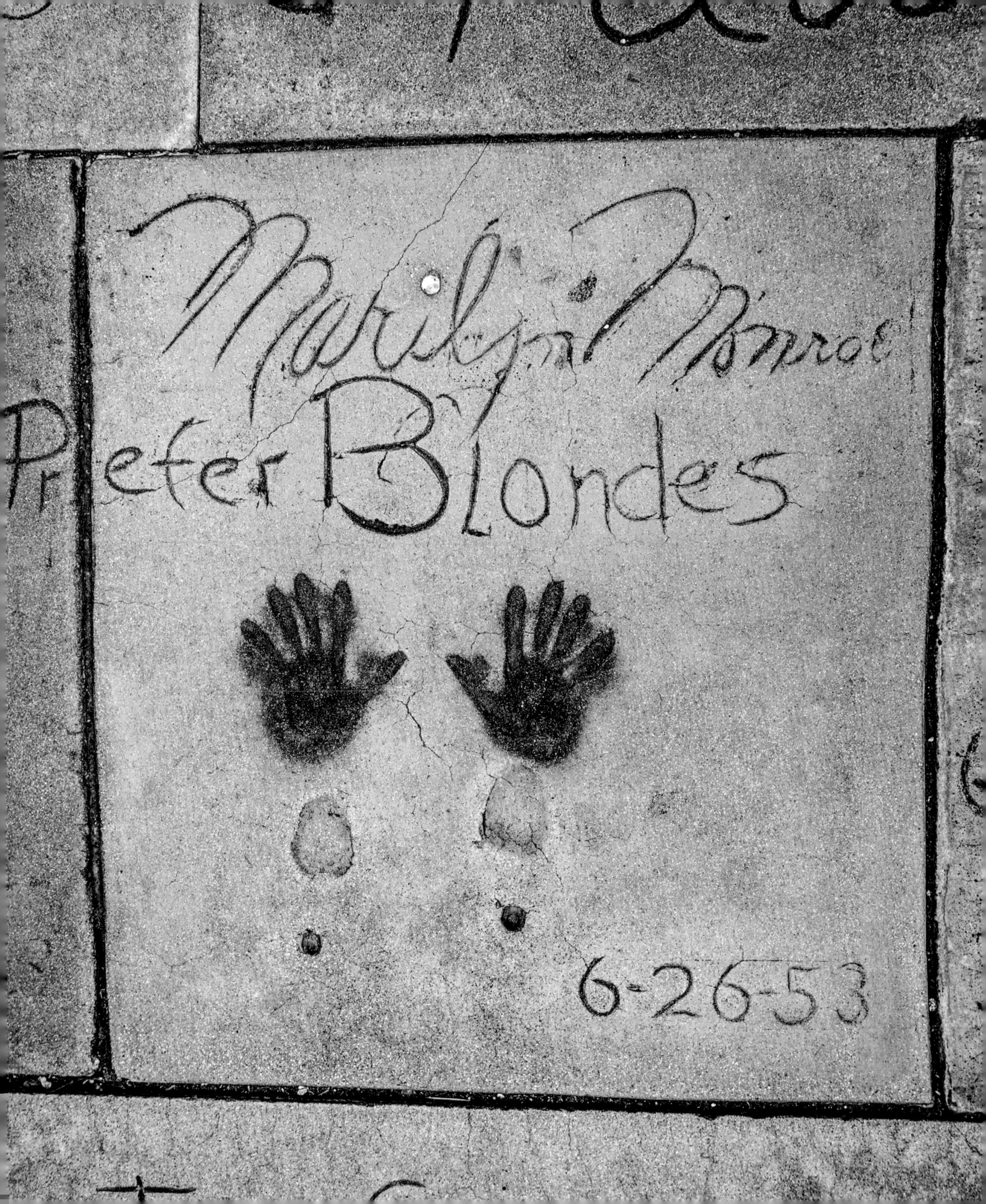
Marilyn Monroe
Prefer Blondes
6-26-53

The Chinese Theatre's Forecourt of the Stars features the handprints of movie stars from Hollywood's golden age to today.

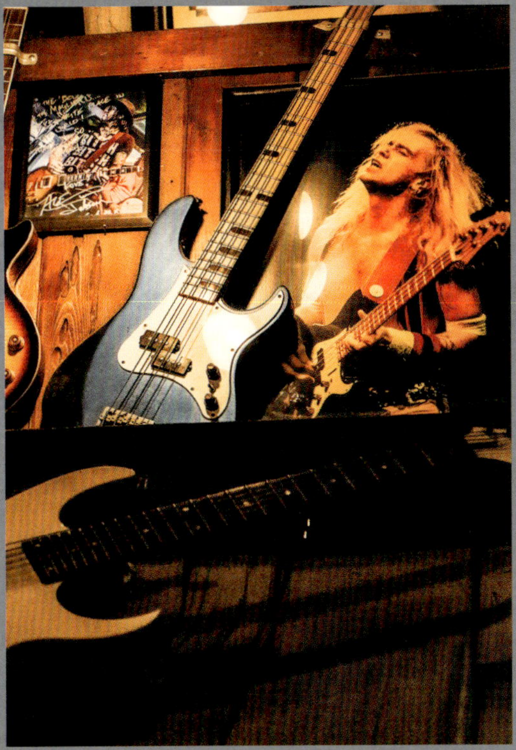

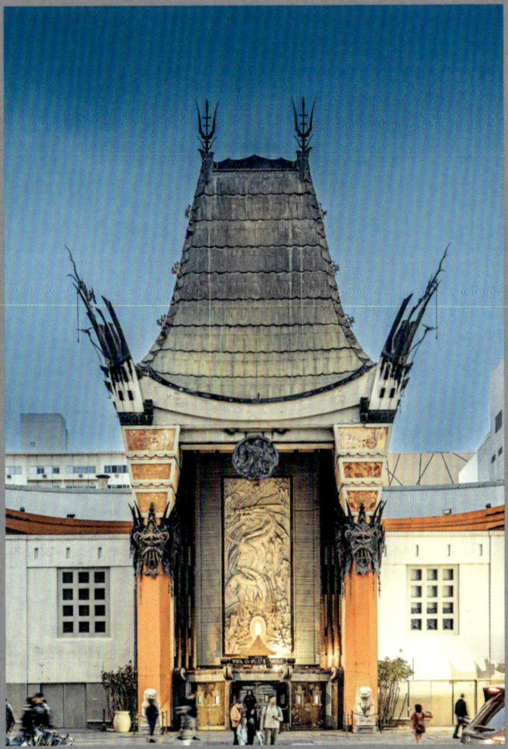

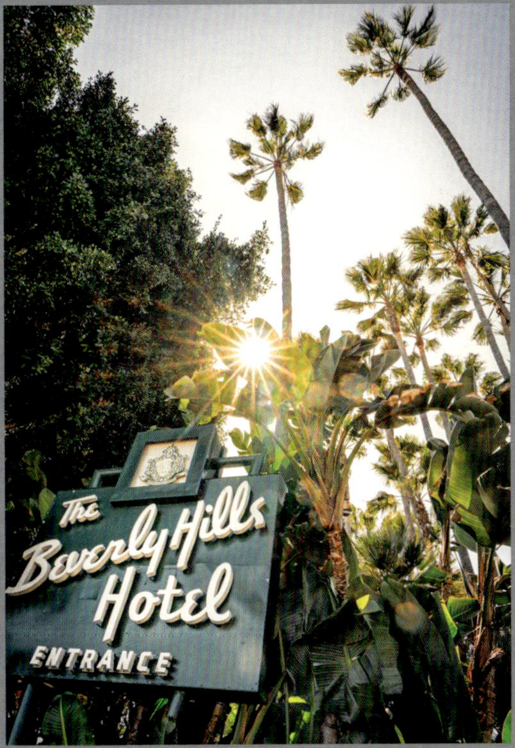

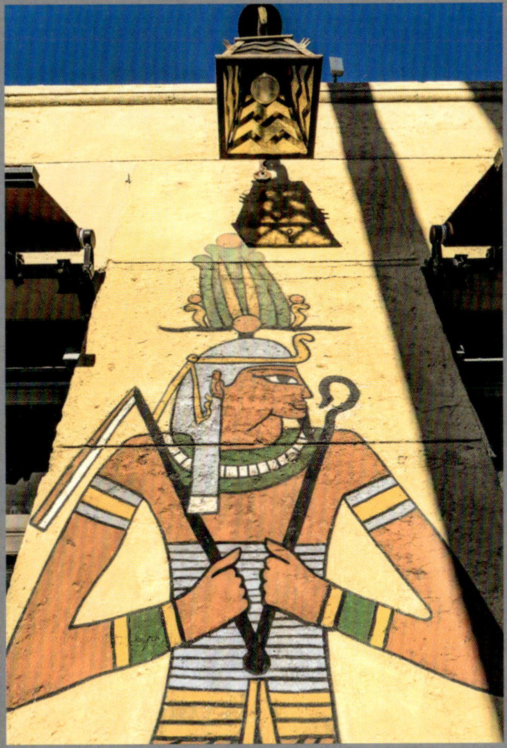

The Rainbow Bar & Grill is a historic watering hole and restaurant on the Sunset Strip and has been frequented by musicians from Elton John to Lemmy Kilmister of Motörhead.

More than four million people a year visit the landmark Chinese Theatre.

The legendary Beverly Hills Hotel is a historic movie star hideaway.

Another landmark themed theater from Sid Grauman, the historic Egyptian Theatre opened in 1922 and is the long-time home of the American Cinematheque.

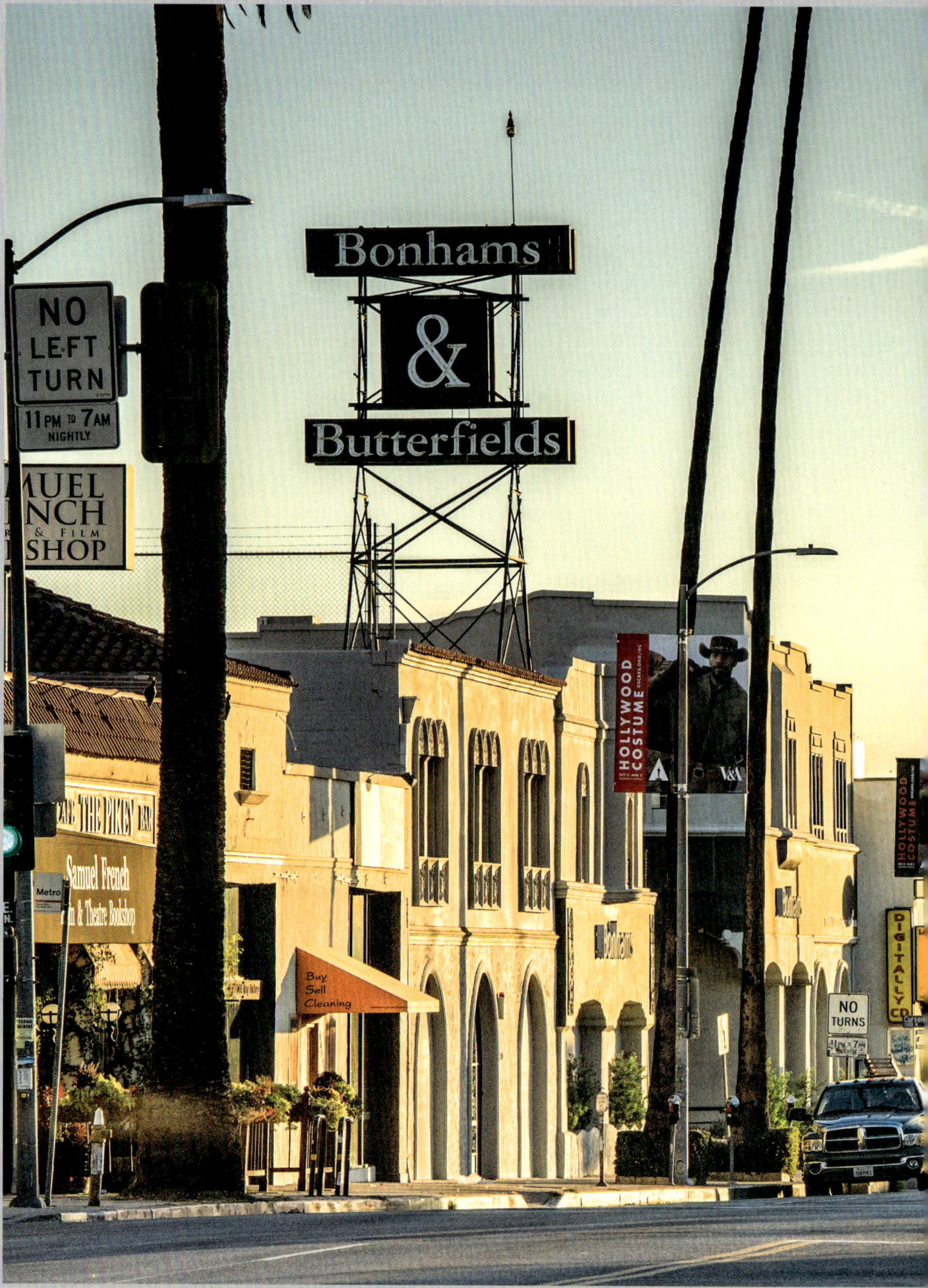

"Like earlier generations of English intellectuals who taught themselves Italian in order to read Dante in the original, I learned to drive in order to read Los Angeles in the original." —architectural critic Reyner Banham

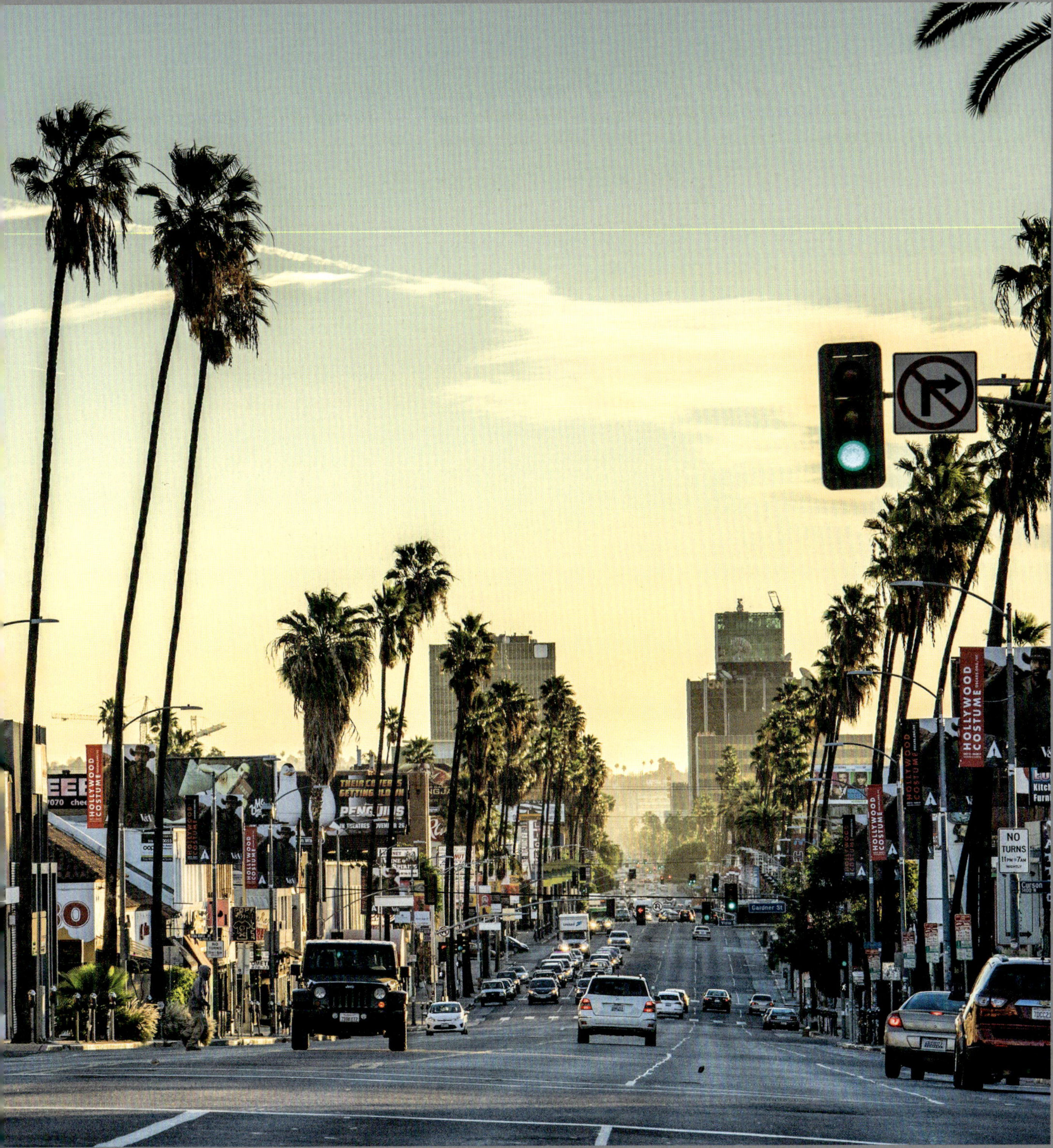
HOLLYWOOD COSTUME
NO TURNS
Gardner St
Curson

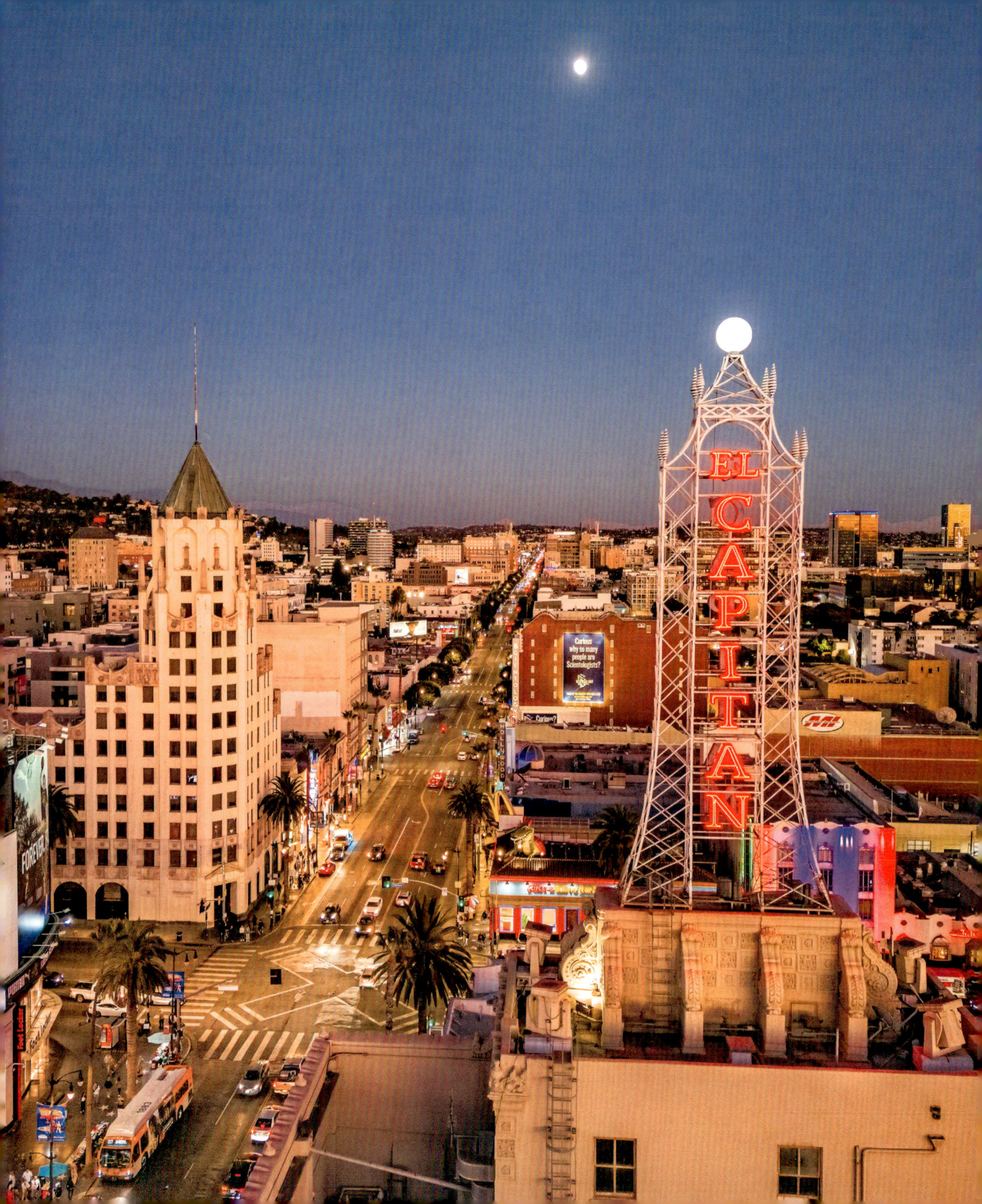
EL CAPITAN
Curious why so many people are Scientologists?
FOREVER

The iconic Hollywood Boulevard lights up at night—and one can still see a movie at the grand 1926 El Capitan Theatre.

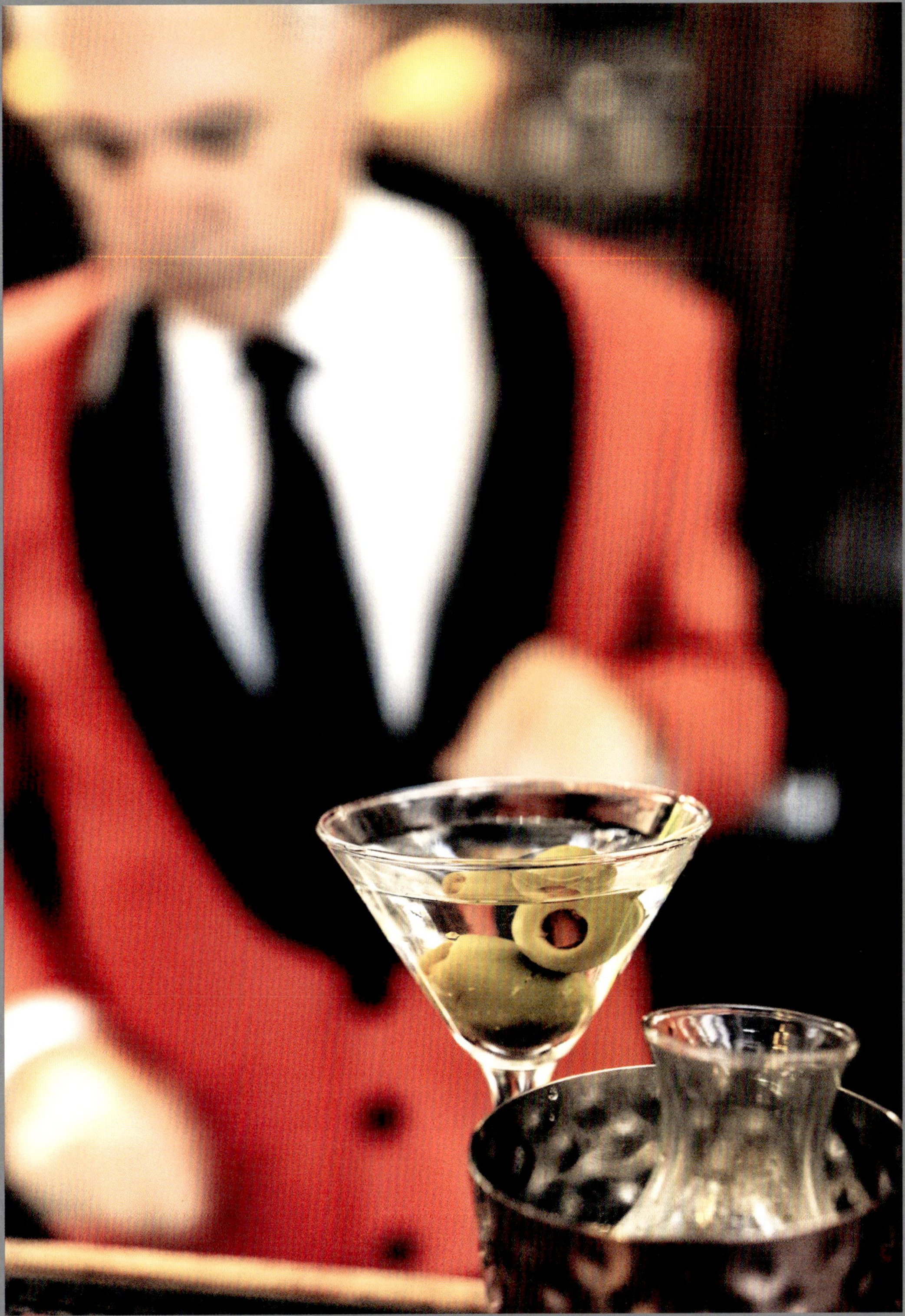

There's nothing more classic than a martini at Musso & Frank's Grill, Hollywood's oldest restaurant.

(Page 128–129) Originally built as a real estate advertisement, the iconic Hollywood sign is more than a century old.

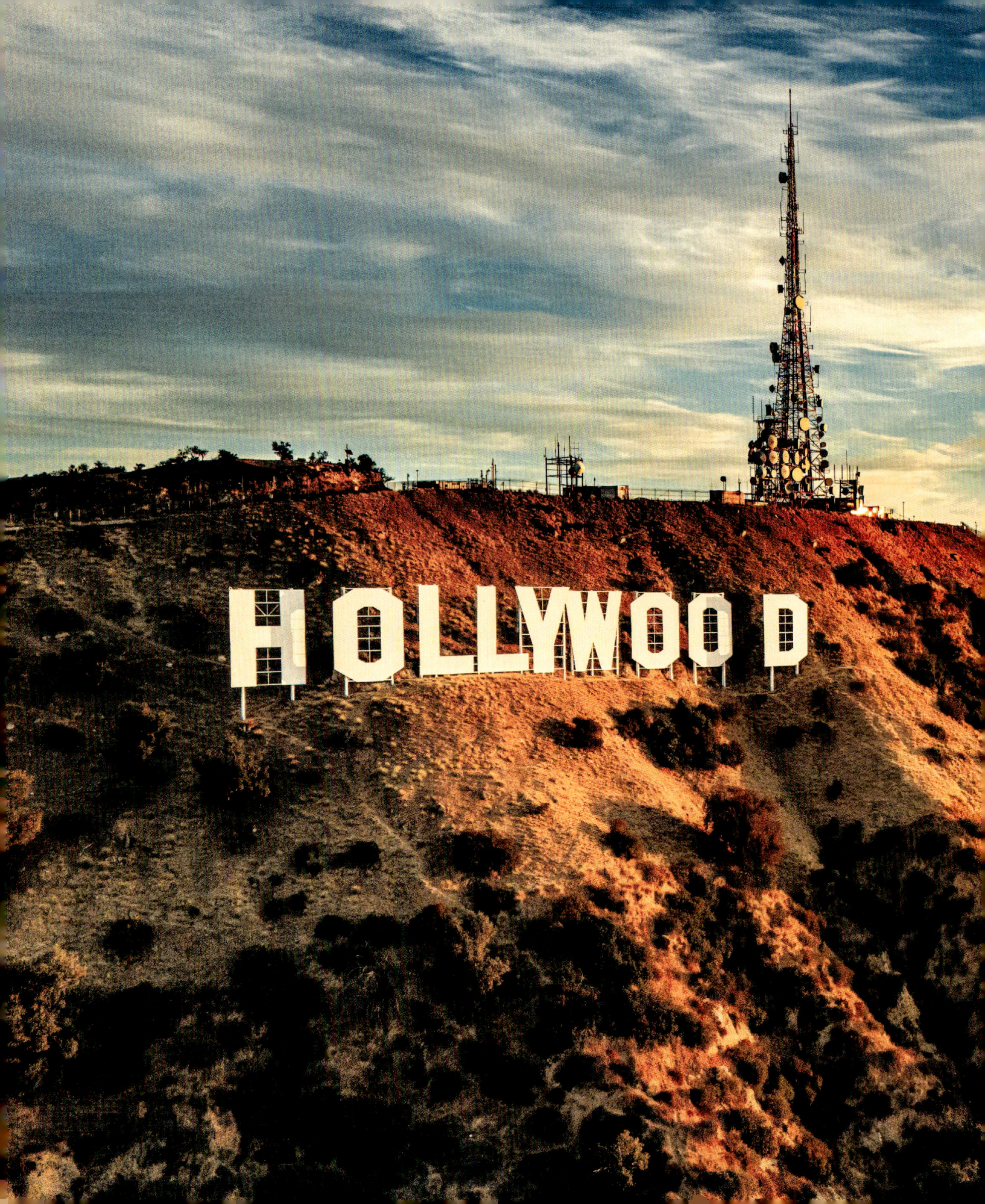
HOLLYWOOD

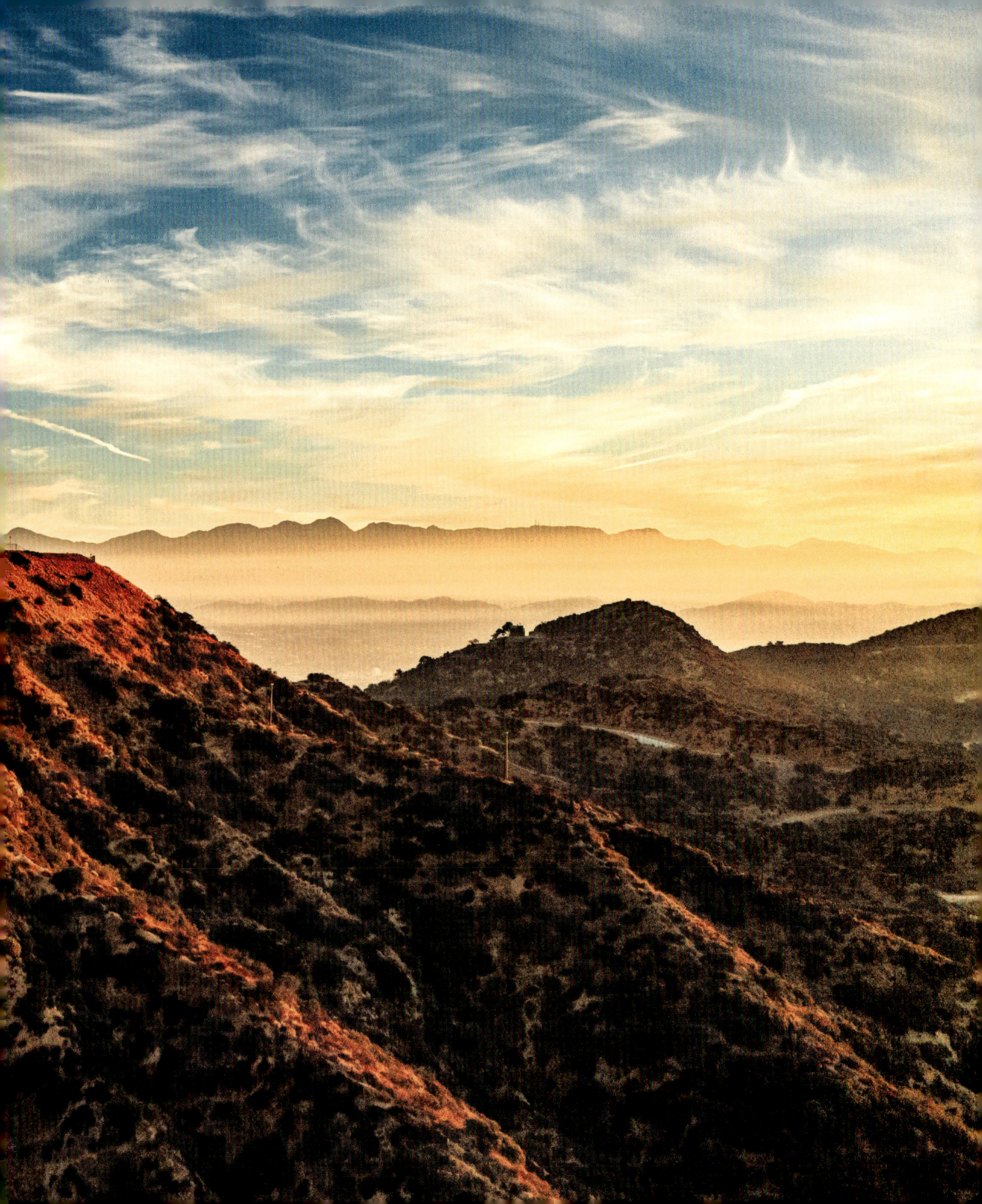

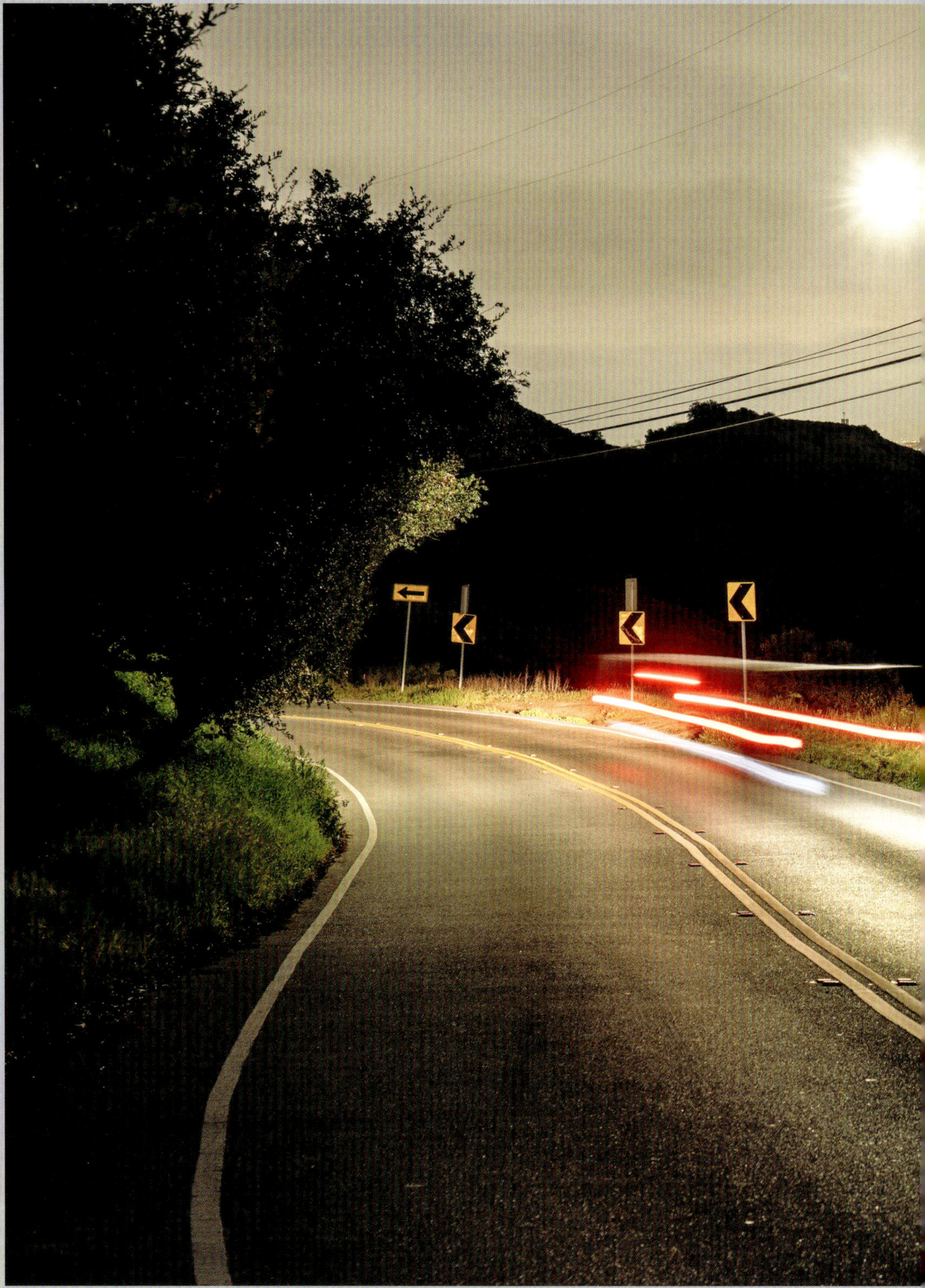

Mulholland Drive curves through the Hollywood Hills and offers stunning views of the city below.

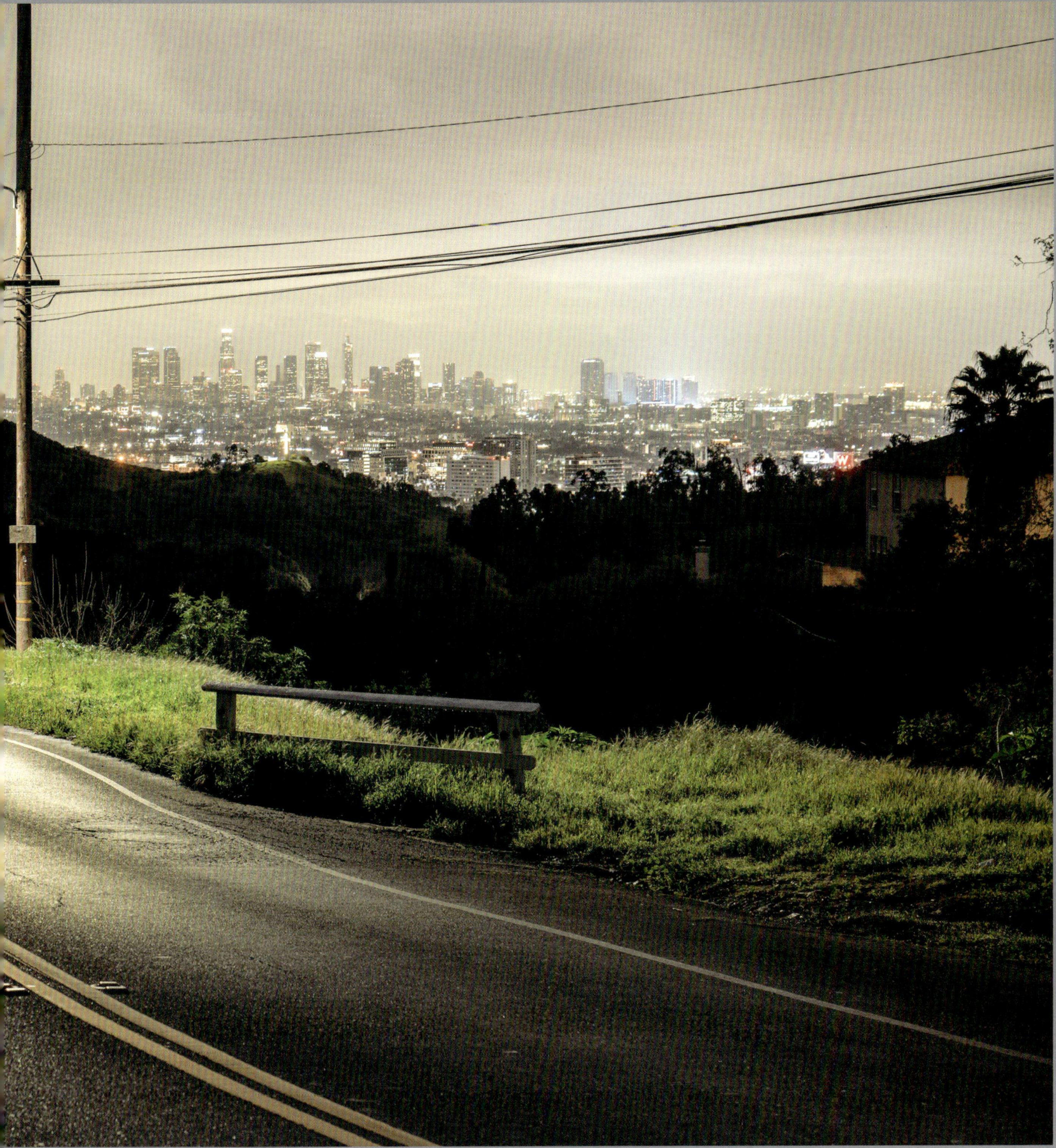

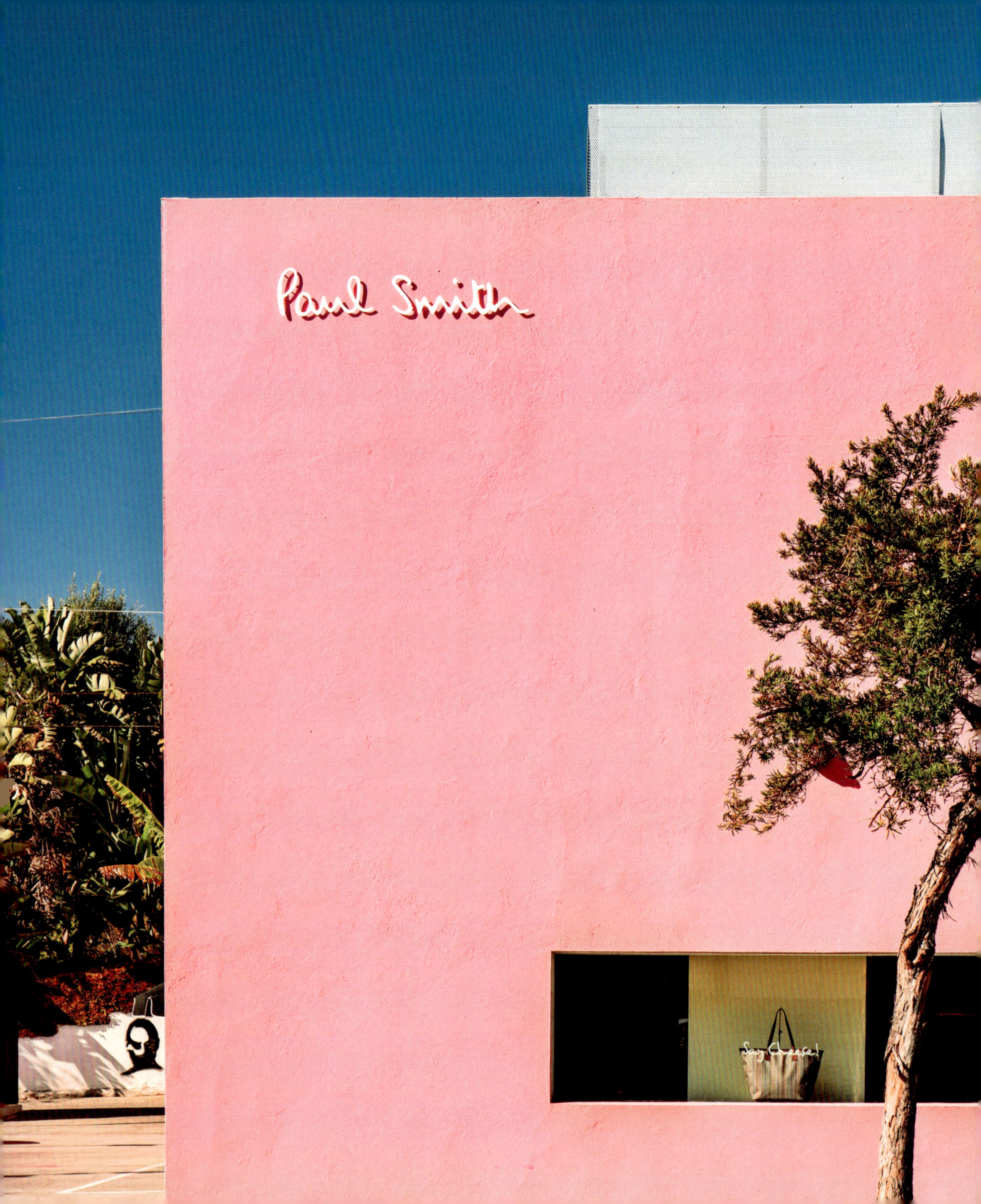
Paul Smith

Another popular shopping district is along Melrose Avenue in Hollywood.

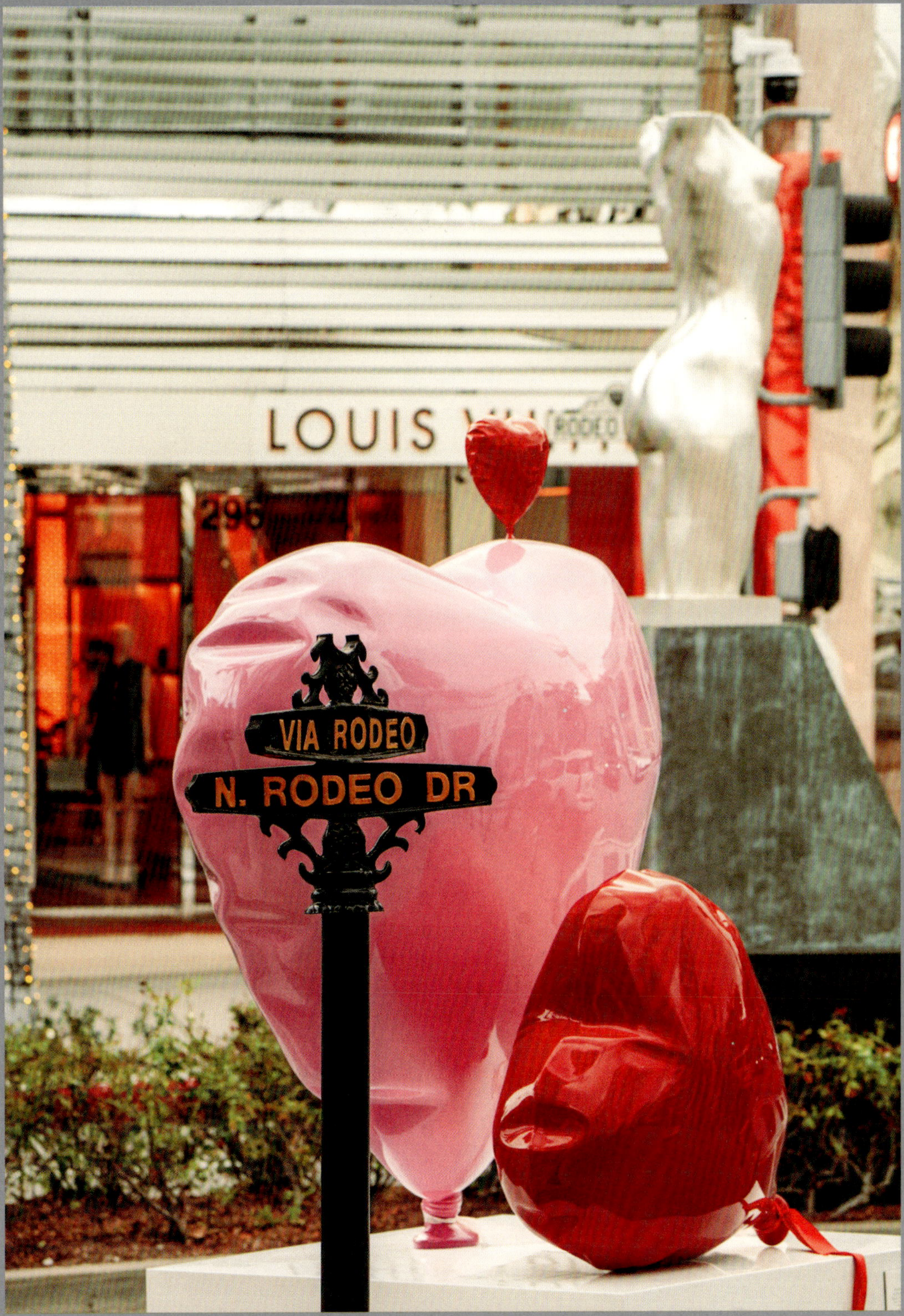

The famed Rodeo Drive, the luxury shopping street, is located in the city of Beverly Hills, not Hollywood, but it's certainly known for its celebrity allure.

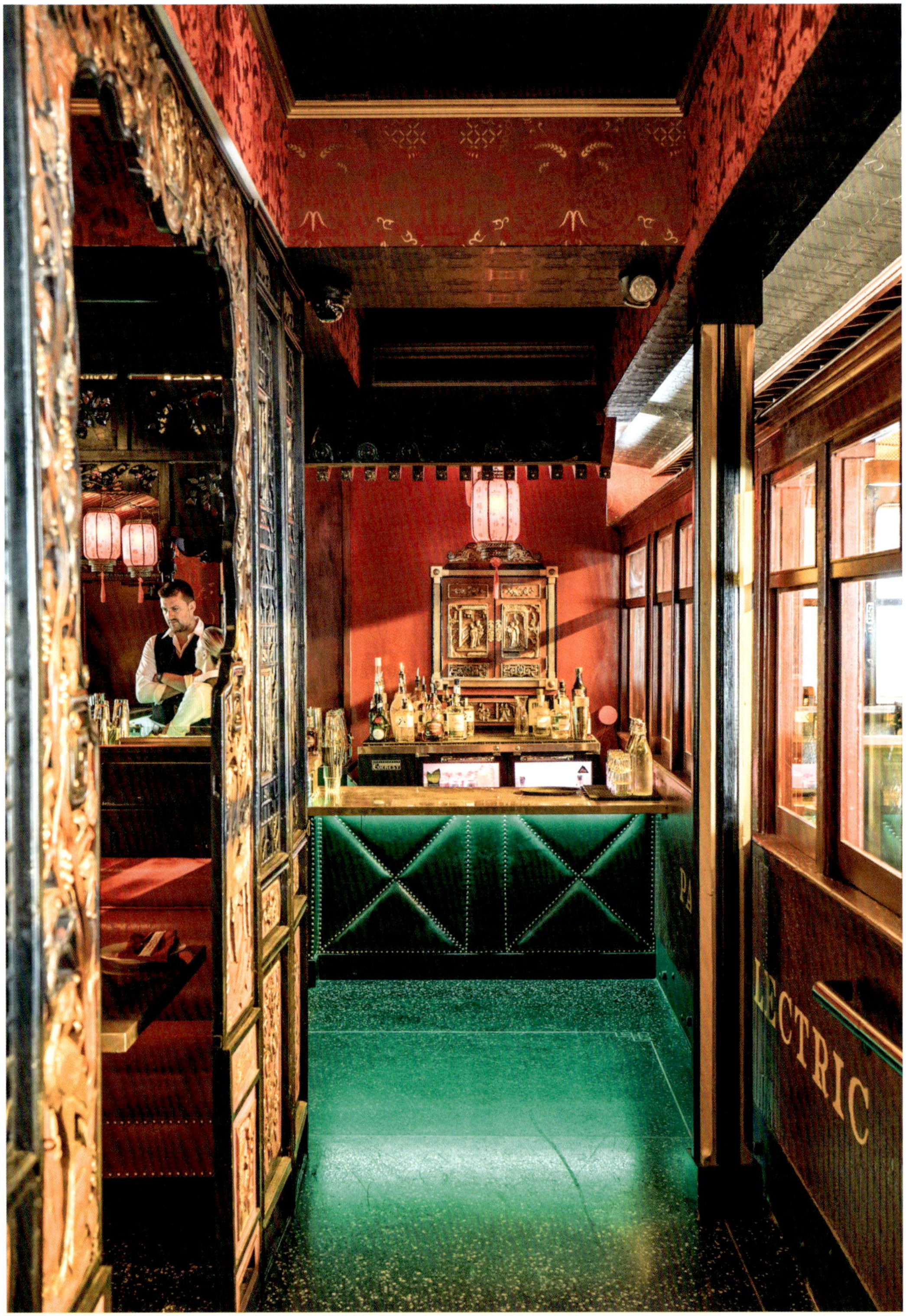

West Hollywood's Formosa Café is the quintessential LA bar—full of history, stories, and great atmosphere.

The Formosa Cafe

A Legendary Hollywood Bar

This iconic bar and Taiwanese-inspired restaurant has a history fitting for an old Hollywood legend—one full of starlets, grande dames, gangsters, and wannabe moguls. More than eighty years old, it's a monument to Hollywood's history.

First opened in 1939, the Formosa Cafe served as the watering hole of choice for a host of film players, many of whom were working across the street at the Samuel Goldwyn Studio. Sinatra, Bogart, James Dean—heck, even Elvis Presley—were patrons, and stories about the stars' antics here abound. (A favorite: Formosa employees once found John Wayne scrambling eggs in the kitchen one morning after a long night). And should the need arise, Bugsy Siegel's safe remains in its original location in the floor under his usual table.

Another bit of history preserved here is an original 1904 red trolley car, the oldest surviving "Red Car" left in existence. Electric trolley cars like this one were part of the Pacific Electric Railway's public transportation system that operated throughout Los Angeles County from the late 1800s until the 1960s.

If the Formosa feels like you've stumbled into a scene of a film, that's because it's been used as a location in several iconic LA films, including *L.A. Confidential*, and a 2019 restoration of the bar involved not only preservationists and historians but also Hollywood set designers. It's Hollywood doing Hollywood, and this is the perfect place for it.

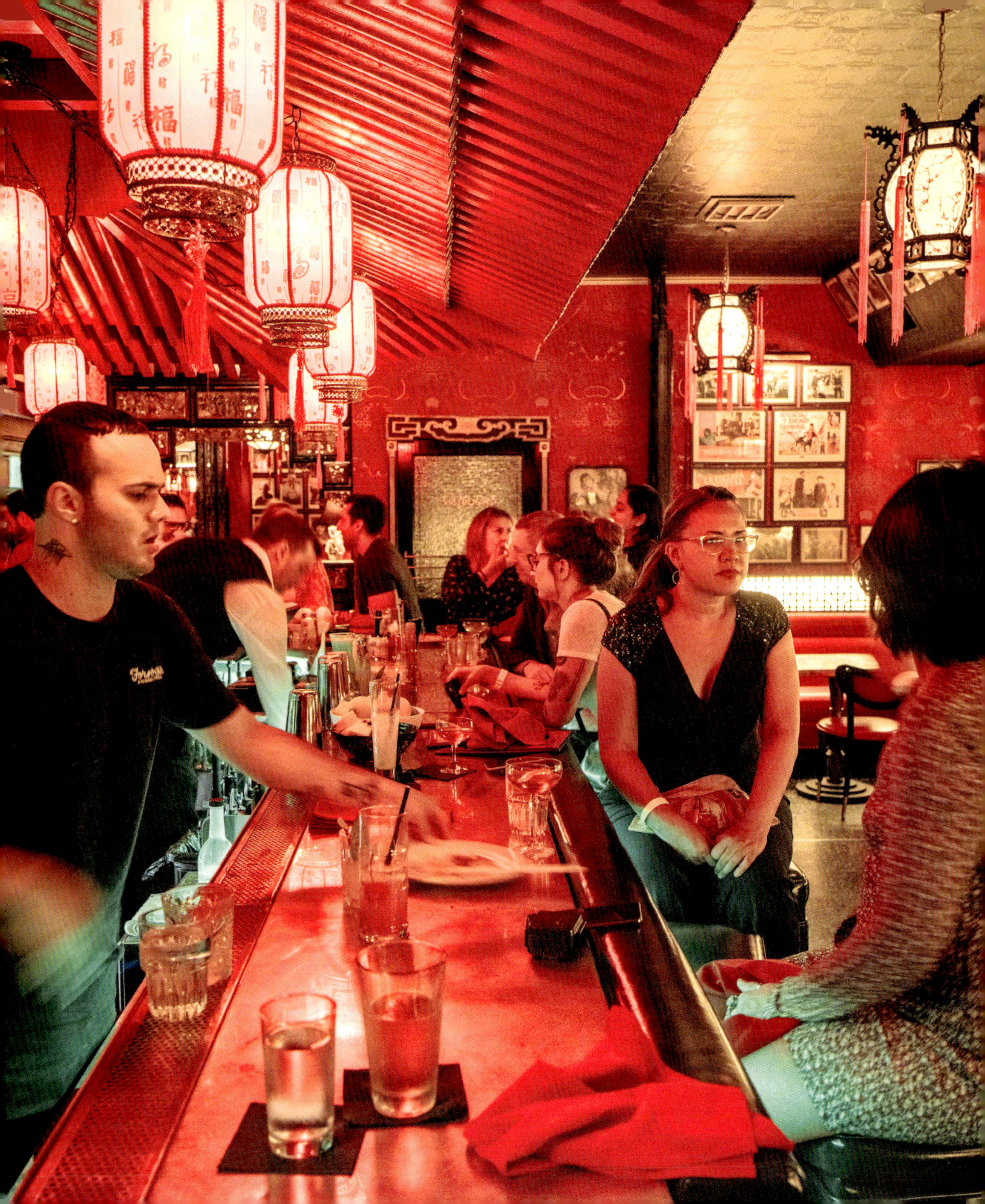

"Hollywood has always been a cage...a cage to catch our dreams." —director John Huston

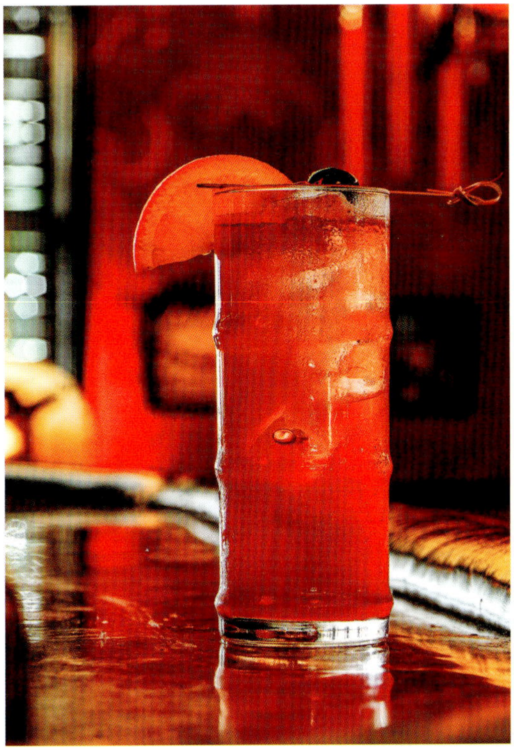

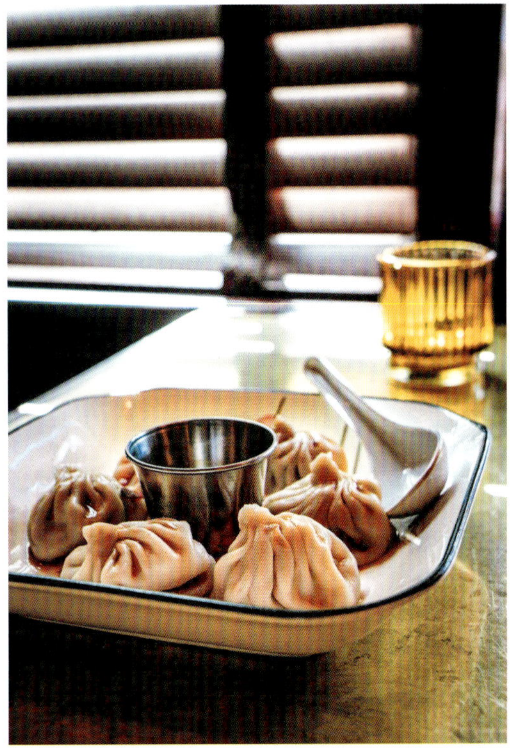

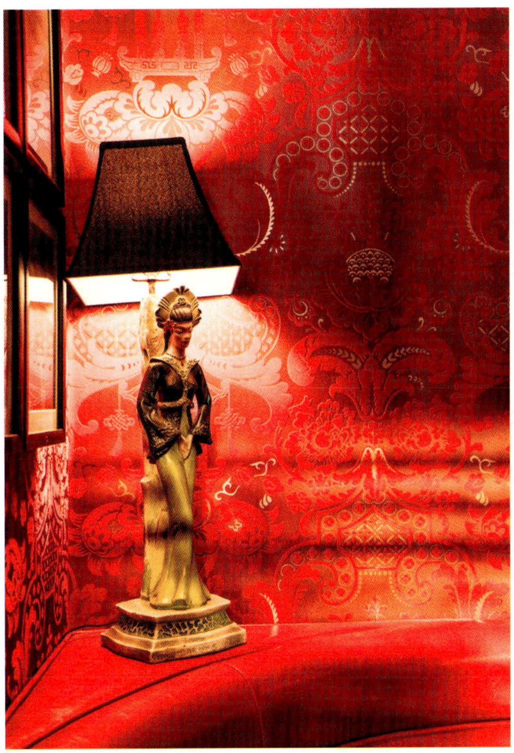

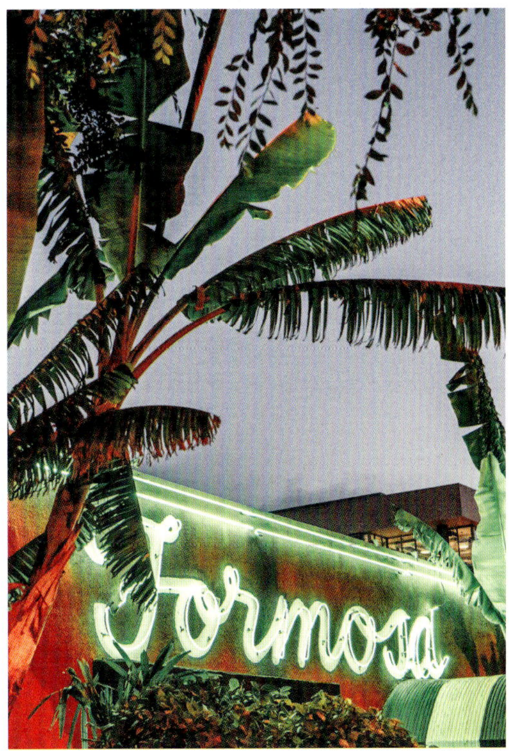

A Singapore Sling cocktail captures the vintage atmosphere of the bar.

Archivists and hospitality notables helped to create the menu, which pays homage to the bar's history and culinary evolution.

Wallpaper designed by Tina Charad, who worked on Tarantino's *Once Upon a Time in Hollywood*, harkens back to the many layers of wallpaper found during the bar's restoration.

The bar is a portal to the past with its Kodachrome-red interior and film noir neon.

Capitol Records Building

Good Vibrations A-Happenin' Here

The world's first circular office building, this 1956 structure was built for Capitol Records, the West Coast's first major record label. Located near the heart of Hollywood (the Hollywood and Vine intersection), it was designed by Louis Naidorf for architect Welton Becket's firm, who designed many of LA's other landmark mid-century buildings such as the Pan-Pacific Auditorium, the Beverly Hilton, the Cinerama Dome, and downtown's Music Center.

While many people say the Capitol Records Building looks like a stack of records, the Los Angeles Conservancy writes that its unique shape was more about efficiency than the structure's function. However, a design feature that has everything to do with the client are the high-fidelity recording studios built underneath the tower, which include underground reverberation chambers designed in tandem with musician Les Paul. These echo chambers have been used to create some of the most distinctive and legendary recordings, such as the Beach Boys' song "Good Vibrations." Among the many other artists who have recorded here are Beck, Frank Sinatra, Billie Holiday, Ella Fitzgerald, Louis Armstrong, the Beatles, and Nat "King" Cole (in fact, the building is referred to by some as "the house that Nat built").

Atop the building is a rooftop spire, which looks like the needle on a record player. When the building was completed in 1956, the granddaughter of Samuel Morse threw the switch to light a red light at the top of the spire that continuously spells out "Hollywood" in Morse code. This light continues to beckon all—and it's joined each year during the December holidays by a Christmas tree that has been lit atop of the building since 1958.

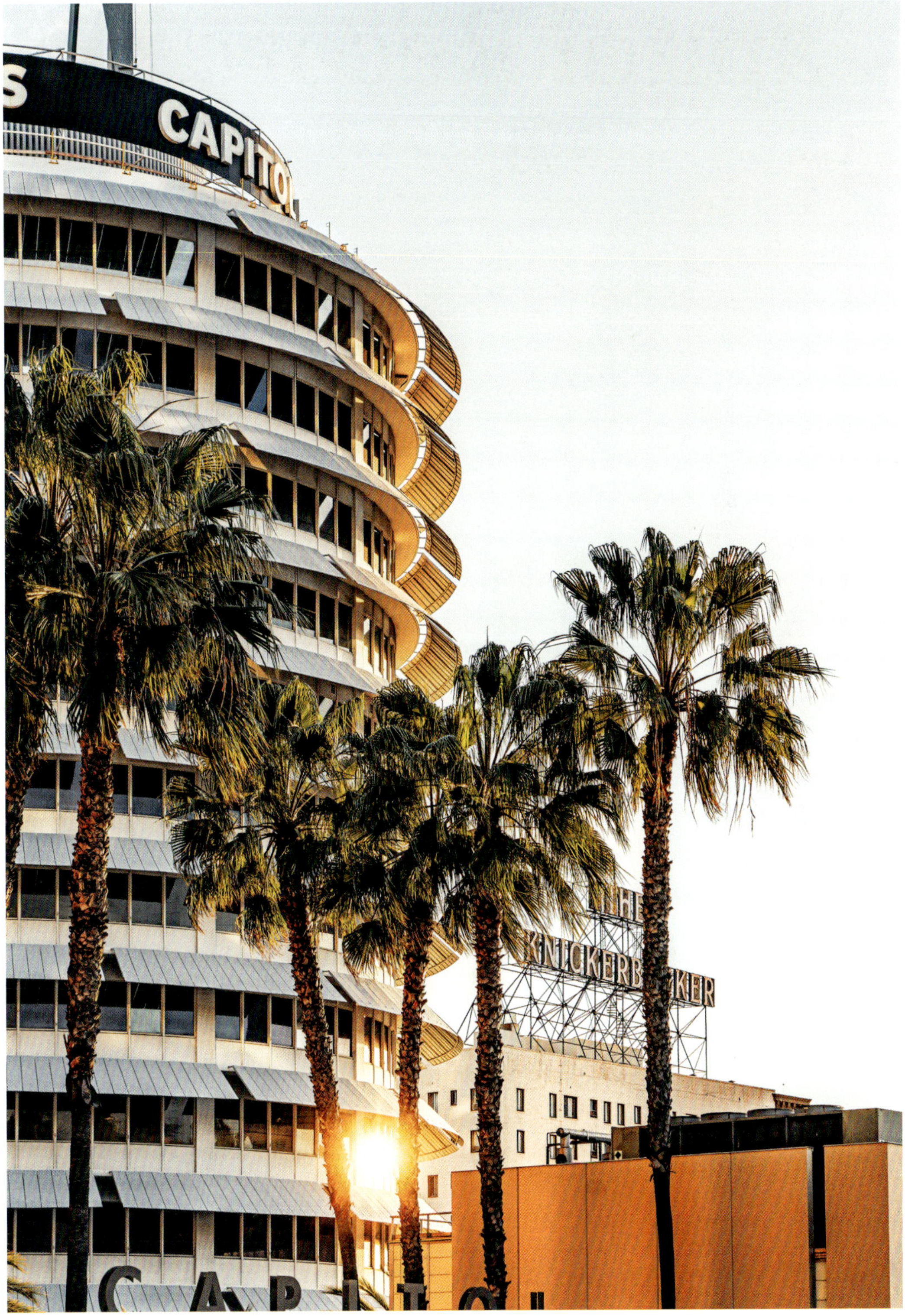

The Capitol Rccords Building's unique porcelain enamel sunshades are designed to create spiral lines of light and shadow that echo the building's cylindrical structure.

(Page 140–141) A view south down Vine Street—the Capital Records Building is located near the heart of Hollywood, the historic intersection of Hollywood Boulevard and Vine.

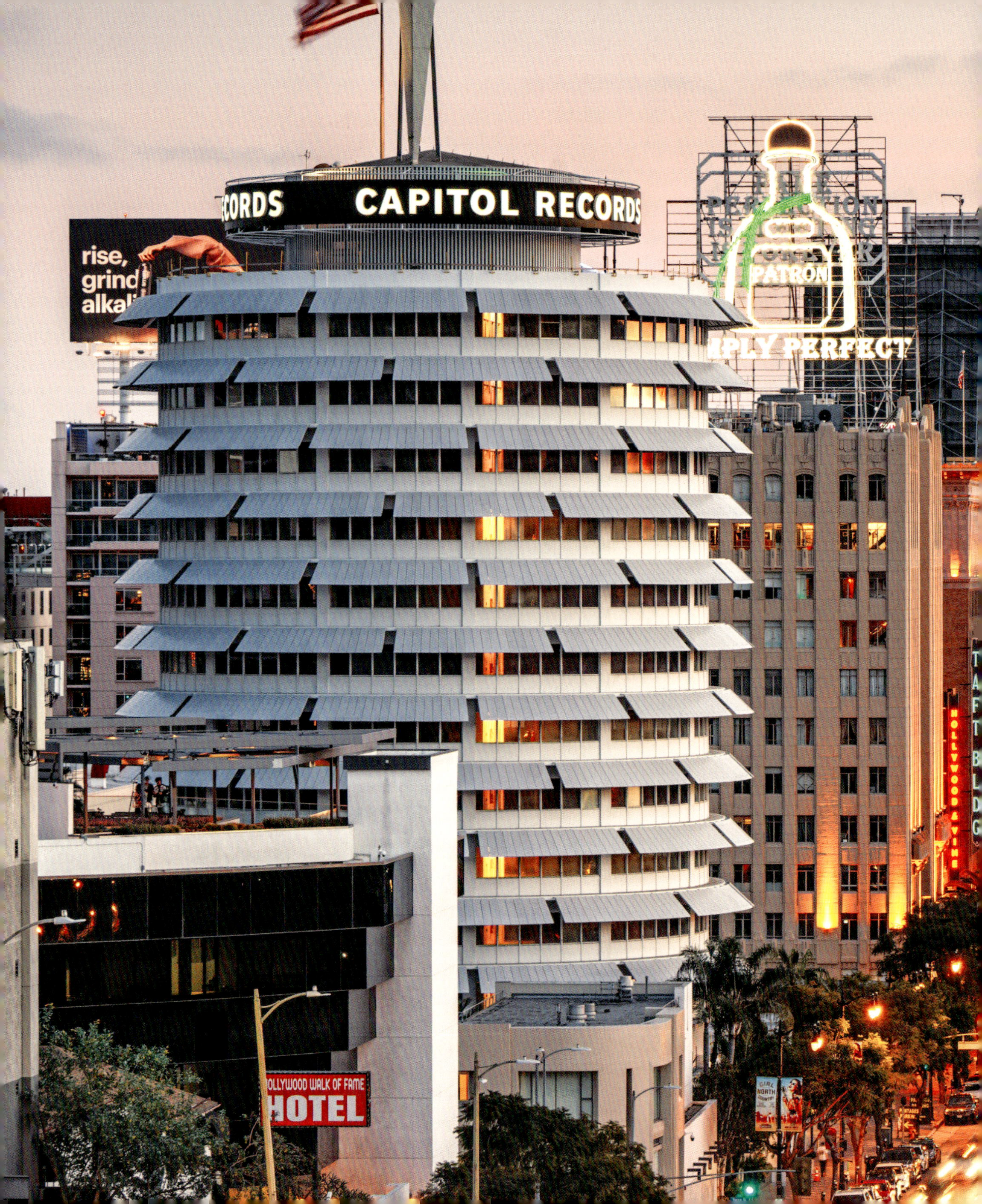
CAPITOL RECORDS
rise,
grind
PATRON
HOTEL

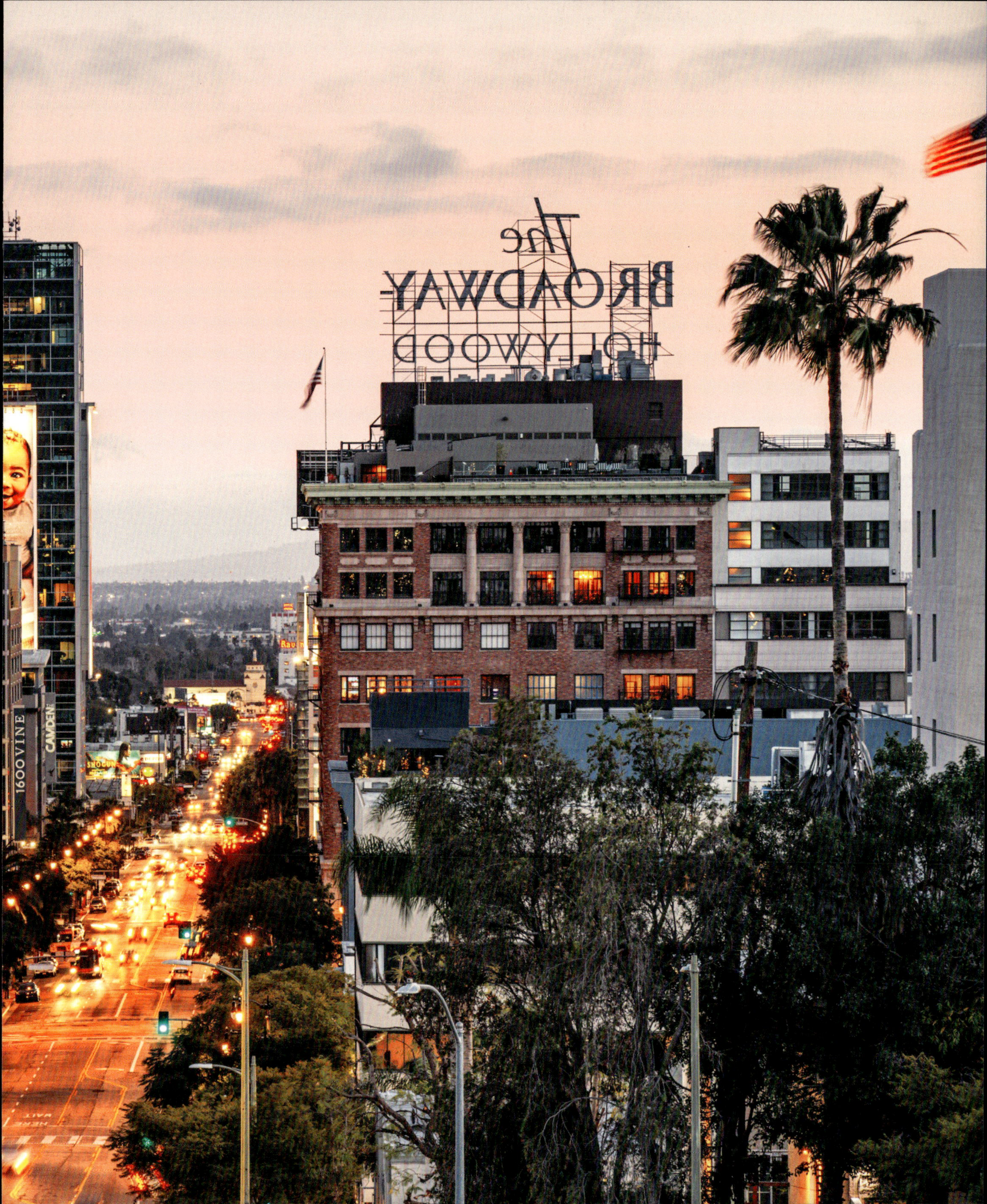
The BROADWAY
HOLLYWOOD
1600 VINE
CAMDEN

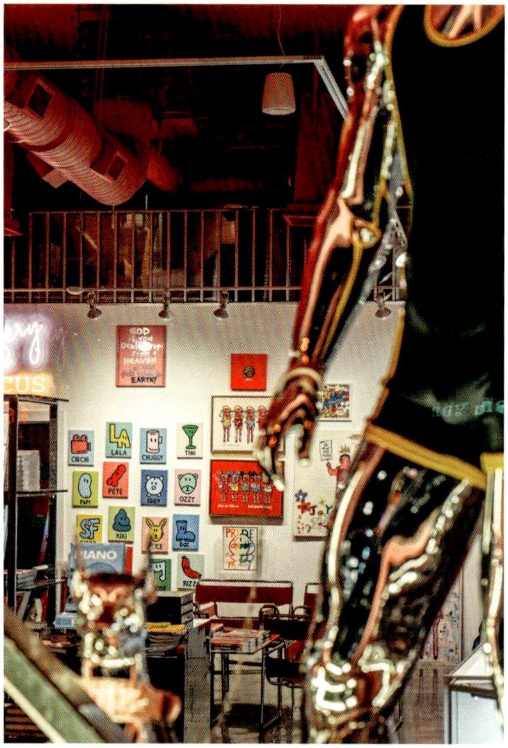

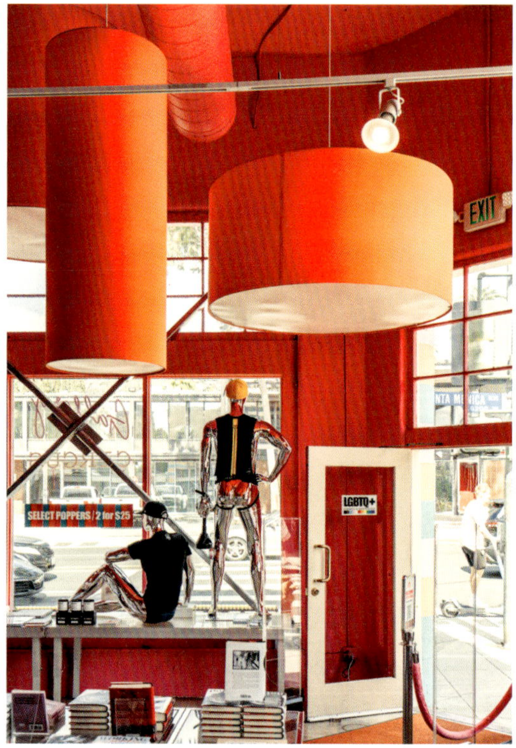

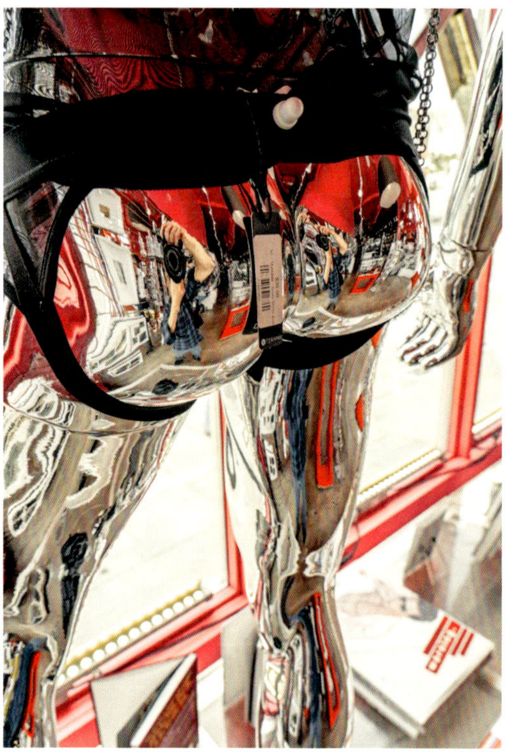

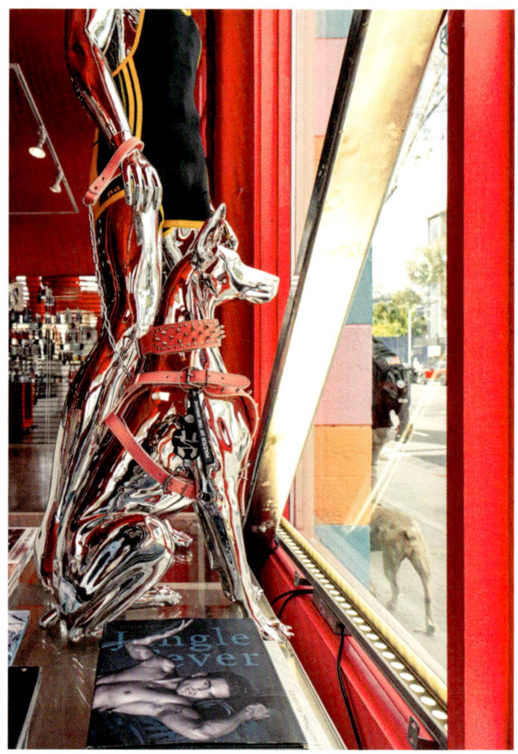

Interior views of Circus of Books shows the new light-filled, upscale boutique complete with an art gallery—it's way different to the darkened shop that once had a cruising spot nicknamed Vaseline Alley behind the store.

Circus of Books

West Hollywood's Queer History Hot Spot

West Hollywood has long been one of the centers of LGBTQ+ culture in Los Angeles—and LA has long been ahead of the rest of the US in fighting for gay rights (look up the Black Cat Tavern protests to see how activity in LA predated Stonewall) and building queer communities and institutions. An unincorporated area of Los Angeles County until 1984, West Hollywood was a haven from the Los Angeles Police Department's enforcement of anti-gay laws in the surrounding city. Gay nightclubs, bars, restaurants, bookstores, and other businesses flourished here as more people moved to Los Angeles in the twentieth century, many of whom had some association with the motion picture industry.

Opened in 1960 as Book Circus, this legendary pornography bookstore became Circus of Books in 1982, when Karen and Barry Mason took it over. Their daughter's documentary film, *Circus of Books*, details the important role the shop had for LA's gay community as well as legally for the rest of the US. The rise of the internet and meet-up apps largely put an end to the shop's business in 2019, but its history as a gathering place and cruisy hookup spot remains. In 2020, the store was reopened by drag queen and director Chi Chi LaRue and reimagined as a high-end boutique, with an art gallery that features LGBTQ+ artists. While it may not be exactly the same, the spirit of the place endures.

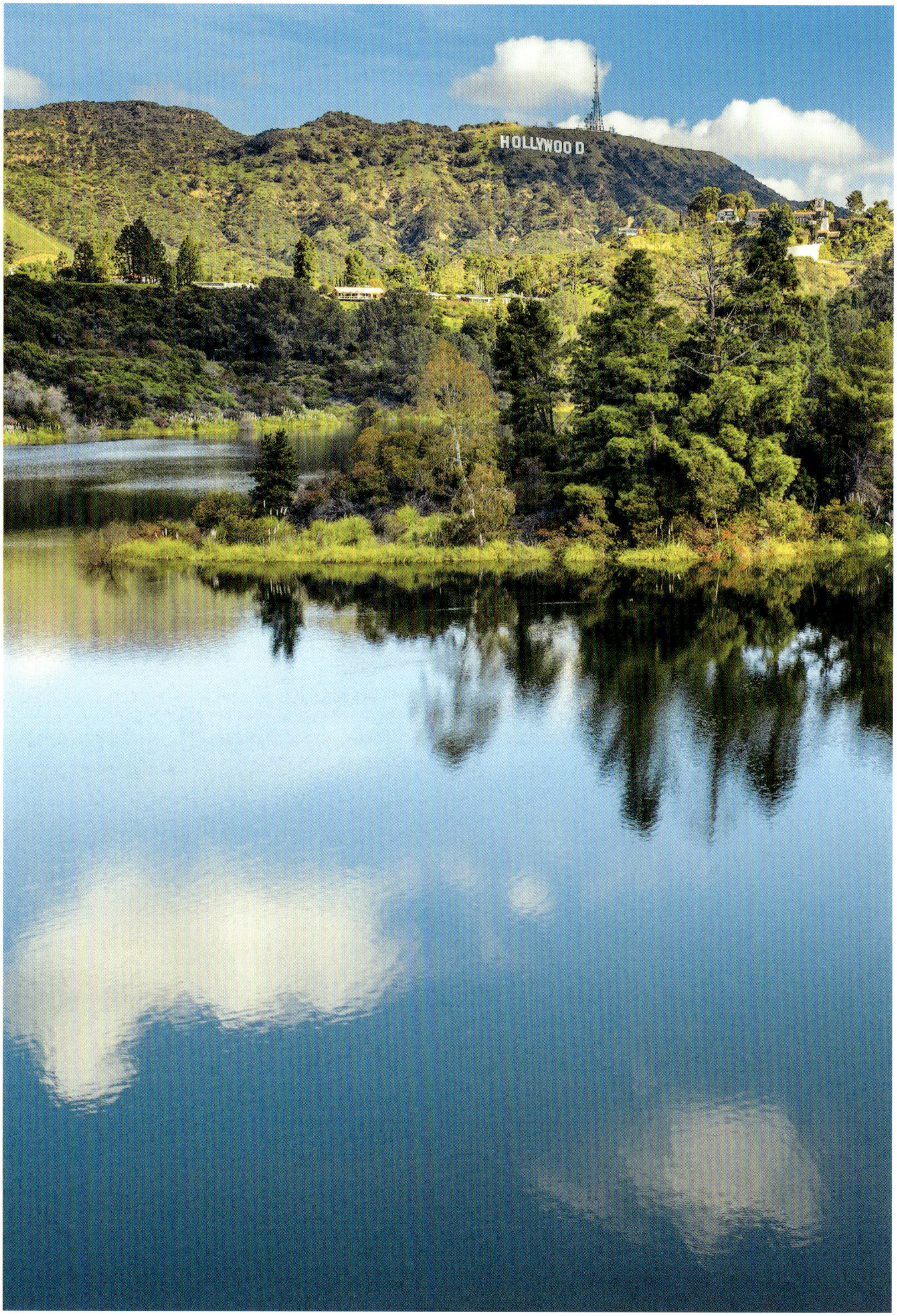

A view of Lake Hollywood at the Hollywood Reservoir shows the iconic Hollywood Sign and some surrounding real estate.

Hollywood Reservoir

Hike Like You Live in the Hollywood Hills

One of the most incredible aspects of life in Los Angeles is that one can be in the wilderness—or at least experience nature—without wandering far from the comforts of urban life. There's no better example of this phenomena than this hidden Hollywood gem, the Hollywood Reservoir (also known as Lake Hollywood). Located in the Hollywood Hills, not far from the Hollywood Sign and the 101 Freeway, this bucolic place contains a gorgeous, man-made lake with a walking path around it, the historic Mulholland Dam, and some of the most incredible views around.

Built in the 1920s under supervision of William Mulholland, the dam created the lake, which holds some 2.5 billion gallons of water from the LA Aqueduct and once served as the main water source for the city. While the dam itself is a piece of art, it's the natural beauty that surrounds it which is even more incredible. A wonderful place for an escape, it would be hard to believe one was still in Hollywood—except that there's a fantastic view of the iconic sign to remind you.

One thing to know: getting to the Hollywood Reservoir can be tricky. There are two different entrances, one on the Valley side and one through the Hollywood Hills, and neither are easy to find. The hours the park is open changes with the seasons, so it's best to check online before visiting. Also, the area is maintained by the Los Angeles Department of Water and Power, not the Los Angeles Department of Recreation and Parks, which operates a nearby park named Lake Hollywood Park.

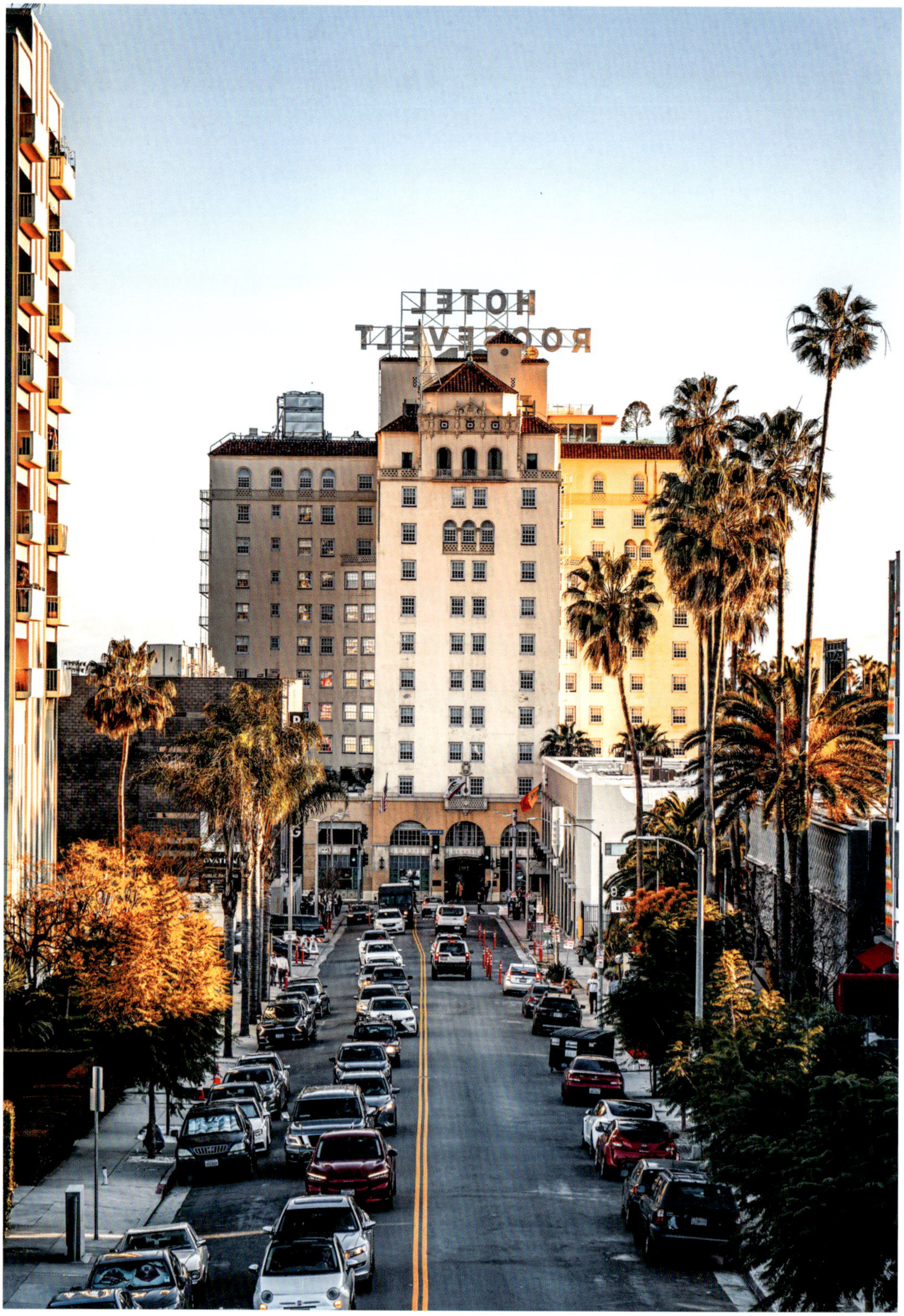

Many stars make the Hollywood Roosevelt Hotel home. Marilyn Monroe lived here for two years.

Hollywood Roosevelt Hotel

Site of the First Academy Awards Ceremony

Named after the popular US president, the Roosevelt Hotel—now the Hollywood Roosevelt—was opened in 1927 by a group of prominent businessmen and Hollywood players, including actors Douglas Fairbanks and Mary Pickford, and theater owner Sid Grauman (the Chinese Theatre, the Egyptian Theatre). Most famously, the hotel served as the site for the first ever Academy Awards ceremony on May 16, 1929, starting the Oscars tradition that continues to this day—albeit in a different location down the street.

A mainstay during Hollywood's Golden Age, the Roosevelt was home to several movie stars who opted for long-term stays in between various houses, including Marilyn Monroe, Montgomery Clift, and Carole Lombard. It is said that the ghosts of a few former residents haunt the halls—or in the case of Clift, room 928 where the brooding actor stayed in 1952 while filming *From Here to Eternity*.

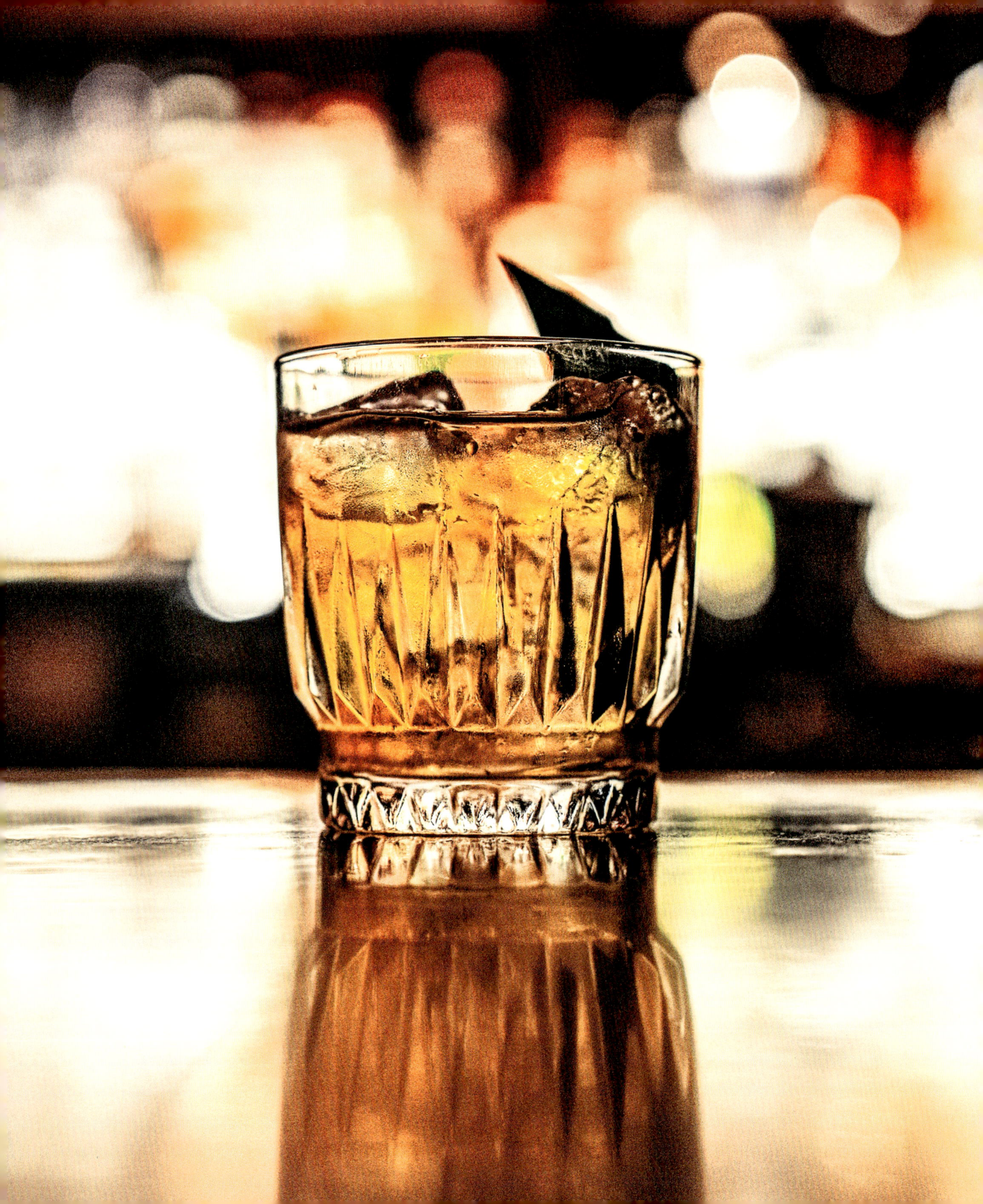

"Hollywood is wonderful. Anyone who doesn't like it is either crazy or sober." —writer Raymond Chandler

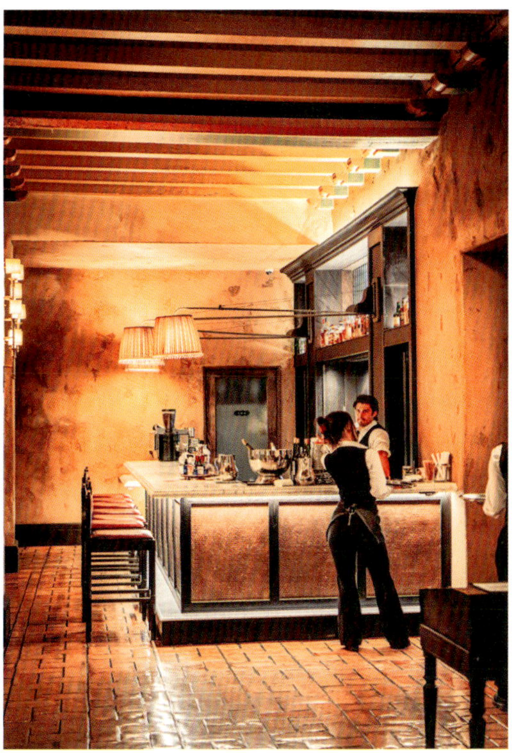

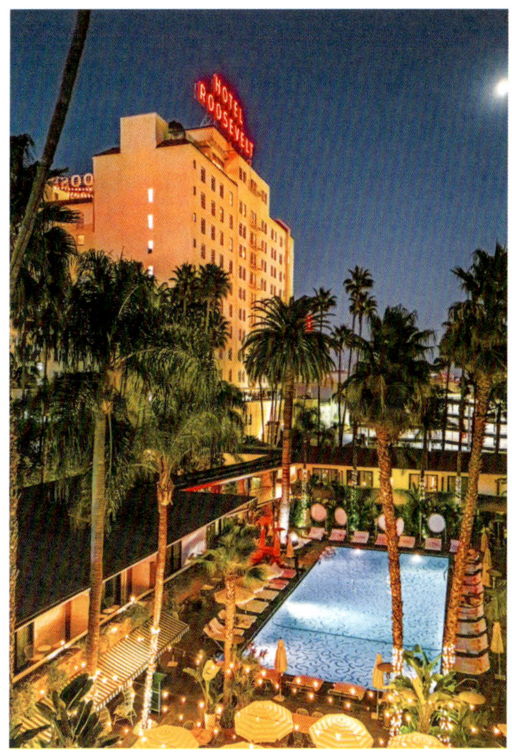

The hotel's golden-era Hollywood atmosphere extends to the bar called the Spare Room—a gaming parlor that features wooden bowling lanes.

The hotel's Tropicana Pool features a mural in the pool painted by painter David Hockney.

Hollywood Forever Cemetery

Cemetery and Cultural Center in the Heart of Hollywood

One of the most unique of the city's cultural sites, Hollywood Forever is a national cemetery, working mortuary, and, oddly enough, a cultural center that hosts an array of hip and fun events. Founded in 1899, it is the final resting place of a host of famous people, from Hollywood legends like Rudolph Valentino and Judy Garland to contemporary artists such as David Lynch and Chris Cornell. It is also the site of one of the oldest active Jewish cemeteries in California.

The cemetery, which is located right next to Paramount Studios, is a wonderful place to walk around for any fan of film history—or if one just wants 62 acres of beautiful landscaping in the heart of Hollywood (entrance is free). But the place really comes to life (ha!) when hosting one of many popular events: there are concerts, regular outdoor film screenings, and an annual Dia de Los Muertos celebration that is much beloved by Angelenos.

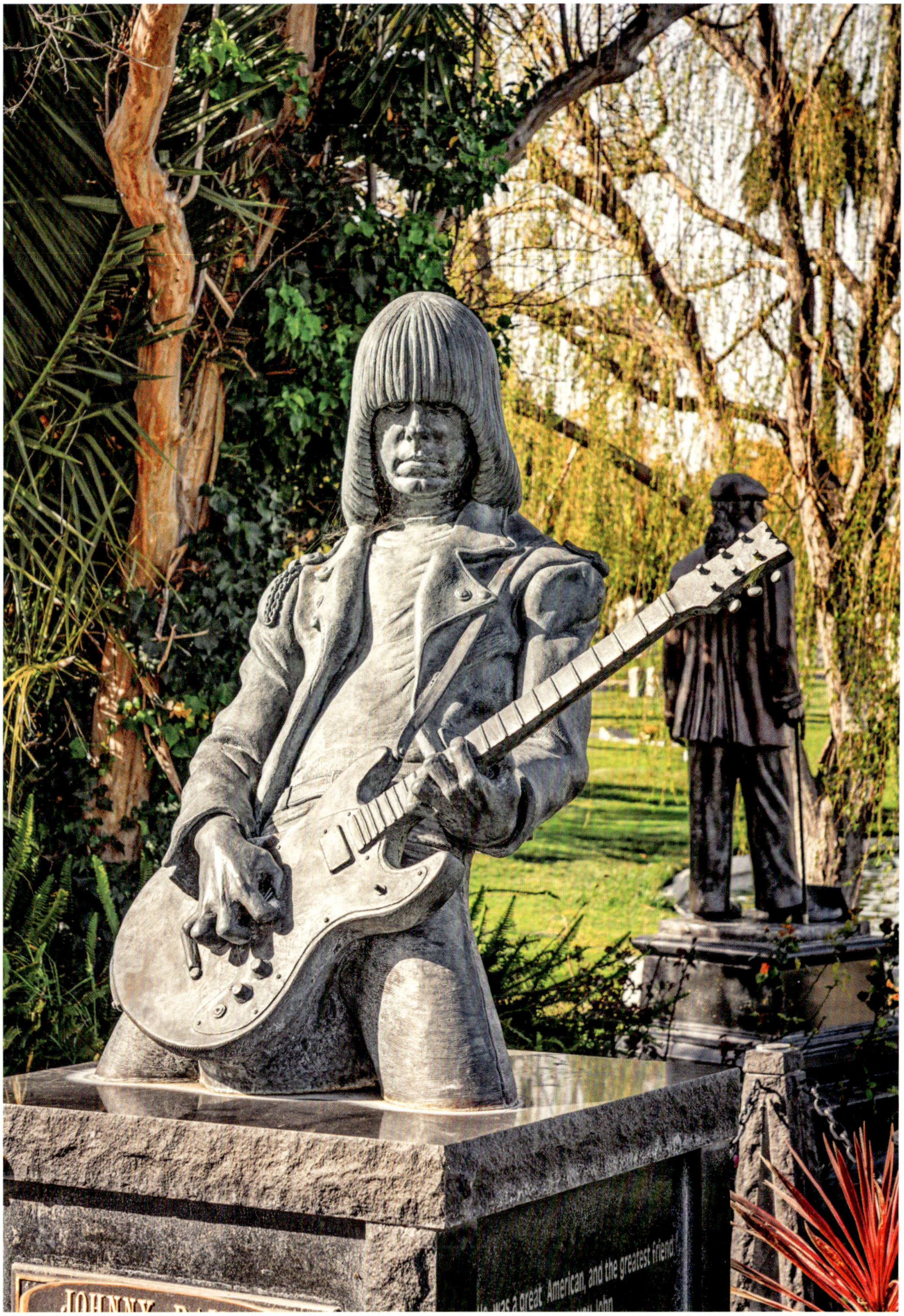

A fitting headstone marks the grave of punk rocker Johnny Ramone, who has a yearly tribute held at the cemetery in his honor. Dee Dee Ramone is also buried at Hollywood Forever.

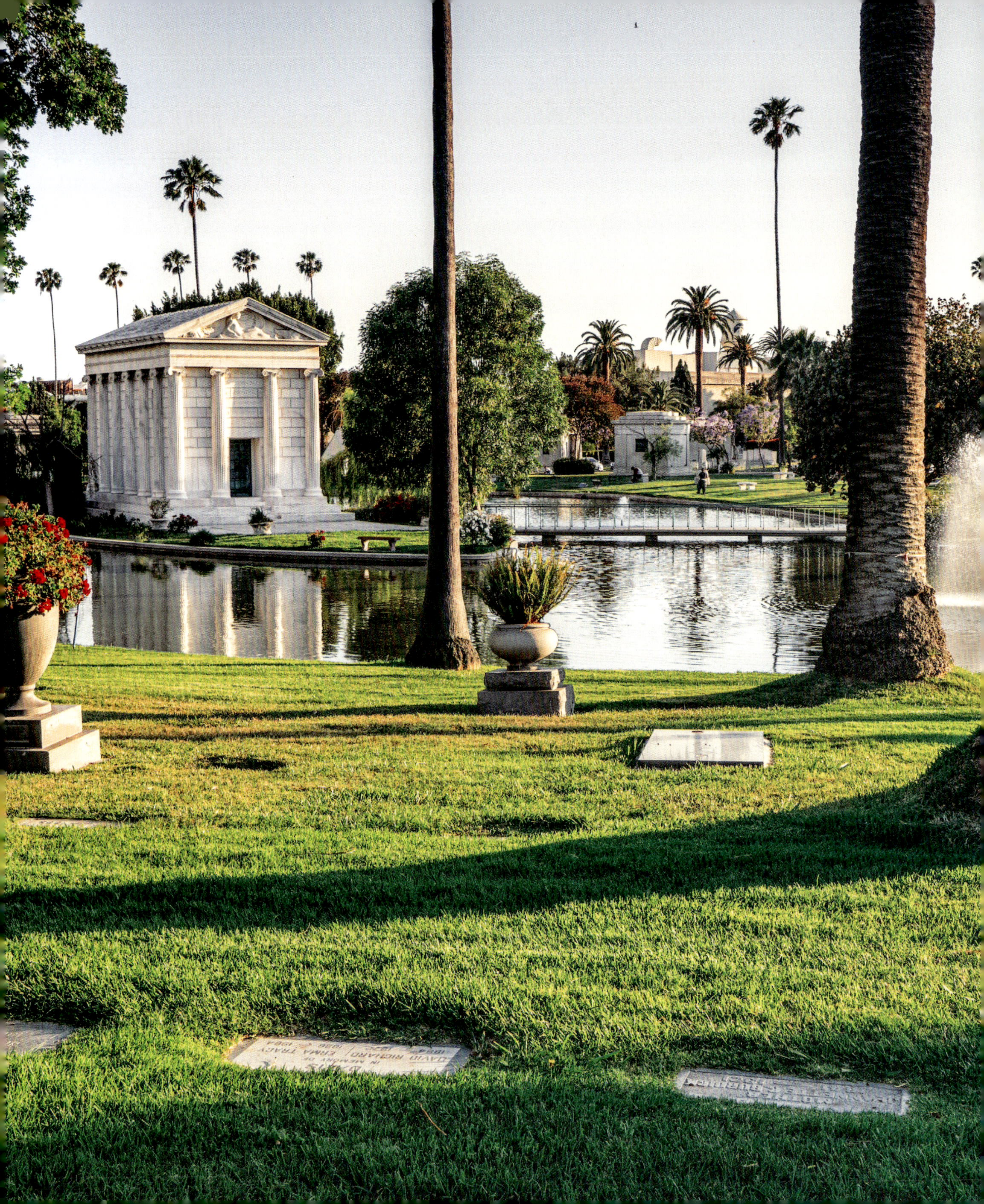

One of the most impressive burial places is a mausoleum located on the island of the cemetery's Sylvan Lake, which belongs to the family of William Andrews Clark, Jr., the founder of the Los Angeles Philharmonic Orchestra.

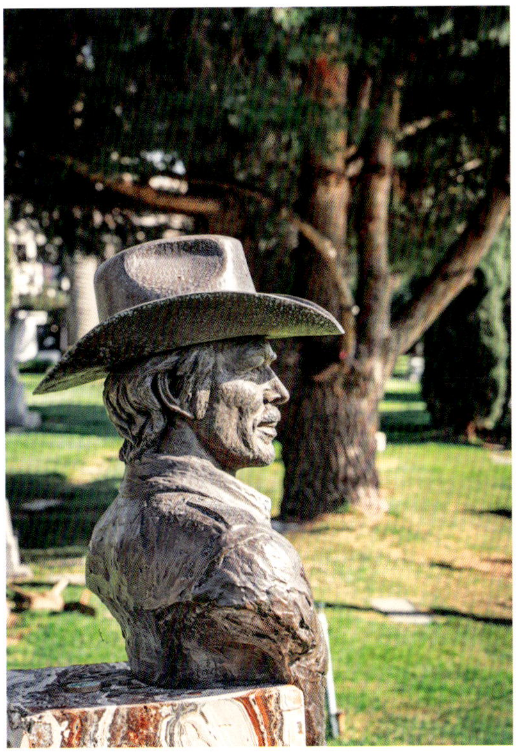

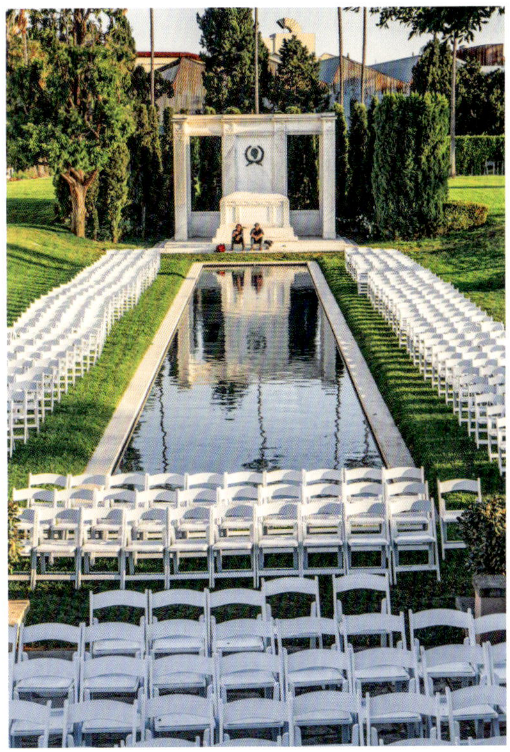

A bust of actor Burt Reynolds marks the Bandit's grave, which also happens to be located near actor Tyrone Power's resting place.

A majestic park in the center of Hollywood, the cemetery is an official historic-cultural monument for the City of LA.

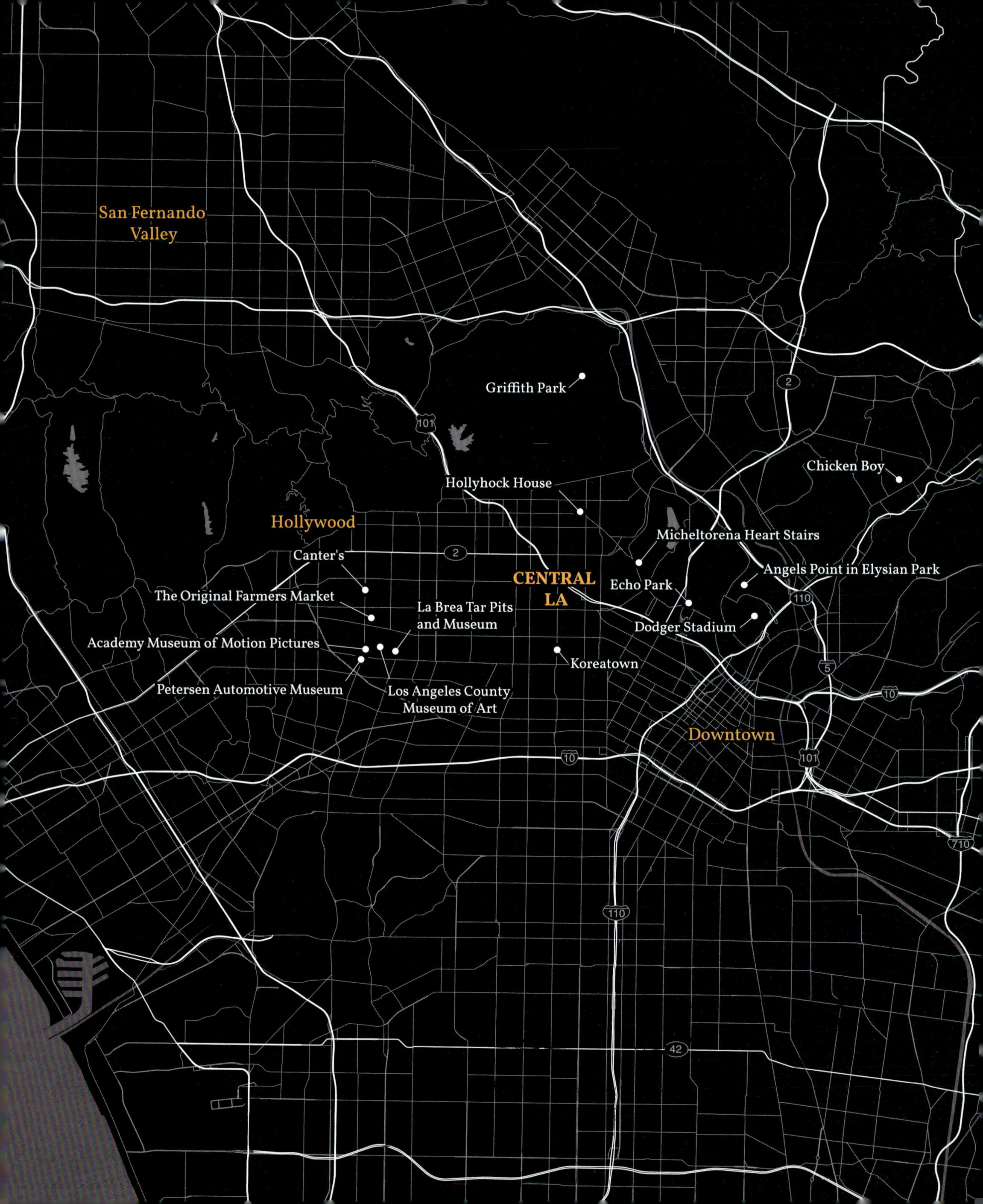

San Fernando Valley
Griffith Park
Hollyhock House
Chicken Boy
Hollywood
Micheltorena Heart Stairs
Canter's
Angels Point in Elysian Park
CENTRAL LA
Echo Park
The Original Farmers Market
La Brea Tar Pits and Museum
Dodger Stadium
Academy Museum of Motion Pictures
Koreatown
Petersen Automotive Museum
Los Angeles County Museum of Art
Downtown
101
2
110
5
10
710
42

Central
Los Angeles

Iconic Sites

Centers Move with Perspective

There's an often-repeated description of Los Angeles that it's "72 suburbs in search of a city." The quote has been attributed to a bunch of different writers, but it's mostly a way for people from the East Coast to dismiss the urbanity of LA because it looks different to what they are used to. Los Angeles doesn't have a traditional center because it is so vast—and each neighborhood has its own character, identity, and histories. The center for most folk who live here is whatever is immediately around them—their street, their neighborhood stores, the nearby parks and attractions. The taco stand one frequents weekly, the closest grocery store, the kids school, the local bar—these are centers. In a city as big and sprawling as LA, there isn't just one center—there are many—and they all have to do with where you are, who you are, and where you want to be.

This doesn't make it easy for the visitor who might just want to see *the* city center—and it certainly doesn't make it easy to divide up the city geographically, because choosing what to call "Central" LA is inherently a political act. What the center is depends on where you live—some Angelenos live most of their days without, say, crossing La Brea Avenue or Vine Street. Others commute hours to work or school, crisscrossing the city mutiple times a day. These are all Angelenos, and they all have different ideas of what the center of the city is.

Determining "Central" LA then is a matter of perspective. For us organizing this book, we've decided to separate the downtown section from "Central" even though pretty much anyone would say downtown *is* Central LA. It's just a matter of there being so many landmarks in the downtown area, we thought it merited its own entity.Similarly, Highland Park is Northeast LA, but here we've stuck it in with Central because, well, being based in Silver Lake, we go there all the time.

These imaginary divisions that separate the city into more digestible bits are, like our freeways or public transportation routes, just meant as tools to help you get from one interesting place to another.

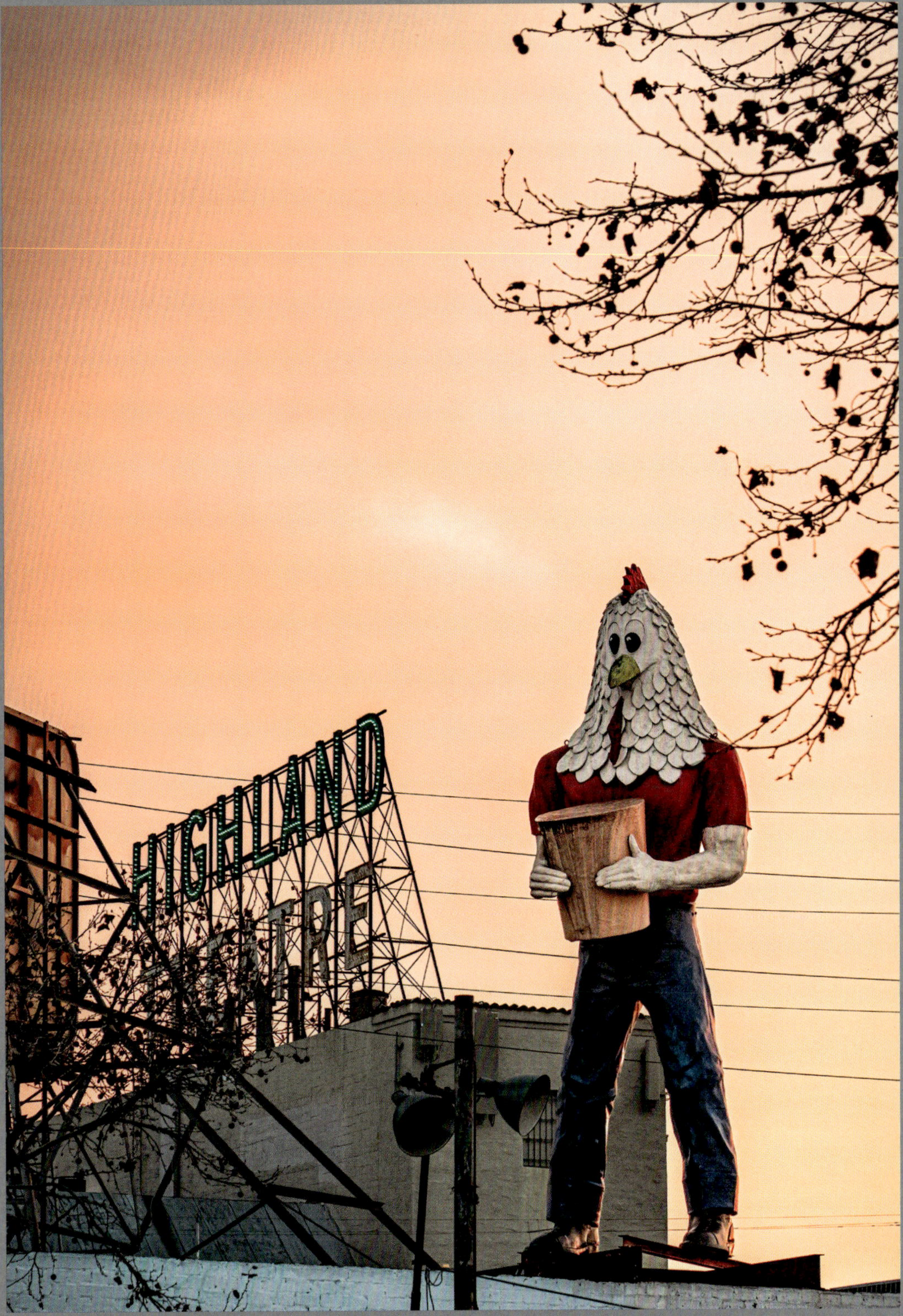

The 22-foot-tall Chicken Boy statue watches over North Figueroa Avenue in the heart of the Highland Park neighborhood; the "Statue of Liberty of Los Angeles" was installed by Future Studio Design and Gallery atop their building located on Historic Route 66.

(Page 158–159) Built on the site of the former Chavez Ravine neighborhood, Dodger Stadium opened in 1962 and is one of the oldest ballparks in Major League Baseball.

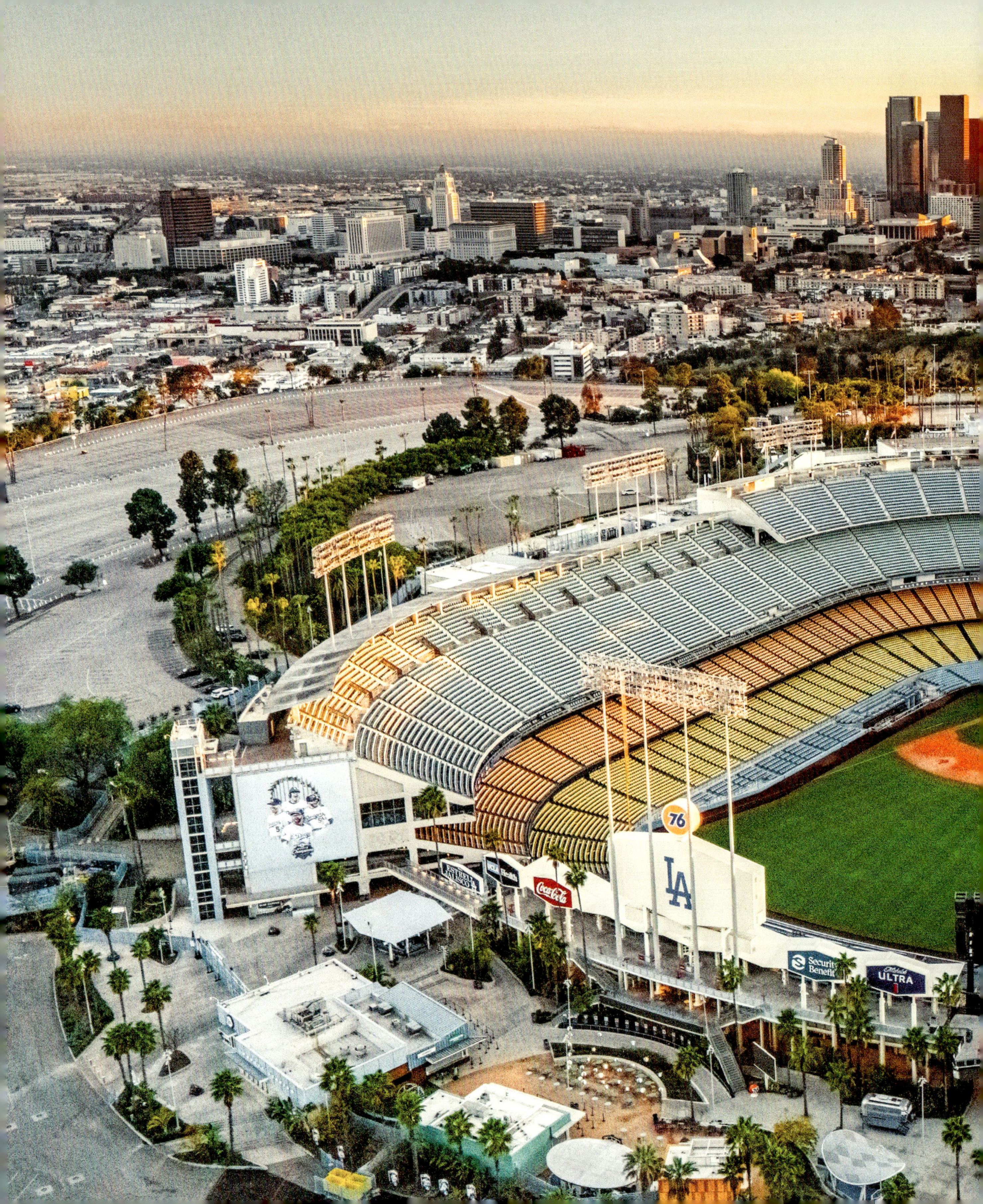
76
LA
Coca-Cola
ULTRA

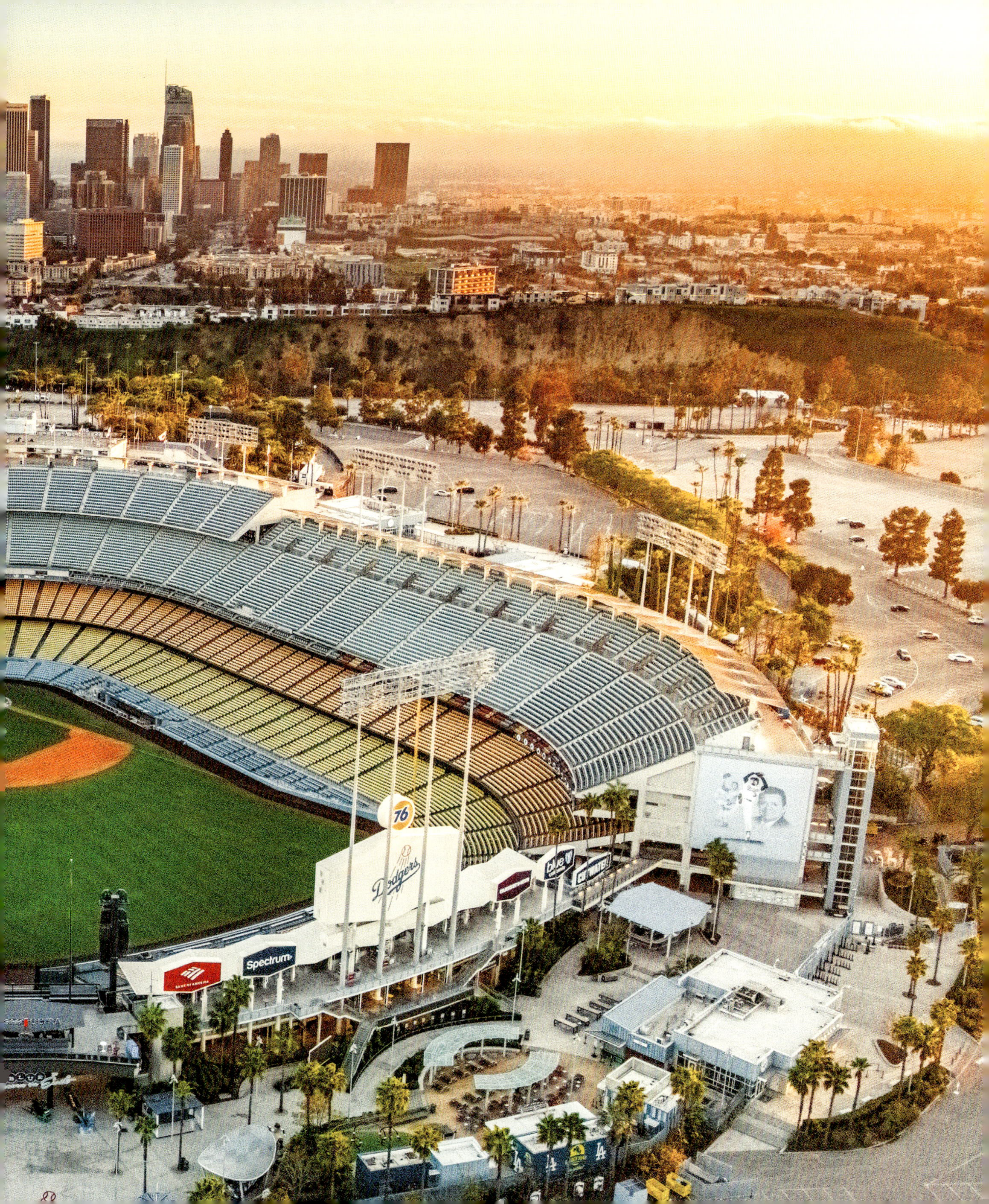
76
Dodgers
Spectrum
BANK OF AMERICA

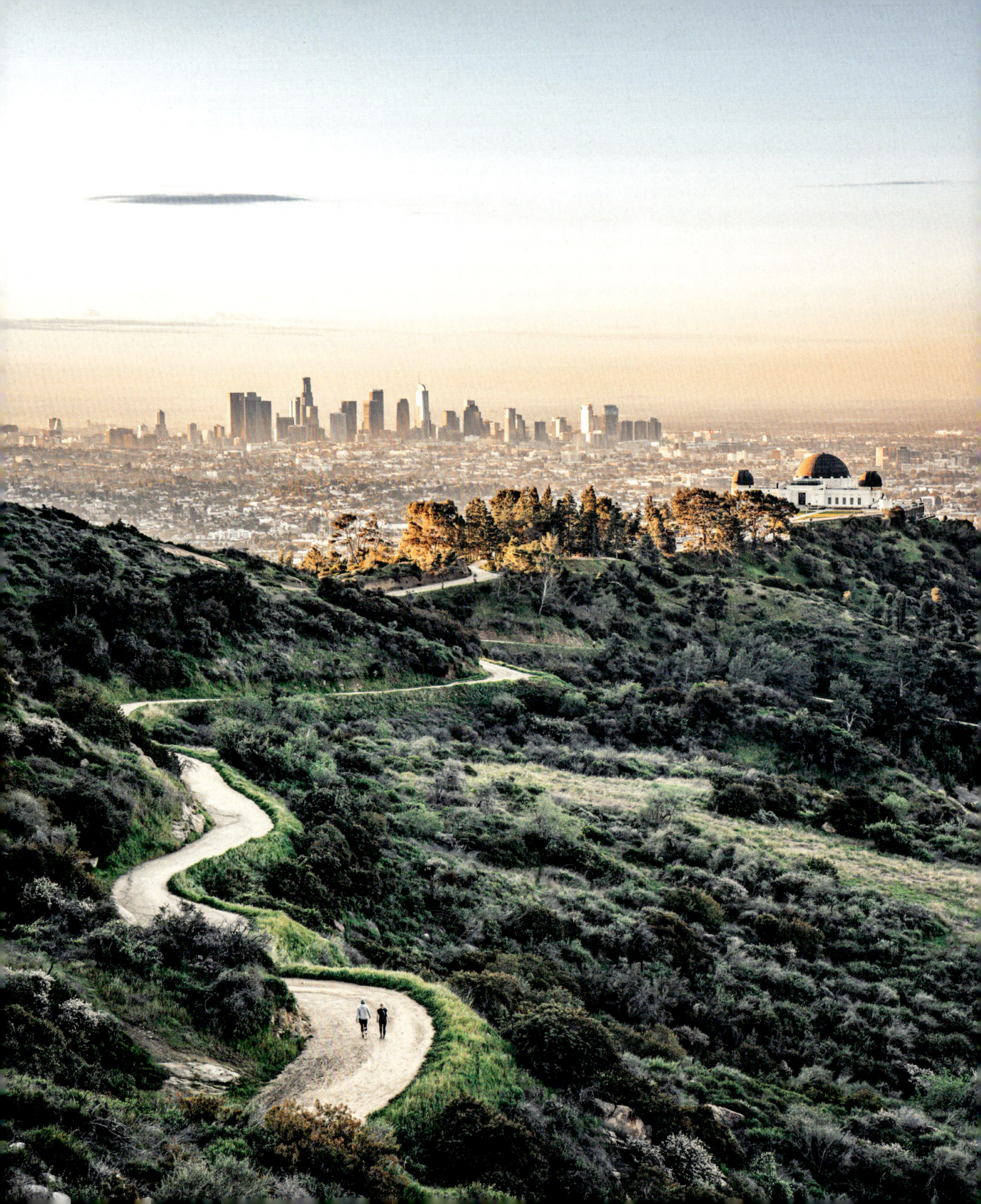

A view from Griffith Park proves fashion designer Isabel Marant true: "In Los Angeles, you can have the city life and feel like you're on holiday at the same time."

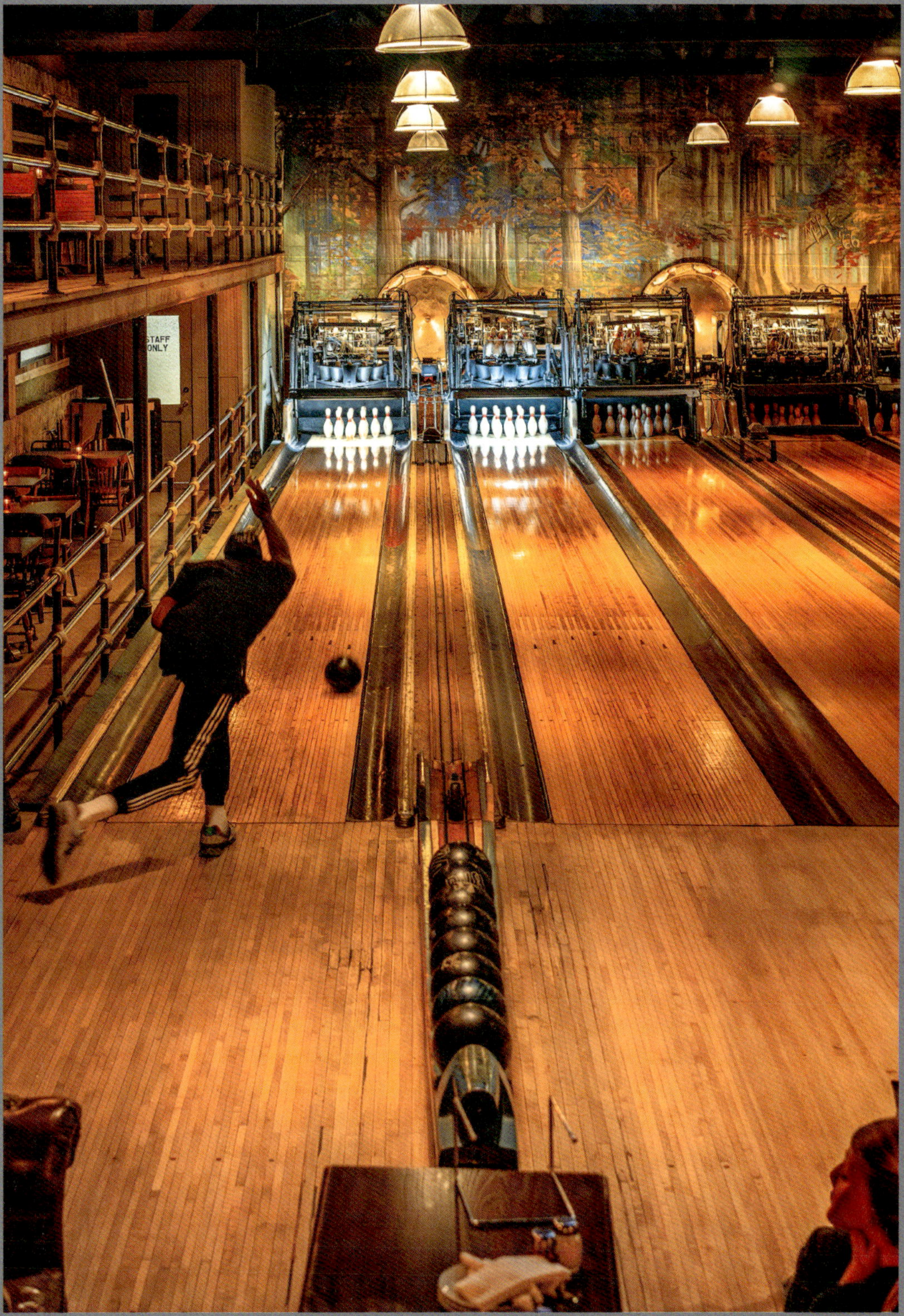

The Highland Park Bowl is a bar in which you'll find one of the city's oldest bowling alleys.

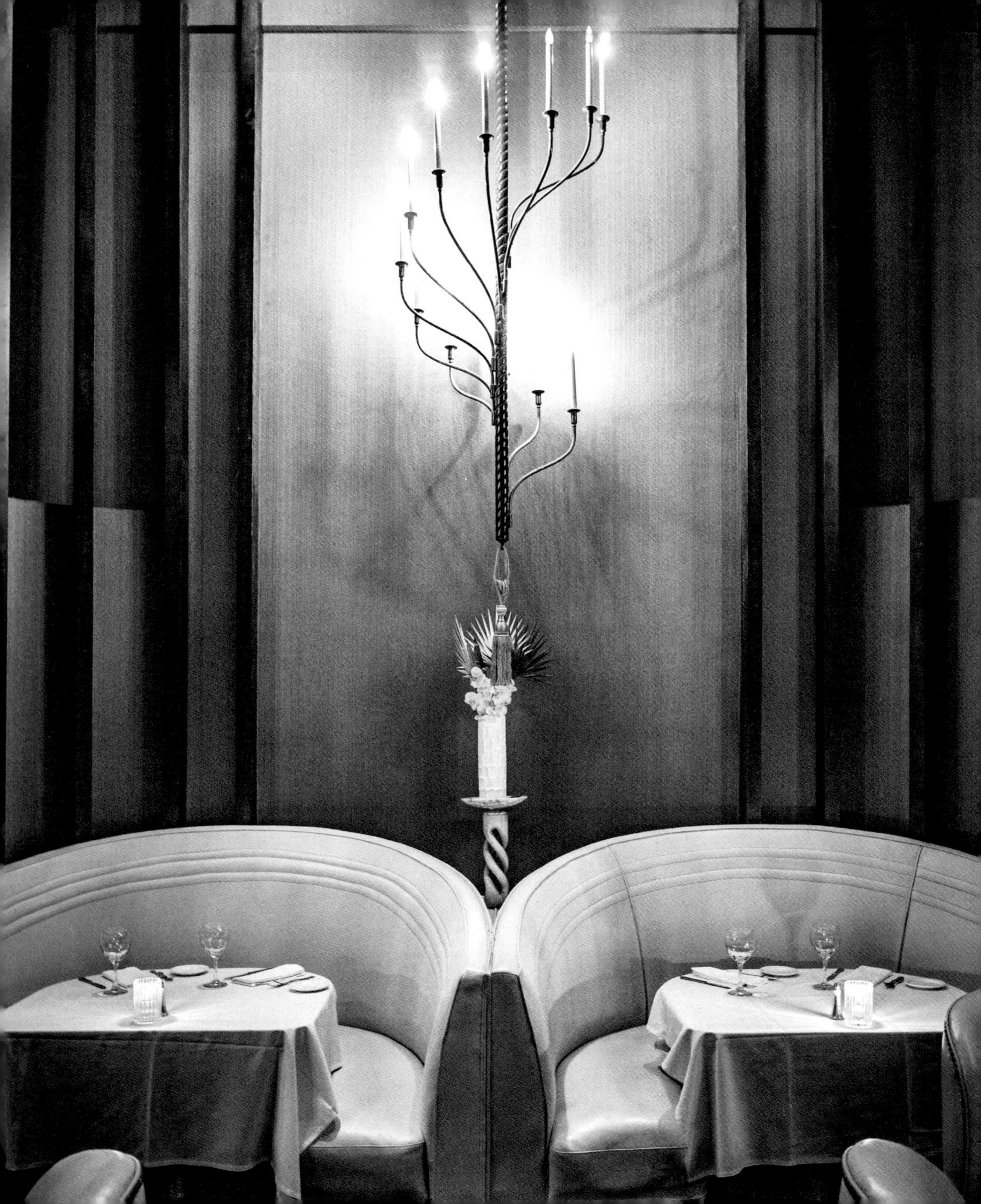

For a taste of mid-century LA, visit the Dresden Restaurant and Lounge in Los Feliz, a classic old Hollywood cocktail lounge that features live music and is a frequent filming location.

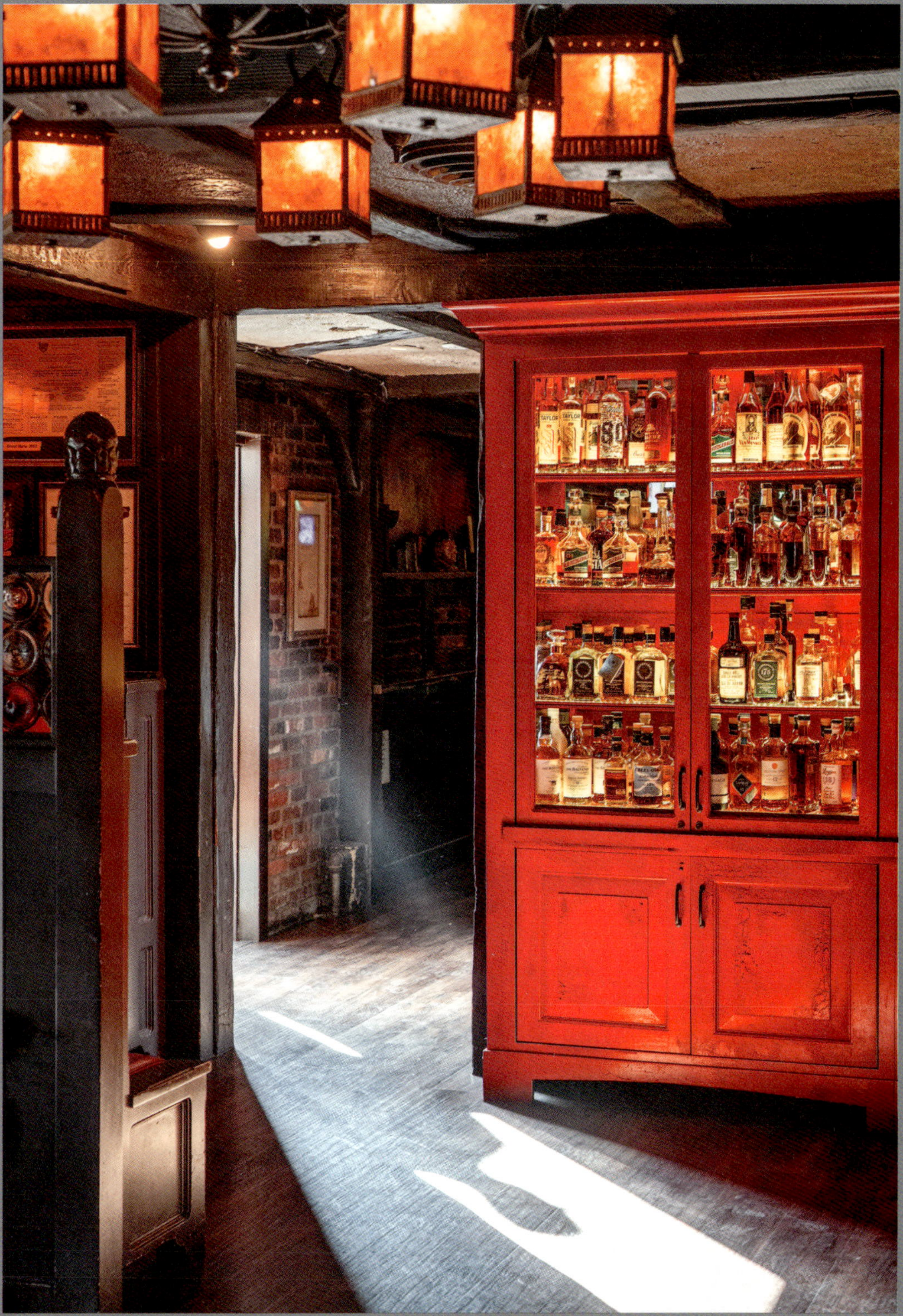

The century-old Scottish steakhouse, the Tam O'Shanter, in Atwater Village, has two major boasts: first, it contines to serve the Moscow Mule invented at the legendary Cock 'n Bull, and second, Disney's early animators used to dine here.

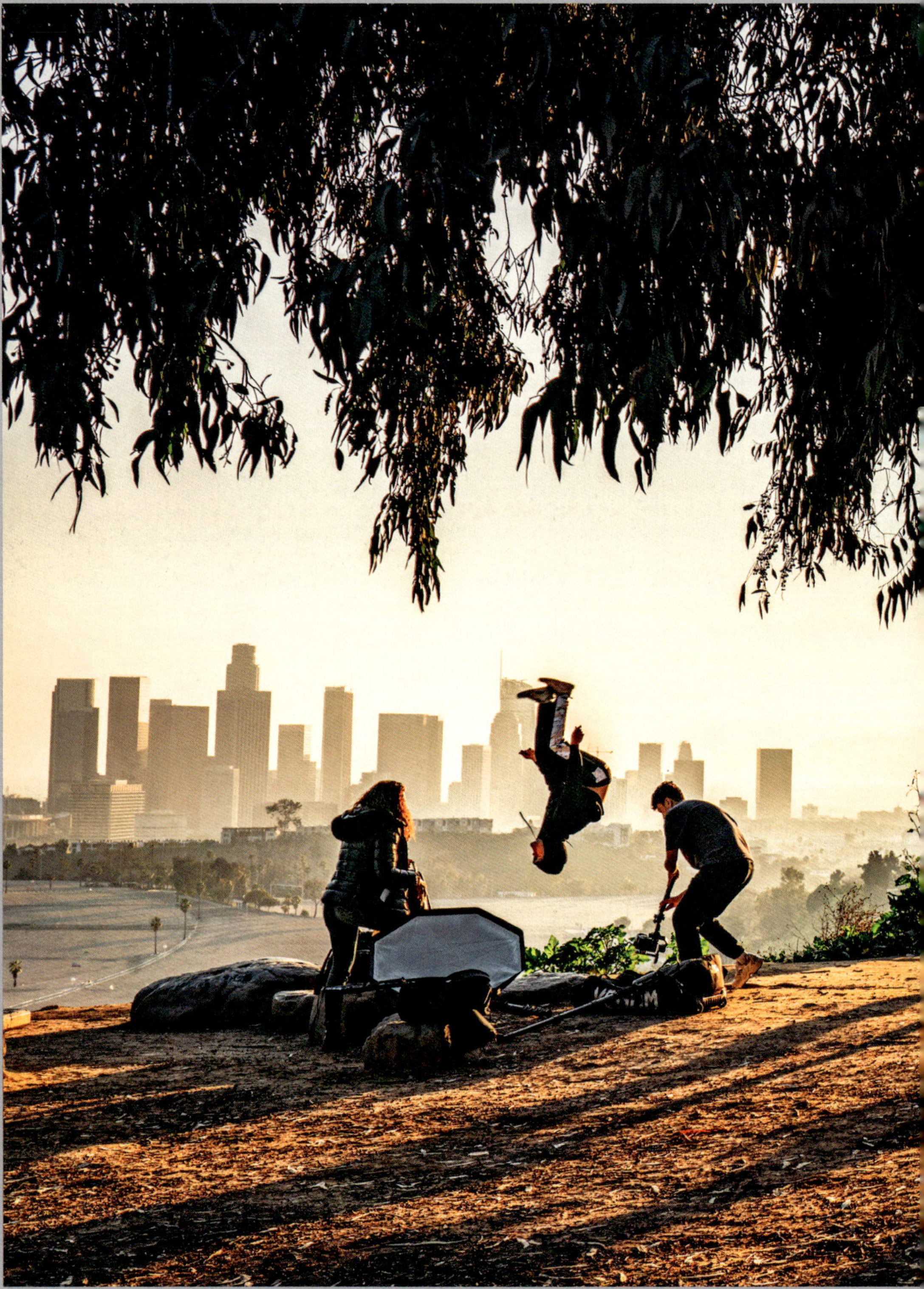

The view from Angels Point in Elysian Park, the city's oldest public park, is incredible, and it's a nice hike to get there.

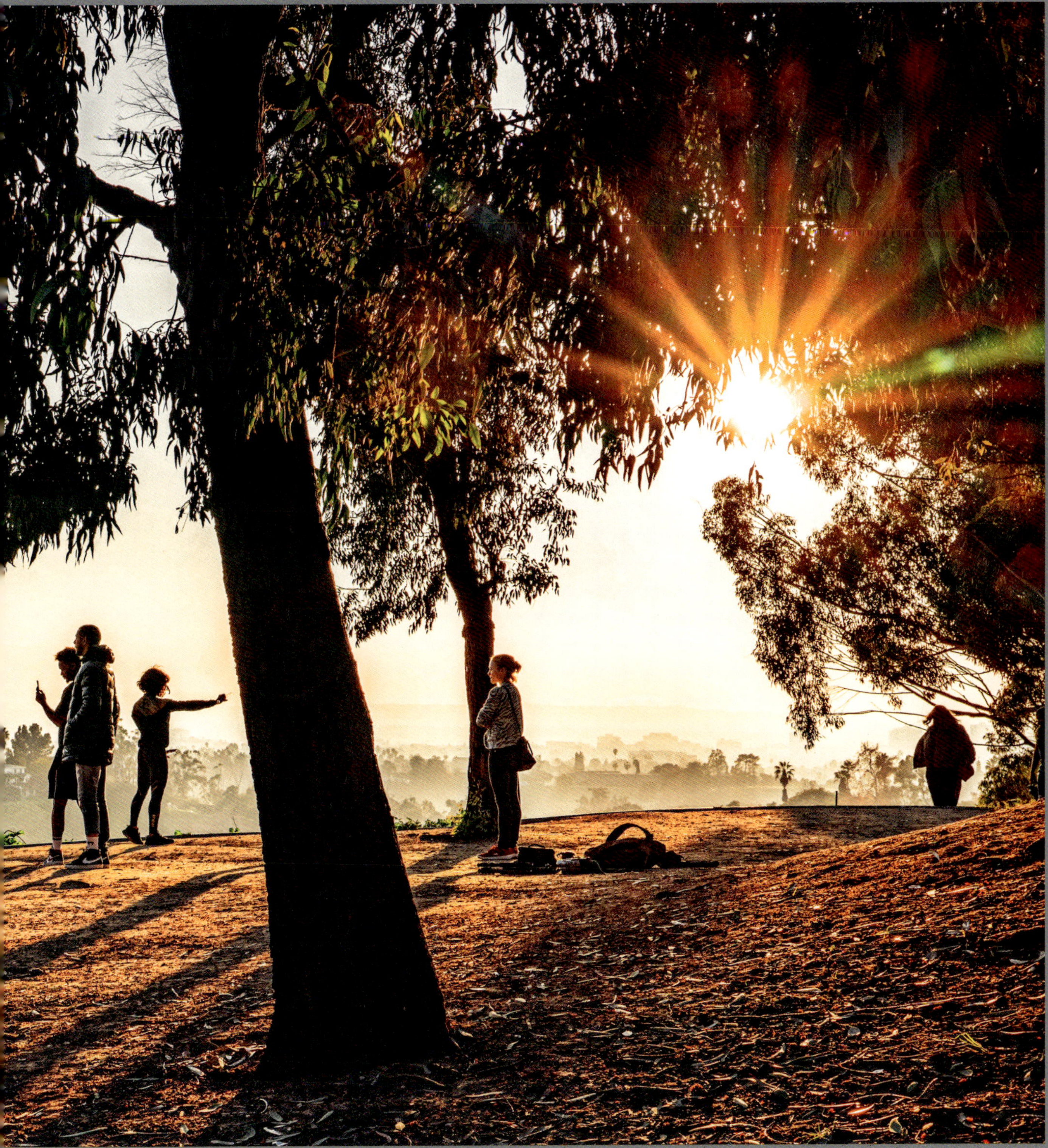

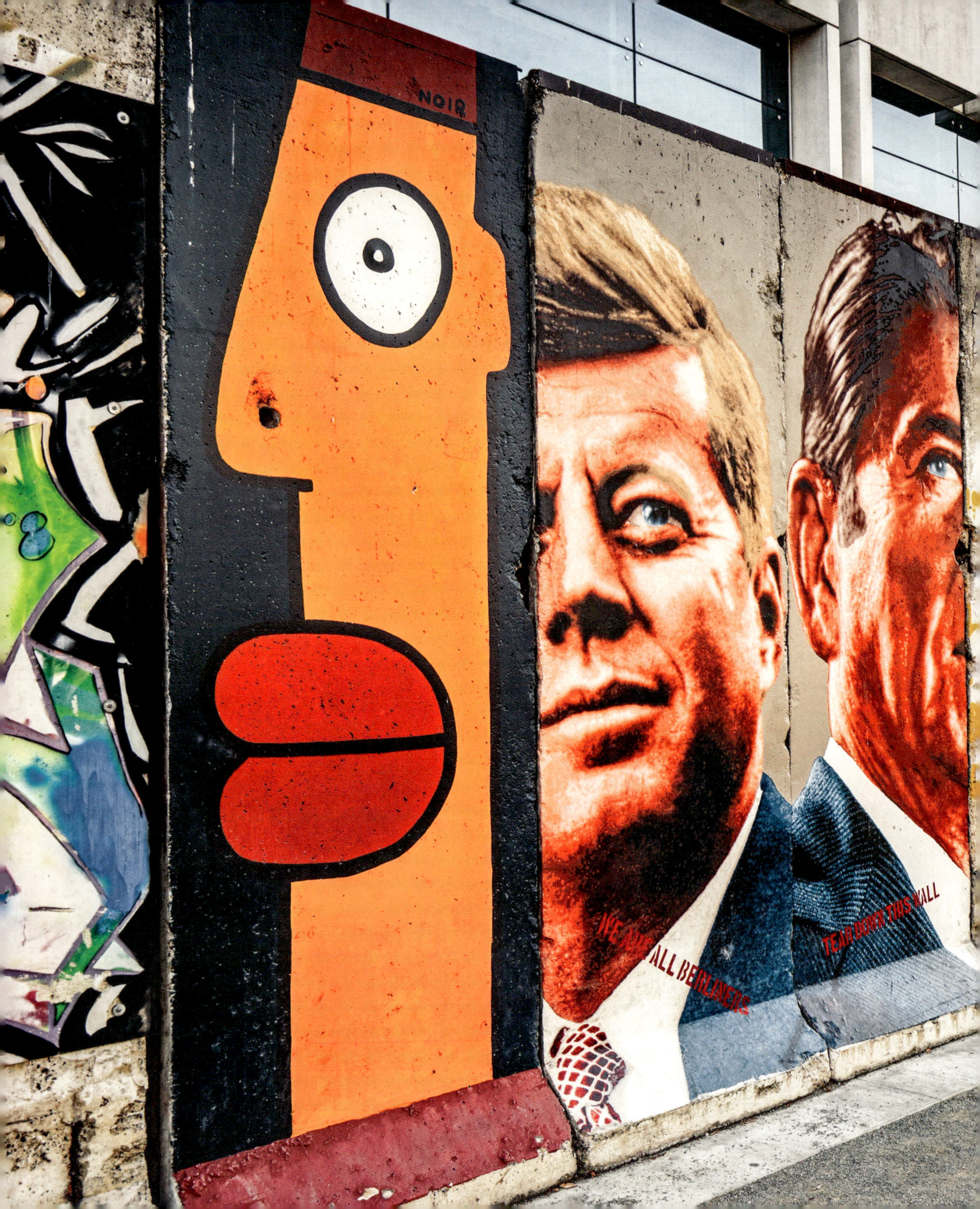
NOIR
ALL BERLINERS
TEAR DOWN THIS WALL

In the Miracle Mile district, pieces of the Berlin Wall are on view along Wilshire Boulevard as part of the Wende Museum's commemoration of the wall's fall.

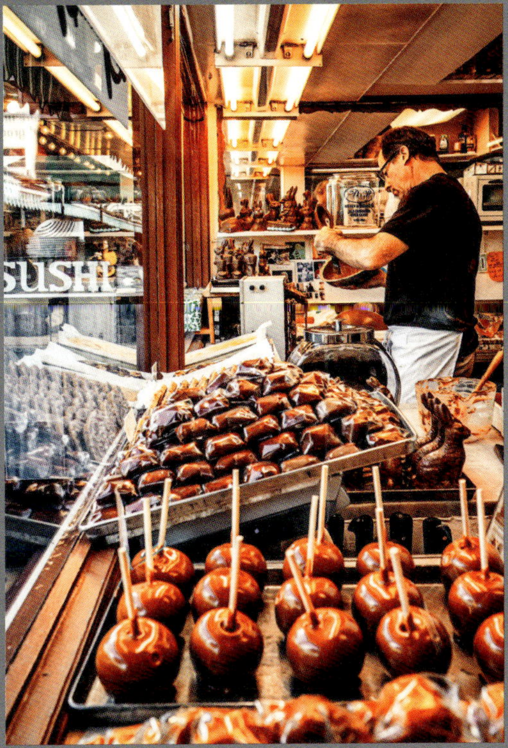

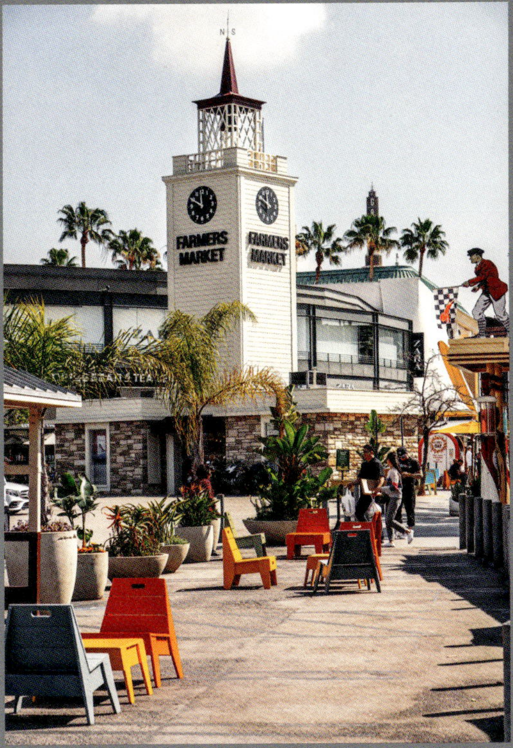

The Original Farmers Market, the first farmer's market in California, has been on the corner of Fairfax and Third Street since 1934 and boasts an incredible variety of merchants and food stalls, all with a big side of history.

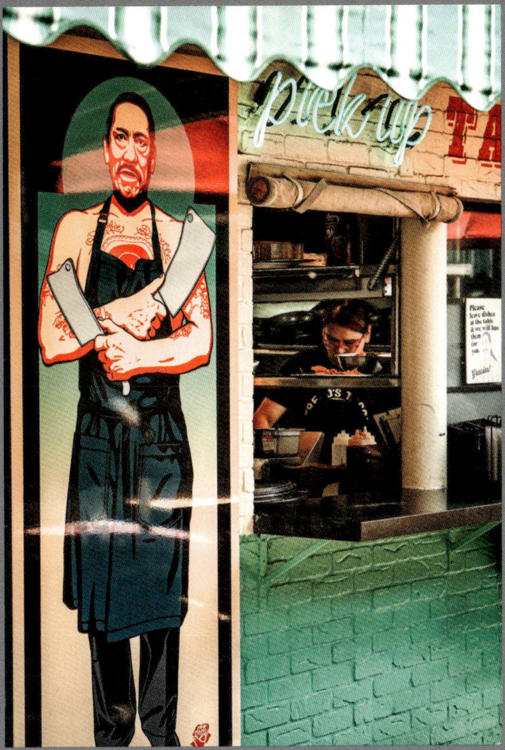

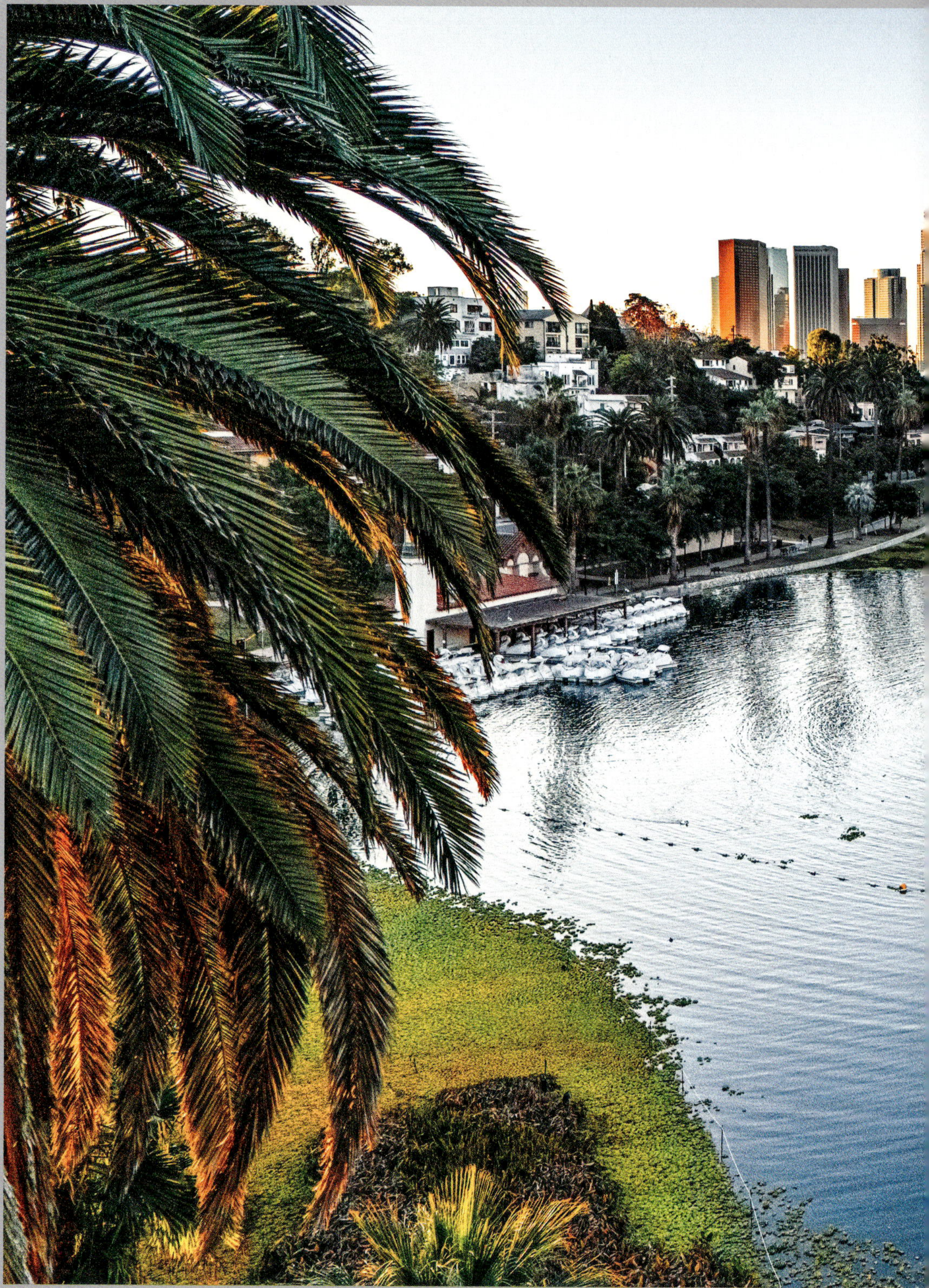

Originally built in 1868 as a reservoir for drinking water, Echo Park Lake is now a recreational park with a walking path around the lake and signature swan boats to ride through it.

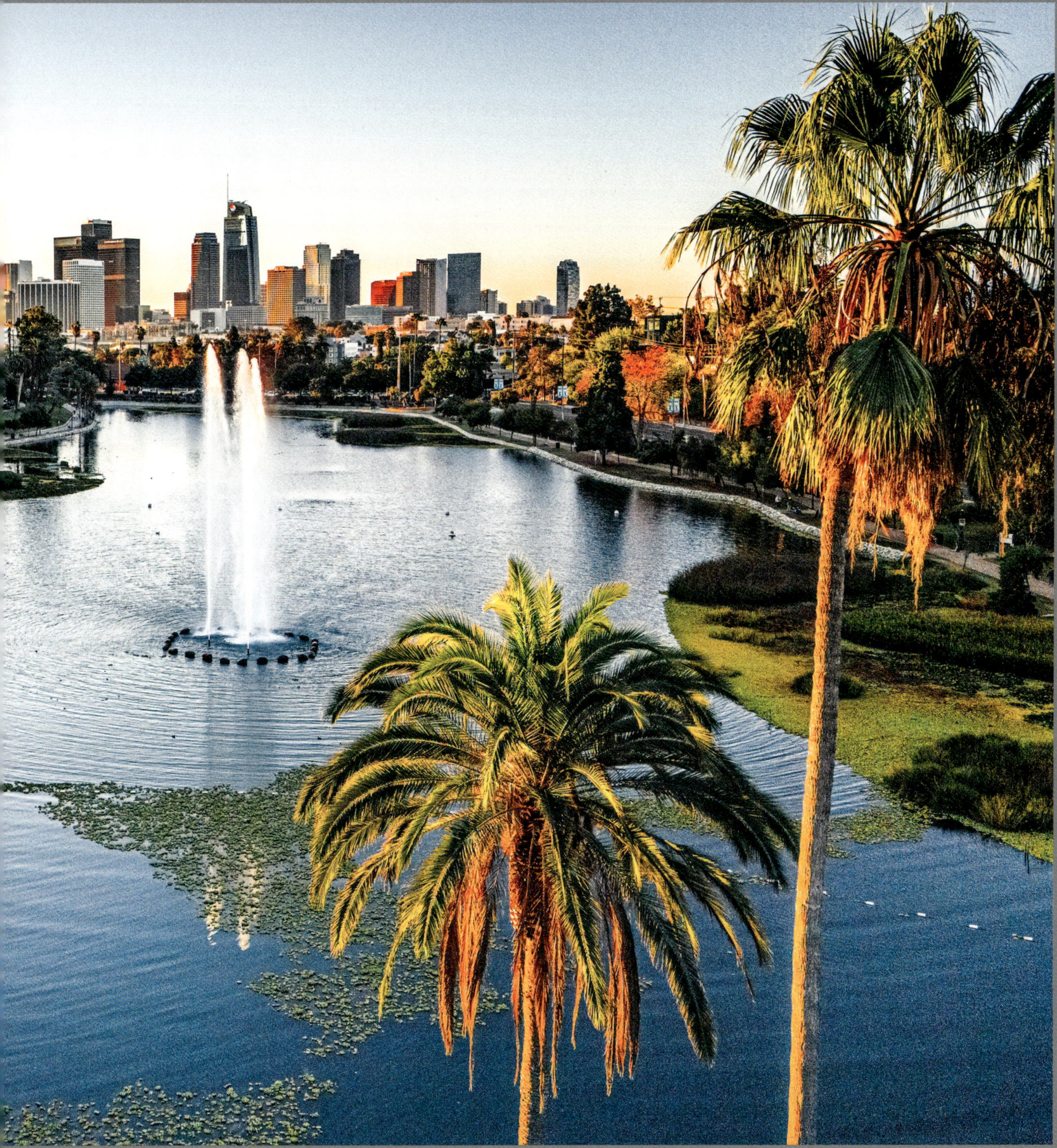

Koreatown

"Second Seoul" and More

The less than three square miles that make up Koreatown are the most diverse and densely populated of all of LA's many neighborhoods. Not only does Koreatown have the largest population of Korean people outside of South Korea, there are also significant populations of Angelenos from Central America, Mexico, Bangladesh, Thailand, Mongolia, and the Philippines who call K-town home. This area is where LA's diversity shines—where the city's multilingual, multi-ethnic, and often immigrant-led influences come together to create vibrant and new cultures. Take, for example, one small example: the Korean-inspired taco, which came to prominence in 2008 with the Kogi taco truck and is now on menus around the world. What could be more LA than a fusion of Korean and Mexican food made in a truck and eaten on the street?

Though today's K-town might be called "a second Seoul," known for its nightlife, restaurants, and as a hub for business, fun, and relaxation (try one of the many jimjilbangs, South Korean-style spas), its roots set down nearly 120 years ago, when Korean immigrants who worked in the citrus industry in Riverside, California, were forced by a freeze to look for work elsewhere. They settled in downtown Los Angeles, and eventually a change in US immigration law in 1965 led to a significant growth of LA's Korean community. For decades, Koreatown and its bustling markets, shops, and services have served as a destination for the Korean American community—and everyone else. As chef David Chang, creator of the Momofuku restaurants and the TV show *Ugly Delicious* told the *L.A. Times*, "I love K-Town—it's probably the most exciting place to eat in America."

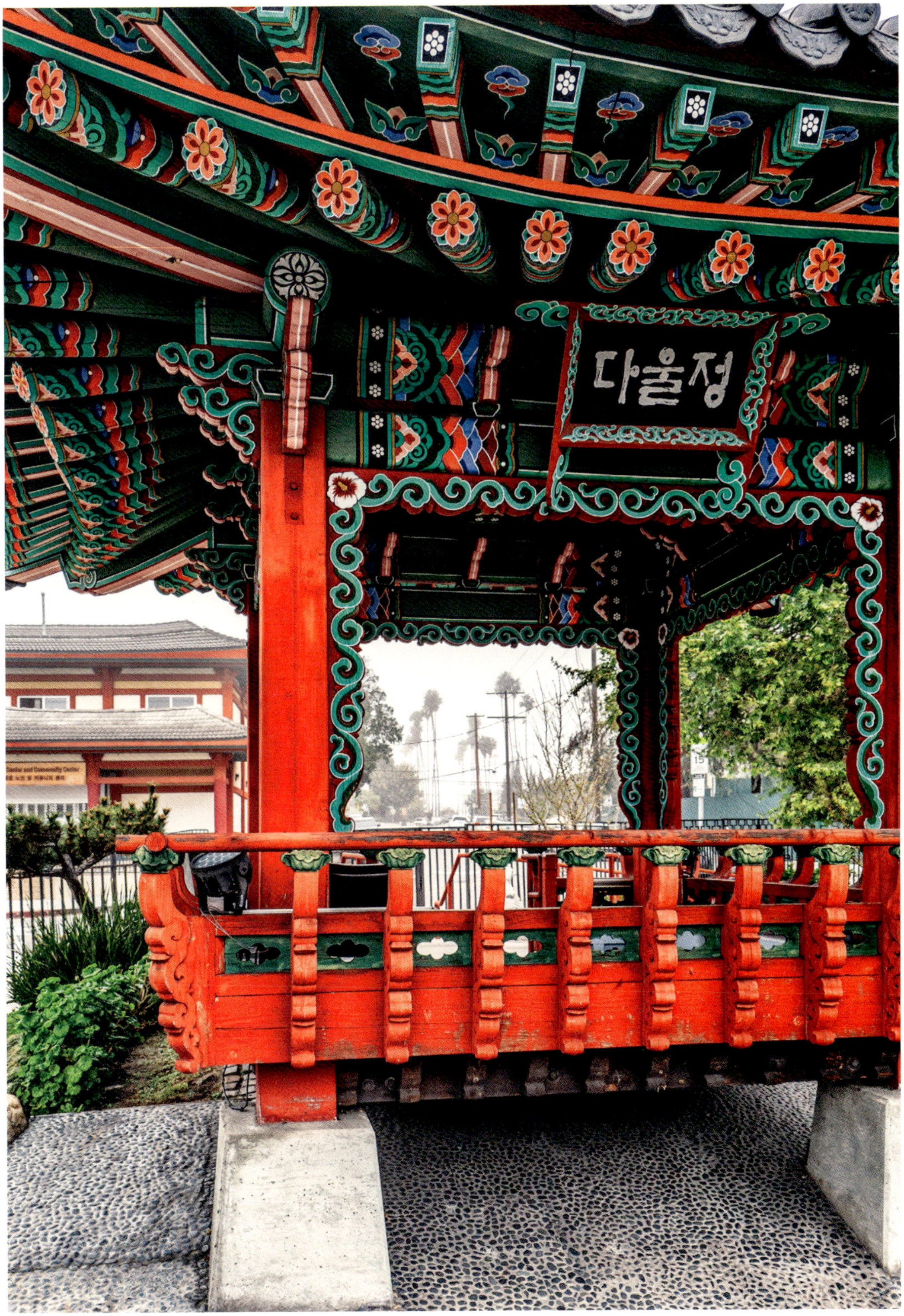

Dedicated in 2006, the Koreatown Pavilion Garden, also called Da Wool Jung (which means harmonious gathering place), is a gateway monument built to symbolize the cultural, economic, and political growth of the Korean American community.

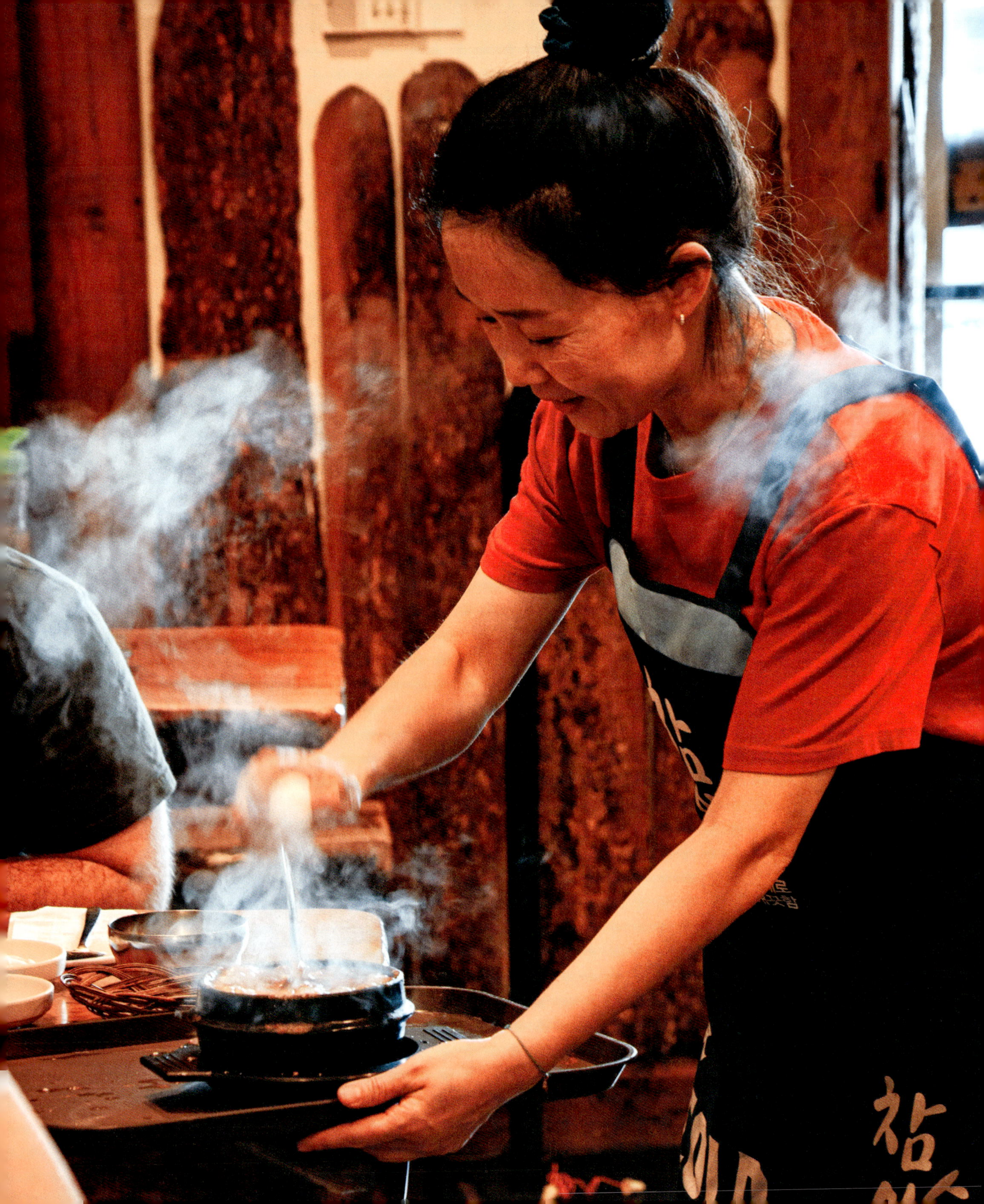

There are so many amazing restaurants in Koreatown, and many excel at a very specific specialty, as at Beverly Soon Tofu, where it was soondubu, a tofu soup.

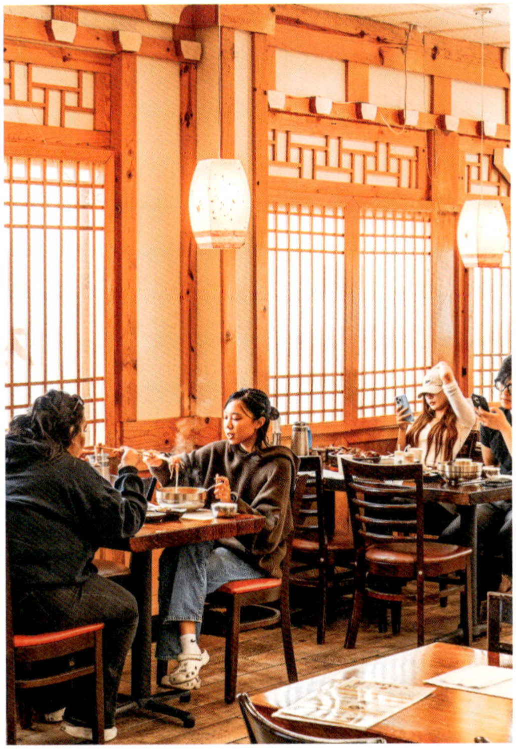

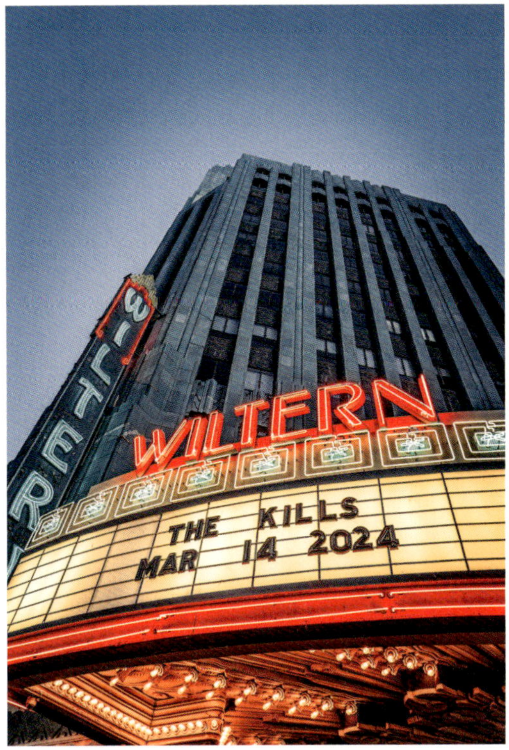

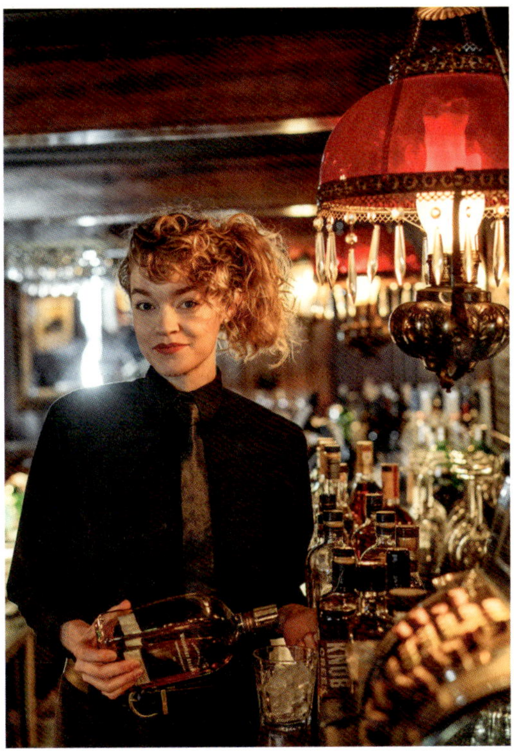

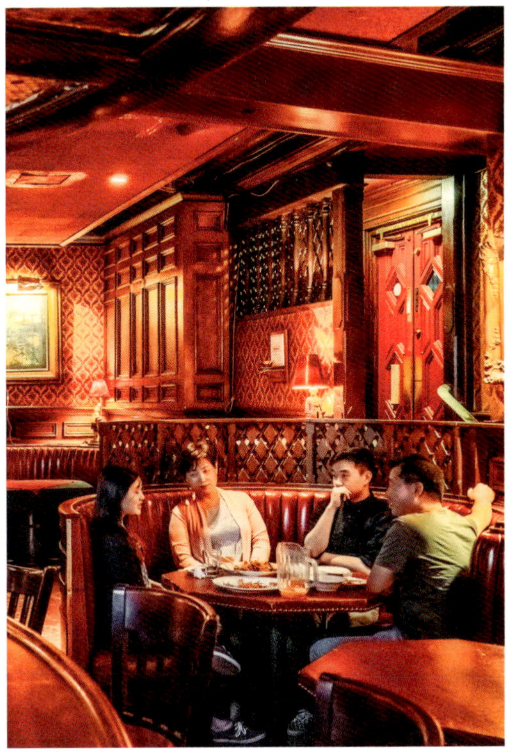

Jinsol Gukbap on West Third Street in Koreatown specializes in gukbap, a pork-based soup.

The Wiltern Theatre, a gorgeous concert venue, is part of the 1931 landmark Art Deco Pellissier Building.

Taylor's Steakhouse opened in 1953 and looks like a film noir location.

The Prince is a popular nighttime spot for drinks and Korean fried chicken—it's also been a film location for *Twin Peaks, Mad Men,* and *Chinatown.*

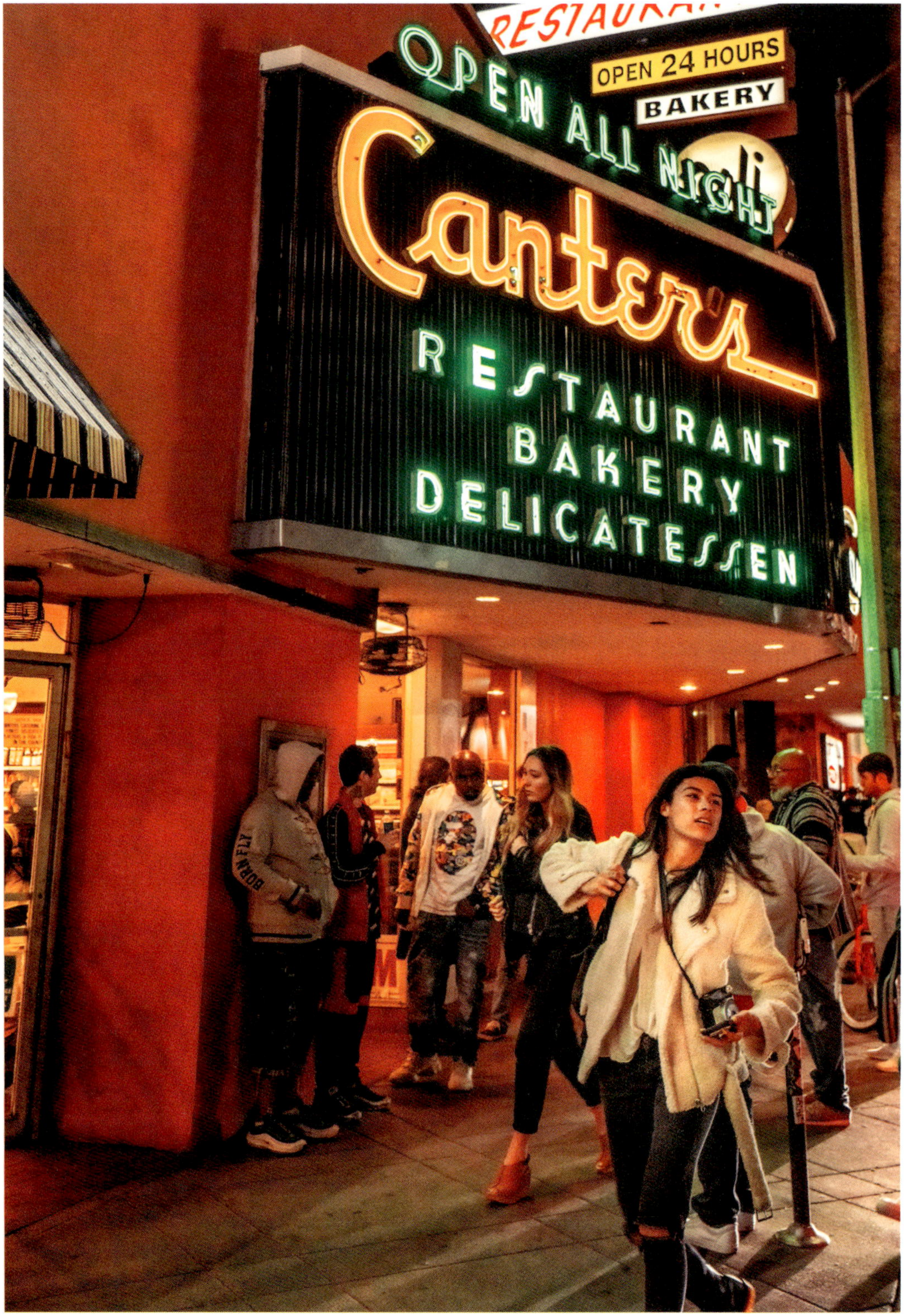

"In Los Angeles, everyone is a star." –actor Denzel Washington

Canter's Delicatessen

Classic Gathering Spot for a Late-Night Nosh

Canter's is a late-night institution—the kind of place one goes with a group of friends, all hankering for the comfort of an early breakfast or a midnight bowl of matzo ball soup, unwilling for the evening to end. It's a legendary spot, an anchor to the historically Jewish neighborhood of Fairfax, which today is a dynamic mix of streetwear shops and the few legacy businesses left that cater to the orthodox community. Everyone comes together at Canter's—hipsters and skaters, old folks, families—and that's how it's been since the deli and bakery first opened in 1931.

Some of Canter's celebrity noshers include Marilyn Monroe, who would come with her husband Arthur Miller, as well as musical legends such as Frank Zappa, Jim Morrison, and Neil Young. The cocktail lounge adjacent to the dining room is known as the Kibitz Room and features a full bar with a stage for live musical performances. In the 1990s, this was a frequent hotspot for local musicians, who would perform or just hang out to eat, drink, and kibitz.

Canter's role as a fixture in rock 'n' roll history is thanks not only to its atmosphere and comforting menu, it's also—as most things are in a city the size of Los Angeles—its location. During the heyday of the Sunset Strip, many of the bands that performed in venues on Sunset came here after. After all, it's right down the street and open twenty-four hours a day.

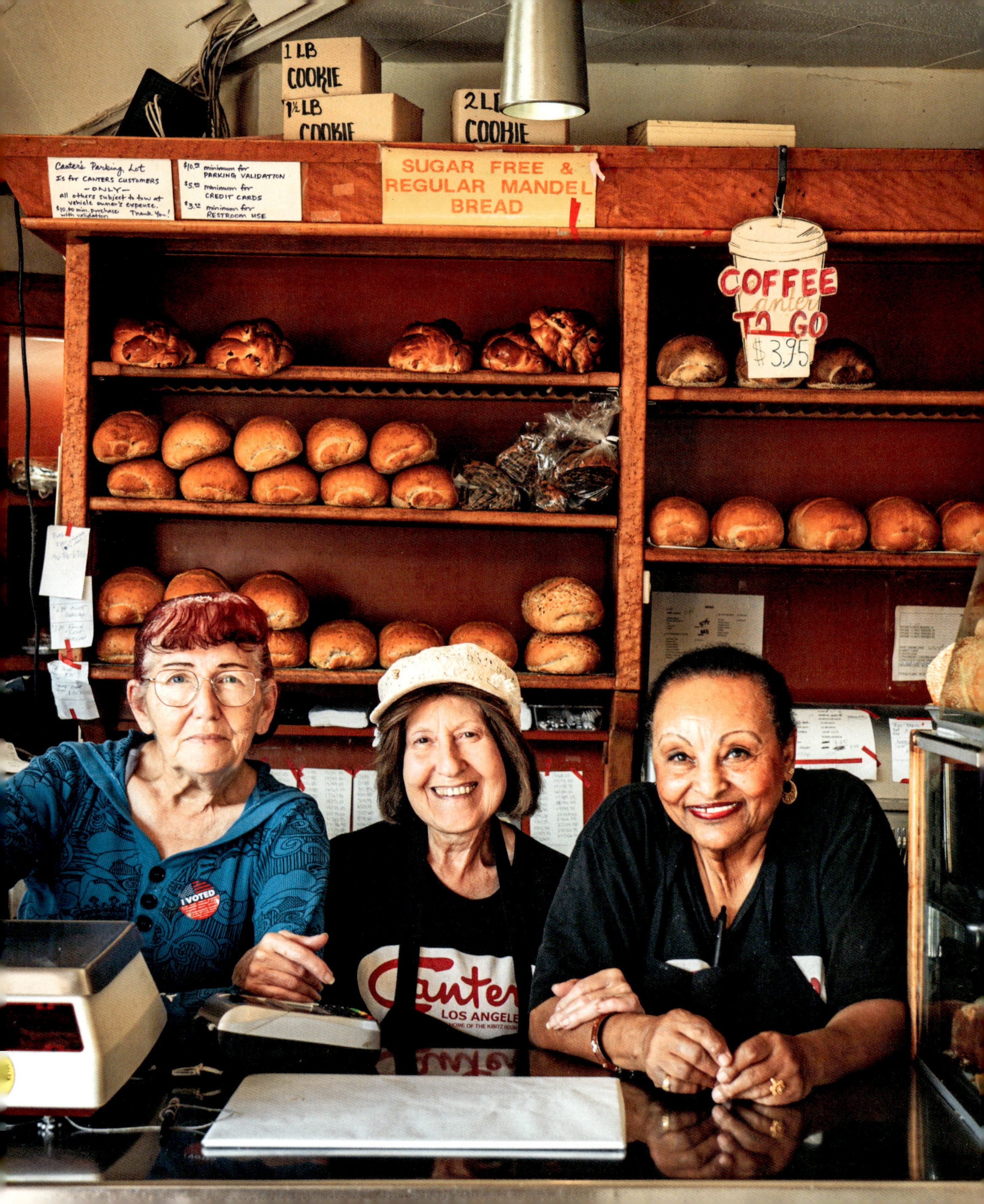
1 LB COOKIE
1½ LB COOKIE
COOKIE
Canter's Parking Lot
Is for CANTERS CUSTOMERS
-ONLY-
all others subject to tow at vehicle owner's expense.
$10.00 min. purchase with validation Thank You!
$10.00 minimum for PARKING VALIDATION
$5.00 minimum for CREDIT CARDS
$3.00 minimum for RESTROOM USE
SUGAR FREE & REGULAR MANDEL BREAD
COFFEE TO GO
$3.95
I VOTED
LOS ANGELE

All varieties of Jewish sweets are available at the bakery, which even President Barack Obama ordered on his visit to the deli in 2014.

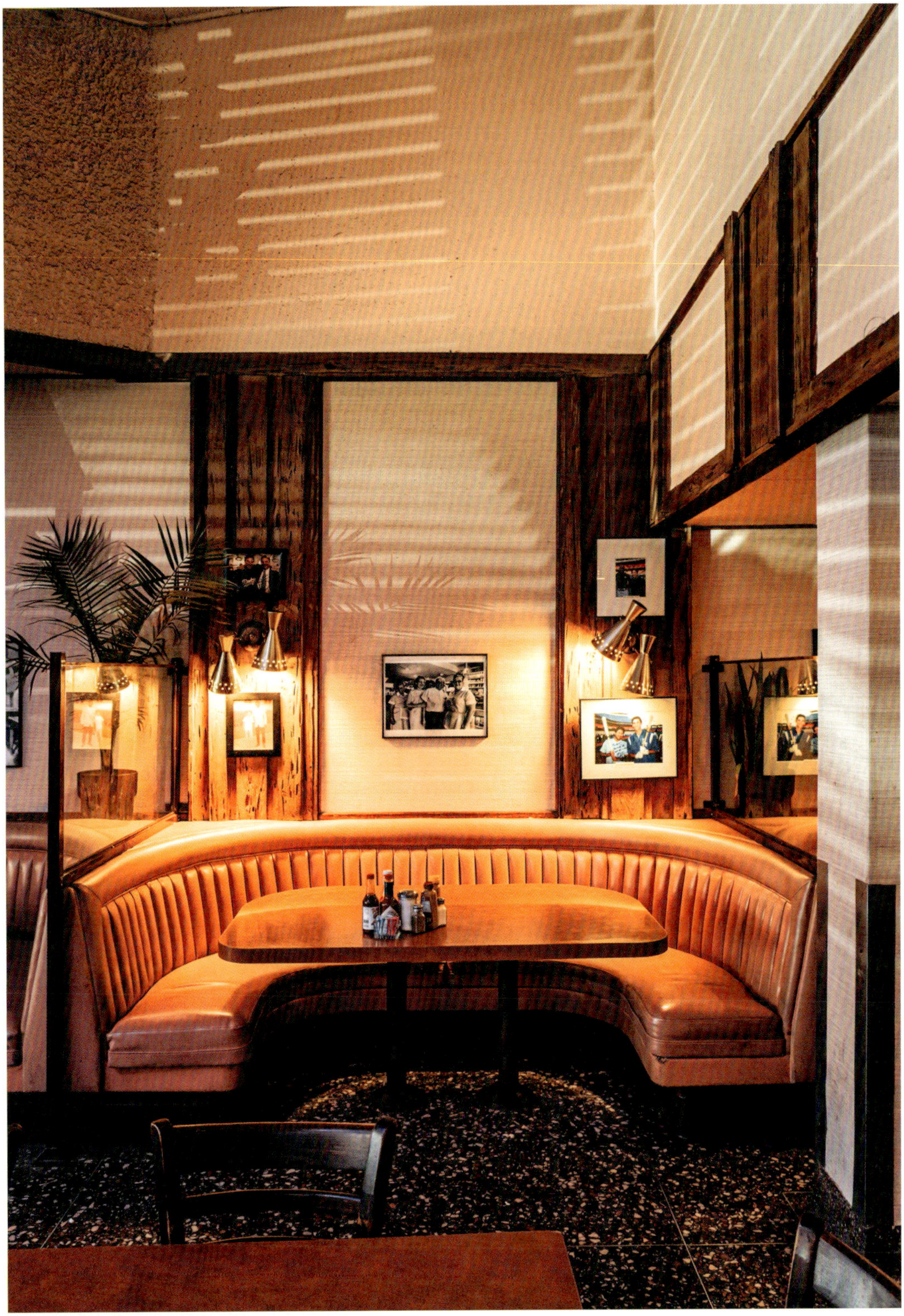

Canter's has booths dedicated to celebrities like Nancy Sinatra and Rodney Bingenheimer, the DJ and club owner who is known as the Mayor of the Sunset Strip.

Hollyhock House

Frank Lloyd Wright's Masterpiece that Birthed California Modernism

Los Angeles is home to eight residences designed by the legendary American architect Frank Lloyd Wright. Located in the East Hollywood/Los Feliz area, Hollyhock House is the architect's first Los Angeles commission and the city's first-and-only UNESCO World Heritage site. Commissioned by Aline Barnsdall as part of a 36-acre arts complex that was never fully realized, the house, guest house, and grounds were built between 1918 and 1921 and serve as a harbinger of what would become California Modernism.

Now owned by the City of Los Angeles, Wright's masterpiece is open to the public for tours—check the website for reservations. The Barnsdall Art Park surrounds the structure and is open daily for picnics and visits. The view of the nearby Hollywood Hills and Griffith Park, as well as the city below, atop what Wright and Barnsdall knew as "Olive Hill," is worth the visit alone—plus, on Fridays in the summer there might be a ticketed wine tasting as well.

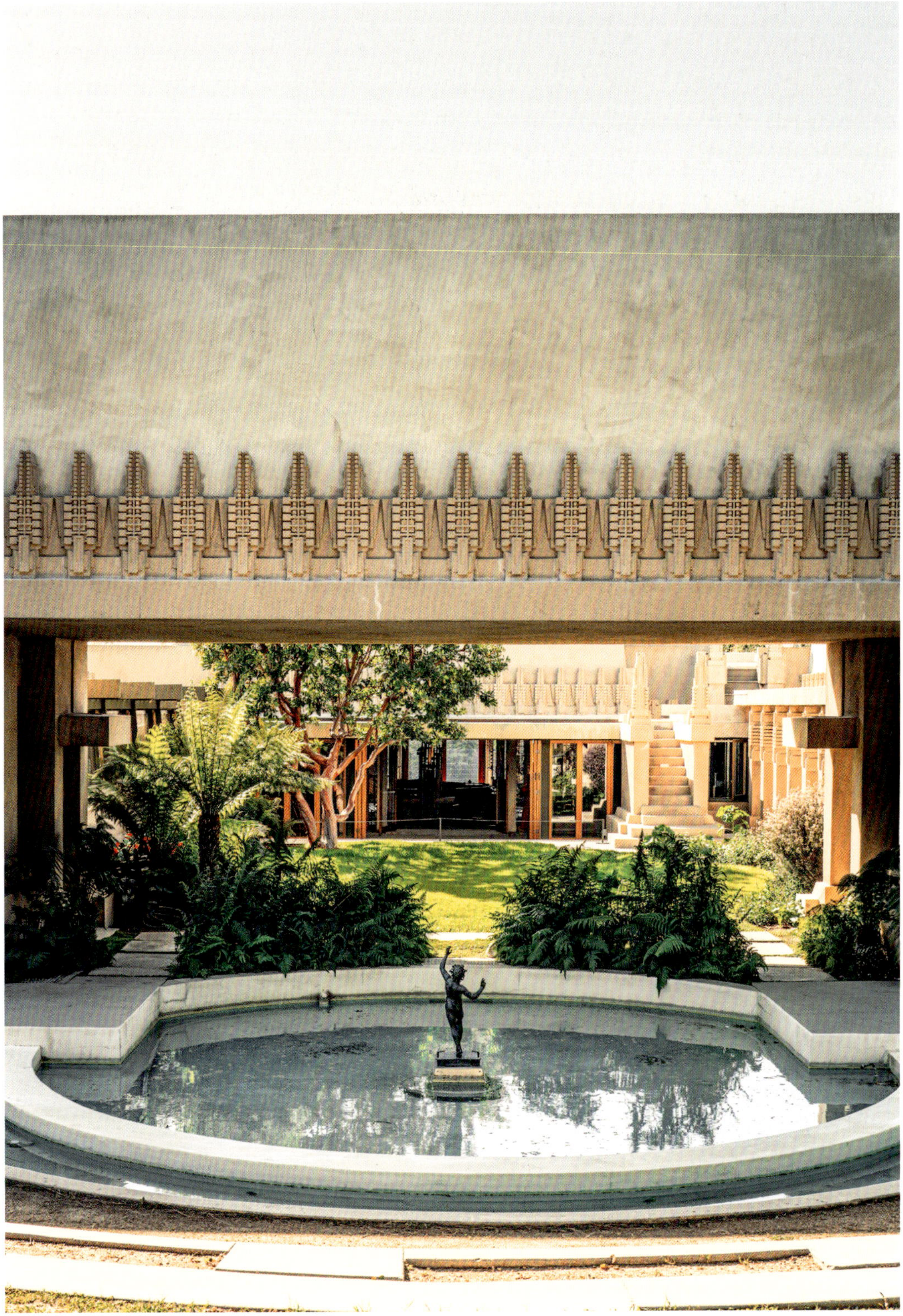

"Study nature, love nature, stay close to nature. It will never fail you." —Frank Lloyd Wright

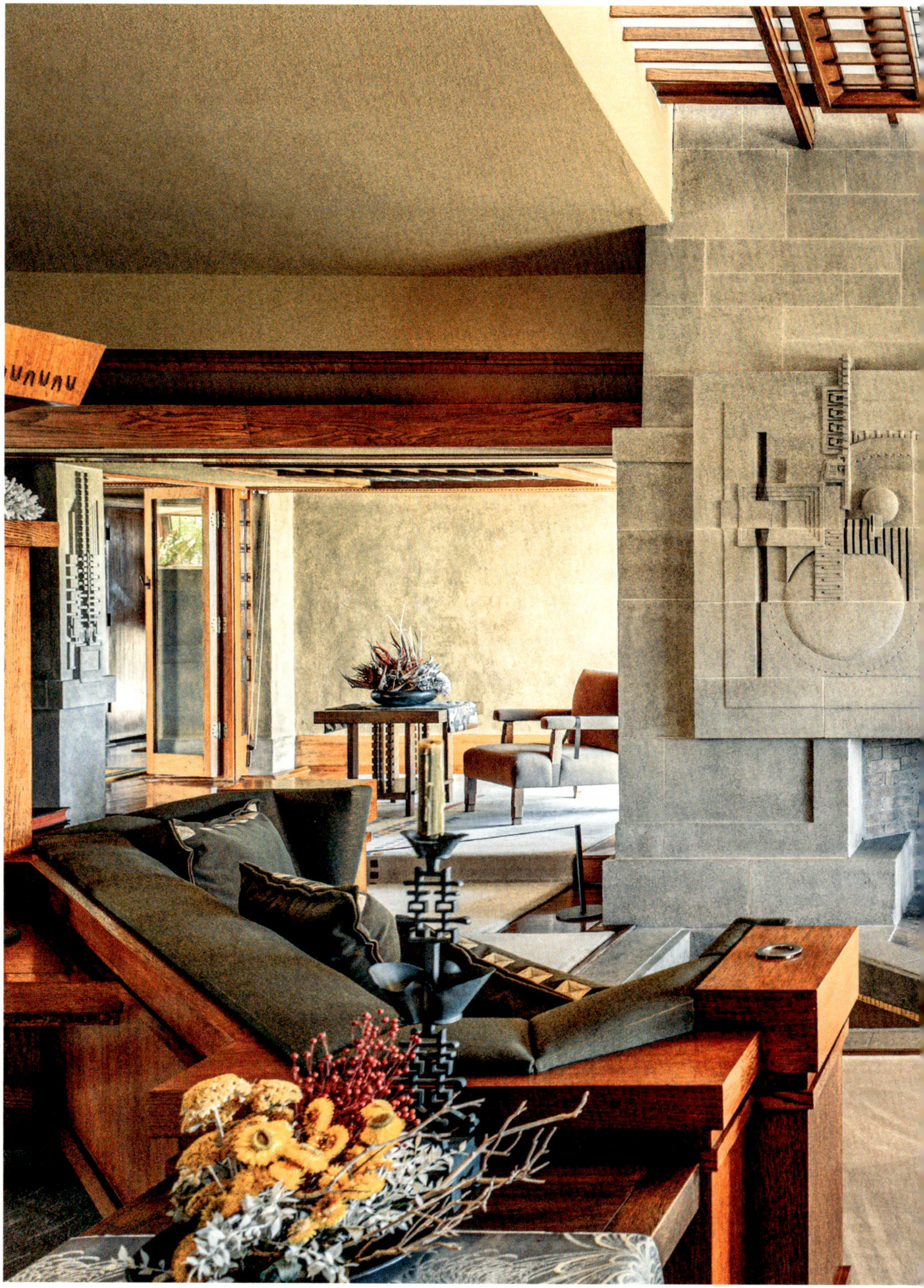

For the dramatic living room, Wright sought to integrate all four elements—fire, earth, air, and water. The monumental fireplace originally had a water feature around it.

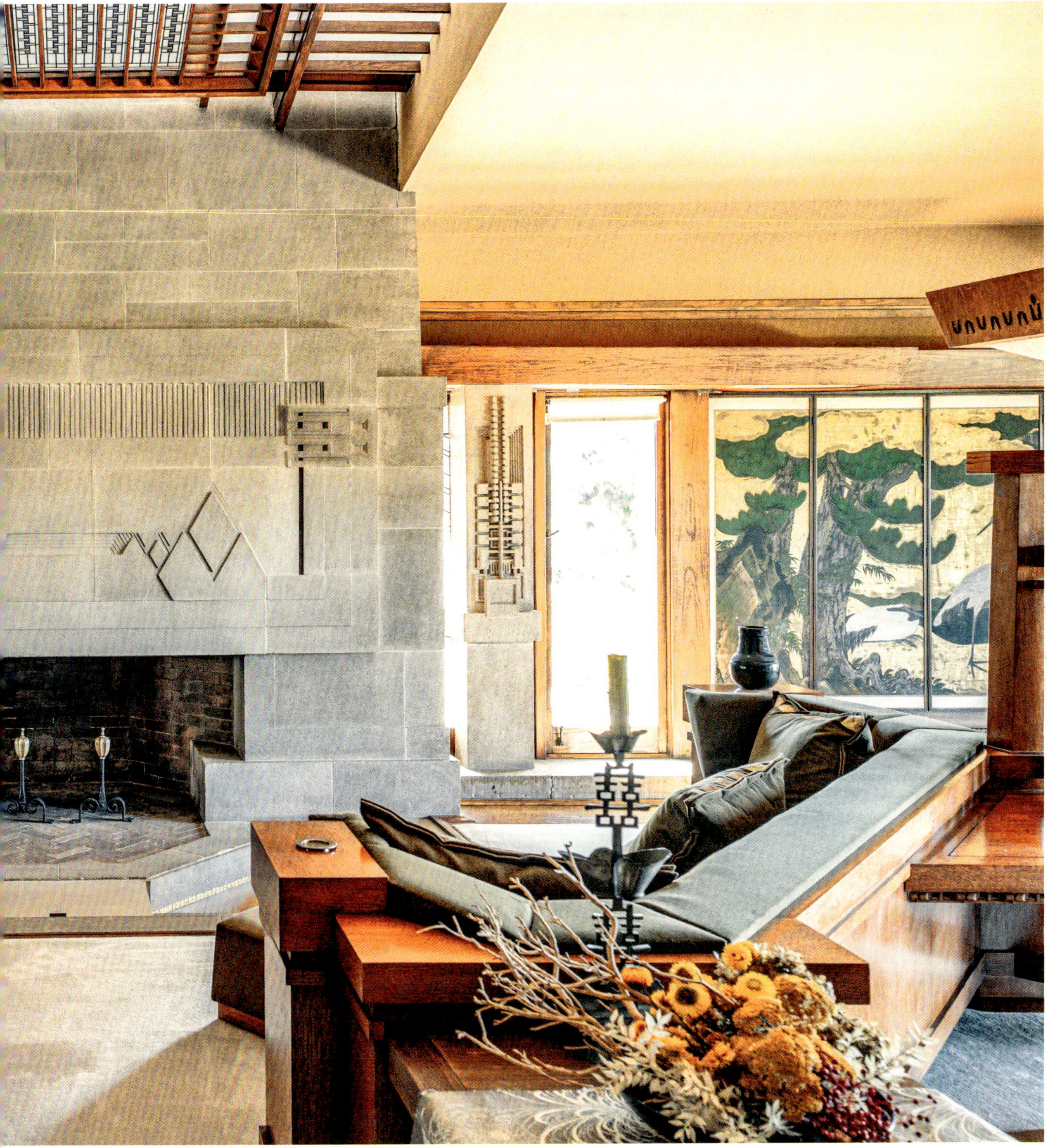

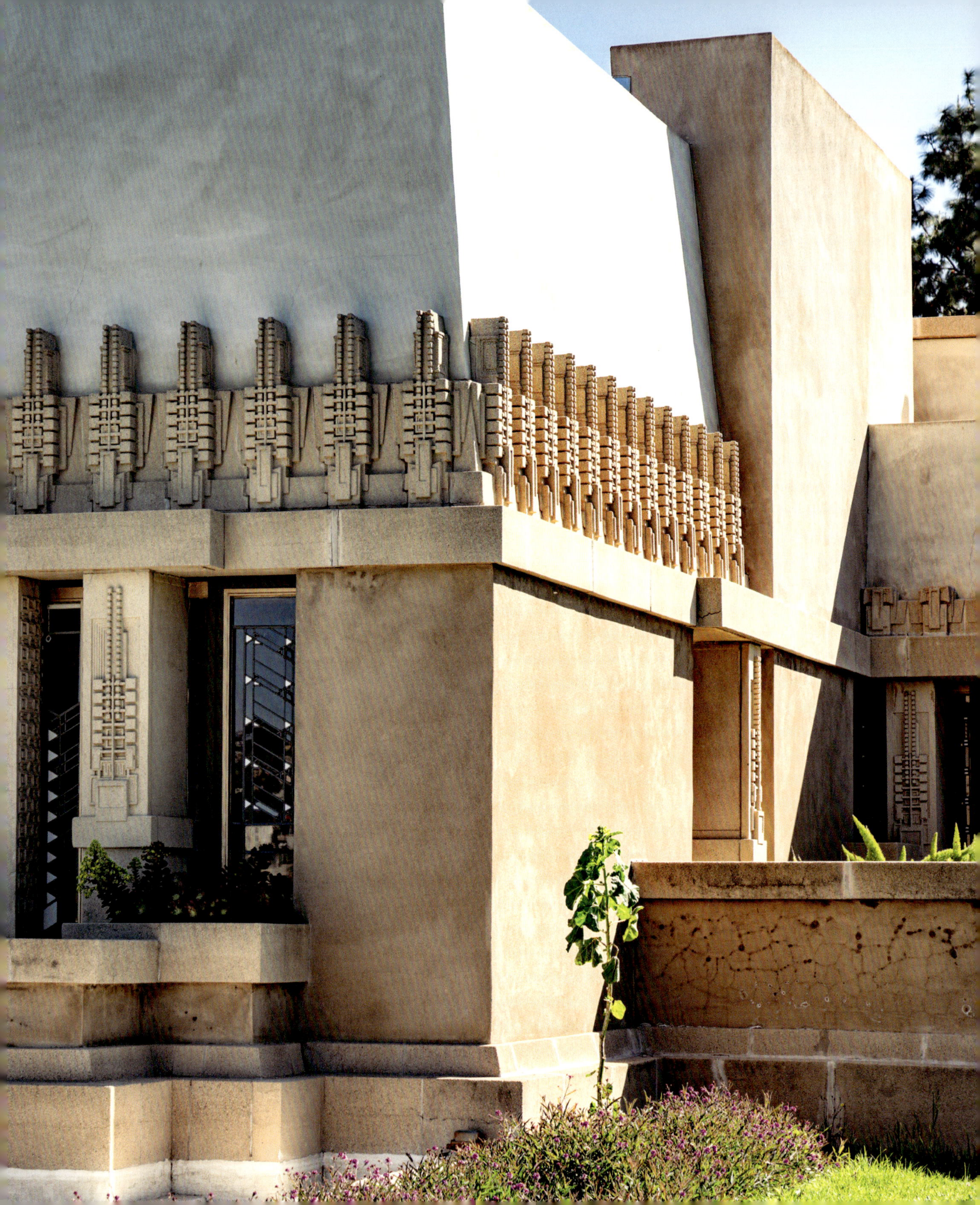

Aline Barnsdall's favorite flower, the hollyhock, serves as a recurrent design motif.

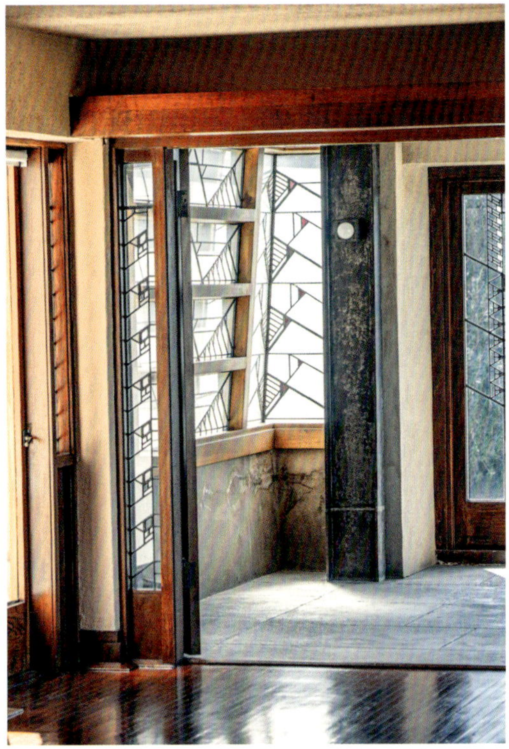

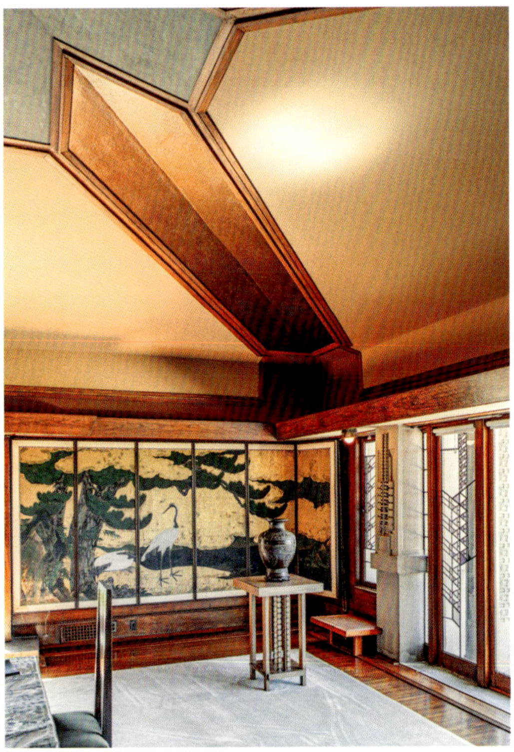

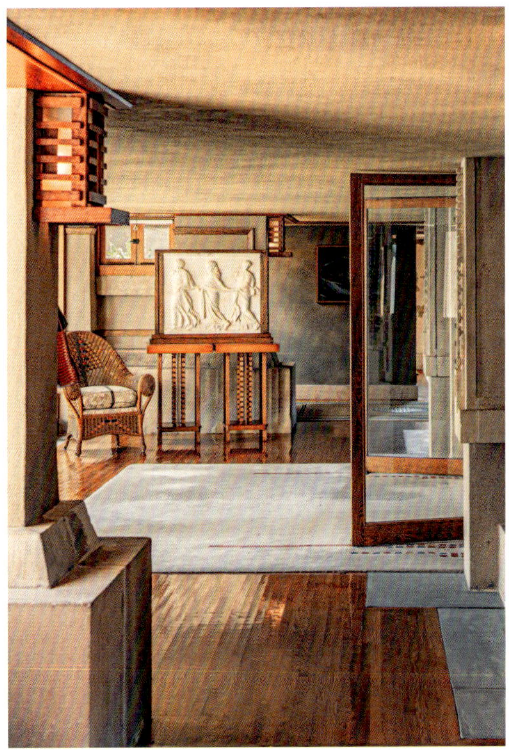

Hollyhock is said to be Wright's ode to California—its freedom and natural beauty. But he and Barnsdall often disagreed on the design, and other architects who worked for Wright were left to finish the project, including Rudolph Schindler and Richard Neutra.

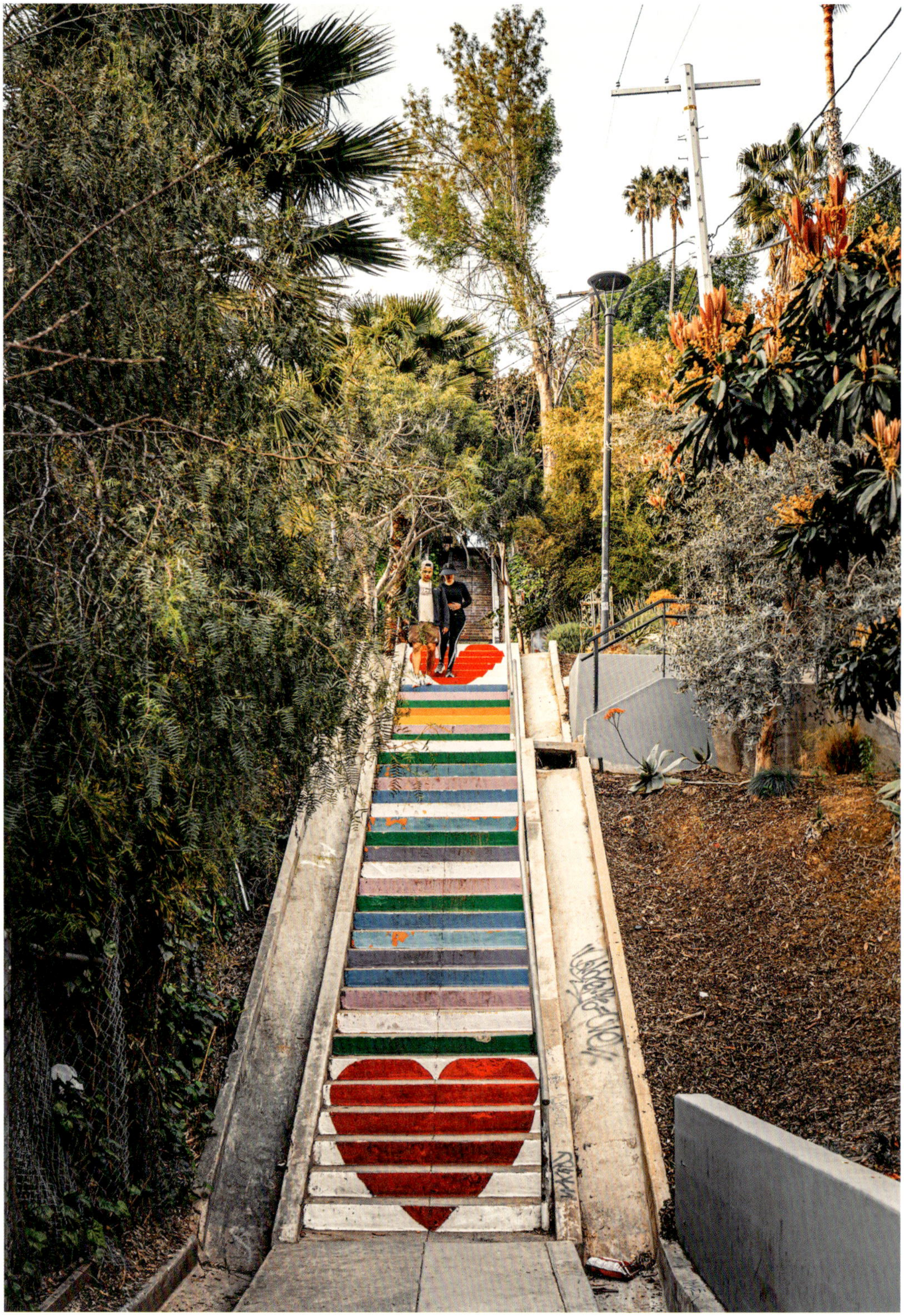

The neighborhood of Silver Lake has a big heart—and big hills. Both are evident at the Micheltorena Stairs located off Sunset Boulevard.

Secret Stairs

Little-Known Fact: the City is Connected by Public Staircases

Most everyone thinks about Los Angeles as a flat city of freeways but, in fact, the city is surrounded by mountains, and with that comes hills and canyons. One of the best secrets of Los Angeles is the network of municipal stairwells built across the city to navigate these hills and connect residential areas to what was once a huge public transportation system of trolley cars. Today, LA still has a great public transportation system, and we highly encourage you to use it! It saves a lot of time, frustration, and fossil fuels.

Journalist and writer Charles Fleming, a long-time contributor to the *Los Angeles Times*, wrote the book on these historic staircases—it's called *Secret Stairs* and is a walking guide, complete with maps, to exploring staircases across the city. The Silver Lake neighborhood is particularly rich in staircases—some counts say there are at least forty—many of which have colorful murals that help tell the history of the area.

Miracle Mile

Home to Bubbling Pools of Tar and Museum Row

During the 1920s, Wilshire Boulevard was the most glamourous street in Los Angeles, especially the part that stretched out of downtown toward Hollywood. The Miracle Mile neighborhood owes it moniker, like much of Los Angeles, to a savvy real estate developer who hoped to extend Wilshire's allure to the west side. One of the most famous parts of the neighborhood is the stretch of Wilshire known as Museum Row, which houses no fewer than six world-class museums: the Los Angeles County Museum of Art (LACMA), the Craft Contemporary, the La Brea Tar Pits and Museum, the Petersen Automotive Museum, and the Academy Museum of Motion Pictures. From bubbling tar pits to great works of art, the largest collection of Academy Award statues can be found across the street from a vault of rare, one-of-a-kind cars. It's a miracle, this abundance of cultural artifacts from all eras sharing the same stretch of earth.

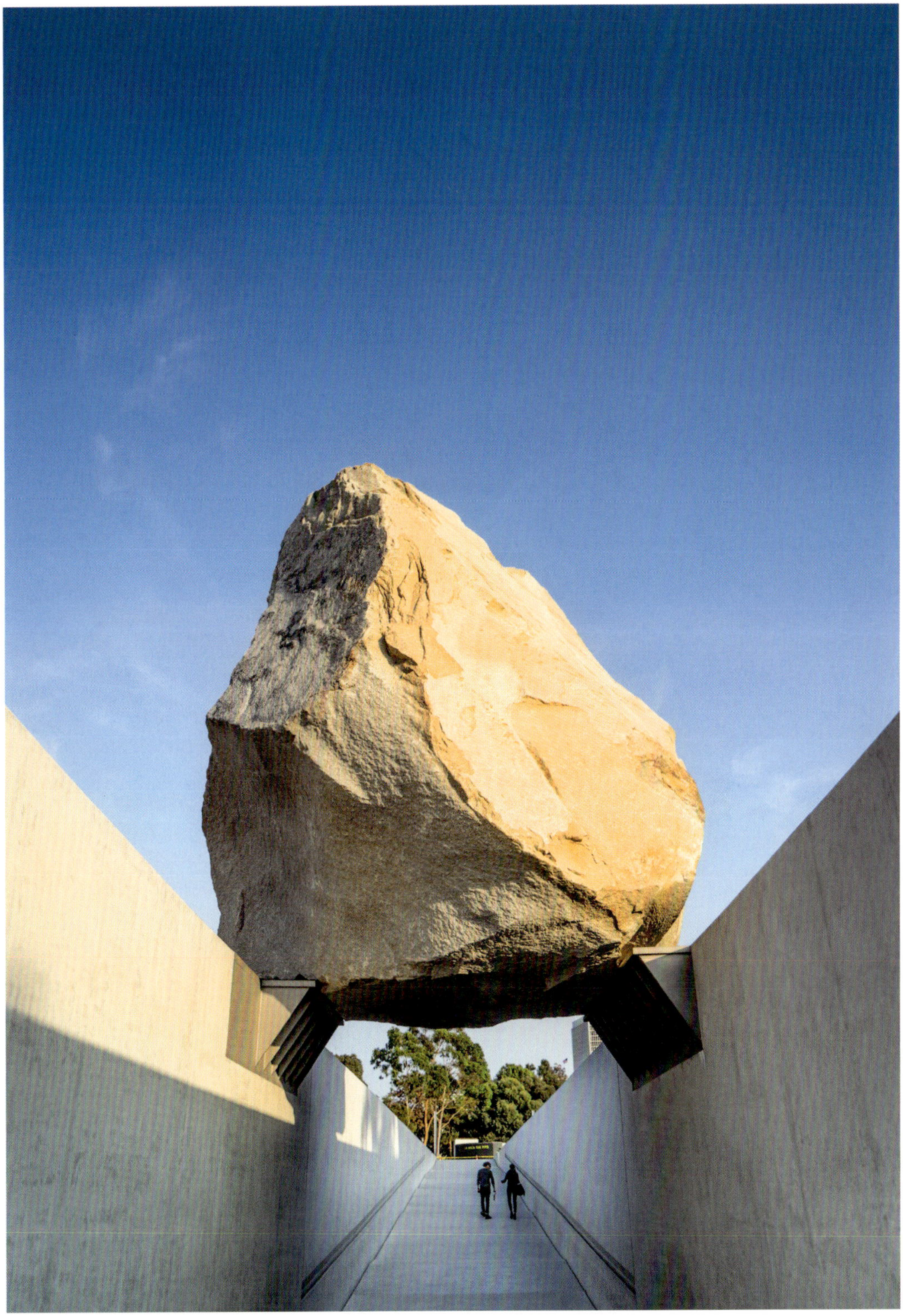

Visitors to LACMA. can walk under "Levitated Mass," an artwork by Michael Heizer that suspends a 340-ton boulder.

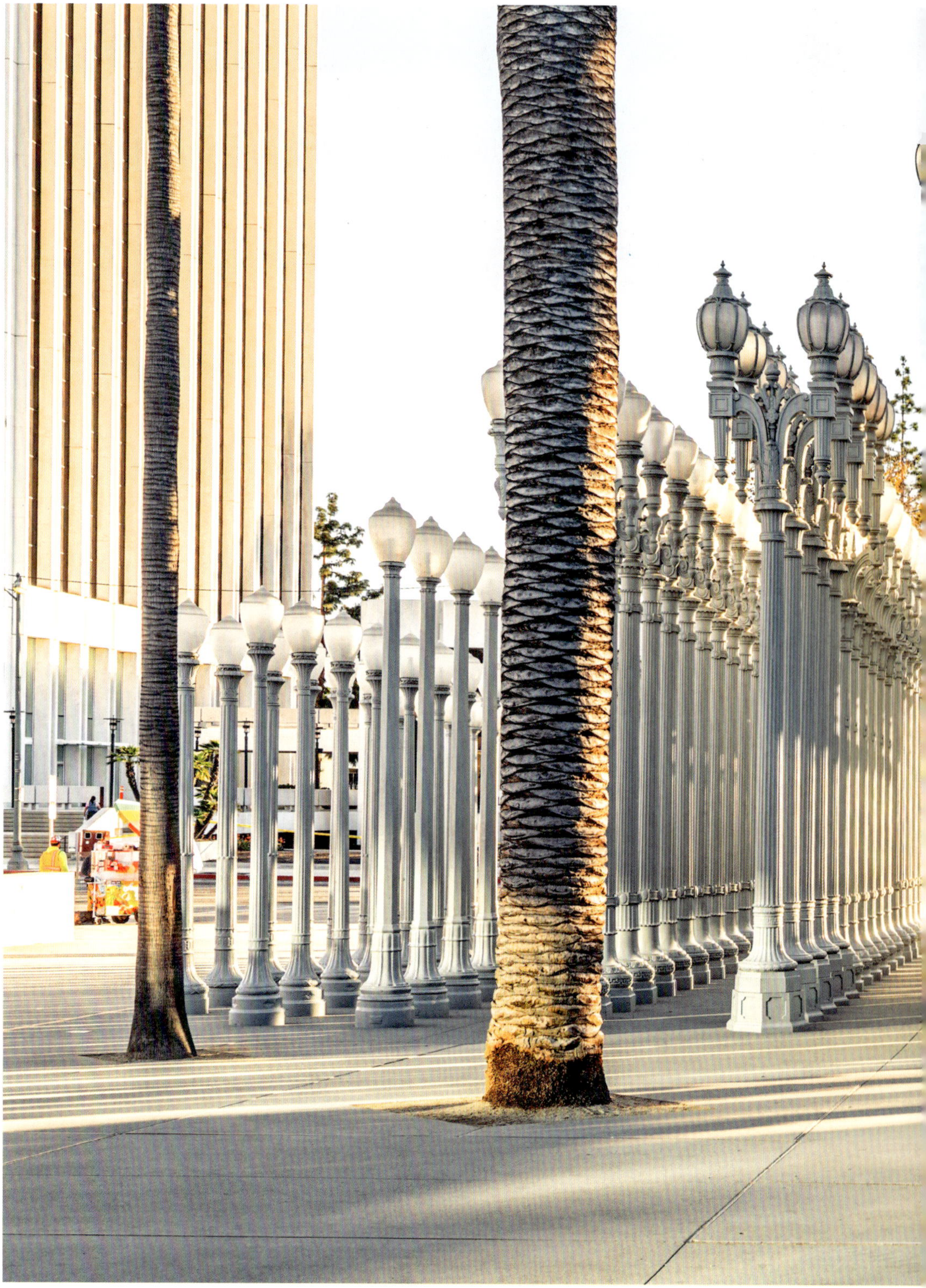

Artist Chris Burden's installation "Urban Light" at the Los Angeles County Museum of Art (LACMA) has become a symbol of the city.

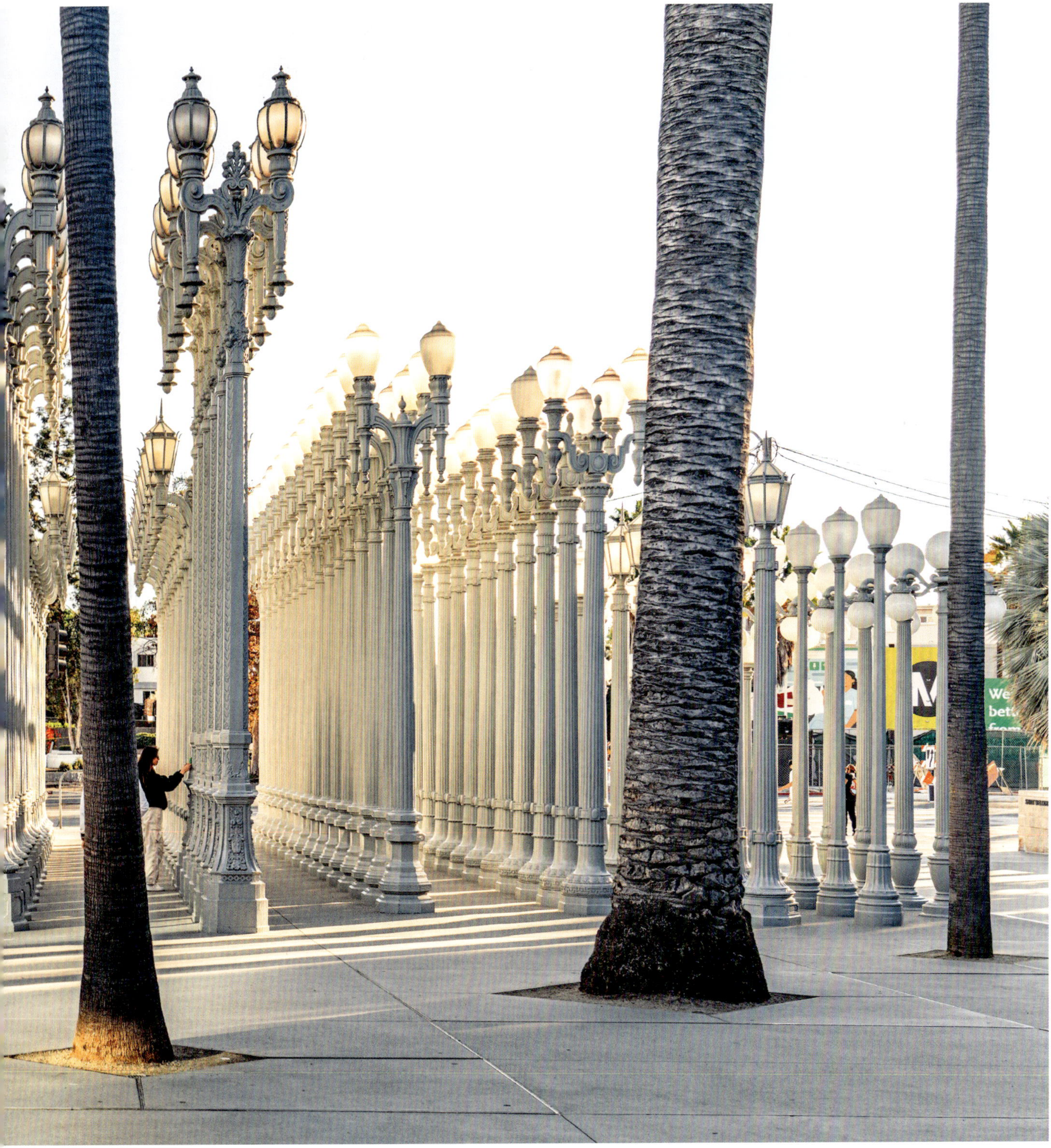

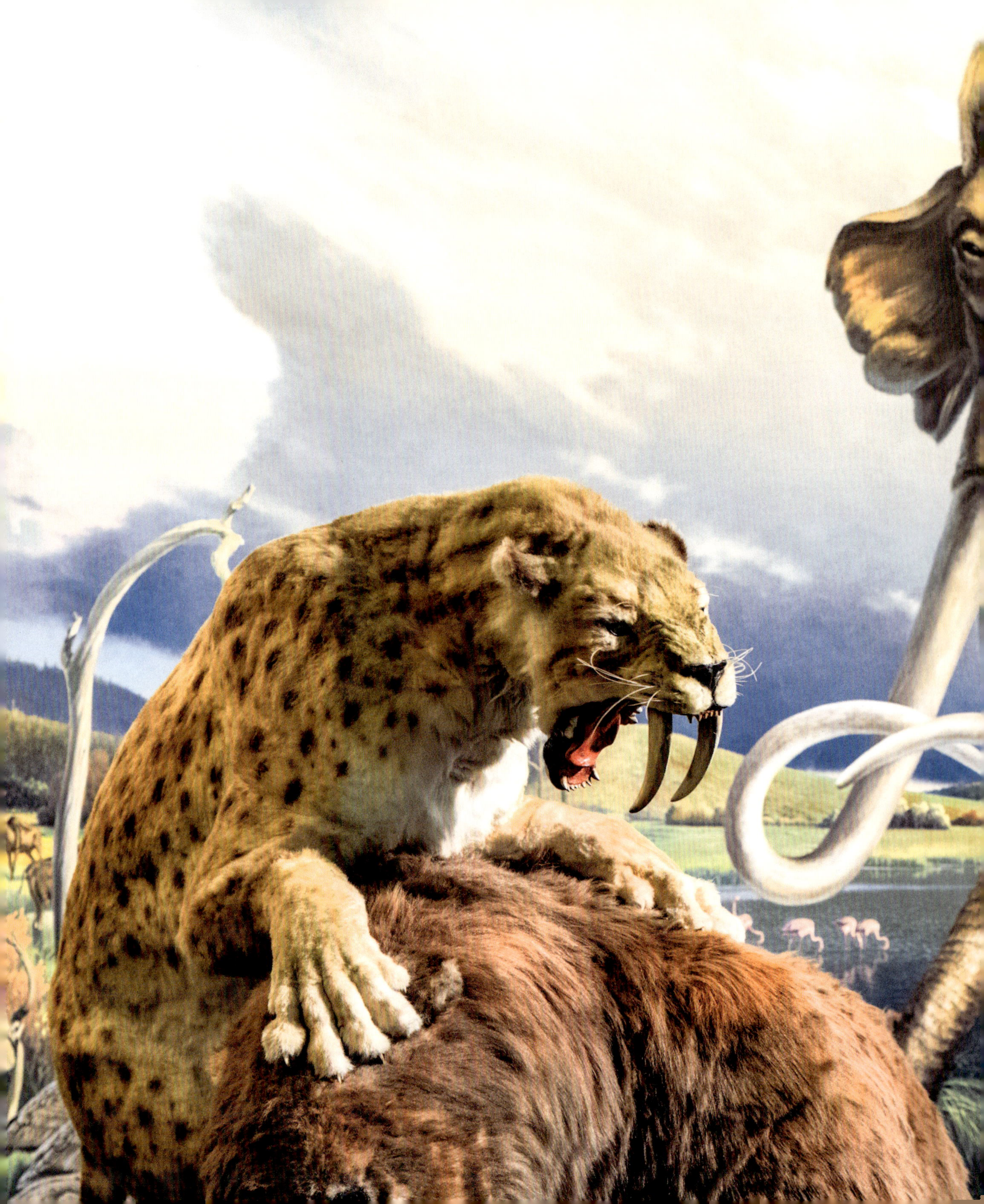

The La Brea Tar Pits and Museum shares the prehistoric history of the land now called LA, including this saber-toothed cat.

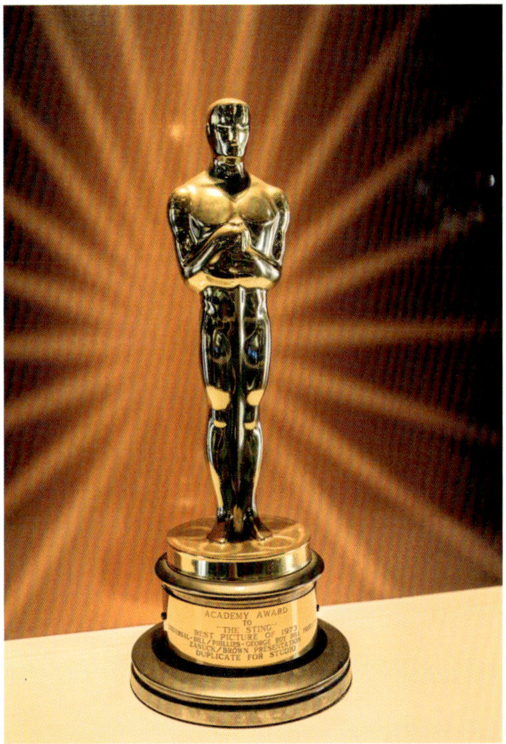

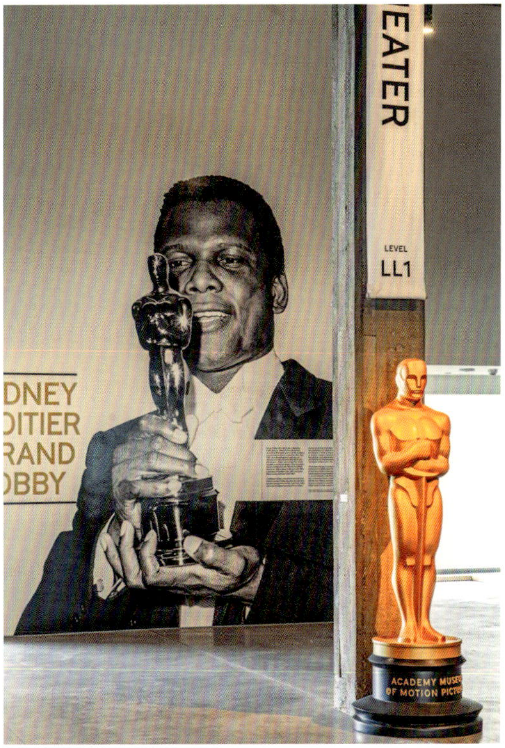

The newest edition to Museum Row is the 2021 futuristic-looking Academy Museum of Motion Pictures, the largest museum in the US devoted to moviemaking.

“If most American cities are about the consumption of culture, Los Angeles and New York are about the production of culture—not only national culture but global culture.” —Barbara Kruger

(Page 192–193) The Academy Museum of Motion Pictures sits across Wilshire Boulevard from the Peterson Automotive Museum, a single intersection of the city devoted to a big slice of LA: cars and movies.

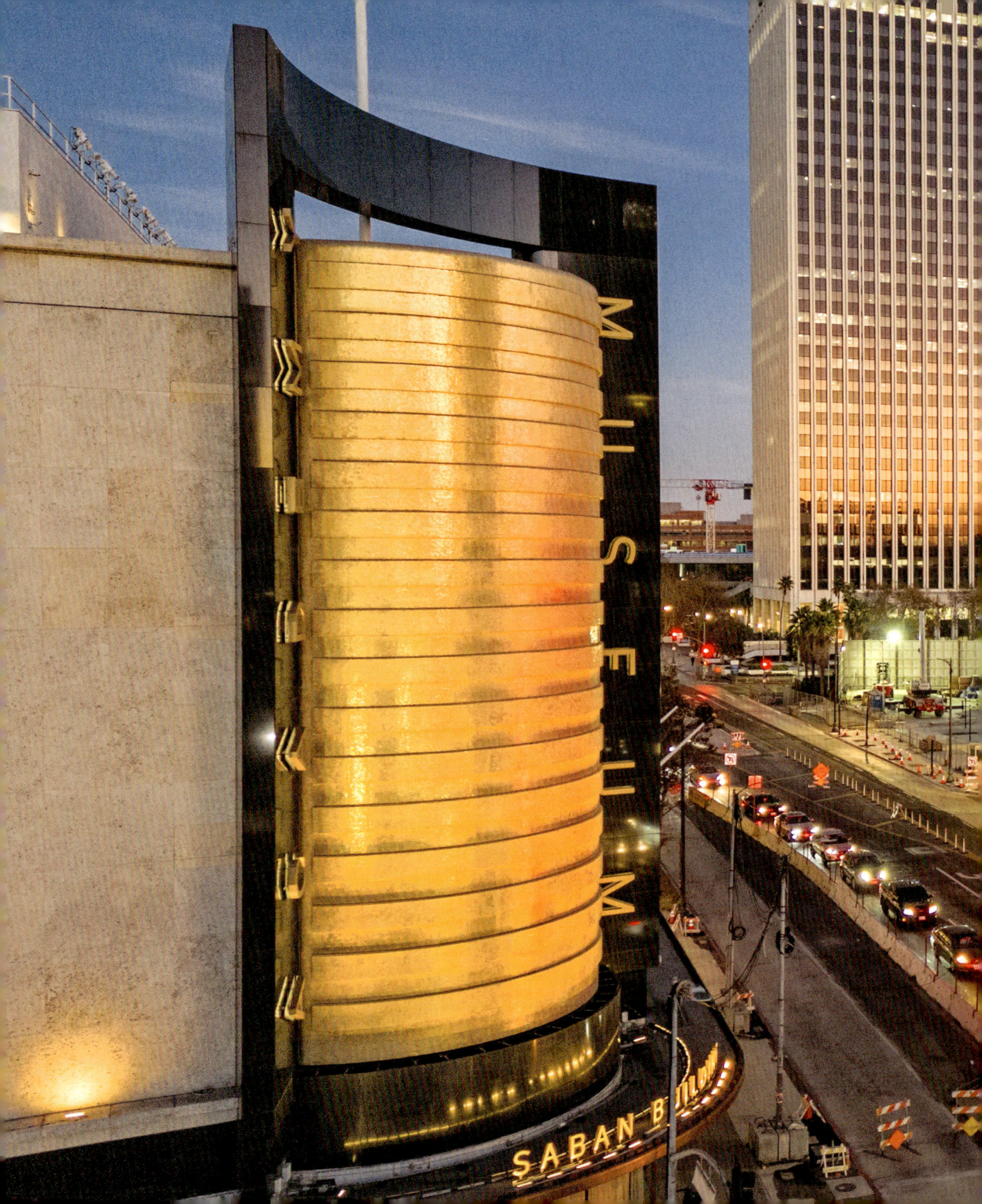
SABAN BUILDING

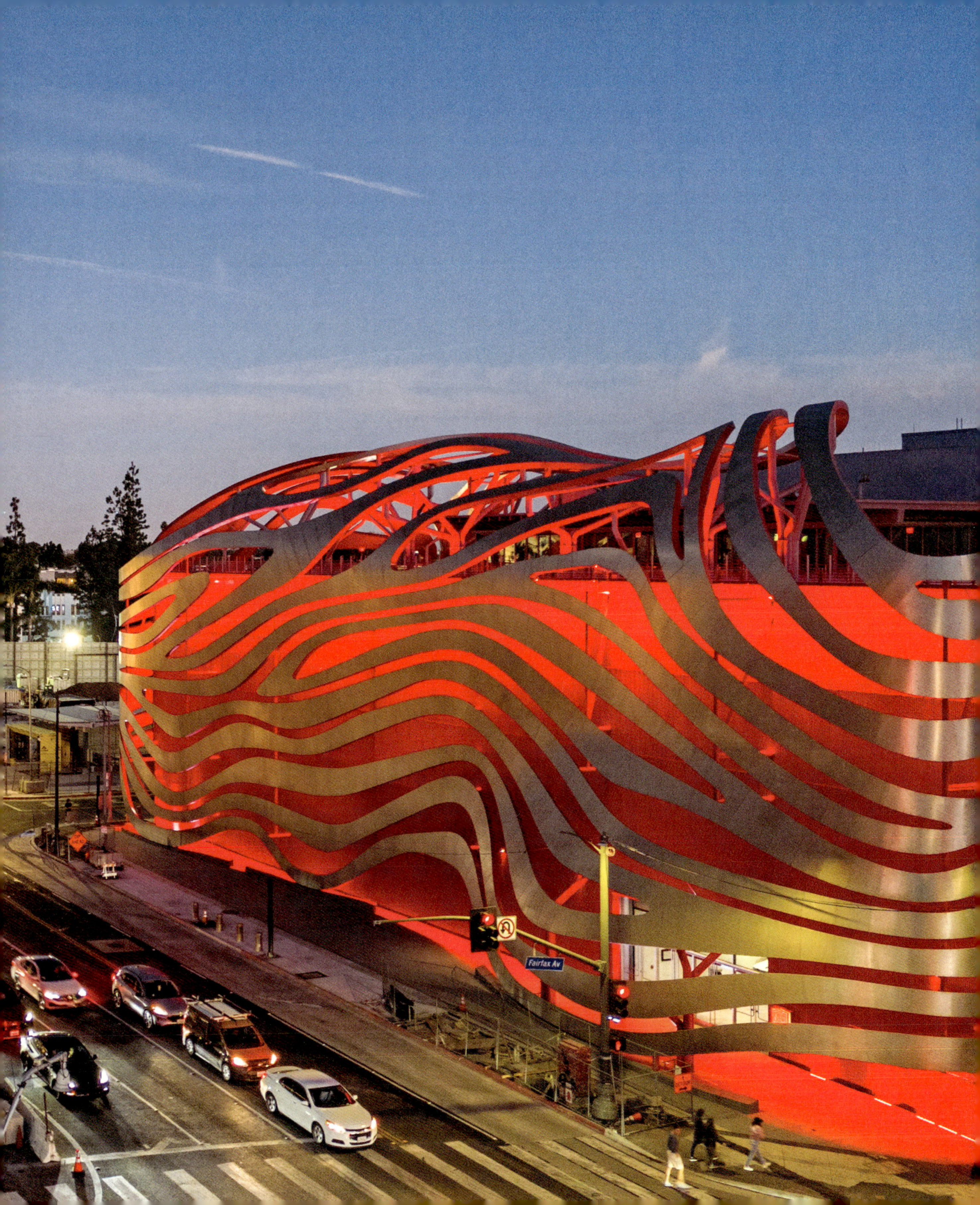
Fairfax Av

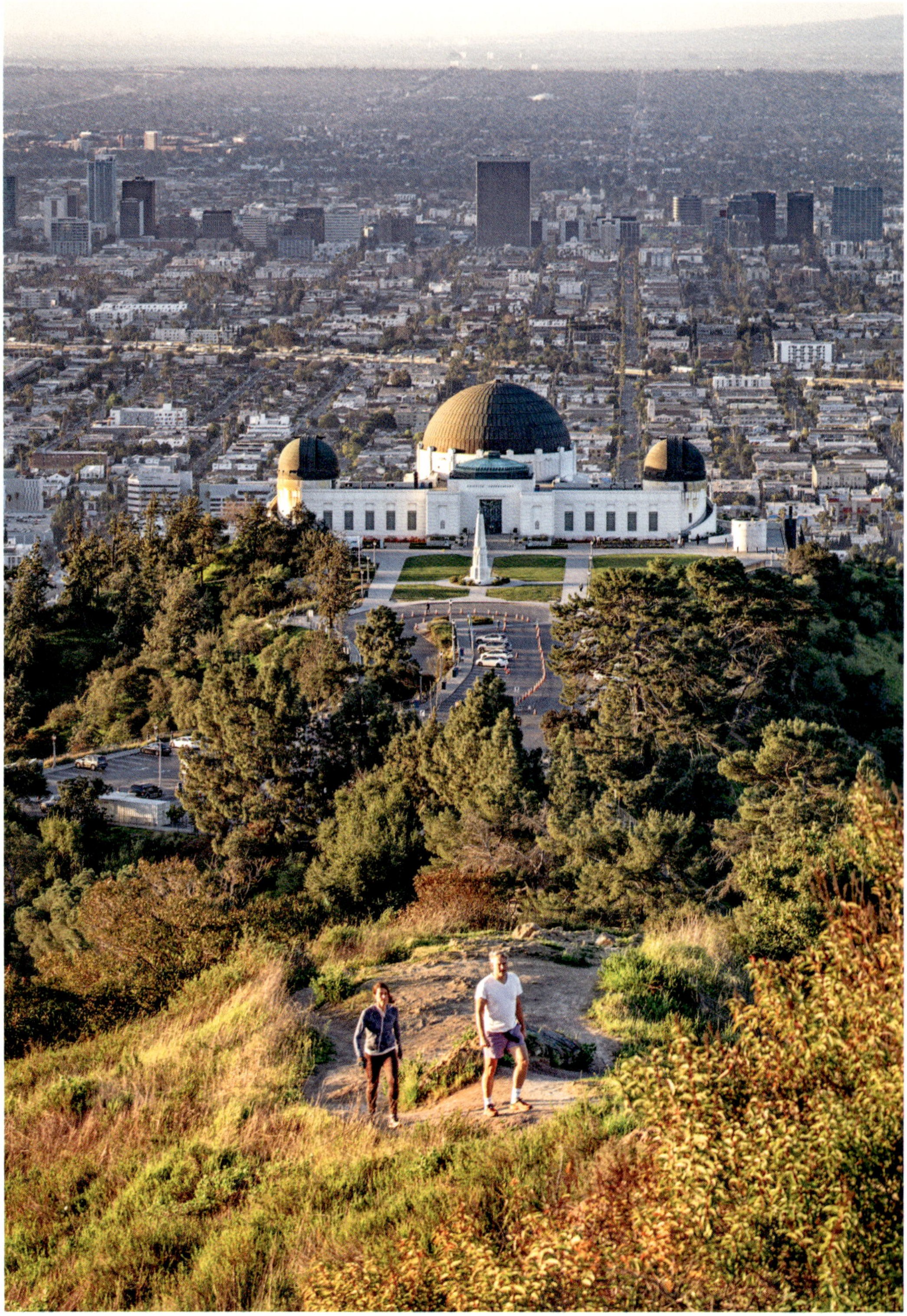

More than fifty-three miles of hiking trails exist in the rugged hills of Griffith Park, and almost all of them offer stunning views of the city below.

Griffith Park

The City's Wild Heart

This 4,210-acre public park looms over Hollywood and the rest of Los Angeles as the largest urban-wilderness municipal park in the US. More than ten million people a year visit its chaparral-covered hills to hike, play, picnic, or visit one of the park's many attractions. The star of the park is, of course, the beautiful Griffith Observatory, opened in 1935, one of the most famous landmarks in Southern California and a symbol of Los Angeles. The observatory's incredible architecture and stunning natural setting atop the Santa Monica Mountains make it a must-see attraction from the outside alone—inside, wonderful exhibits and programs bring the universe home.

There's so many more park attractions as well: several playgrounds, including the inclusive Shane's Inspiration; a historic Merry-Go-Round (the one that inspired Walt Disney to build Disneyland); the Los Angeles Zoo; the Autry Museum of the American West; the Greek Theatre; golf courses and tennis courts; Travel Town Museum; a small train to ride (Griffith Park & Southern Railroad); plus many trees to climb and fields to play on. There's also twenty-six miles of hiking trails, which can be traversed by foot or horse. One trail even leads to the iconic Hollywood Sign.

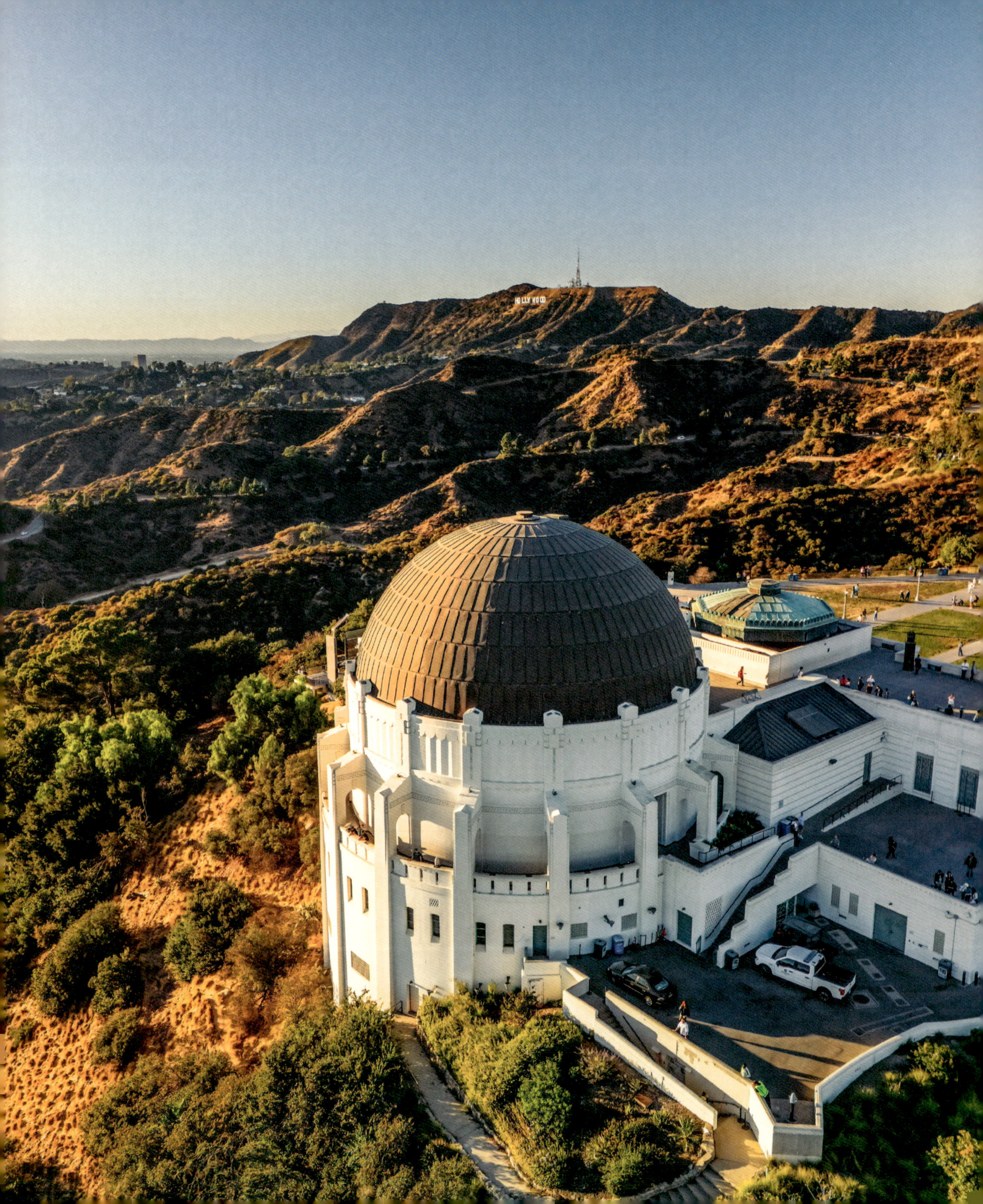

One of the best views of the iconic Hollywood Sign is from Griffith Observatory. While one can hike toward the sign along the park's trails, you cannot get too close to the actual sign—it's best just to enjoy the natural beauty that surrounds you.

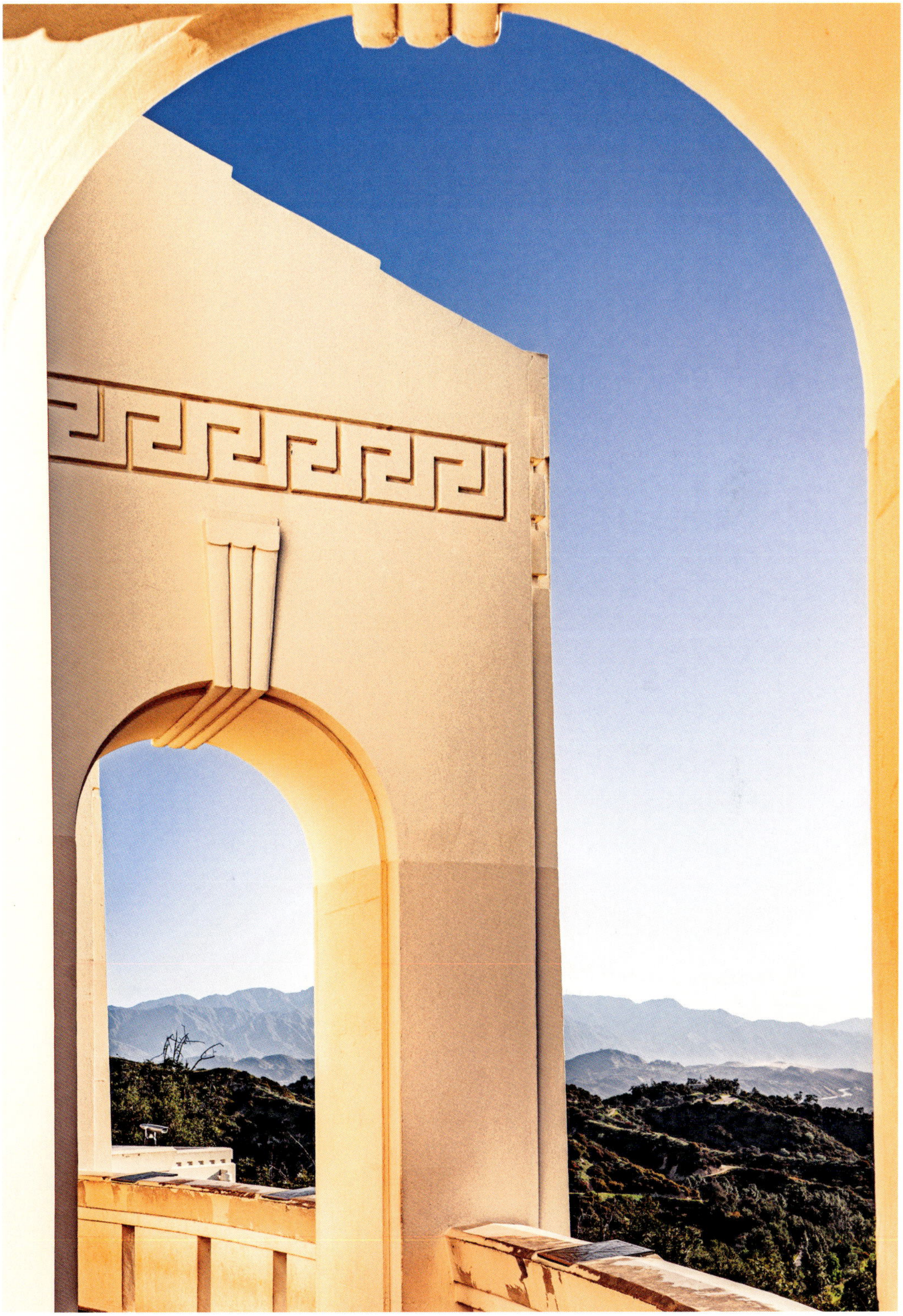

Of course a structure as beautiful as Griffith Observatory is a popular film location—the building has been featured in hundreds of films and television shows, most famously 1955's *Rebel Without a Cause.*

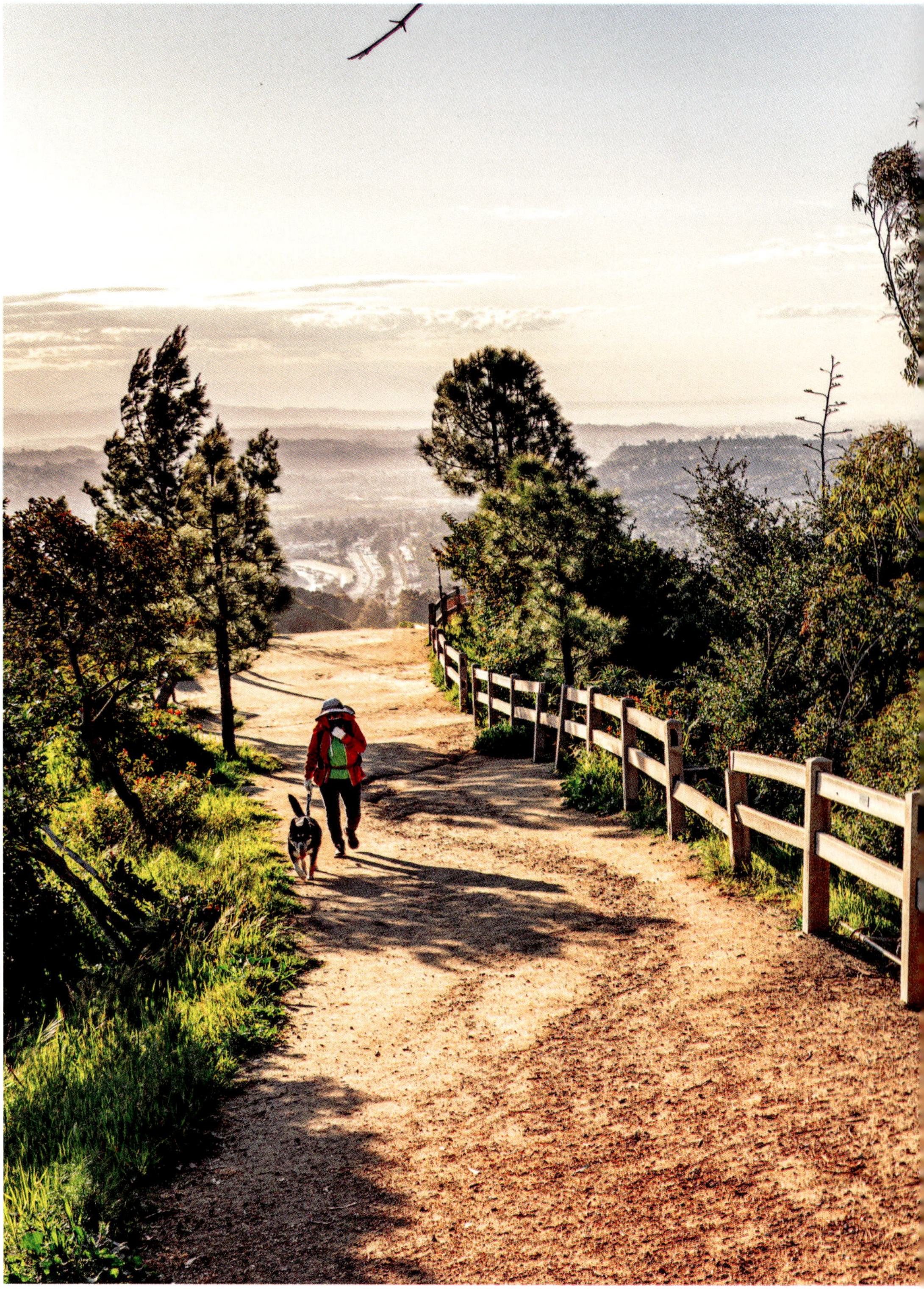

Dante's View is a special site in Griffith Park along the Mount Hollywood Trail where Angeleno Dante Orgolini once cultivated a garden. It offers a scenic vista of the entire LA basin to the Pacific Ocean, and like all of the park, is stewarded by the nonprofit Friends of Griffith Park.

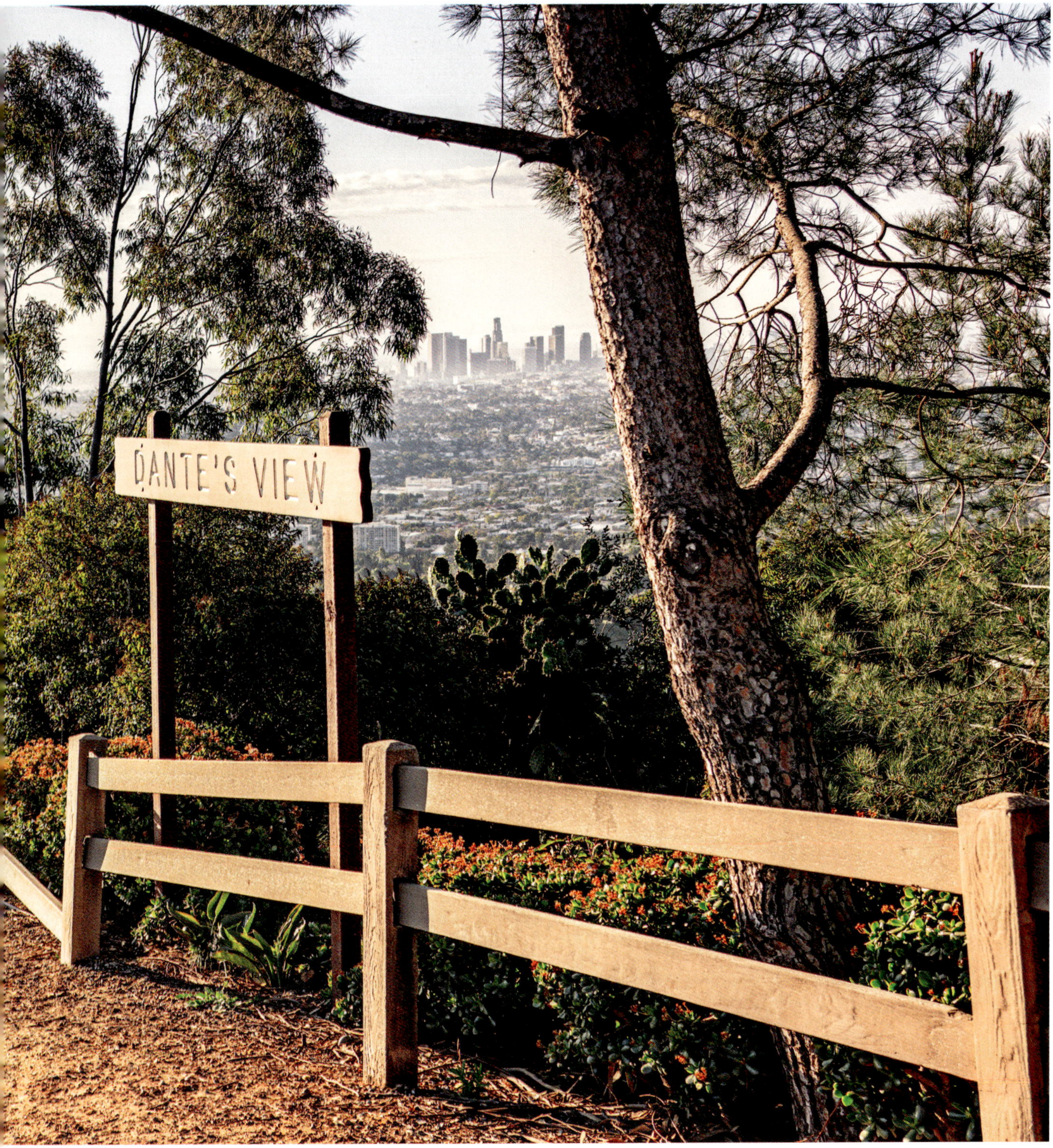
DANTE'S VIEW

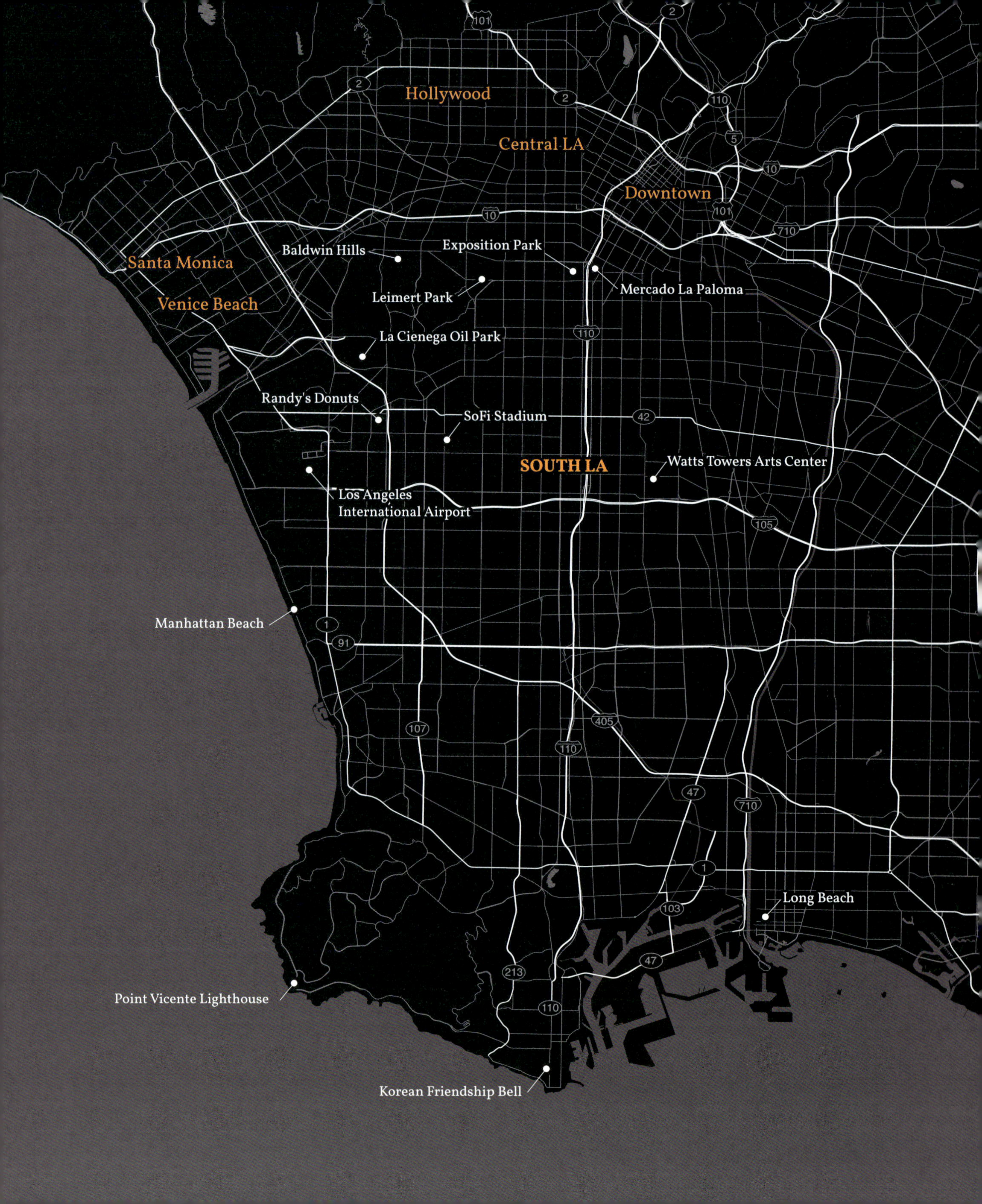

Hollywood
Central LA
Downtown
Santa Monica
Venice Beach
Baldwin Hills
Exposition Park
Leimert Park
Mercado La Paloma
La Cienega Oil Park
Randy's Donuts
SoFi Stadium
SOUTH LA
Watts Towers Arts Center
Los Angeles
International Airport
Manhattan Beach
Long Beach
Point Vicente Lighthouse
Korean Friendship Bell

South Los Angeles

Iconic Sites

Vibrant Neighborhoods with Rich Cultural Histories and Vibrant Communities

As stated earlier, splitting the city up into geographical areas is tricky because Los Angeles is a big, sprawling metropolitan region, full of other cities and also unincorporated areas that are part of the metro region if not part of the city of LA. For instance, Beverly Hills, Santa Monica, Inglewood, Compton, Pasadena, and Long Beach are all cities in their own right, whereas (confusingly) Studio City, Venice, San Pedro, and most of the San Fernando Valley are actually part of the city of Los Angeles. Moving about, one hardly notices the differences in these designations—it all feels like part of LA—but there there are larger stories behind each place.

What is "South LA" then? It's a vibrant and diverse region comprised of many neighborhoods—Baldwin Hills, West Adams, Crenshaw, Exposition Park, Jefferson Park, Historic South Central, and Leimert Park, to name just a few—as well as a few cities such as Inglewood and Compton that are geographically south of downtown and the 10 freeway. This area is also known as South Central, given its proximity to Central Los Angeles, and has long been a center of Black life and community in LA.

Whether you call this broad area—which we made even bigger by including the South Bay and Long Beach—South Central, South Los Angeles, or the newest nickname, SOLA, what you find remains: incredible history, culture, architecture, art, parks, and lots of community spirit. It's home base for hip-hop history: Ice Cube, Dr. Dre, Eazy-E, Kendrick Lamar, and Snoop Dogg are all from South LA. Today, Crenshaw, Leimert Park, and West Adams are thriving centers of Black Los Angeles; Compton, which once was a sought-after suburb for the Black middle class, is now 70 percent Latino. Torrance has the second-largest population of Japanese Americans in the US. South Los Angeles is so diverse because, historically, it was one of the places new immigrants or people of color could lease land or rent or buy homes due to restrictive racial covenants in other parts of the city.

A little-known fact is that the first Olympic Village was built in South Los Angeles—constructed in Baldwin Hills for the 1932 games. How fitting that so many of the 2028 events will also be held in South Los Angeles.

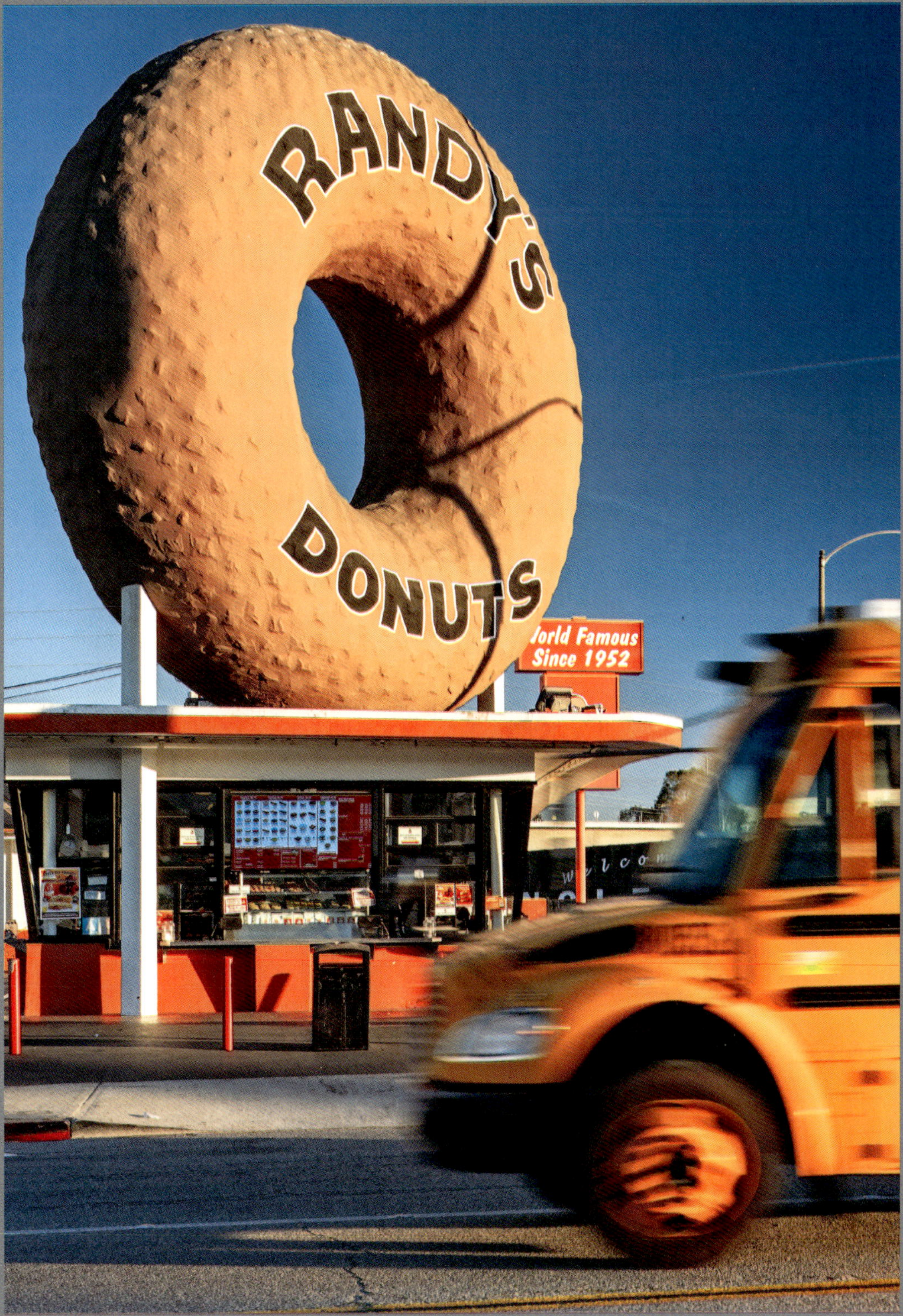

Opened on Manchester Boulevard in Inglewood in 1952, the original location of Randy's Donuts is the most recognized donut shop in the world.

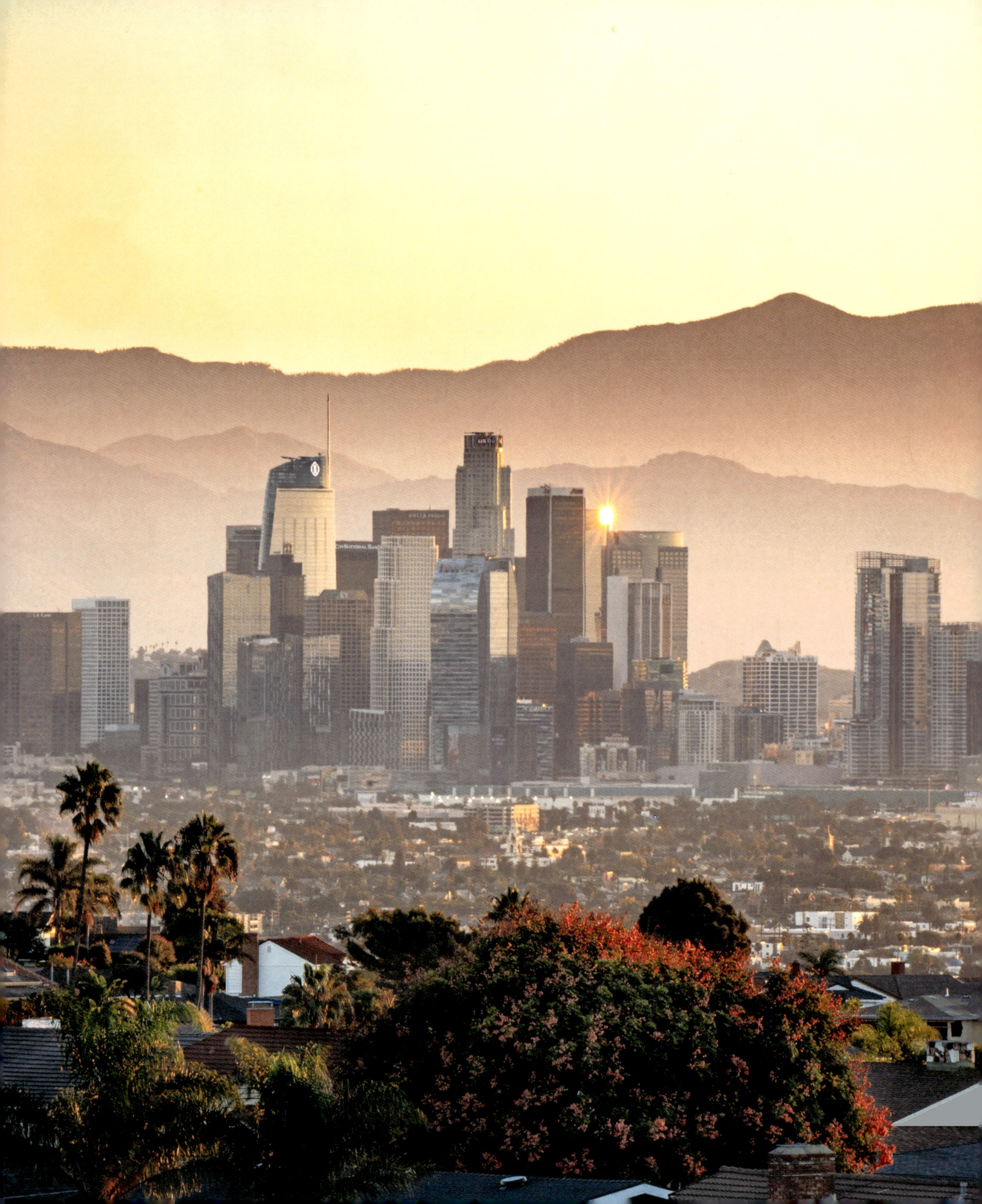

A panoramic view of the downtown skyline from the viewpoint in the Kenneth Hahn State Recreation Area is only one of the many offerings at this expansive park located in Baldwin Hills.

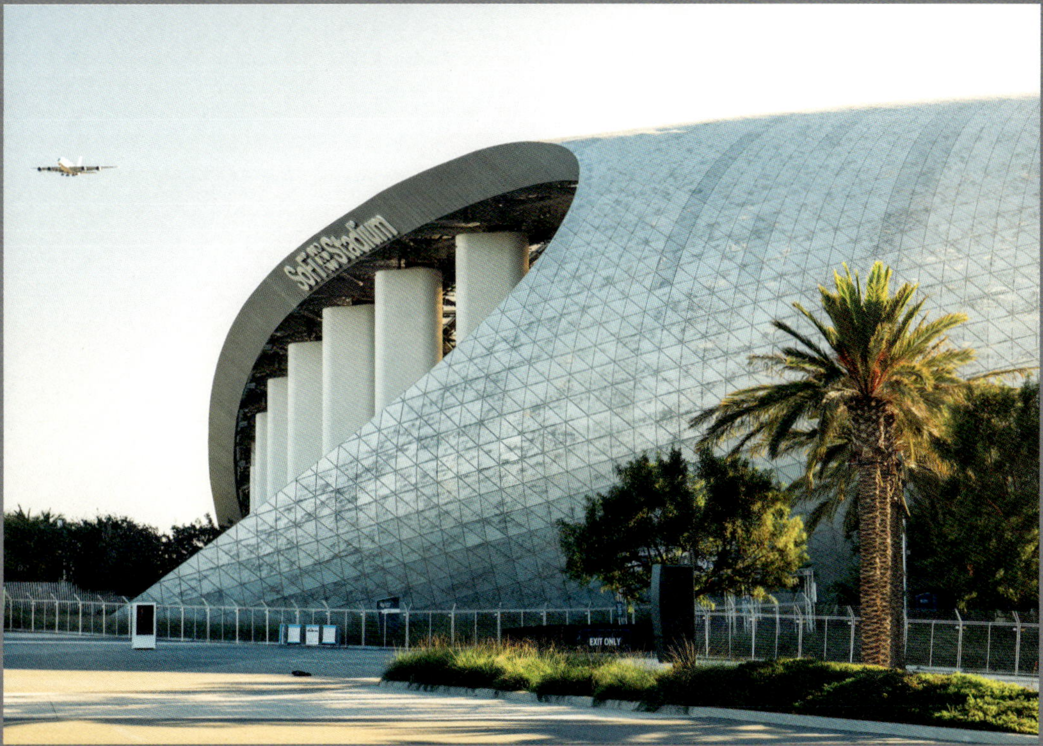

Home of two NFL teams, Inglewood's SoFi Stadium is one of three major sports venues in the neighborhood; the others are the Kia Forum and the Intuit Dome.

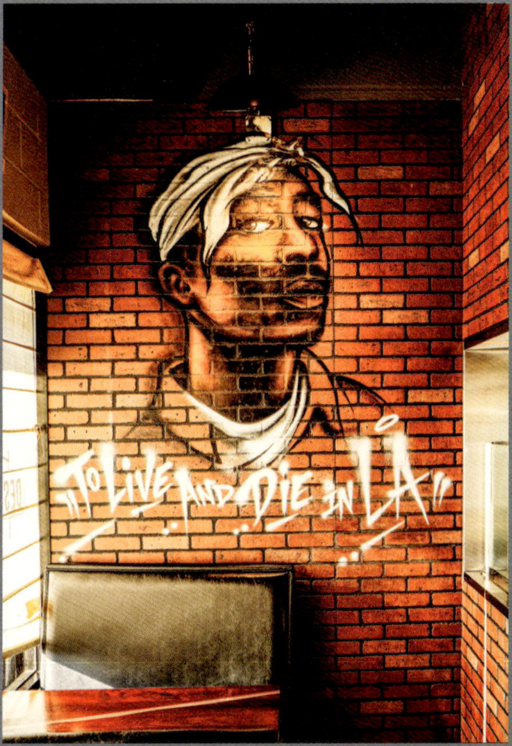

A mural in a restaurant features rapper Tupac Shakur, whose song "To Live and Die in L.A." is an anthem to the city and a love song for South LA.

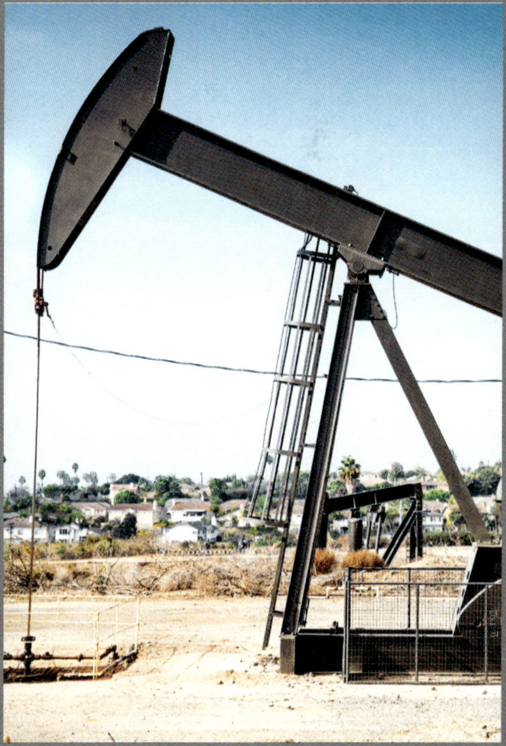

While efforts have been made to end oil drilling in the city, residents in some areas of South LA have lived next to oil wells for decades.

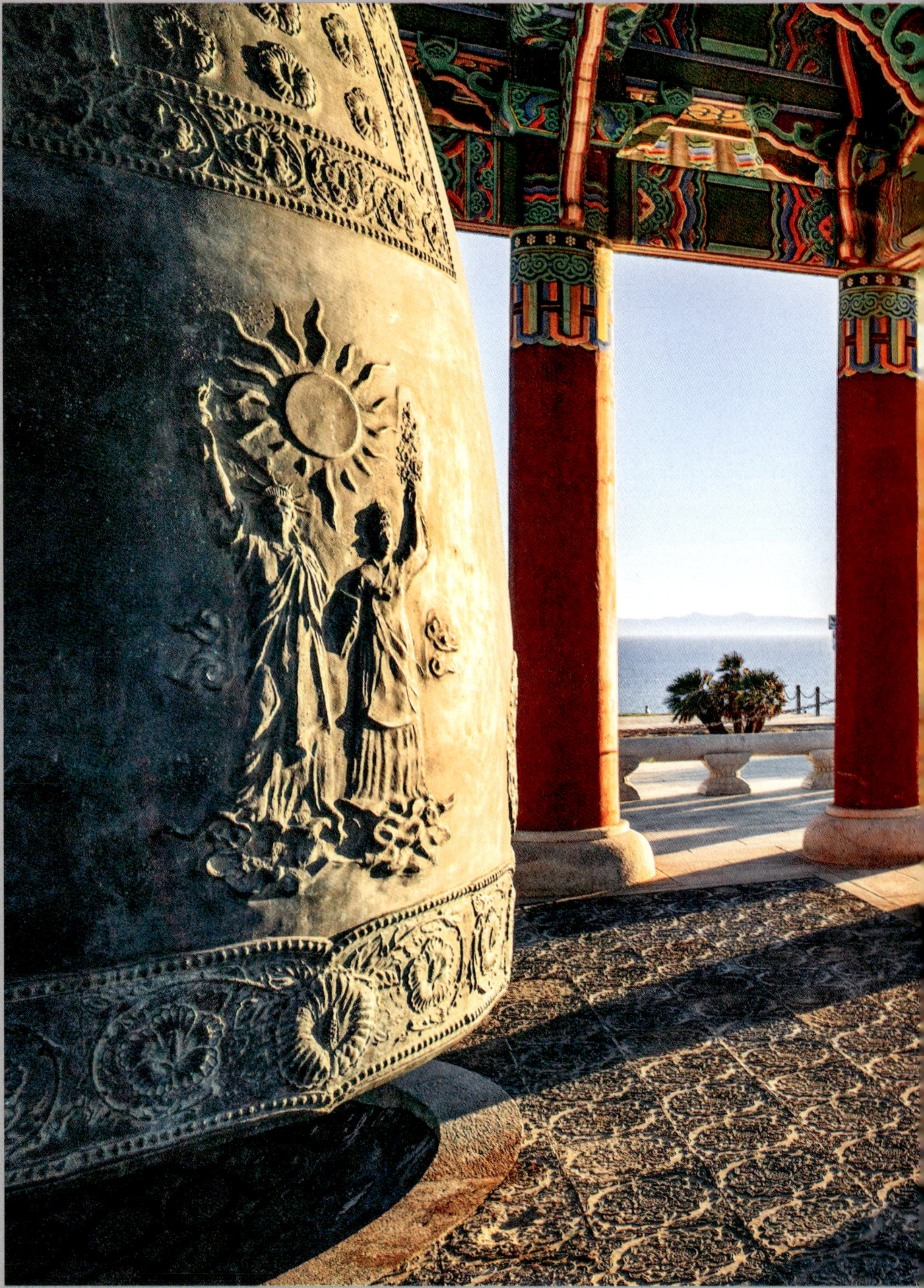

The Korean Bell of Friendship is a gift from South Korea, perched on an idyllic spot in San Pedro's Angels Gate Park.

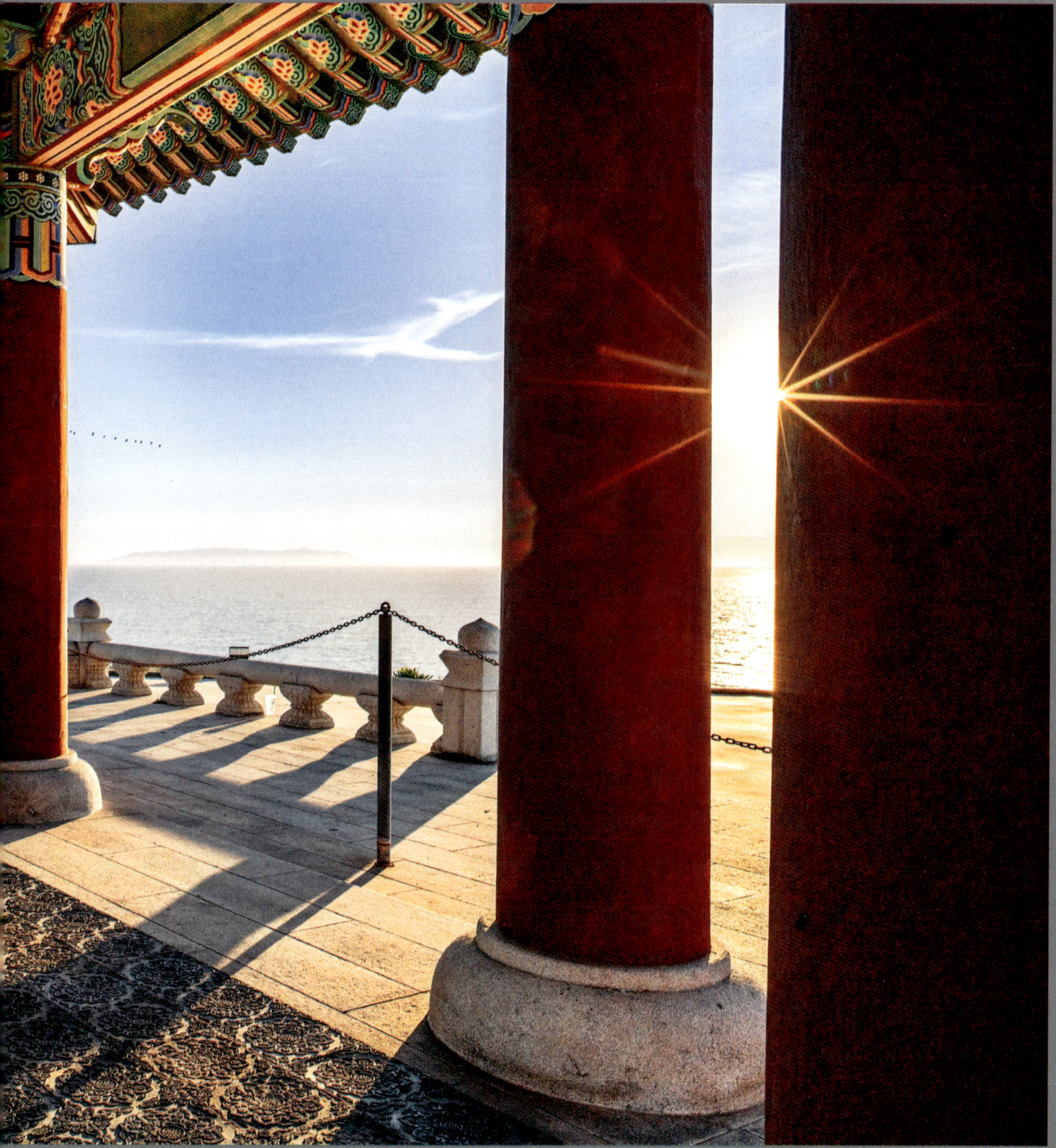

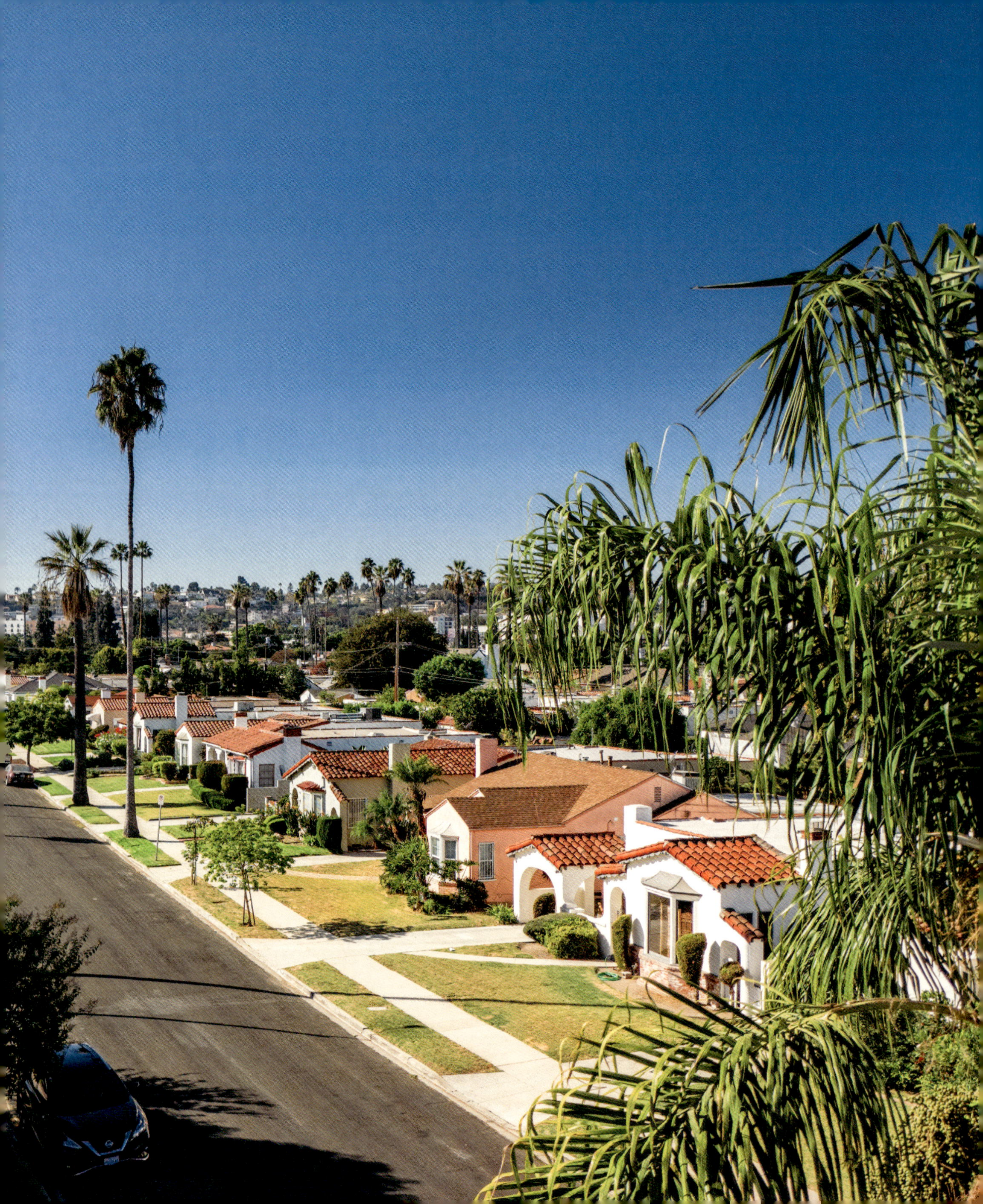

The Leimert Park neighborhood is a center of Black culture in LA. Former residents include musicians Ella Fitzgerald and Ray Charles, and the public park that is the hub of the neighborhood hosts a legendary drum circle.

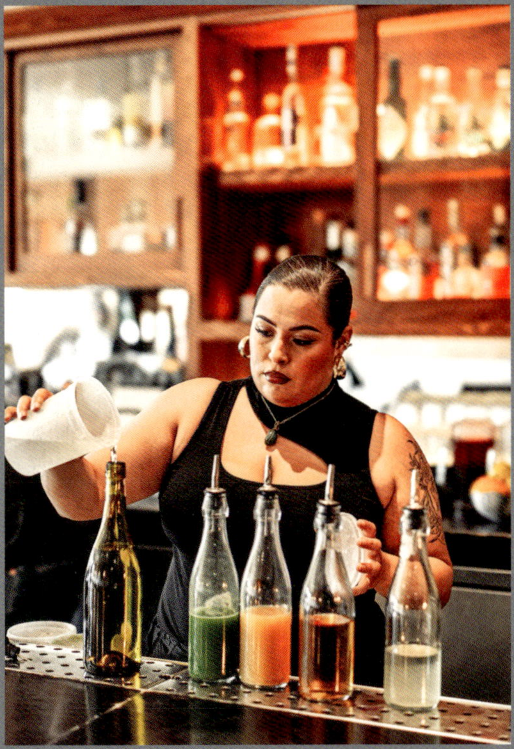

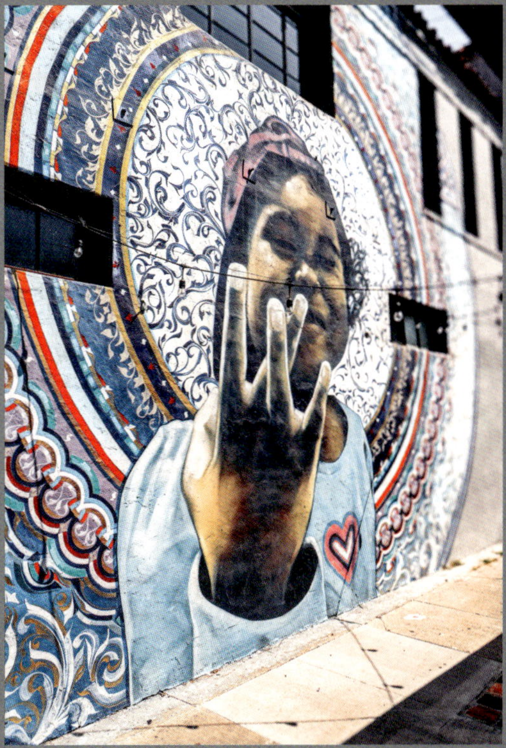

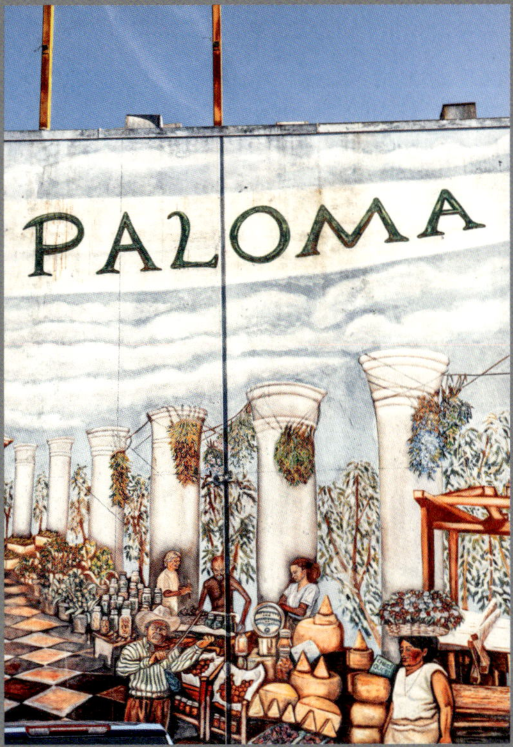

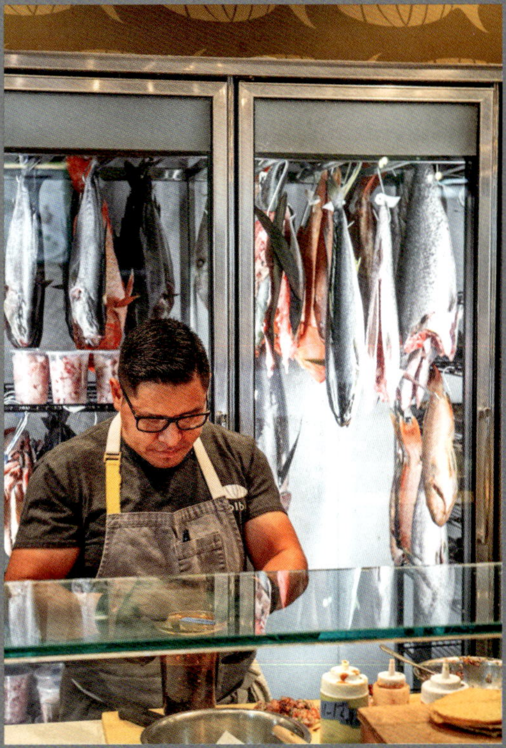

Located in the historic West Adams neighborhood, the Alta Adams restaurant is a community hub frequented by stars such as Issa Rae and Tracee Ellis Ross.

Outside Alta Adams is a mural by LA artist AiseBorn.

A former garment factory in South Central LA, Mercado La Paloma is a community gathering space with a fantastic food hall.

Holbox, one of many vendors in the Mercado La Paloma, is a Michelin-star rated Mexican seafood restaurant.

(Page 210–211) Home of the second largest port in the US, the Long Beach International Gateway bridge has to be tall enough for container ships to pass through—it is the first long-span, cable-stayed bridge in California.

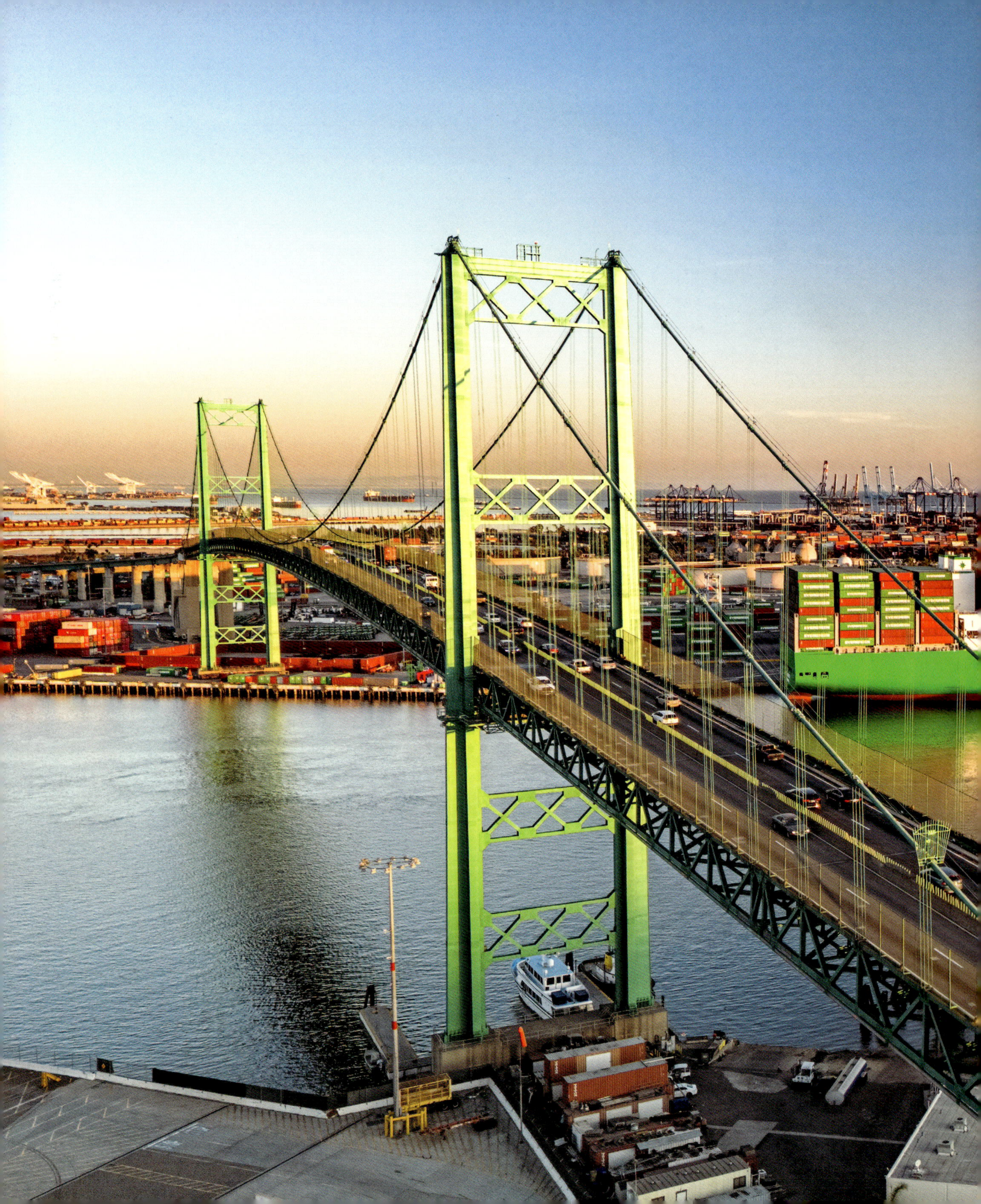

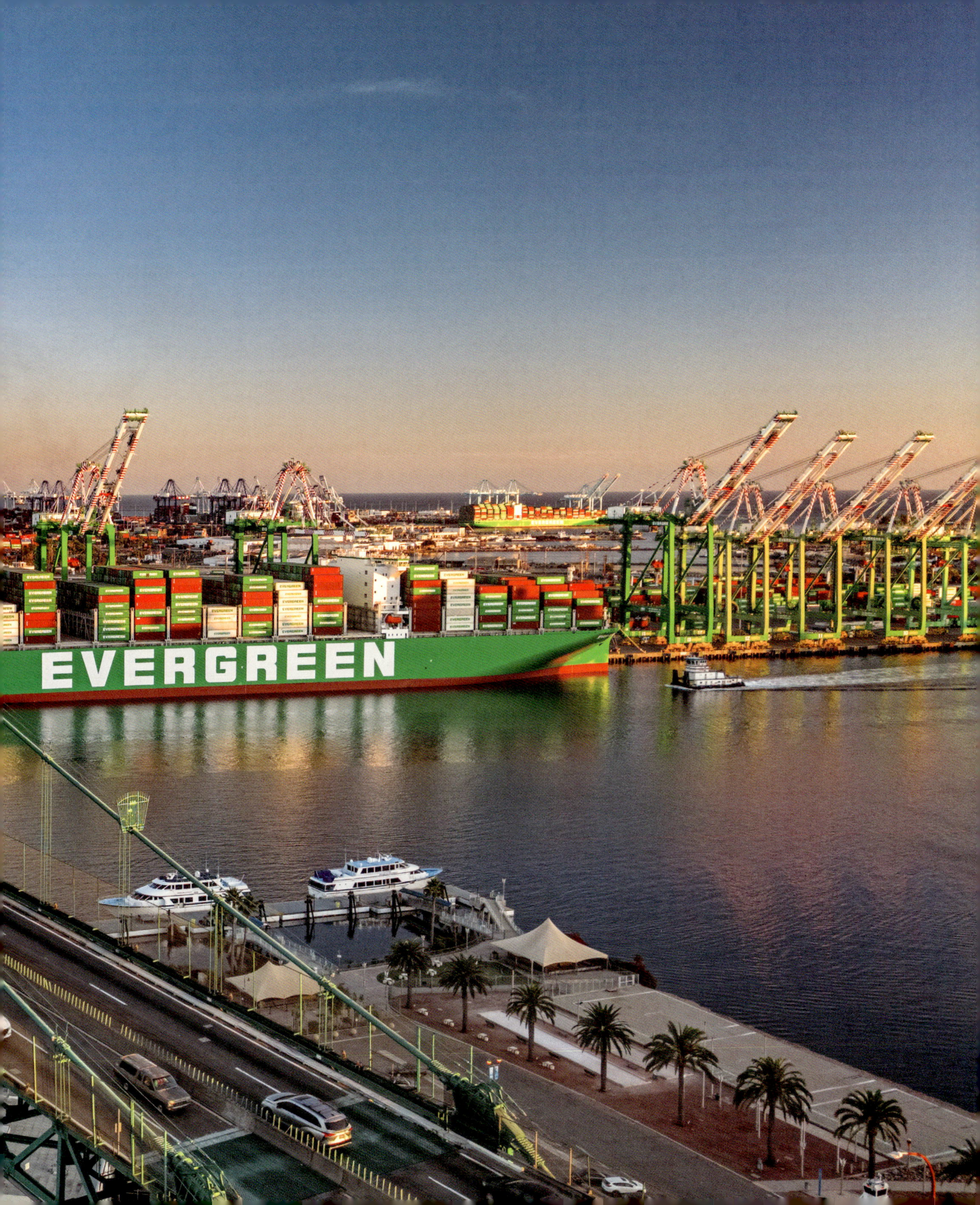
EVERGREEN

Exposition Park

Crossroads of Culture, Community, and Sport

To call this collection of museums, sports arenas, and entertainment venues a park seems like a huge understatement—this 160-acre complex is a world-class cultural center. Located in South Los Angeles, near the University of Southern California and the neighborhoods of University Park, West Adams, and Jefferson Park, this grand expanse of public recreation and educational resources was founded in 1913 on the site of a former agricultural park. Back then, the timing of the grand opening for the new park and museum coincided with the opening of the Owens River Aqueduct, the water conveyance system that takes water from the Sierra Nevada mountains to supply a significant portion of LA's water. When the park was originally dedicated, the fountain in the middle of the sunken rose garden spewed a jet of water into the air.

More than a century later, the area continues to be a public gathering place for a variety of activities, from browsing the world-class collections in the museums to being part of the epicenter of LA sports. There's something to do for everyone, even if it's just sitting in the shade of one of the park's historic trees or having a picnic on the lawn of the Natural History Museum.

As far as the sports venues go, there's an impressive array in Exposition Park. BMO Stadium is the home of both the Los Angeles Football Club and the Angel City Football Club teams, and will host flag football and lacrosse in the 2028 Olympics. The LA 84 Foundation/John C. Argue Swim Stadium, which was built for the 1932 Olympic Games, will be used for diving competitions. Of course, the granddaddy of all sports stadiums in the city, Los Angeles Memorial Coliseum, home of the opening and closing ceremonies, is the first venue in history to have hosted events for three different Olympic Games.

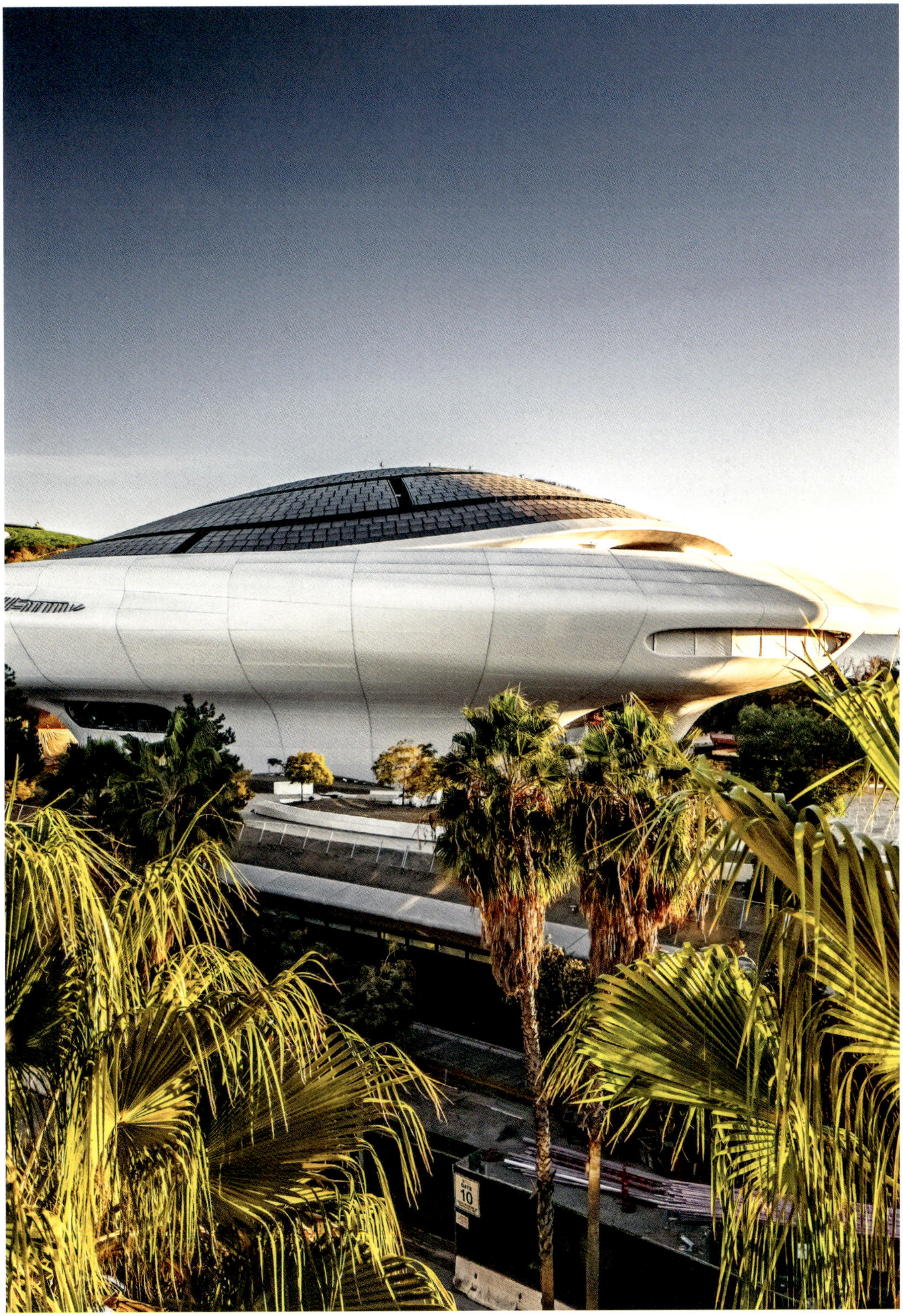

The spaceship-shaped Lucas Museum of Narrative Art, a 300,000-square-foot museum, is one of four major museums located in Exposition Park—the others are the California African American Museum, the California Science Center, and the Natural History Museum of Los Angeles County.

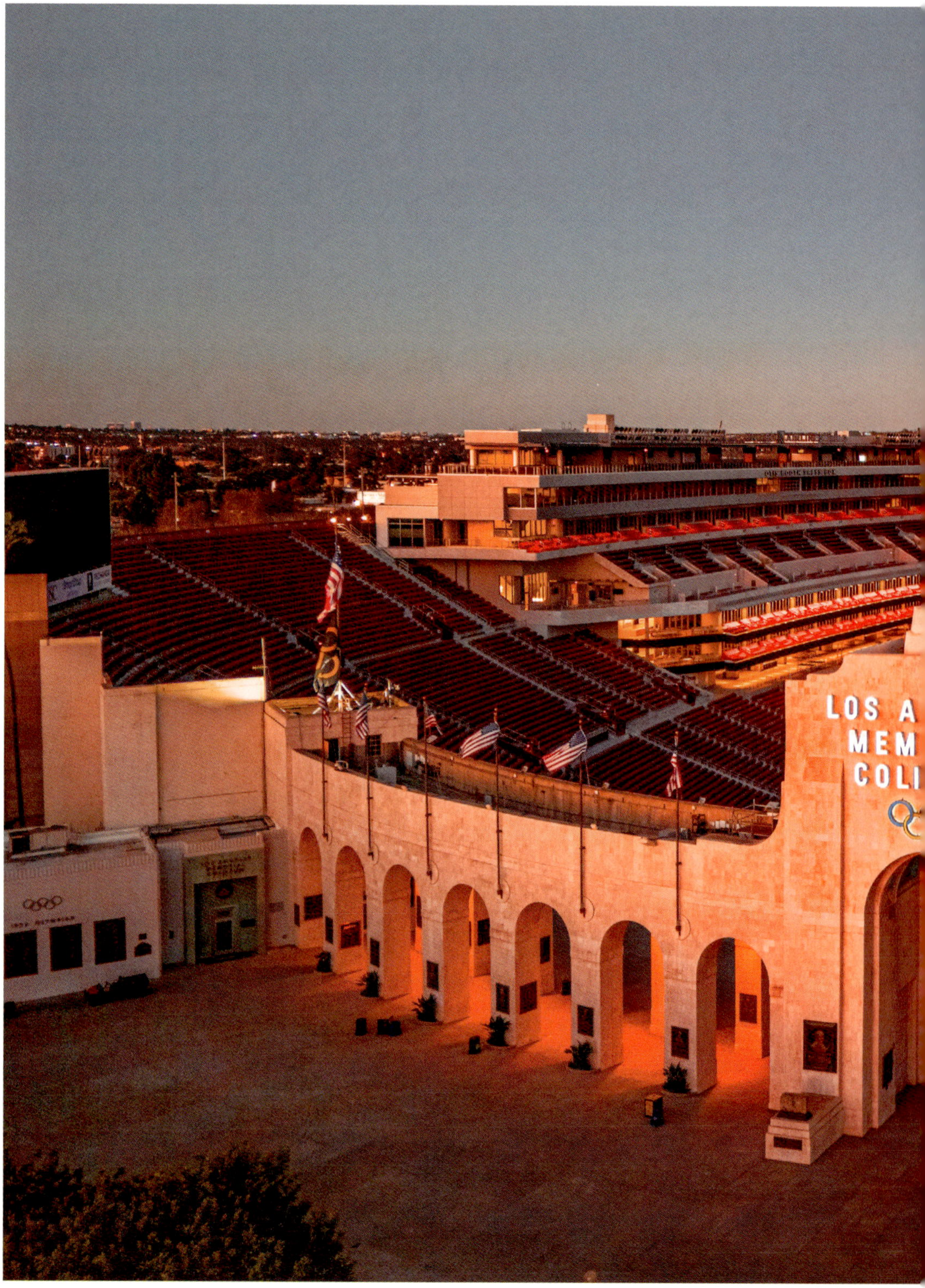

Los Angeles Memorial Coliseum, built in 1923, is known as the Greatest Stadium in the World and has hosted two summer Olympiads (1932 and 1984)—and will host a third in 2028—as well as many professional sports teams, world leaders, and pop stars—from Mick Jagger to Martin Luther King, Jr.

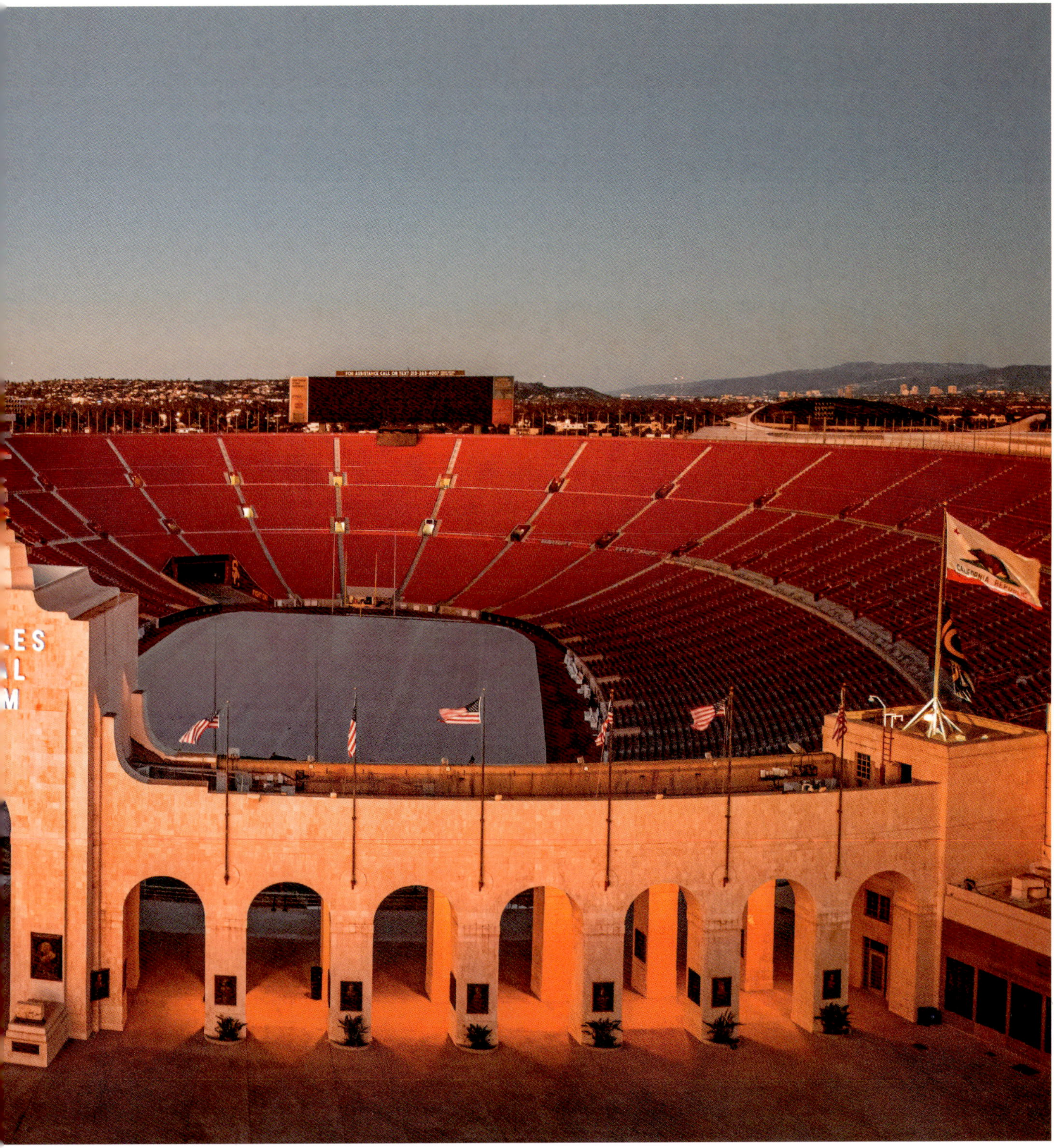

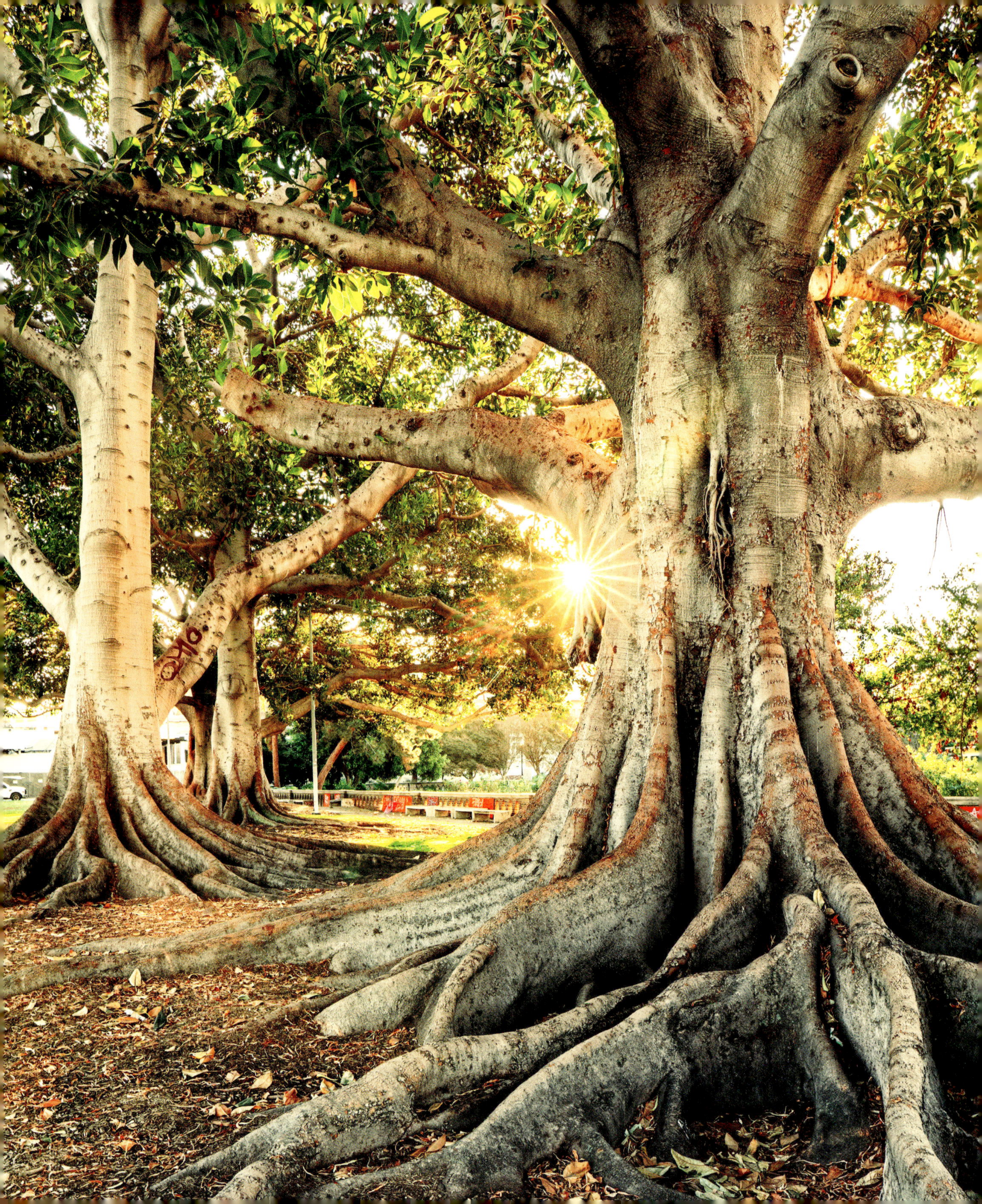

A row of Moreton Bay fig trees grow near Exposition Park's Rose Garden.

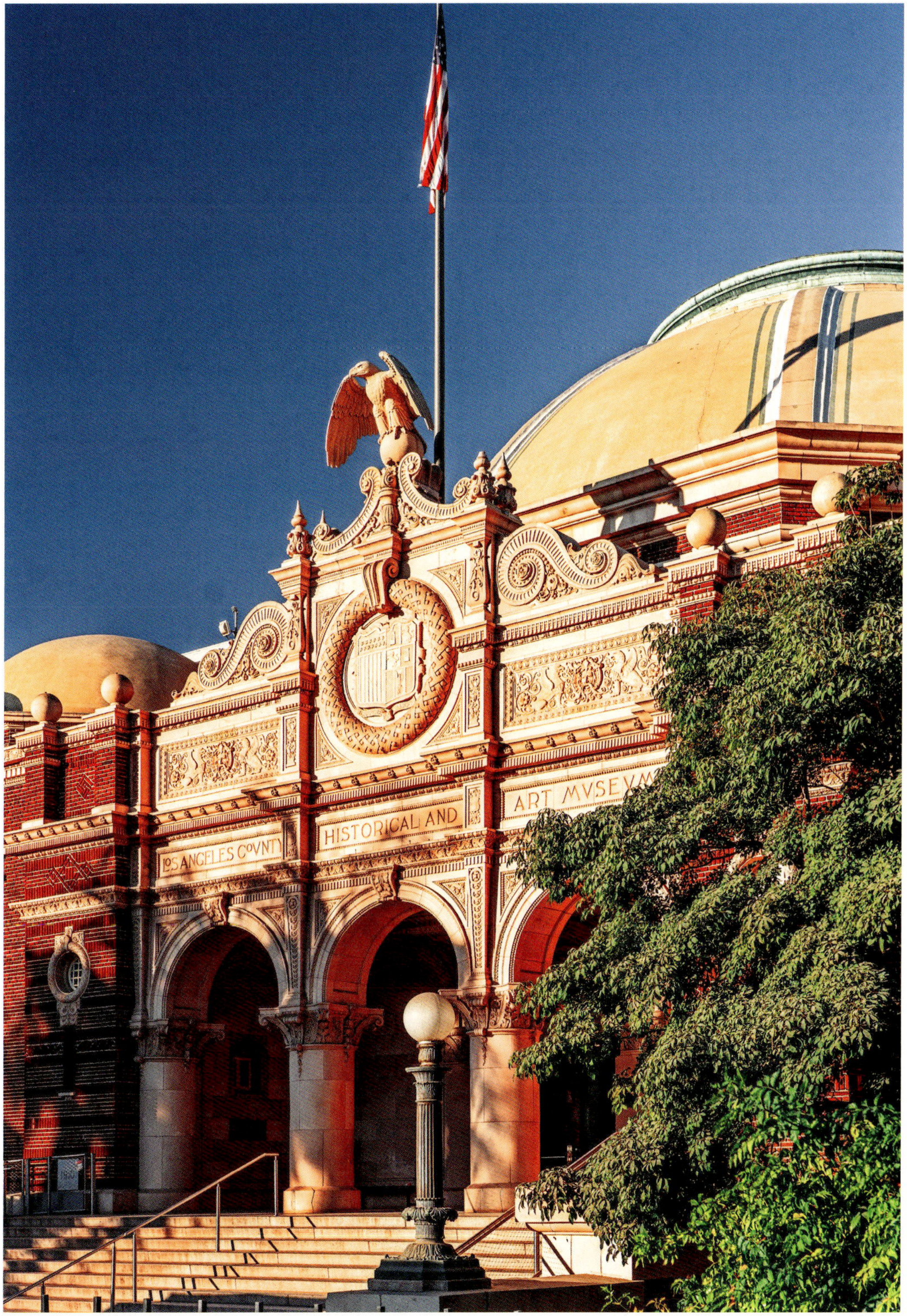

Facing the rose garden in Exposition Park, the original 1913 building was for many years the sole museum for Los Angeles. Today, there are more than 800 museums in LA, and the city is known for having more museums per capita than any other metropolis.

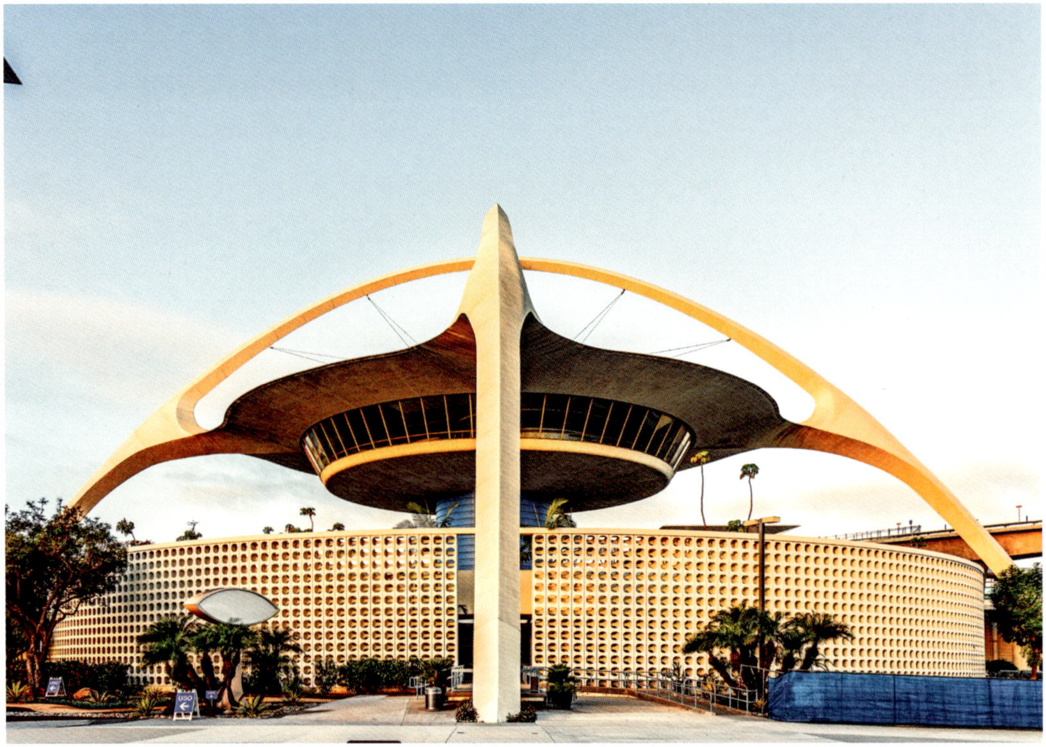

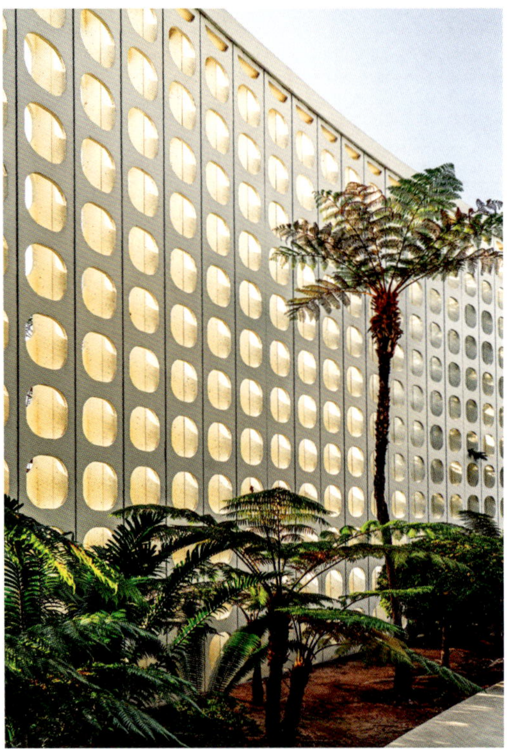

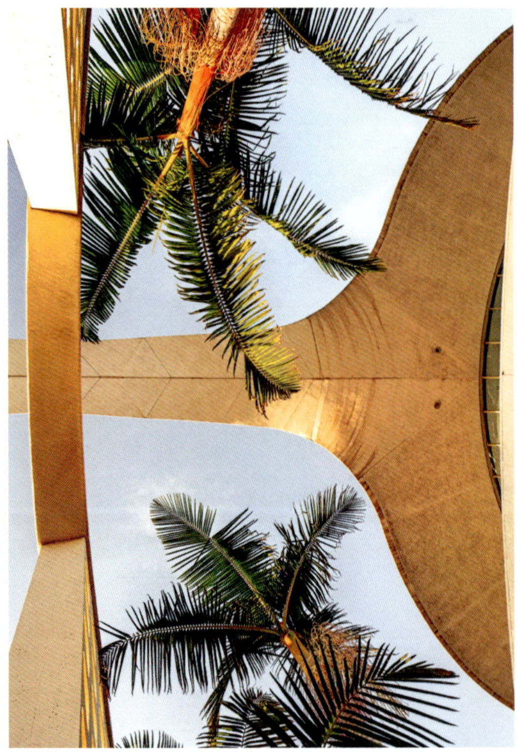

Completed in 1961, LAX's Theme Building is a modern icon that once had a restaurant in its center—hopefully it will again!

Concrete blocks encircle the Theme Building, adding to the mid-century vibe.

Great architecture and palm trees greet visitors from the very beginning.

(Page 220–221) "We are all citizens of Los Angeles because we have seen so many movies." —Writer D.J. Waldie

LAX

The City of the Future Today

Love it or hate it, Los Angeles International Airport (LAX) will probably be the first spot on any itinerary (unless one flies into a smaller regional airport), so why not take a second to appreciate how cool it really is. More than 75-million passengers a year use the airport and its iconic, space-age design captures the spirit of the city—optimistic, retro-futuristic, and dramatic.

Originally founded as Mines Field in 1928, commercial airline service didn't start here until 1946—and it's been busy ever since. An expansion in the 1960s added the U-shaped terminals with the fantastic, spider-like Theme Building in its center. Designed by the architectural firm Pereira & Luckman, this mid-century masterpiece offers a fitting welcome to the city.

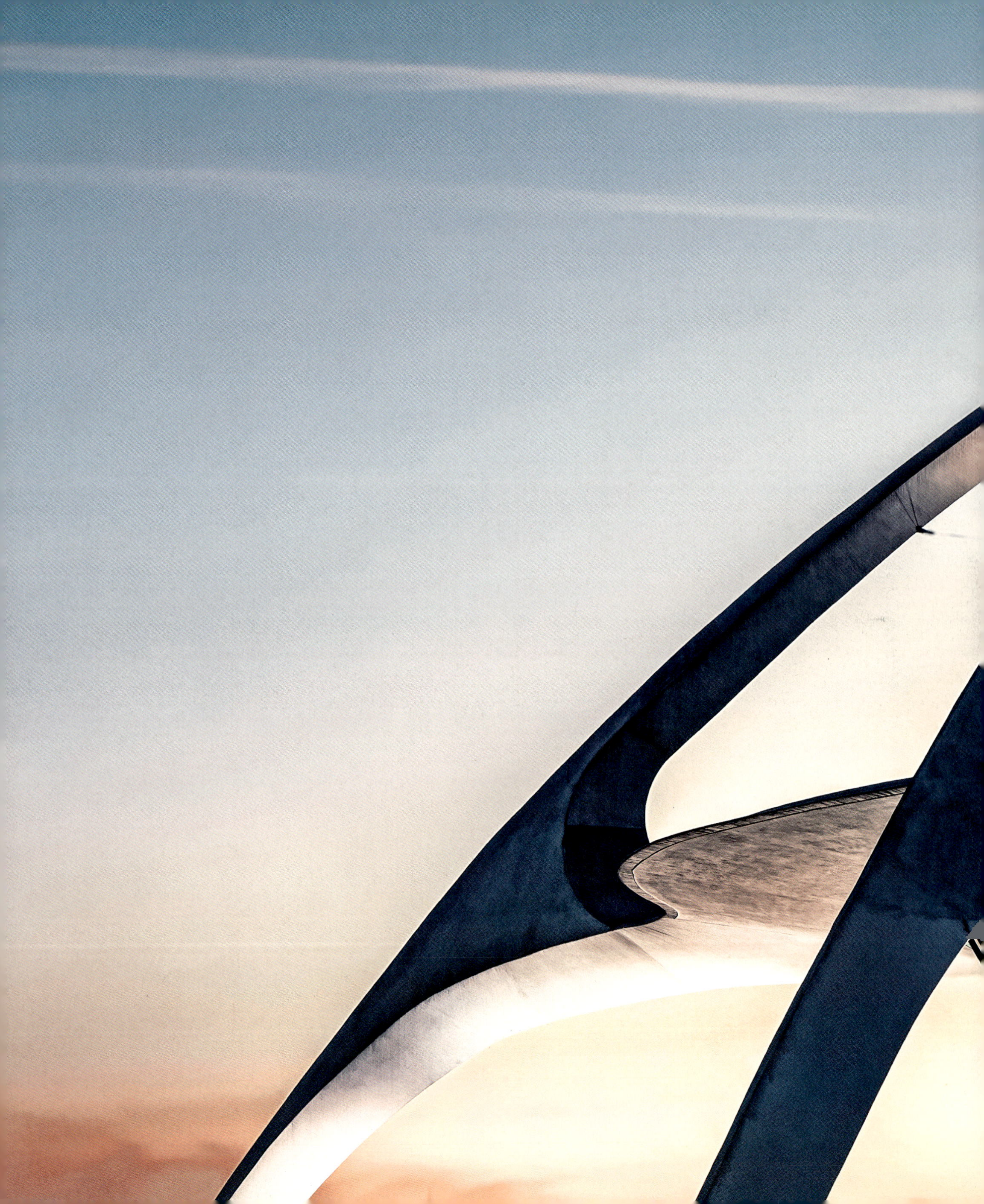

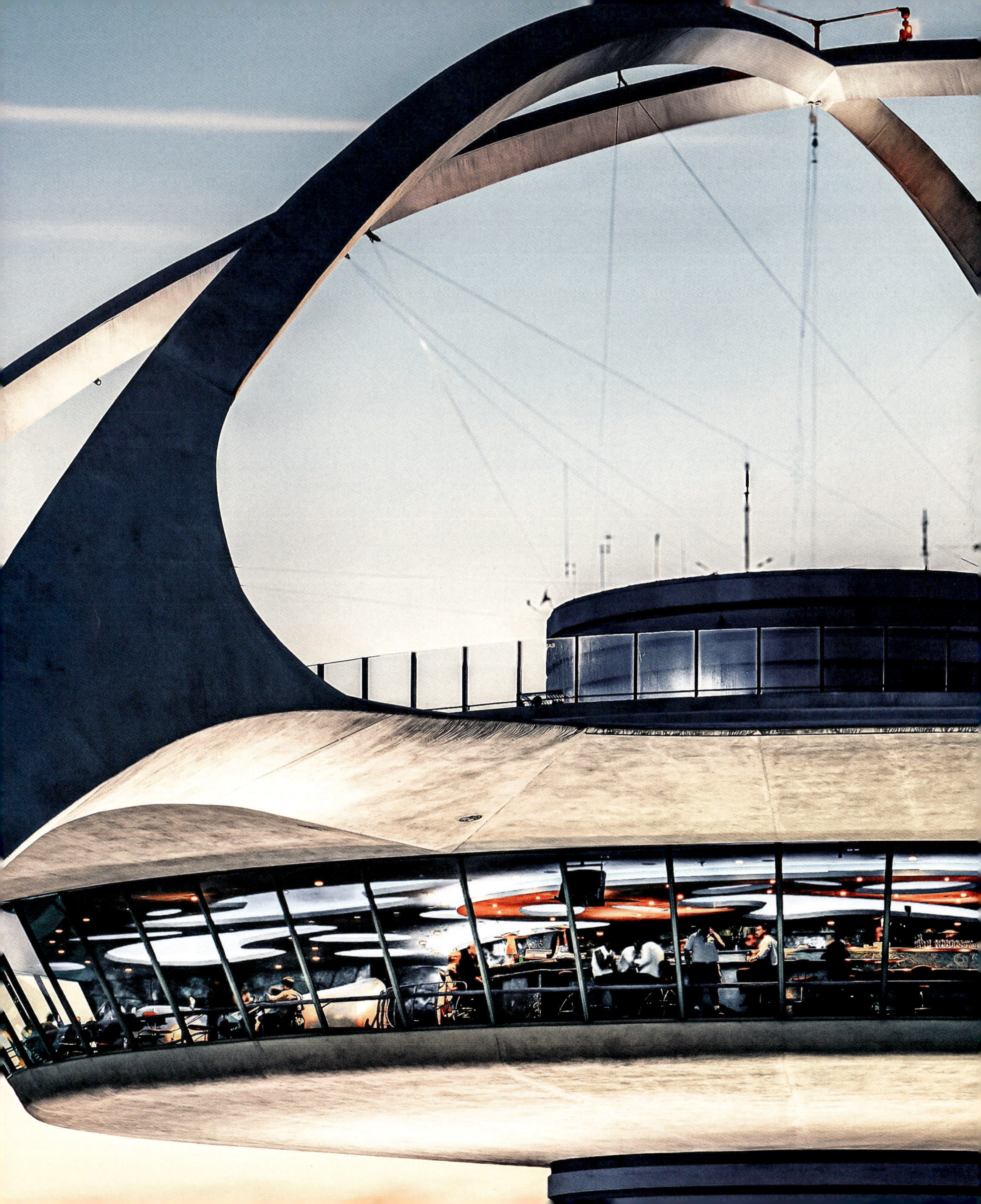

Watts Towers Art Center

Visionary Work of Art, Beacon of Creativity, and Hub of Community

Built by Italian immigrant Simon Rodia over the course of thirty-four years, the towering, colorful Watts Towers are a monument to community and creativity. Located in the community of Watts in South Central LA, these seventeen, interconnected sculptures have been called "the paramount work of folk art of the twentieth century in the United States," and serve as the world's largest single construction created by a single person. Rodia called his masterpiece "Nuestro Pueblo" or "Our Town," and the steel sculptures, fortified by thin-shell concrete and covered with mortar embedded with beautiful shards of tile, ceramics, and glass, have become a symbol of the city. Stretching up to the sky, as colorful and visionary as the city around it, this work of art is a singular expression of Los Angeles that should not be missed.

Along with the towers, the Watts Towers Arts Center hosts exhibitions of contemporary art with programming and classes for the community. The Center offers guided tours of the Watts Towers certain days of the week, so check the website before going. Prepare to be inspired by Rodia's towers as so many great artists have been, from musician Charles Mingus to poet Robert Duncan.

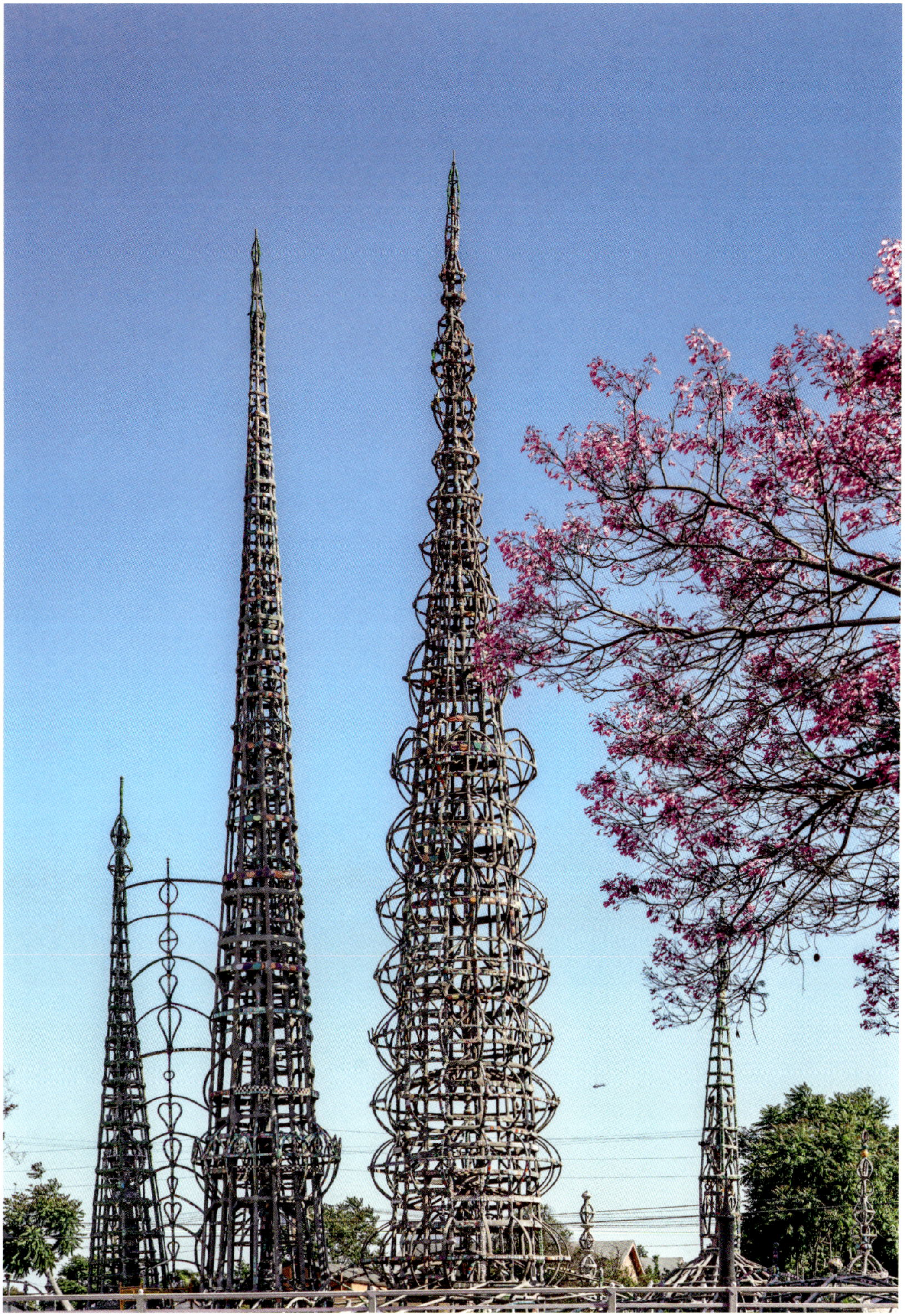

The 2006 documentary film *I Build the Tower* is a visual history of the construction of the towers.

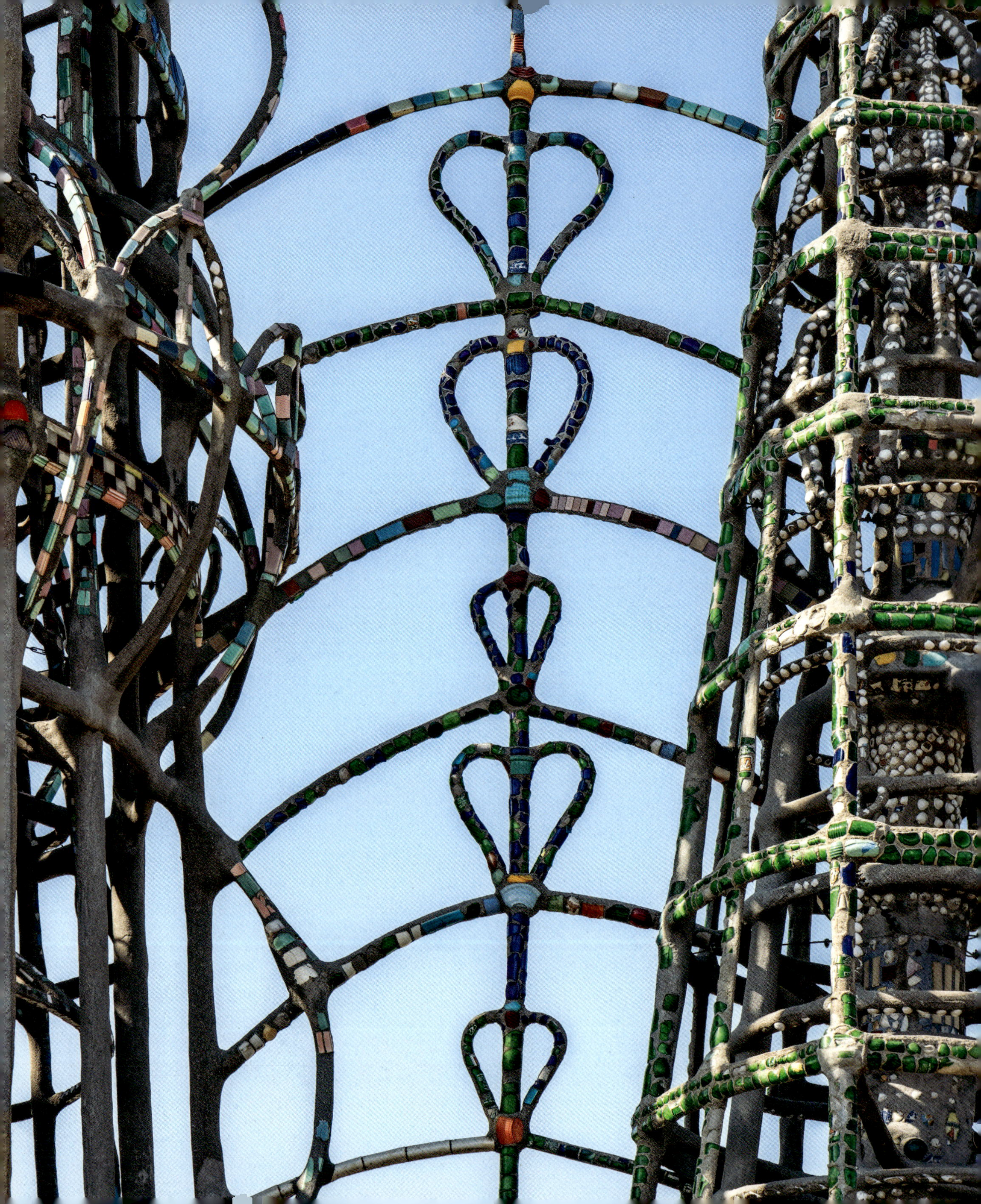

"A real monumental site—these big, tall, cold towers made out of broken cans, glass. You have to see it. When I first went out there, as a kid, I didn't know about the history of Watts, the riots. I had to grow into that, had to learn that."
—Musician Kendrick Lamar

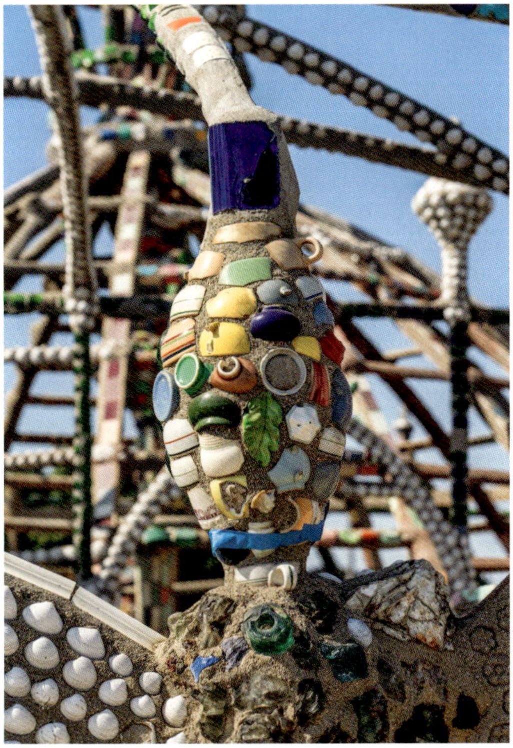

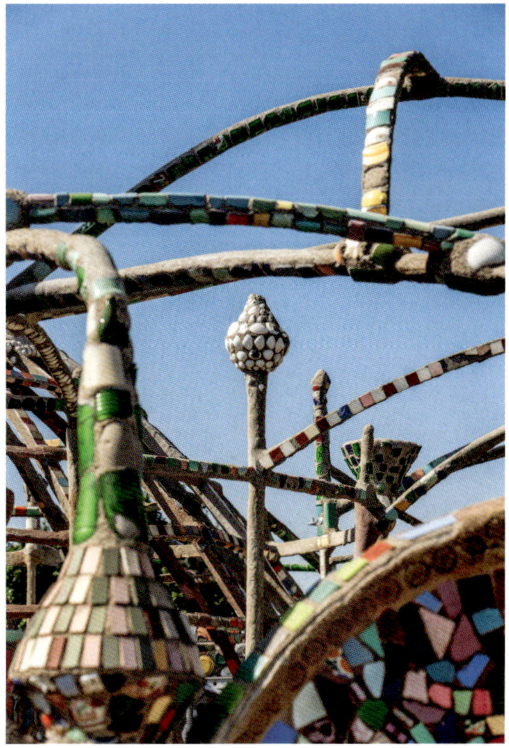

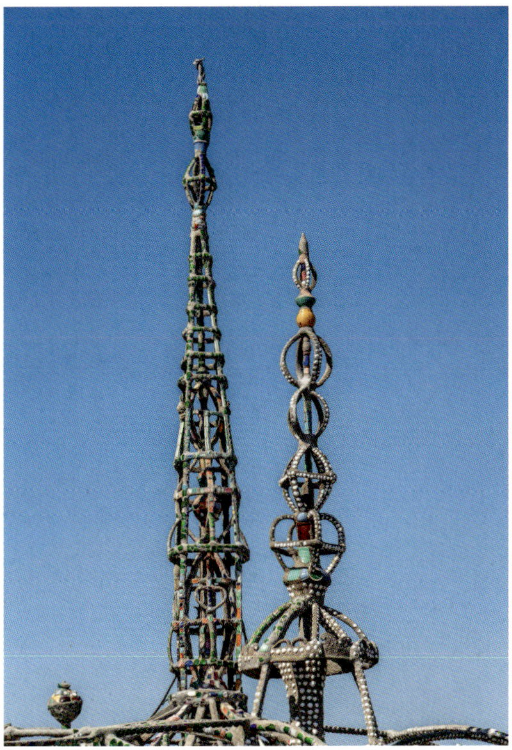

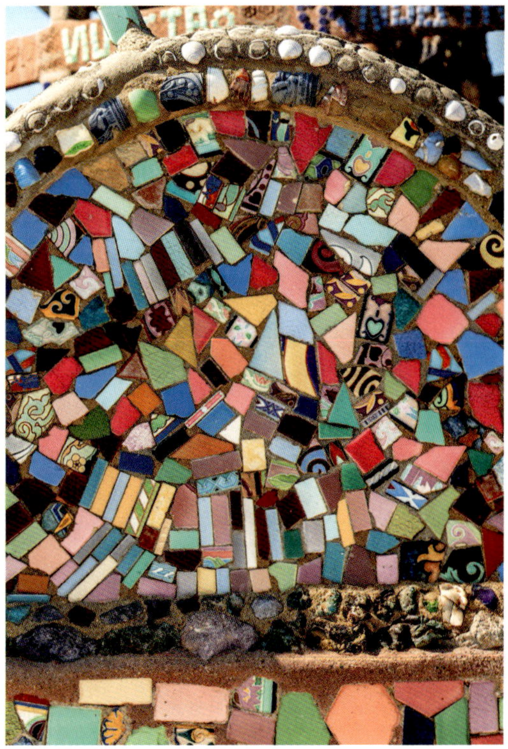

Details of the tower sculptures show Rodia's innovative use of materials. The artist wired scrap pieces of rebar together, wrapped it with wire mesh, and reinforced with thin concrete, using mortar to create colorful mosaics from found materials like California pottery, mirrors, and sea shells.

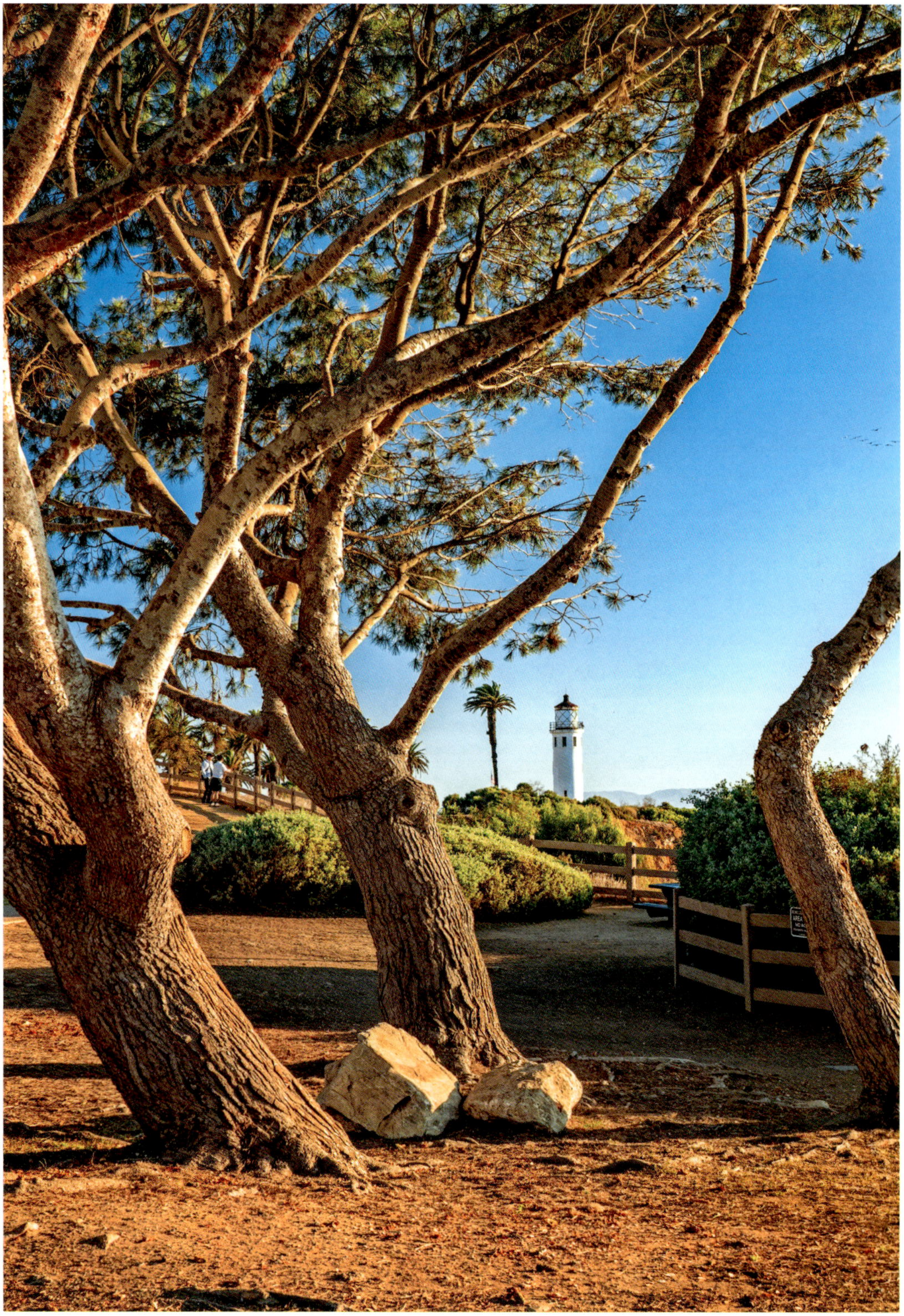

A view of the lighthouse from the adjacent park; below these cliffs are the Pacific reefs of the Palos Verdes Peninsula.

Point Vicente Lighthouse

A Historic Lighthouse and Surrounding Park Perched Above the Pacific

Erected in 1926 to help mariners navigate the dangerous waters of the north end of the Pacific Coast's Catalina Channel, this historic lighthouse is a beacon of beauty perched in the cliffs of the Palos Verdes Peninsula. The 67-foot-high tower has been owned by the US Coast Guard since 1939 and is opened once a month for visitors inside. It's said to be haunted by a ghost known as the "Lady of the Light," so watch for her.

Not only does the lighthouse add to the scenic view, it also has a surrounding park in a beautiful landscape and the Point Vicente Interpretive Center, a natural history museum. Admire the serene beauty, explore tide pools, or go off on an adventurous hike.

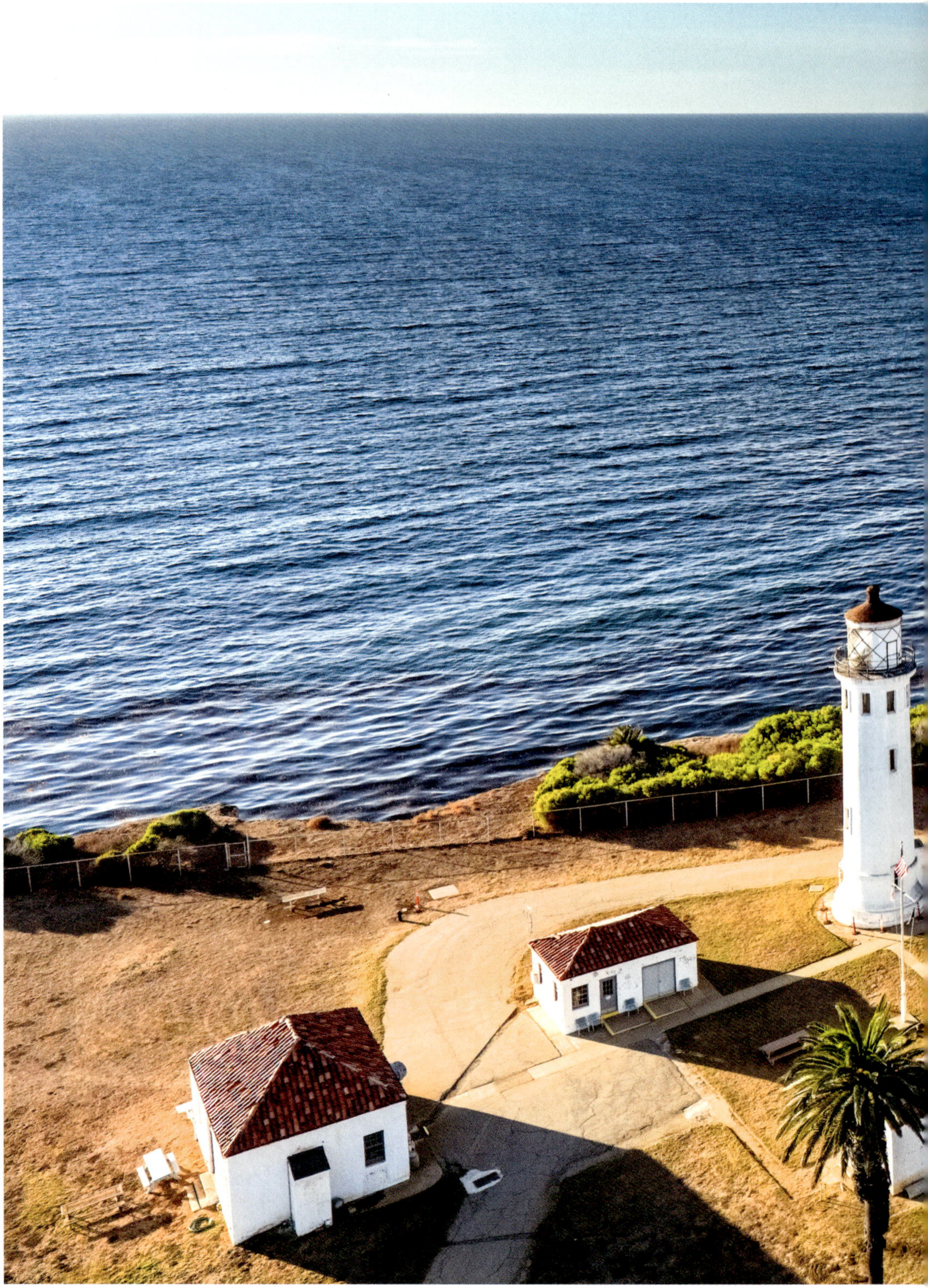

The dramatic coastline of Palos Verdes makes even a lighthouse seem small.

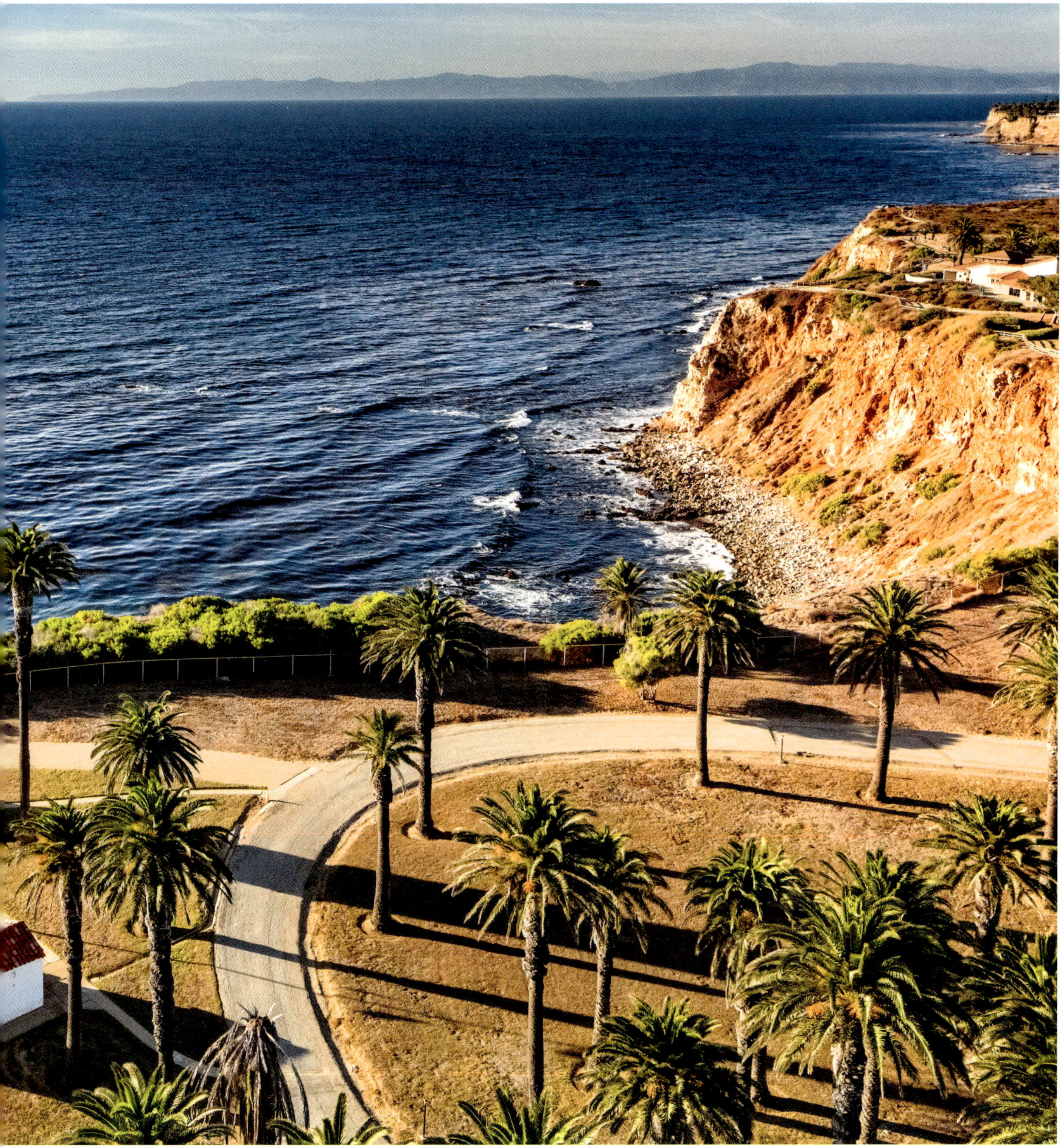

Manhattan Beach

One of the Beautiful Beaches of the South Bay

Home to both LAX and the Port of LA in Long Beach, the South Bay (named for its geography as the southern part of the Santa Monica Bay) is a hub for transport, but it's also got a host of beautiful beaches that aren't Santa Monica or Venice Beach. Which means these classic SoCal beaches—Manhattan Beach, Hermosa Beach, Redondo Beach—are likely to be far less crowded. There's even a pier-to-pier walk between the Manhattan Beach Pier and the Hermosa Beach Pier.

Of these beautiful, laid-back beaches, perhaps the most coveted is Manhattan Beach, confusingly named by developer John Merrill in the early twentieth century after a resort on Coney Island, NY. With more than two miles of coastline, this is the beach of California dreams—the opening credits of the TV show *The O.C.* were shot along the Manhattan Beach strand. The ultrasmooth sand is legendary—in fact, the sand quality and quantity here are so good that the city used to ship sand to Waikiki in Hawaii. The high-quality sand also inspired the birth of the modern beach volleyball movement in 1930. Today, Manhattan Beach is still considered the "Beach Volleyball Capital of the World."

The biggest landmark is the 1920 Manhattan Beach Pier, with its beautiful roundhouse at its end. While today the structure houses an aquarium, during Prohibition it was used for rum-running operations that happened offshore. (Another, perhaps related, bit of city lore is that a converted lifeguard tower served as the city's first jail.)

Aside from its status as one of Southern California's most beautiful beaches, Manhattan Beach is also taking strides to improve upon its exclusive and racist past. Early in the twentieth century, the African American Bruce family purchased land and established a resort catering to Black families. That land was stolen from them in 1924, when the city of Manhattan Beach used eminent domain to acquire the land for a park. In 2022, the Los Angeles County Board of Supervisors returned the ownership of Bruce's Beach to the living heirs of Charles and Willa Bruce.

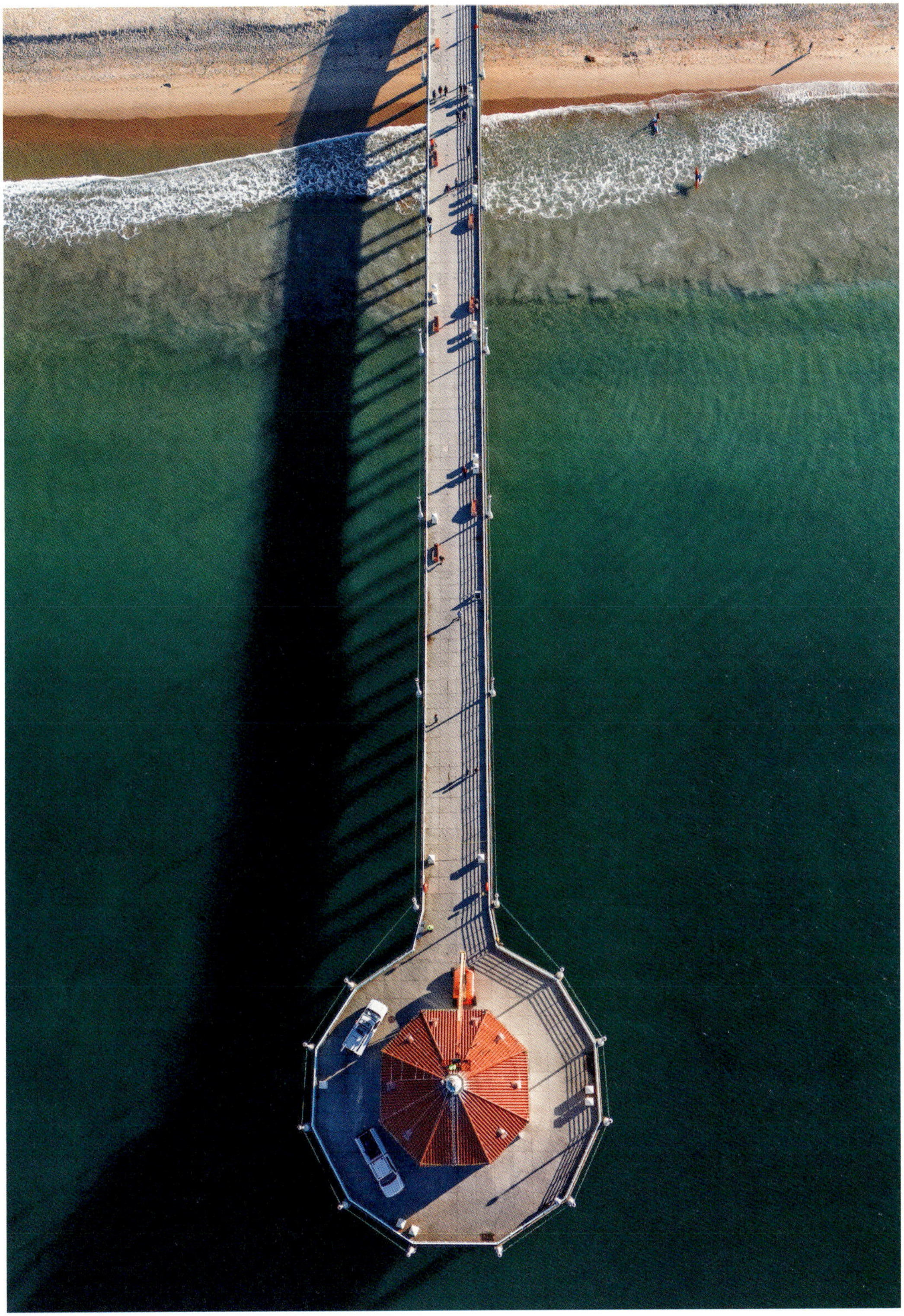

Built in 1920, the Manhattan Beach Pier is the oldest concrete pier on the West Coast and has the stunning Roundhouse Aquarium at its end.

(Page 232–233)
The view atop the Manhattan Beach Pier is a panoramic view of the entire Santa Monica Bay; from below, the gorgeous Pacific.

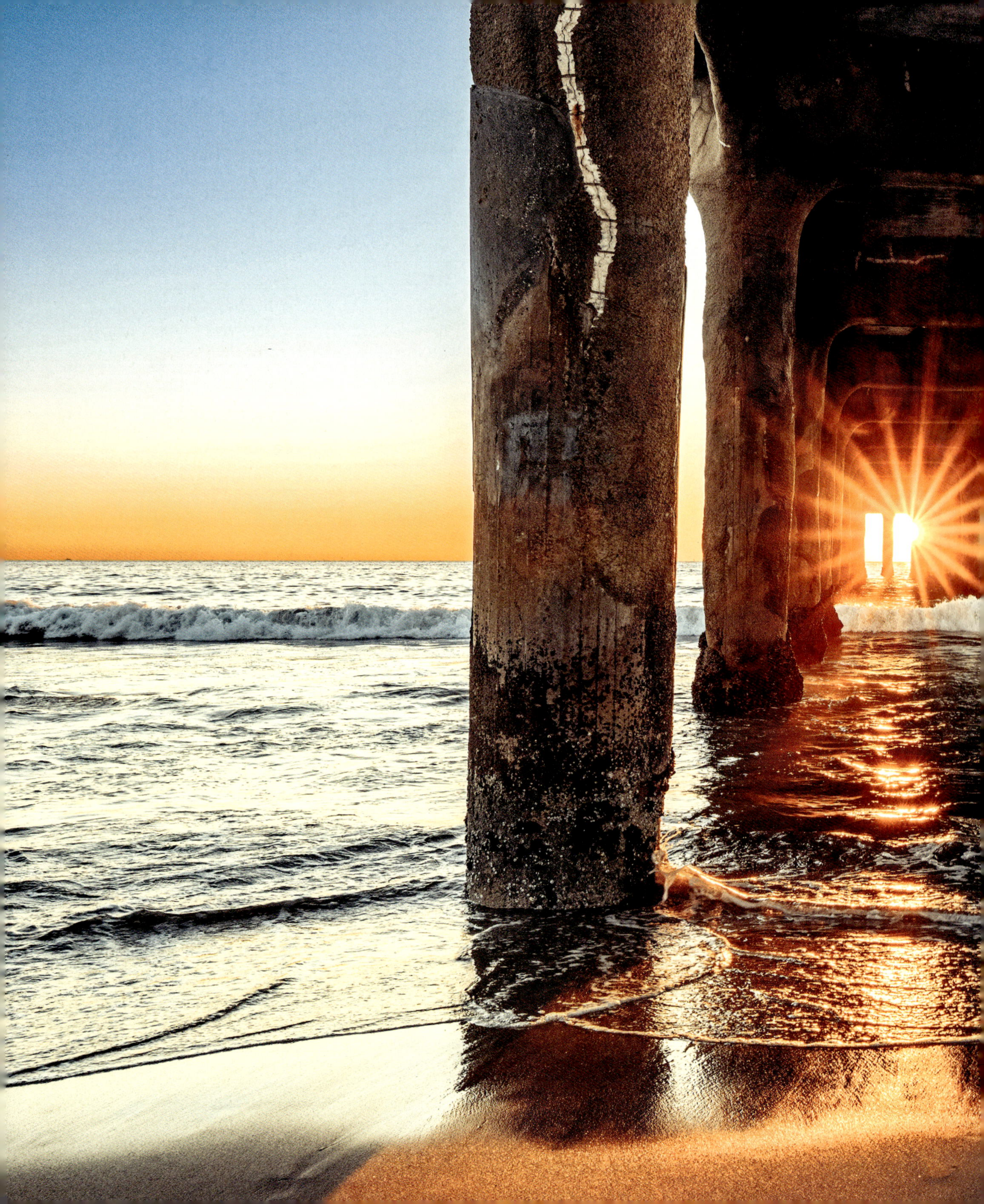

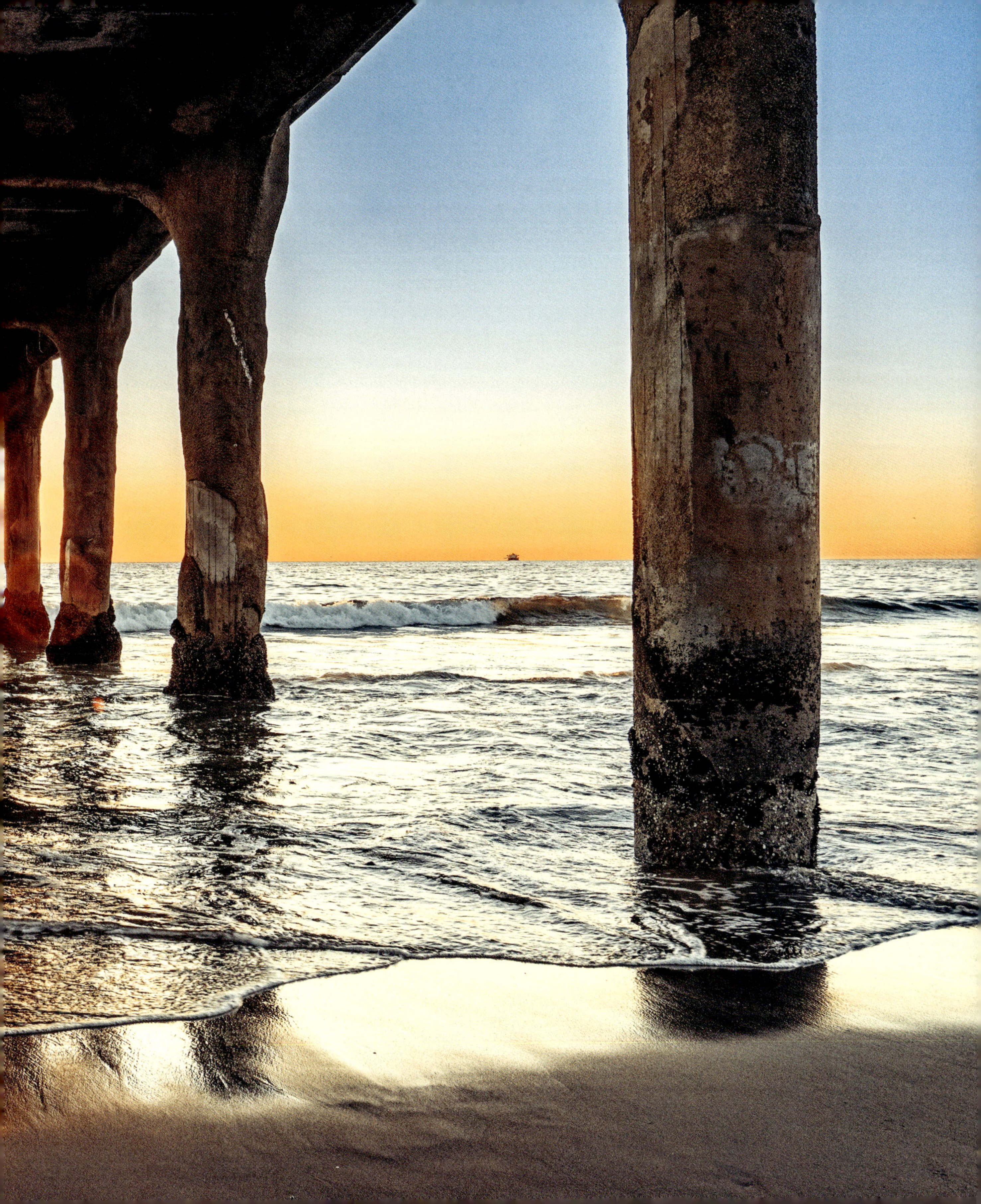

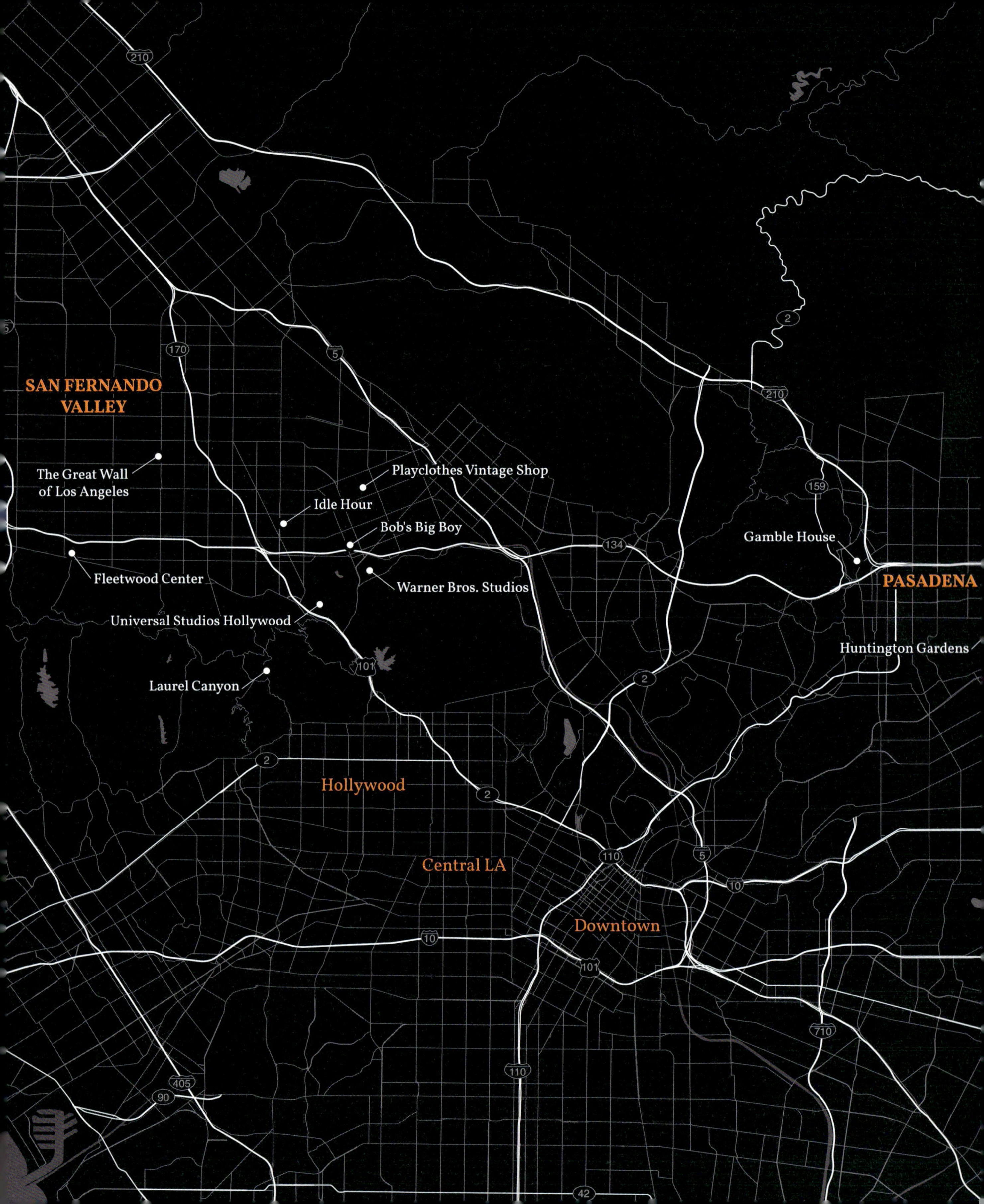
SAN FERNANDO VALLEY
The Great Wall of Los Angeles
Playclothes Vintage Shop
Idle Hour
Bob's Big Boy
Fleetwood Center
Warner Bros. Studios
Universal Studios Hollywood
Laurel Canyon
Gamble House
PASADENA
Huntington Gardens
Hollywood
Central LA
Downtown
210
170
5
2
159
134
101
110
10
710
405
90
42

The San Fernando Valley and Pasadena

Iconic Sites

Los Angeles's Dynamic Geology

One aspect that some visitors to LA are surprised to realize is how mountainous the area is. The Los Angeles Basin, the low-lying coastal plain that makes up most of Central Los Angeles, is surrounded by mountain ranges—and nearly half of Los Angeles County is comprised of mountains. These east-west ranges create geographic divides, creating peaks, valleys, and canyons, and are the site of some of its most dynamic geological activity—the earthquakes, fires, and mudslides the city is famous for. Two important ranges—the Santa Monica Mountains and the San Gabriel Mountains—are the most prominent within the central city. The Santa Monica Mountains are the 50-mile coastal range that stretch from Hollywood Hills all the way up the coast to Point Mugu in Ventura (the iconic mountains of Malibu and Griffith Park, visible most everywhere in the central city). A second range of mountains—the San Gabriels—mark a northeastern boundary, dividing the LA Basin from the Mojave Desert. The city of Pasadena lies at the base of the San Gabriels and is the largest city in the San Gabriel Valley.

The Santa Monica Mountains separate the central city from the infamous "Valley"—aka the San Fernando Valley, which is largely north and northwest of Central LA, whereas the San Gabriel Valley is to the northeast. The two areas are distinct; both have beautiful natural areas and dense residential and commercial neighborhoods which offer more space than those in the central city below. Of course, the San Fernando Valley looms large in the cultural imagination as the birthplace of Valley-speak (like, that's totally bitchin') and as the former hub of the adult film industry (check out the film *Boogie Nights*). But there's certainly way more than these stereotypes suggest, so get "over the hill" and check out these vibrant sections of the city.

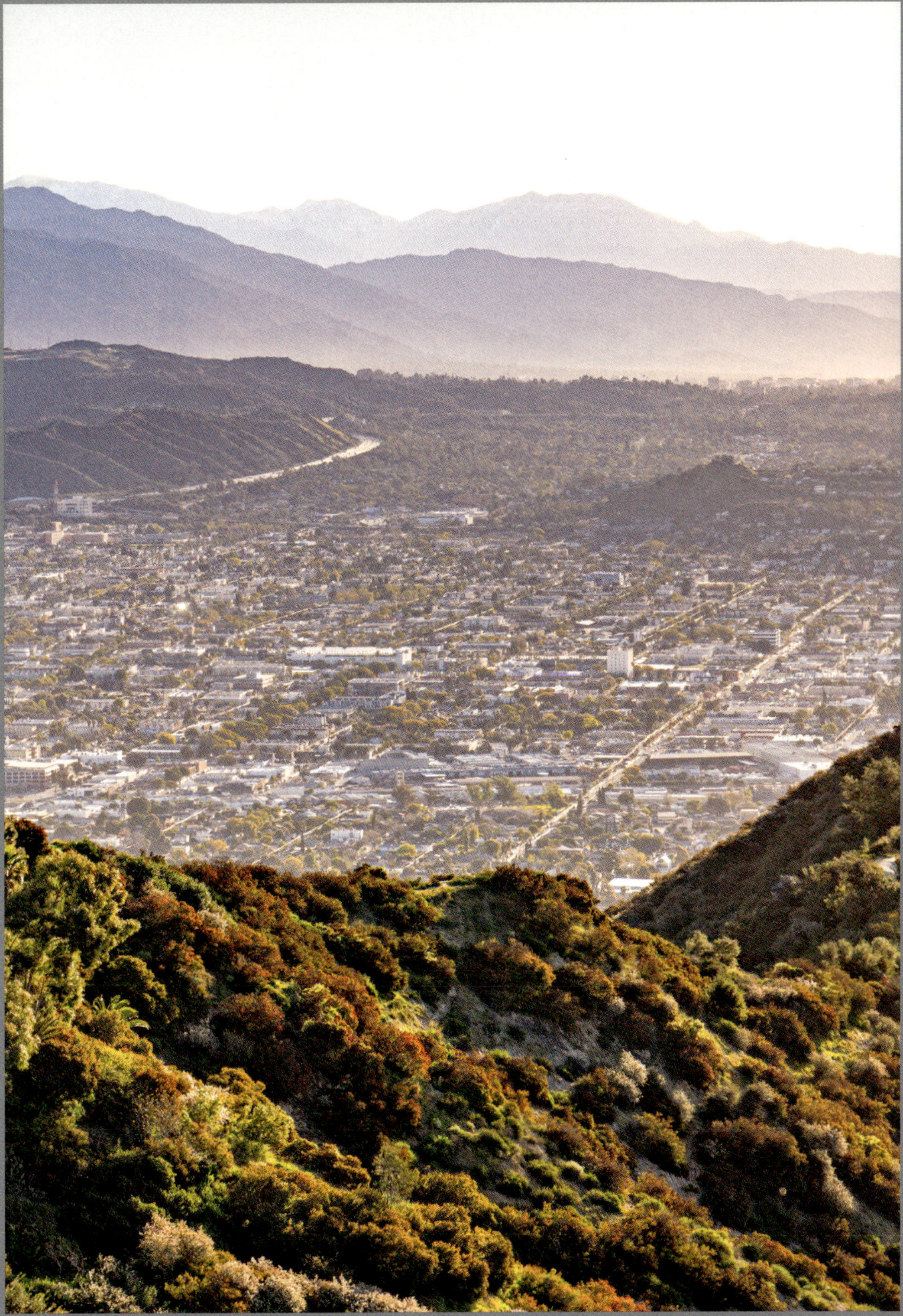

"The San Fernando Valley has always been epic to me. I would watch *Lawrence of Arabia* and think of my equivalent: Ventura Boulevard." —director Paul Thomas Anderson

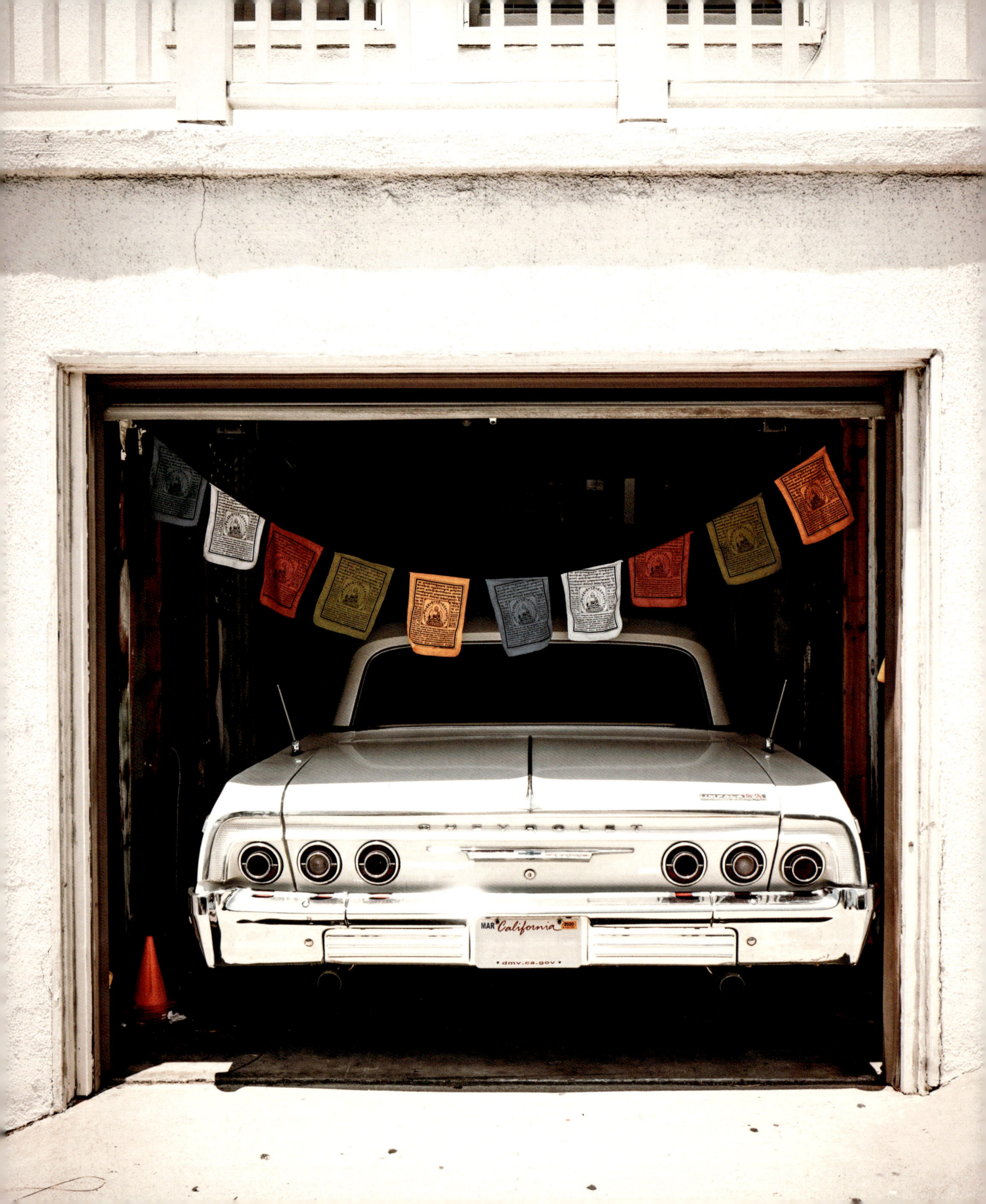
CHEVROLET
MAR
California
dmv.ca.gov

Writer Kevin Roderick says the relationship between the Valley and Central LA is like "step-siblings who have grown closer over time, but who should never be mistaken for blood family."

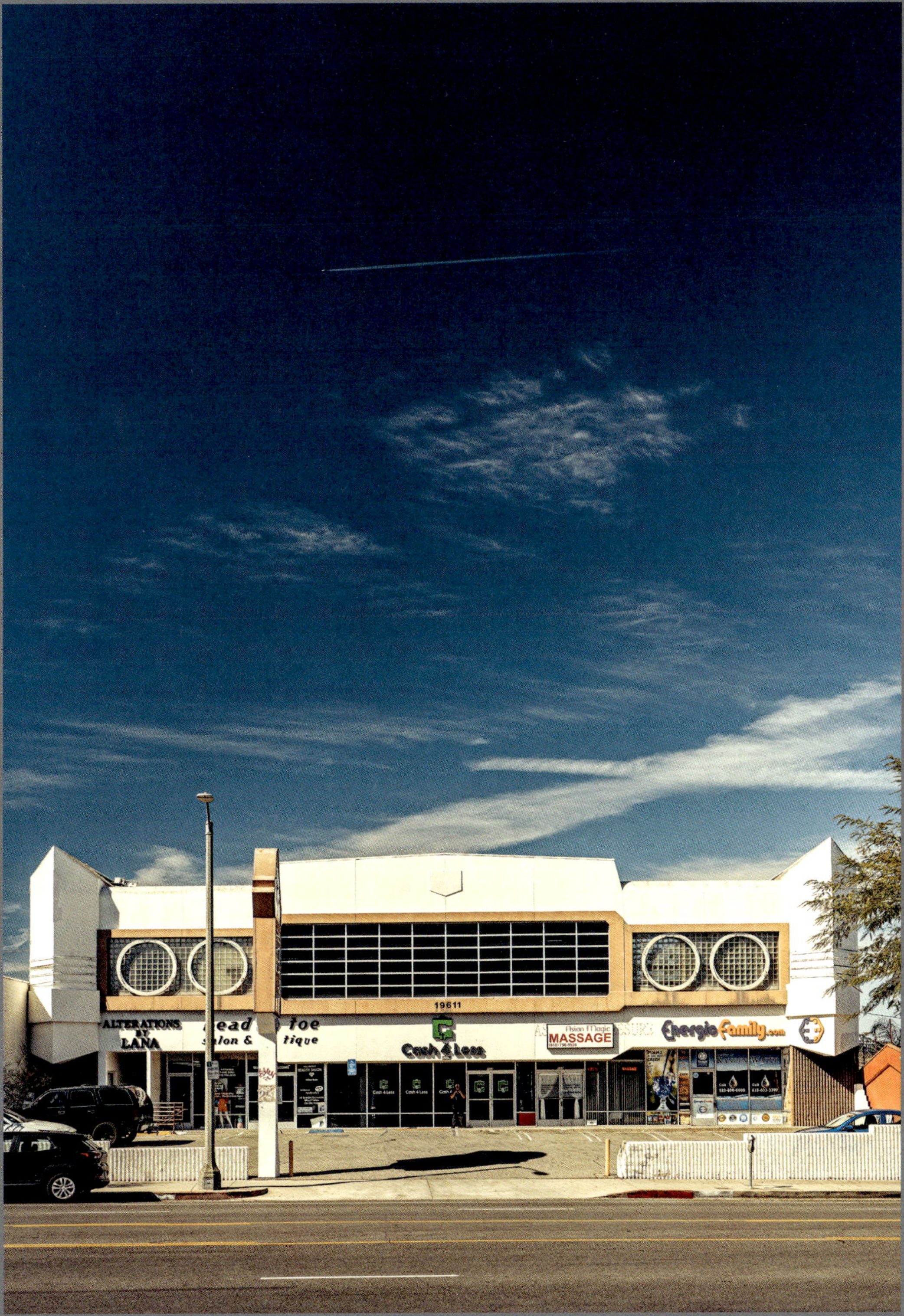

The Fleetwood Center, a strip mall on Ventura Boulevard in the Tarzana neighborhood, boasts a famed building façade—the front of a Cadillac car.

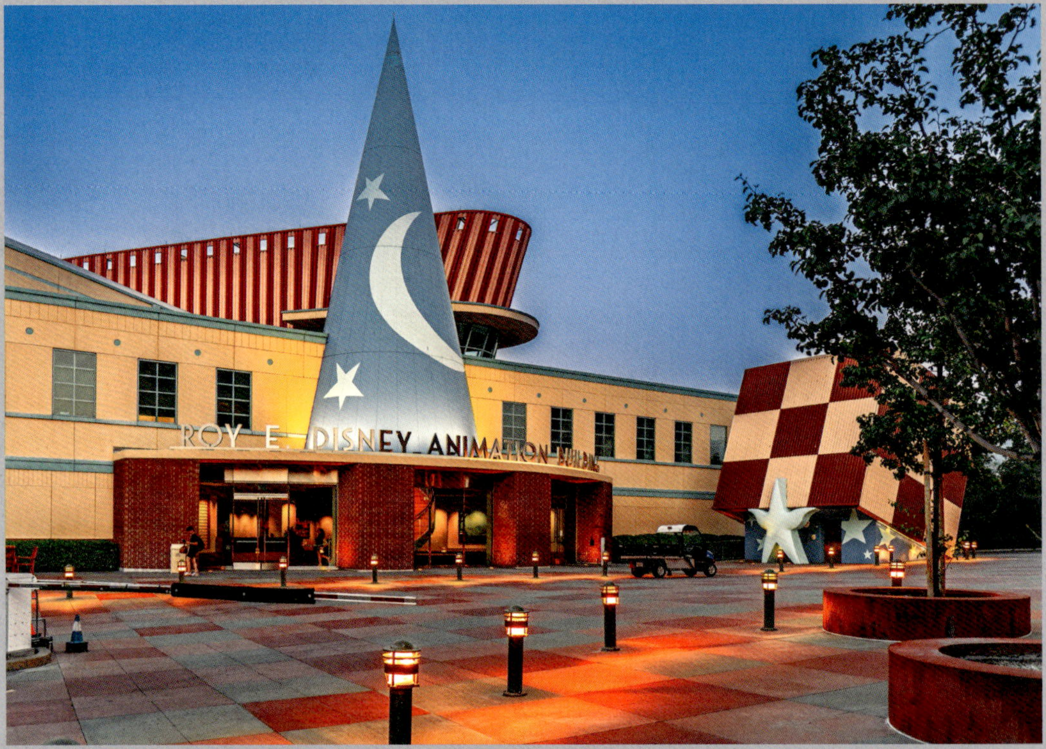

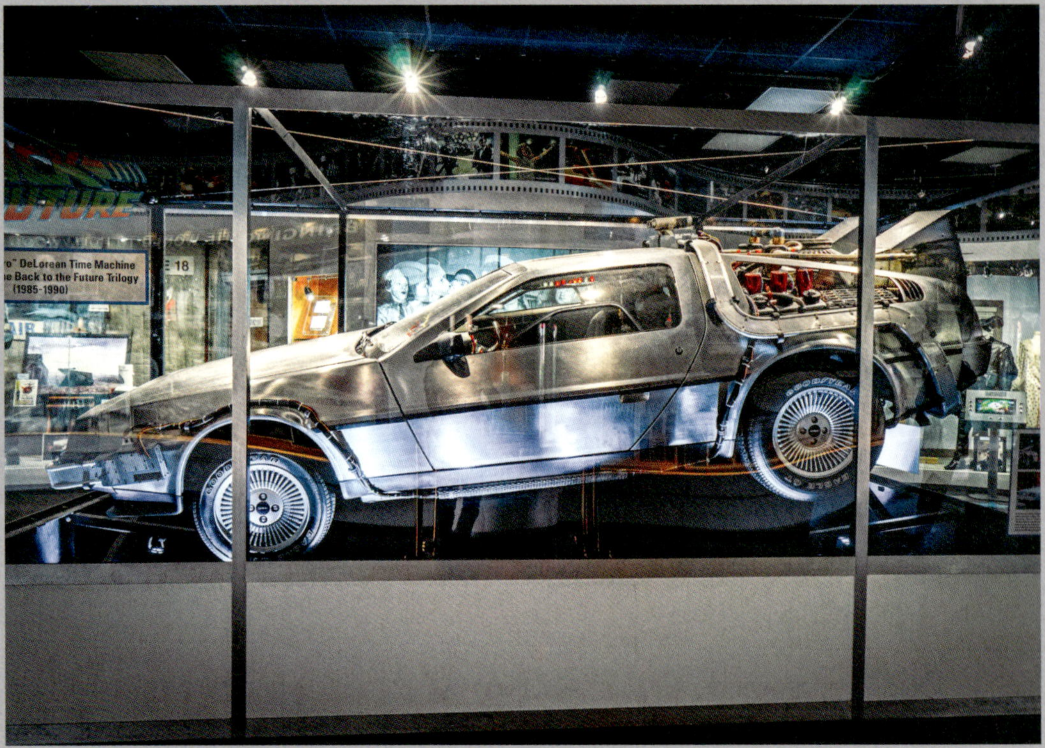

Mickey Mouse's sorcerer's hat serves as the entrance to the Feature Animation Building at Walt Disney Studios in Burbank.

The Delorean from the *Back to the Future* film franchise awaits time-traveling fans at Universal Studios Hollywood.

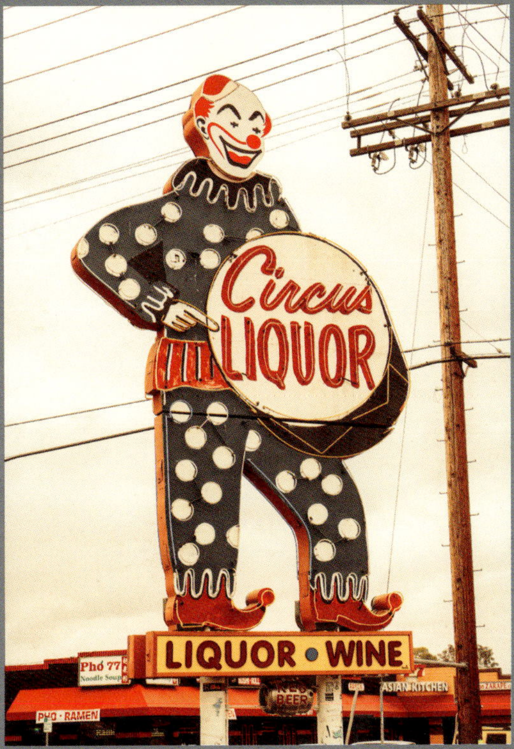

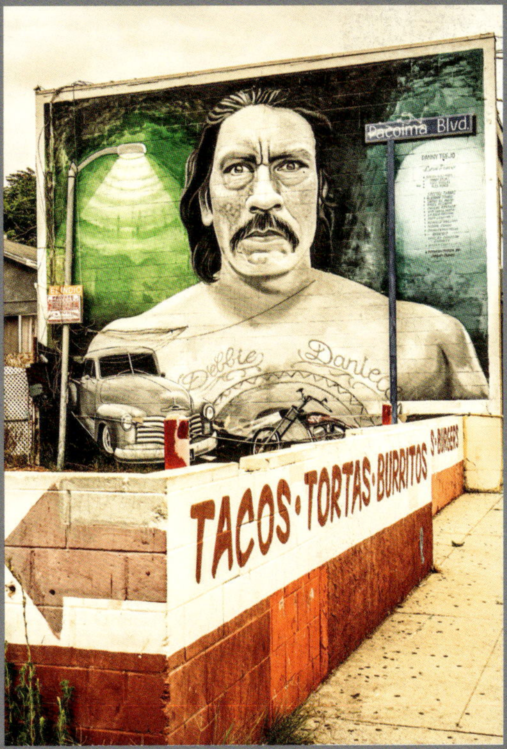

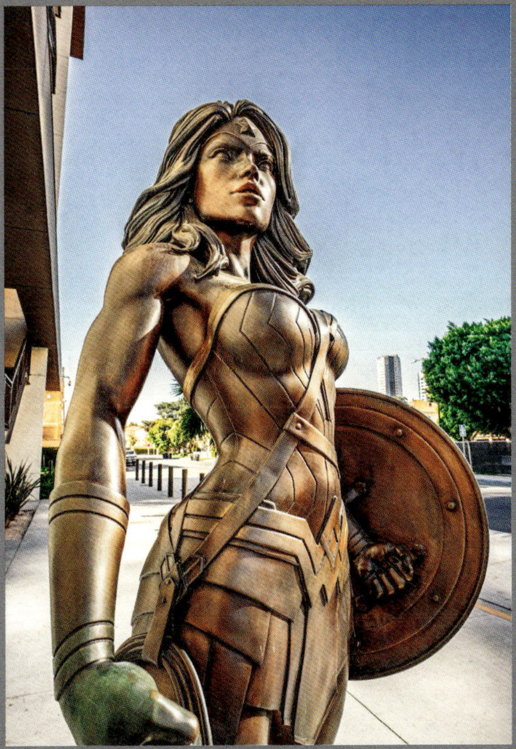

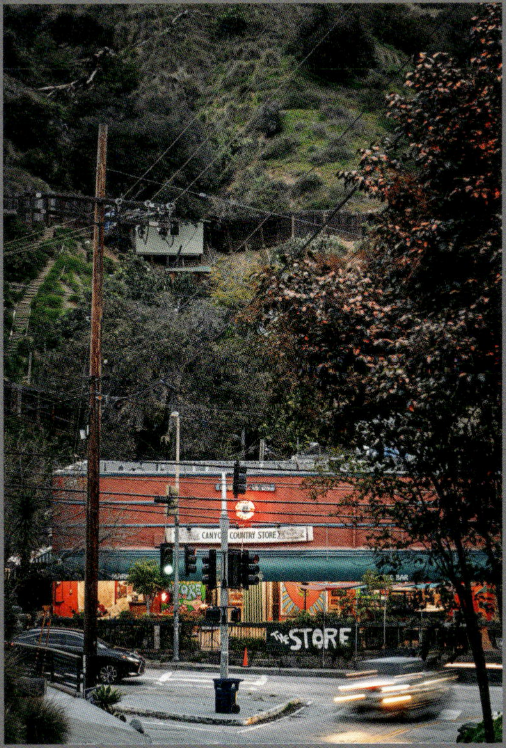

Nicknamed "Valley," the iconic 32-foot neon sign outside a North Hollywood liquor store is a film and TV star with perhaps his most notable appearance in *Clueless*.

Actor Danny Trejo is the star of a mural by artist Levi Ponce on Pacoima's Mural Mile; Trejo founded a number of taco stands around LA as well.

A statue of Wonder Woman guards the Warner Brothers Studio in Burbank.

Laurel Canyon's famed Canyon Country Store is the hippest snack stop on the way to the San Fernando Valley from Hollywood.

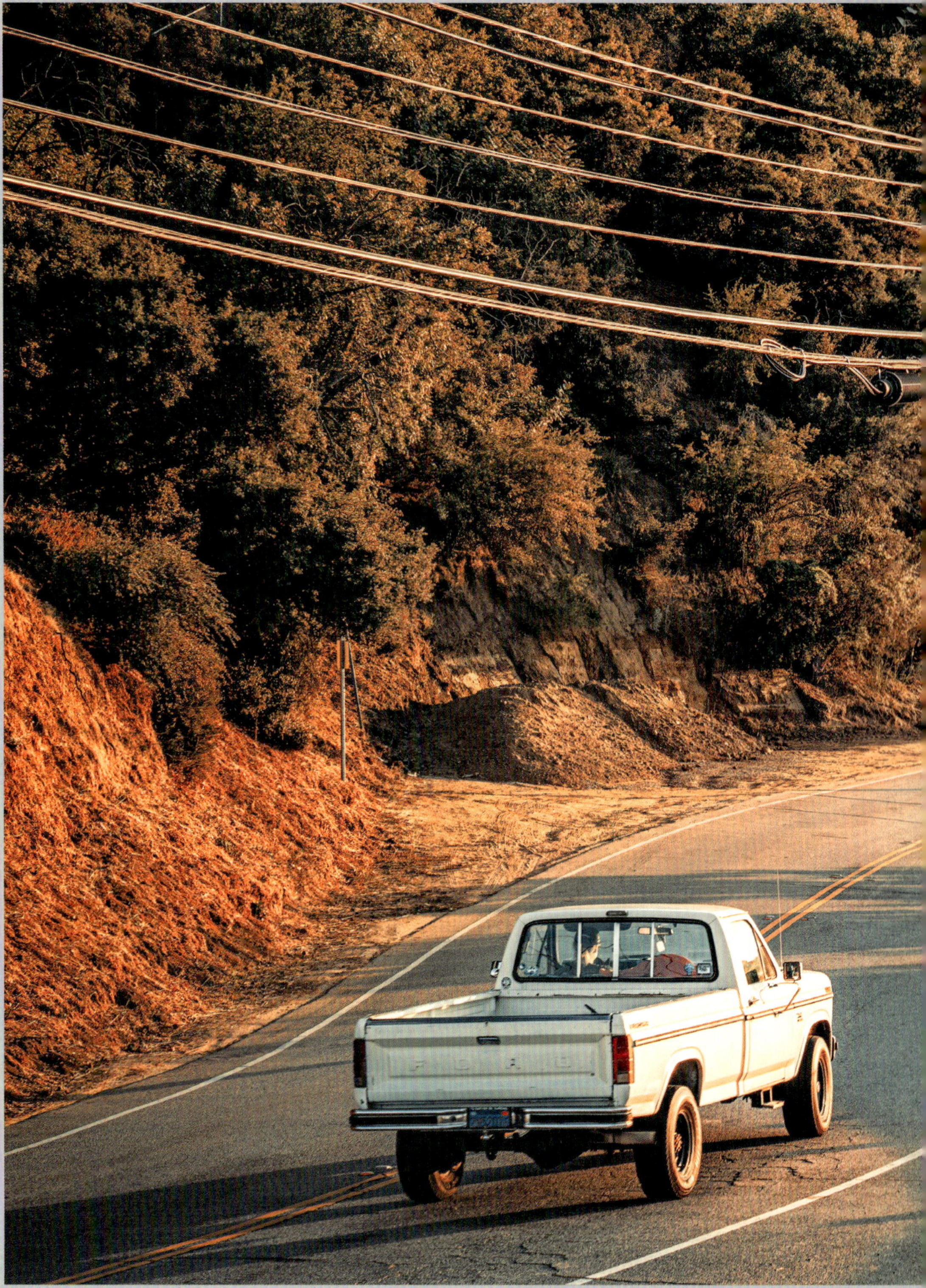

It's a rustic drive on Mulholland to the beautiful Fryman Canyon Park in Studio City.

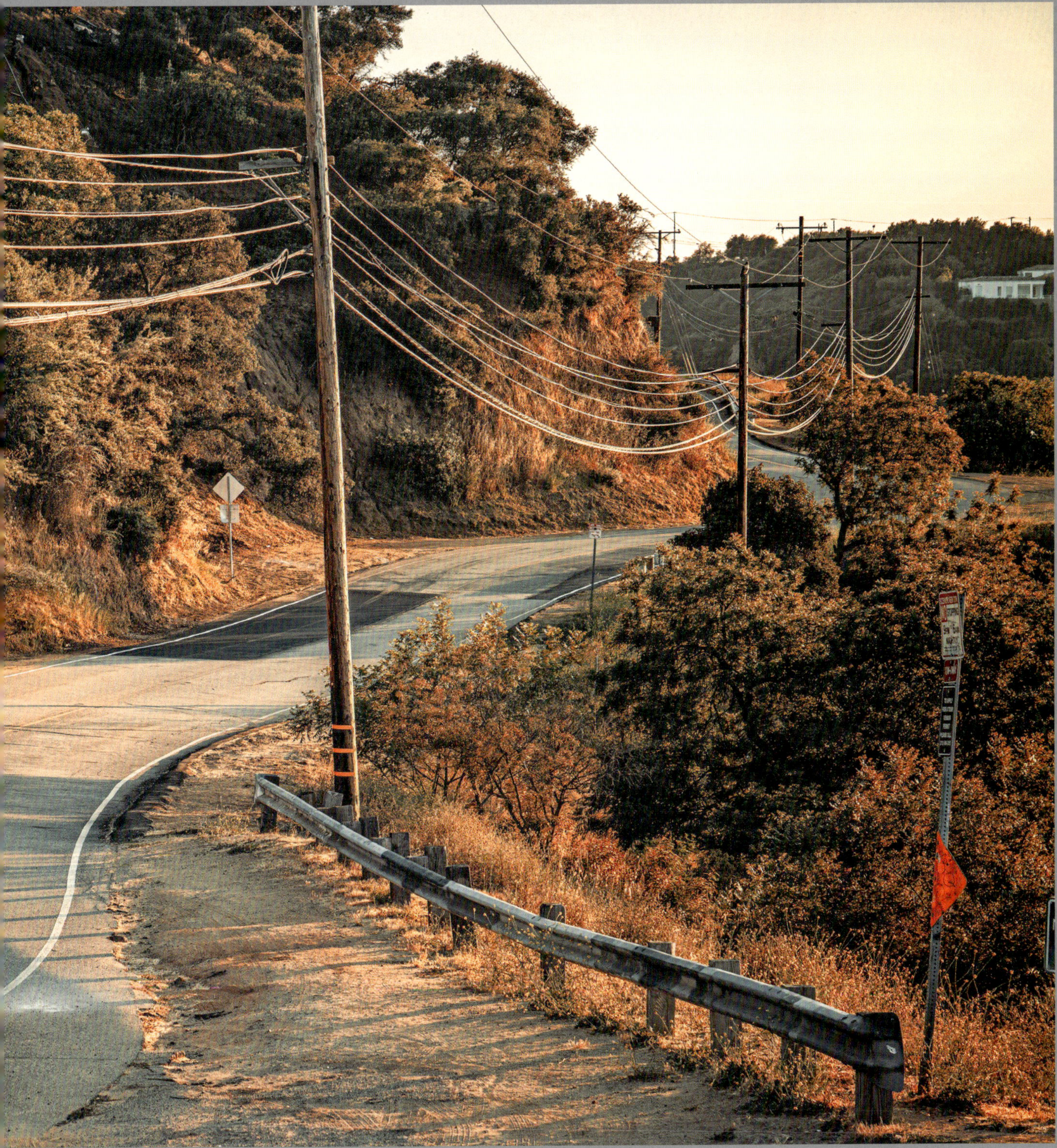

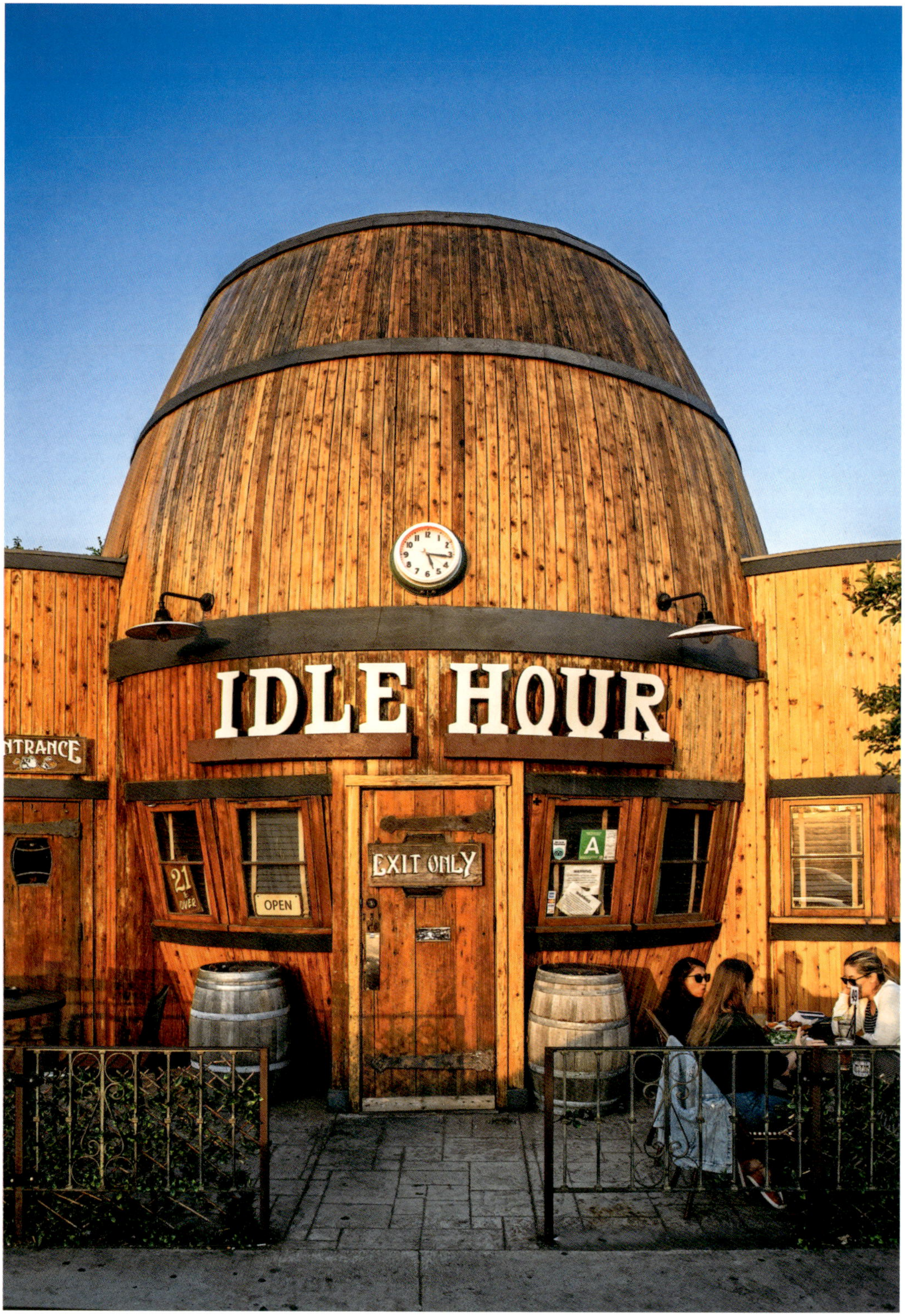

A bar shaped like a barrel? In LA all things are possible.

The Idle Hour

Programmatic Architecture Plus Drinks

Los Angeles is known for some fine examples of what is called programmatic architecture, a style popular in the 1920s and '30s in which a building physically resembled its purpose. Over the decades, the city has boasted a hot-dog stand in the shape of a hot dog (Tail O' the Pup); a famous Hollywood restaurant shaped like a hat (The Brown Derby); a camera store shaped like a camera (The Darkroom); and many donut shops shaped like donuts (Randy's Donuts, The Donut Hole). The appeal of these structures was that they could easily be seen—and serve as advertisements for their products—from a moving car. As the automobile became more popular as a mode of transport, so did these roadside wonders, luring drivers in to enjoy the goods.

Built in 1941, North Hollywood's Idle Hour is a prime example of this type of architecture—it's a bar in the shape of a whiskey barrel. The distinctive-shaped building was, fittingly, a tavern until the 1970s, when Dolores Fernandez, a famous Flamenco dancer, and her husband bought the building and renamed it La Caña Restaurant and Flamenco Club. For nearly a decade the couple performed there and had many old Hollywood stars as patrons. Closed in the 1970s, the building deteriorated for decades until it was restored and reopened in 2015 by the 1933 Group (see the Formosa Cafe, page 131). A great bar with fantastic cocktails and a really fun dance floor, this slice of Americana, perched perfectly in the cradle of the San Fernando Valley, is a joyful expression of LA.

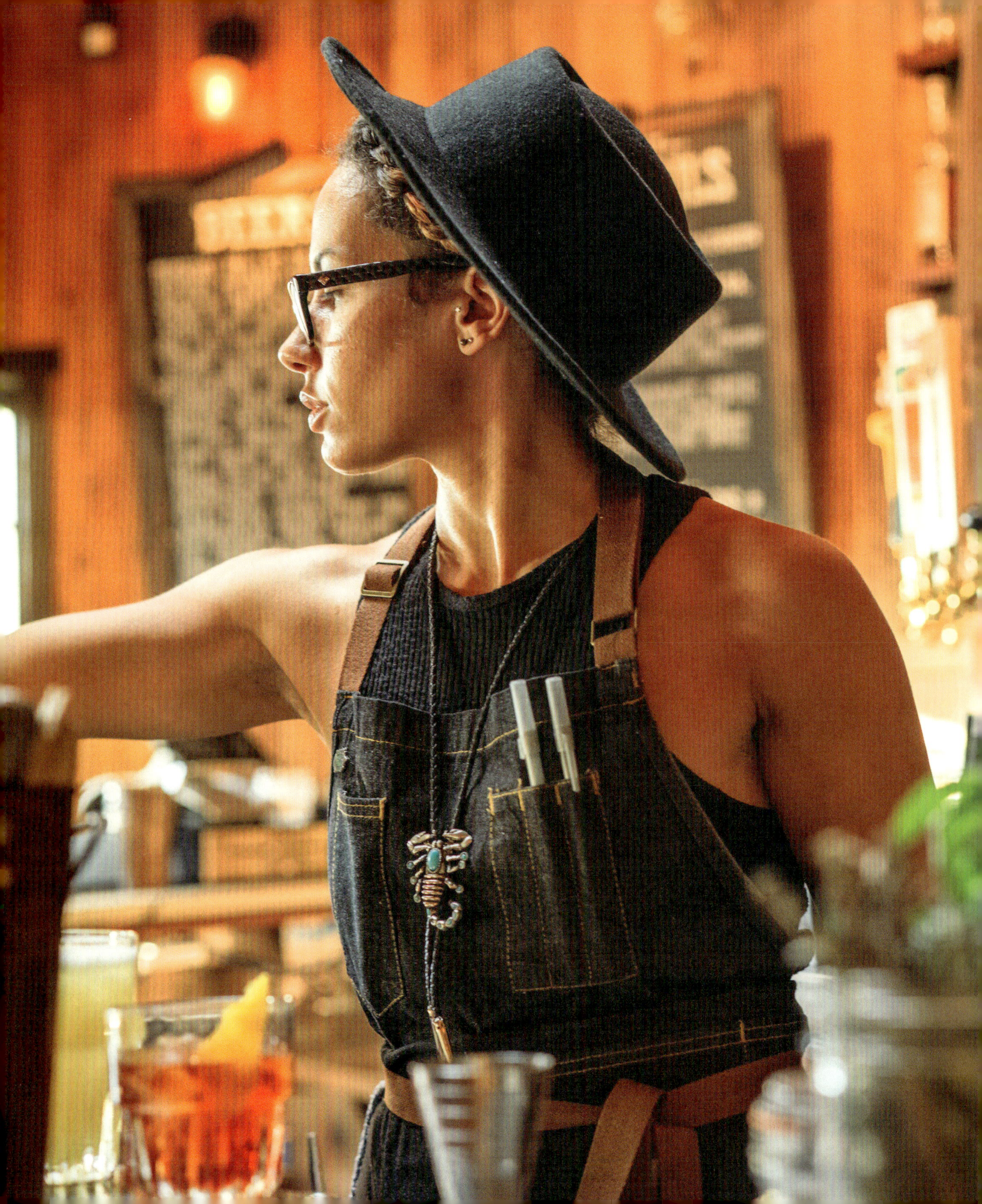

A historic bar and restaurant that serves American fare and great craft cocktails, the Idle Hour's building is a Los Angeles Historic-Cultural Monument.

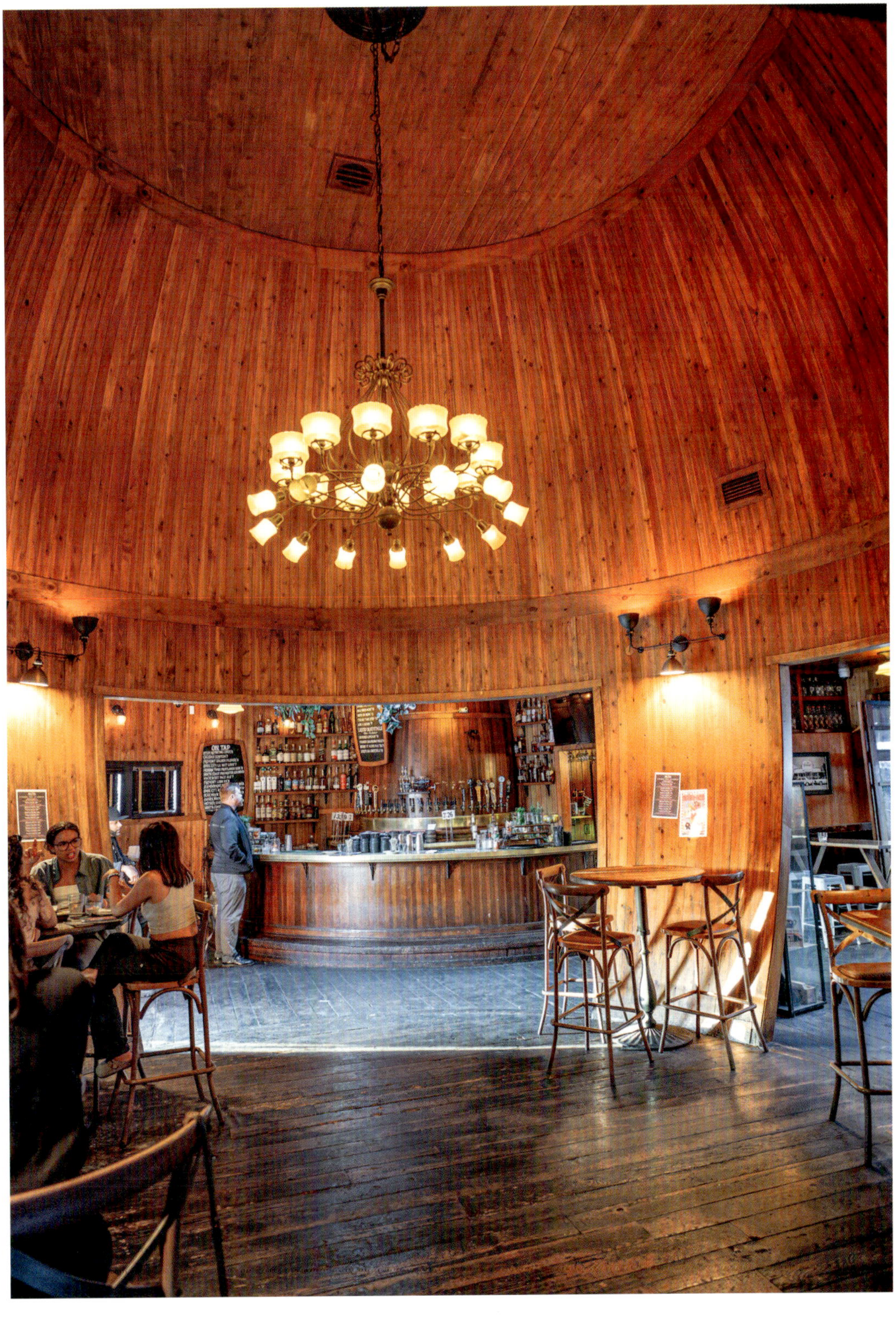

As is fitting for a former flamenco school, the Idle Hour often has dancing in the middle of the barrel.

The Huntington

Rare Books and Rare Plants All in One Place

Henry E. Huntington, a railroad tycoon, purchased the 600-acre San Marino Ranch near downtown Los Angeles in 1903, and ten years later set about collecting an incredible library, art, and botanical collection with his wife, Arabella Duval Huntington. In 1928, the couple's collections were open to the public as the nonprofit institution it remains today—albeit bigger, with the internationally renowned collection of art, books, and botanicals growing through the years.

Today, a visit to the Huntington means trapsing through some of the most beautiful gardens in the world. There are more than 200 acres on the grounds between the gardens, the museum, and the library, so wear walking shoes. Everything is elegant in presentation—as is fitting to a former railroad magnate—and the grounds give off the old monied vibe Pasadena (and the suburb of San Marino, where the Huntington is) is known for. The art museum is housed in the Huntington's former residence, and its most famous work, Thomas Gainsborough's 1770 *The Blue Boy*, has a brilliant contemporary work in dialogue with it from across the room: Kehinde Wiley's 2021 *A Portrait of a Young Gentleman*. The Huntington Library boasts an impressive exhibition of rare books from its collection, and one thing not to miss in the garden collection is an Amorphophallus titanium nicknamed "Green Boy," more commonly called a corpse flower, which when it blooms emits a fragrance similar to that of rotting flesh.

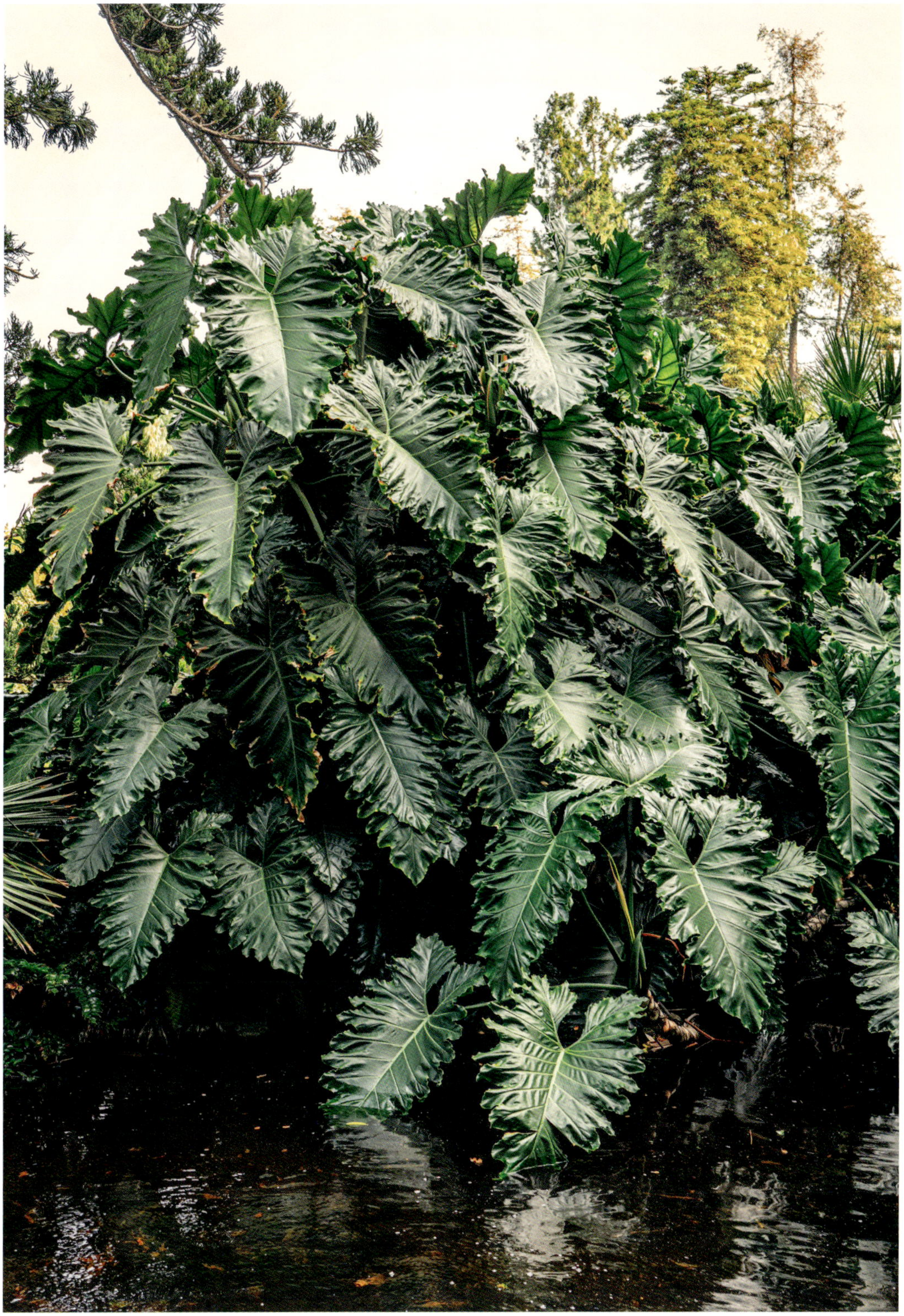

Sixteen themed gardens make up the Huntington's 130-acre botanical collection.

(Page 250–251) Known as the Chinese Garden, Liu Fang Yuan, the Garden of Flowing Fragrance, is one of the largest classical-style Chinese gardens in the world.

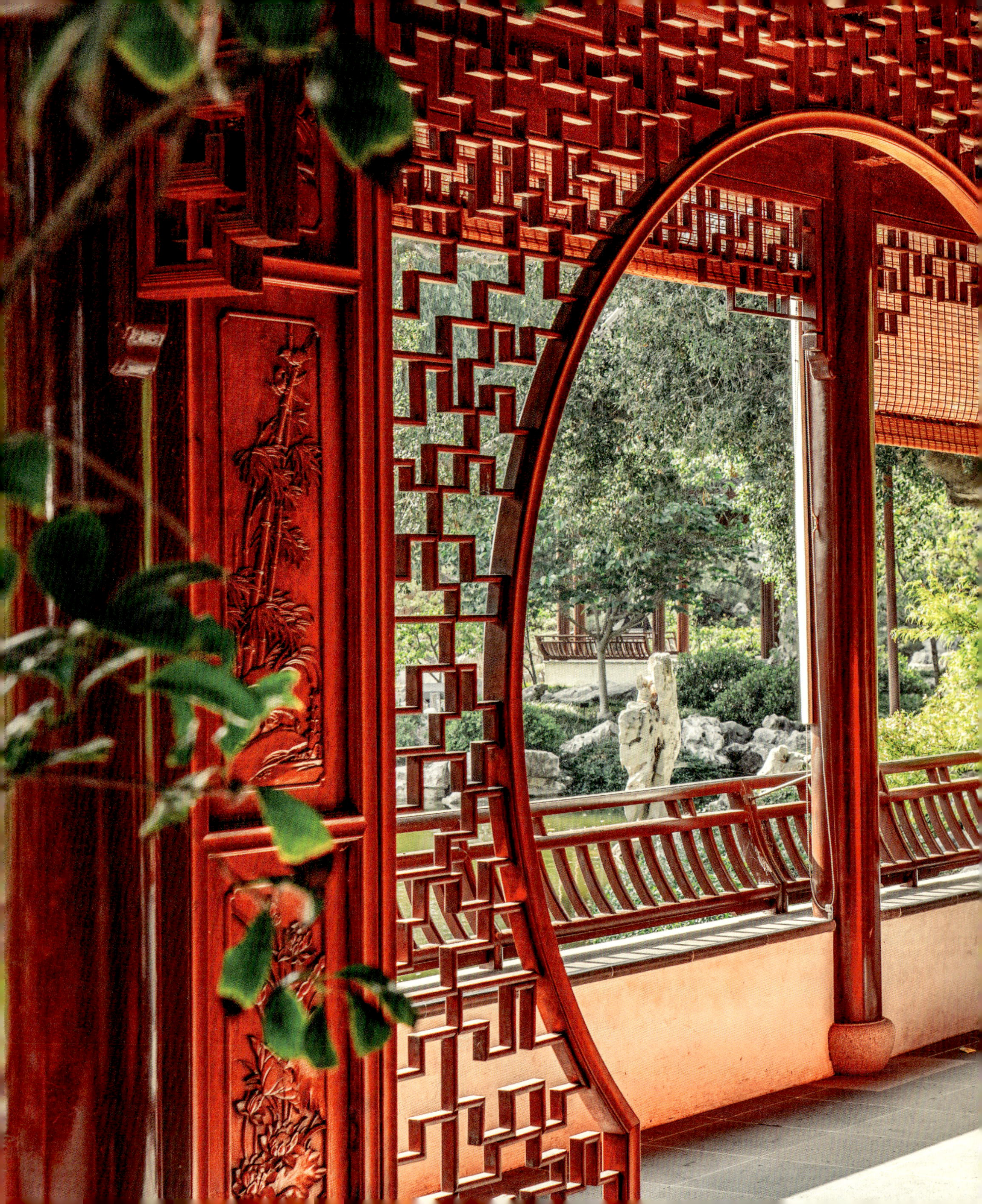

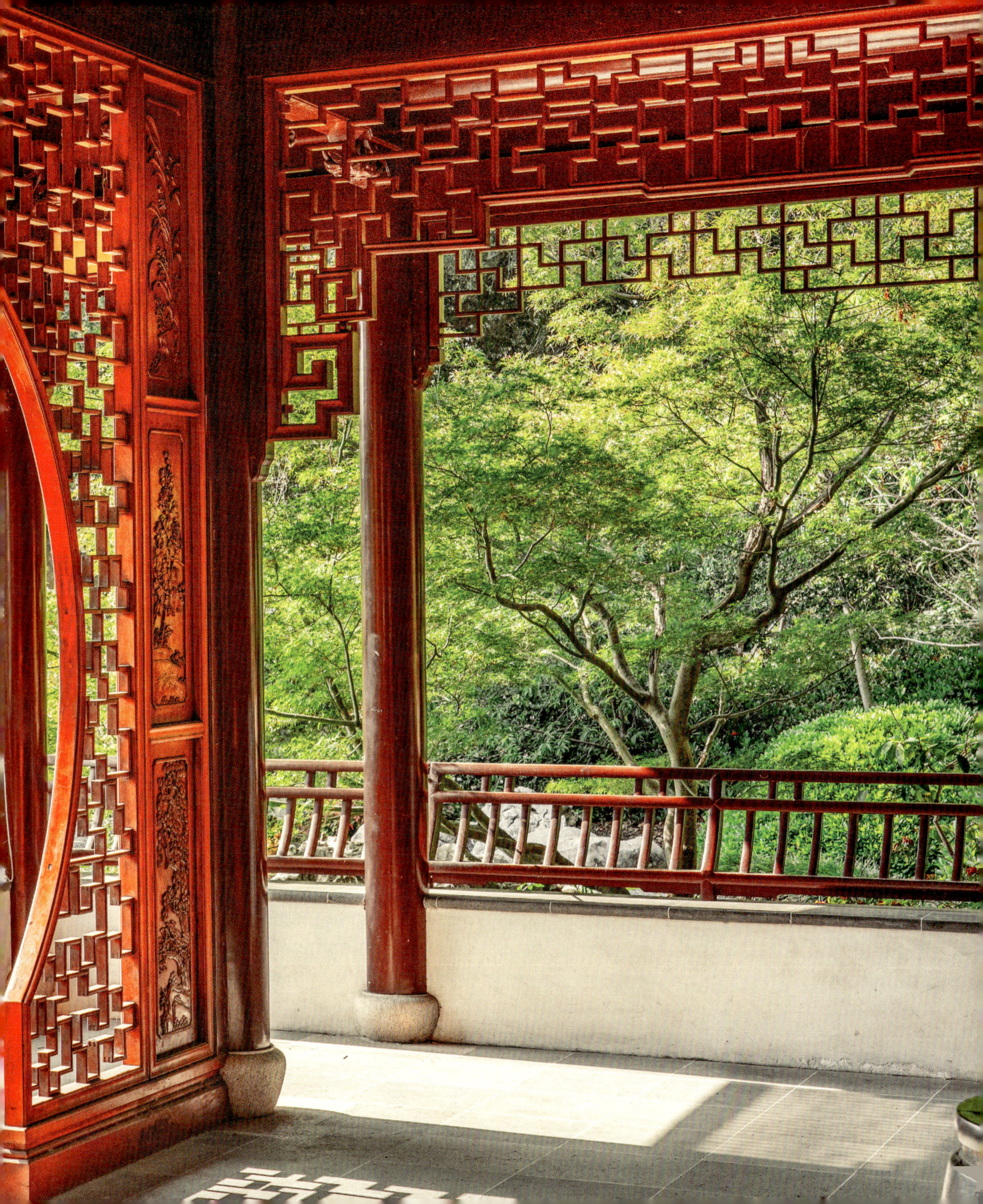

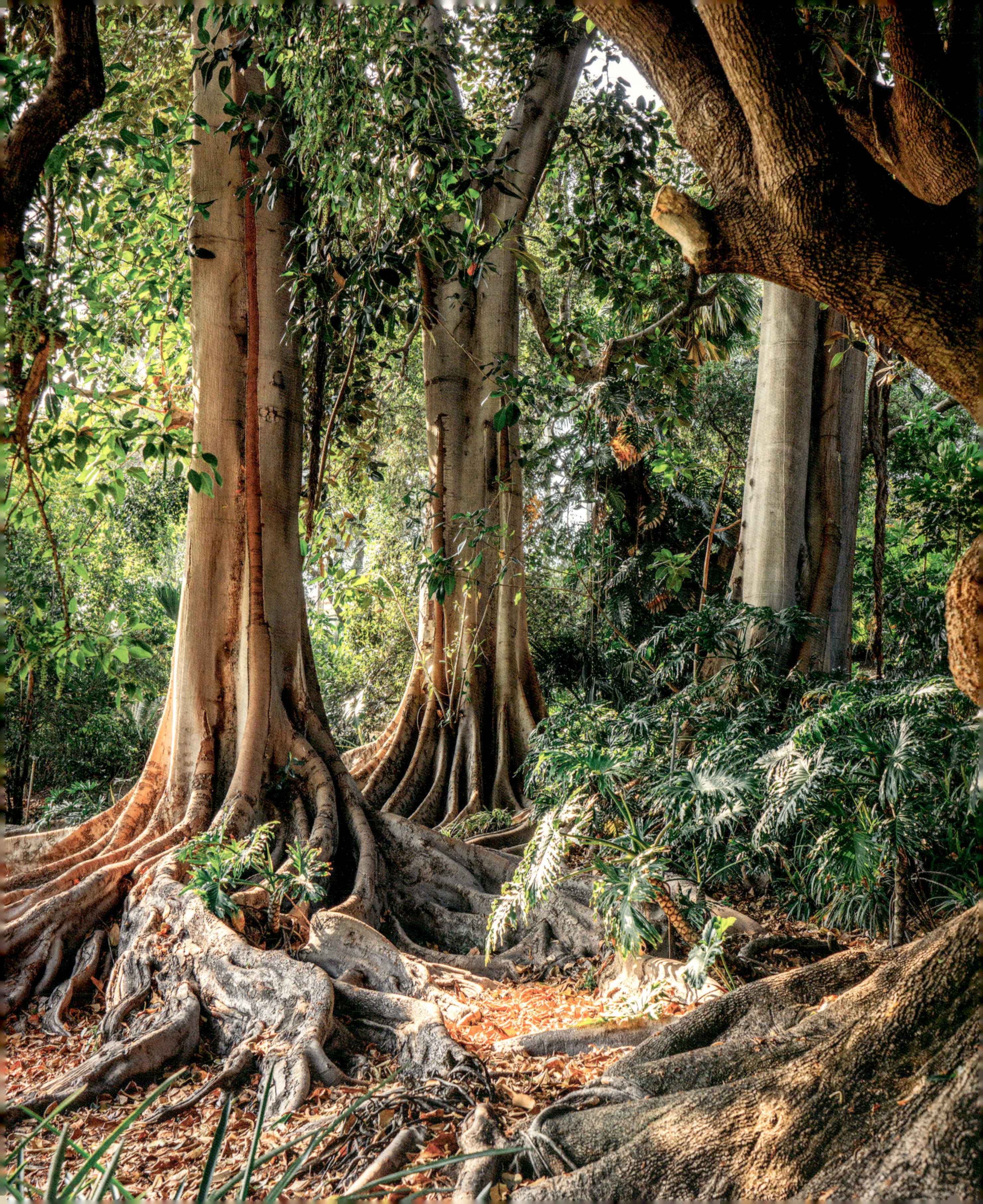

A frequently used location for film and television shows—and for weddings—the Huntington appears in wedding movies like *My Best Friend's Wedding* and *The Wedding Singer.*

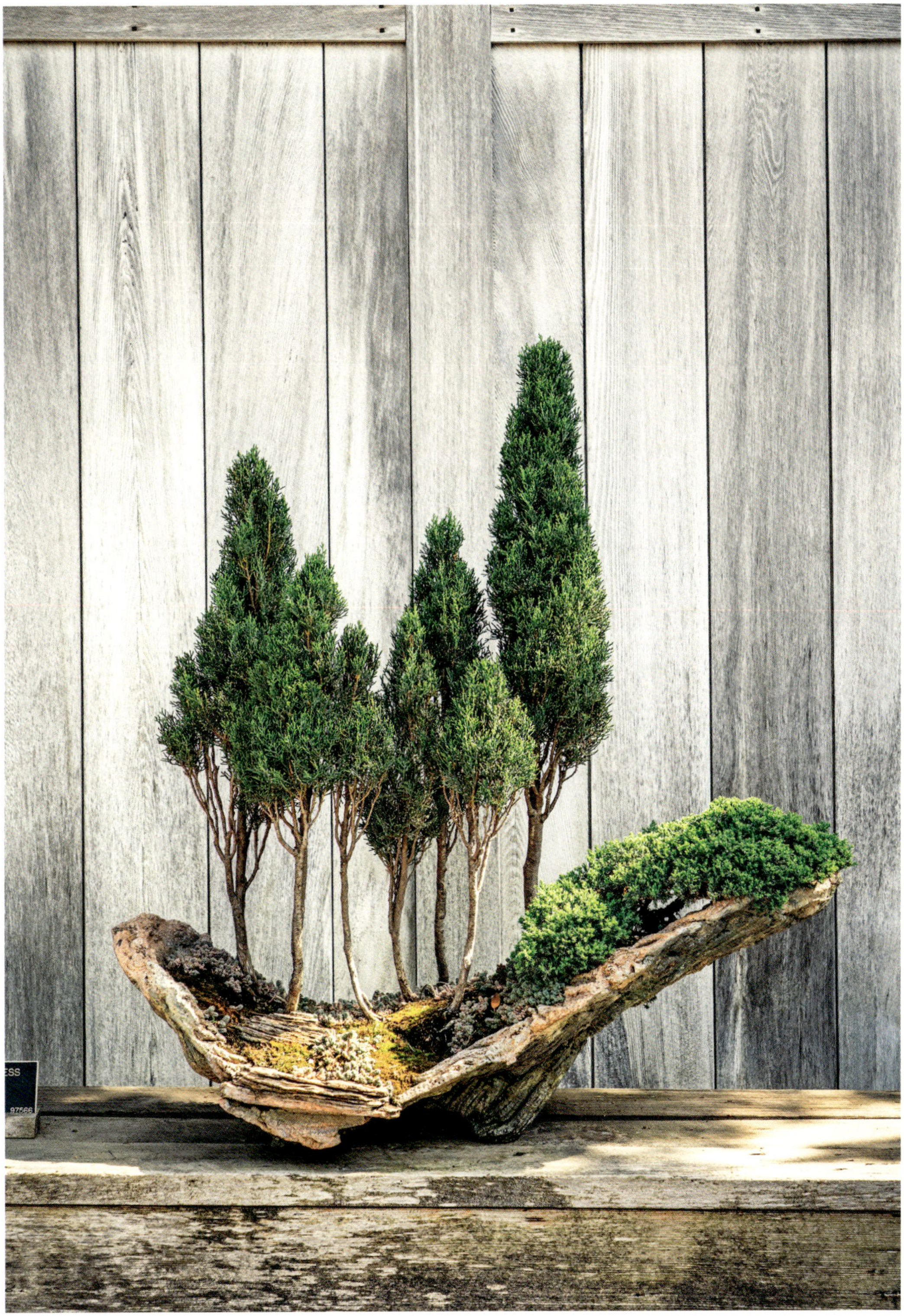

The Huntington's bonsai collection is one of the largest collections of bonsai trees in the US and contains some trees that are over a thousand years old.

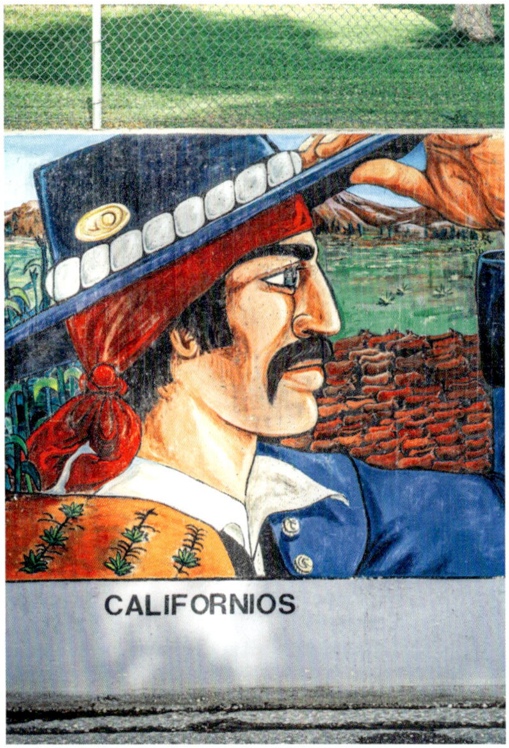

The wall's imagery tells the story of the city's history in a nonlinear fashion, making connections across time and space. Deconstructing the myth of the city's discovery, the mural shows "Californios," the ruling class of early California, dominating the land and exploiting indigenous labor.

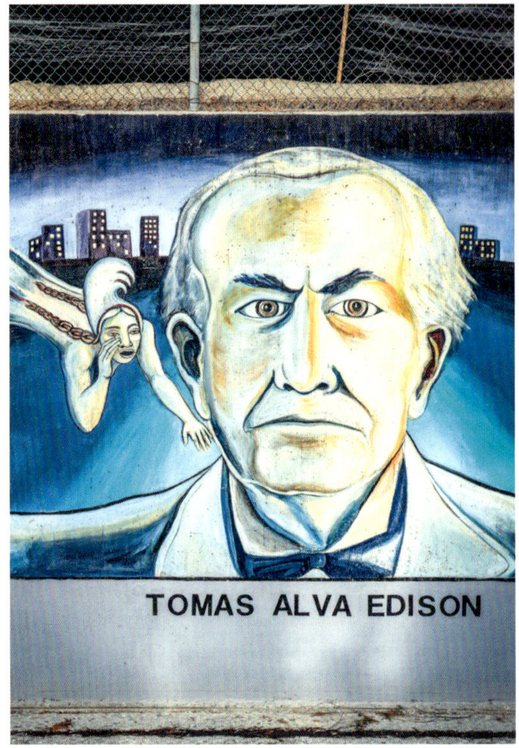

Inventor Thomas Alva Edison, whose inventions gave rise to the birth of cinema and thus LA's film industry, is depicted with Chicomecoatl, the Mexica corn goddess, whispering in his ear—harkening back to a legend that Edison was born in Mexico.

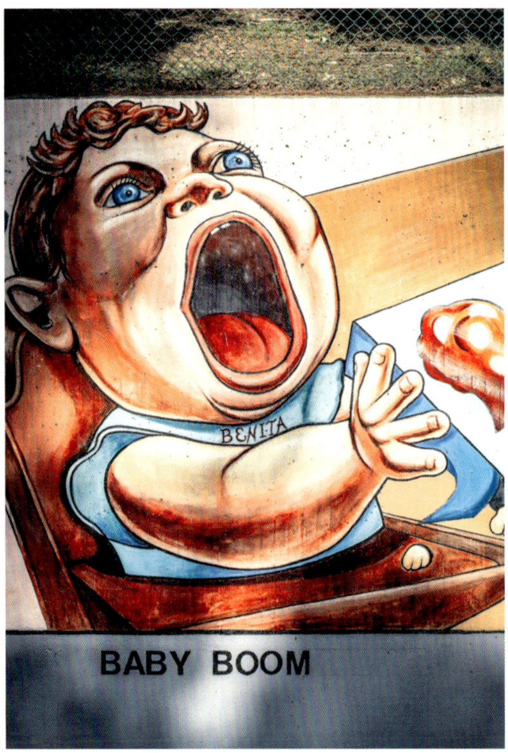

A big, hungry baby symbolizes the post-WWII baby boom and its economic abundance—for some. The name "Benita" means "blessed," and the surrounding scenes make it clear that while white Americans prospered, much of life remained unchanged for people of color. Even those who had fought in the war were still without basic rights.

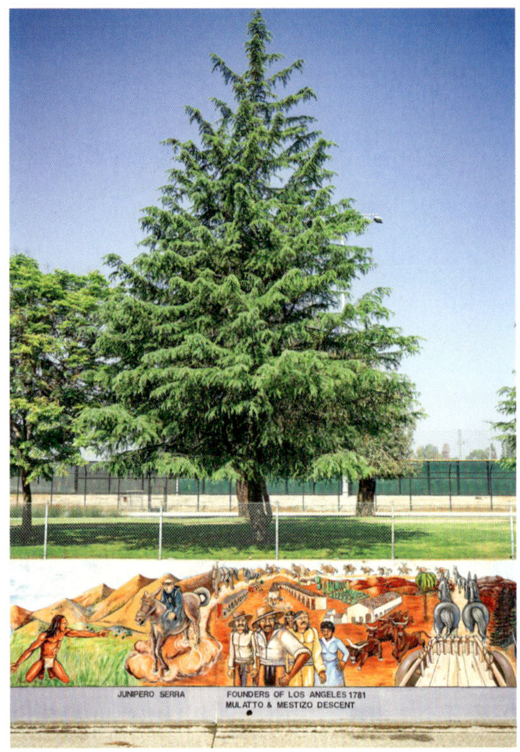

A view from the sidewalk shows the park that surrounds the epic mural.

The Great Wall of Los Angeles

Artist Judy Baca's Ode to the History of California

Conceived of by Los Angeles artist Judith F. Baca, *The Great Wall of Los Angeles* is a half-mile long mural located along the Tujunga Flood Control Channel in the San Fernando Valley. Creating the mural took a decade (1974–1984), and it was made by hundreds of paid participants—local youth and their families—as the first public art project for the nonprofit Social and Public Art Resource Center (SPARC), which Baca founded. Part of a larger park with a fantastic bike path, the mural depicts the history of California through historical figures and events that prioritize the contributions of the state's often overlooked or historically marginalized communities. It's a people's history—created by and for the diverse, working people who shaped the state.

Bob's Big Boy

A Diner Beloved by Car Enthusiasts and David Lynch

LA is blessed by several great Googie coffee shops, and Bob's Big Boy, located in beautiful Burbank, is one of them. Built in 1949, this location is the oldest remaining outpost of the burger chain and serves American diner fare like hamburgers, French fries, and delicious, thick milkshakes. Bob's is a time capsule—like *American Graffiti* come to life.

The most striking feature of Bob's is its dramatic architecture, a sterling example of what became known as Googie or "coffee shop modern." Homegrown in Los Angeles, this mid-century, space-age style was created in response to the area's burgeoning car culture—buildings were designed to lure the passing motorist with dramatic architecture, ample signage, and use of the most modern of building materials. Designed by architect Wayne McAllister, a master of the eye-catching architectural style, Bob's has been officially declared a California State Point of Historical Interest thanks to the Los Angeles Conservancy. It's also allegedly where director David Lynch liked to eat lunch every day at 2:30 p.m. in the early days of his career—ordering the same meal each time: tuna melt, fries, black coffee, and a chocolate milkshake. Some folks say Lynch actually ate at a now-closed location of Bob's on Wilshire Boulevard, but when the director died, his impromptu memorial was here. Fans left offerings at the foot of the Big Boy statue.

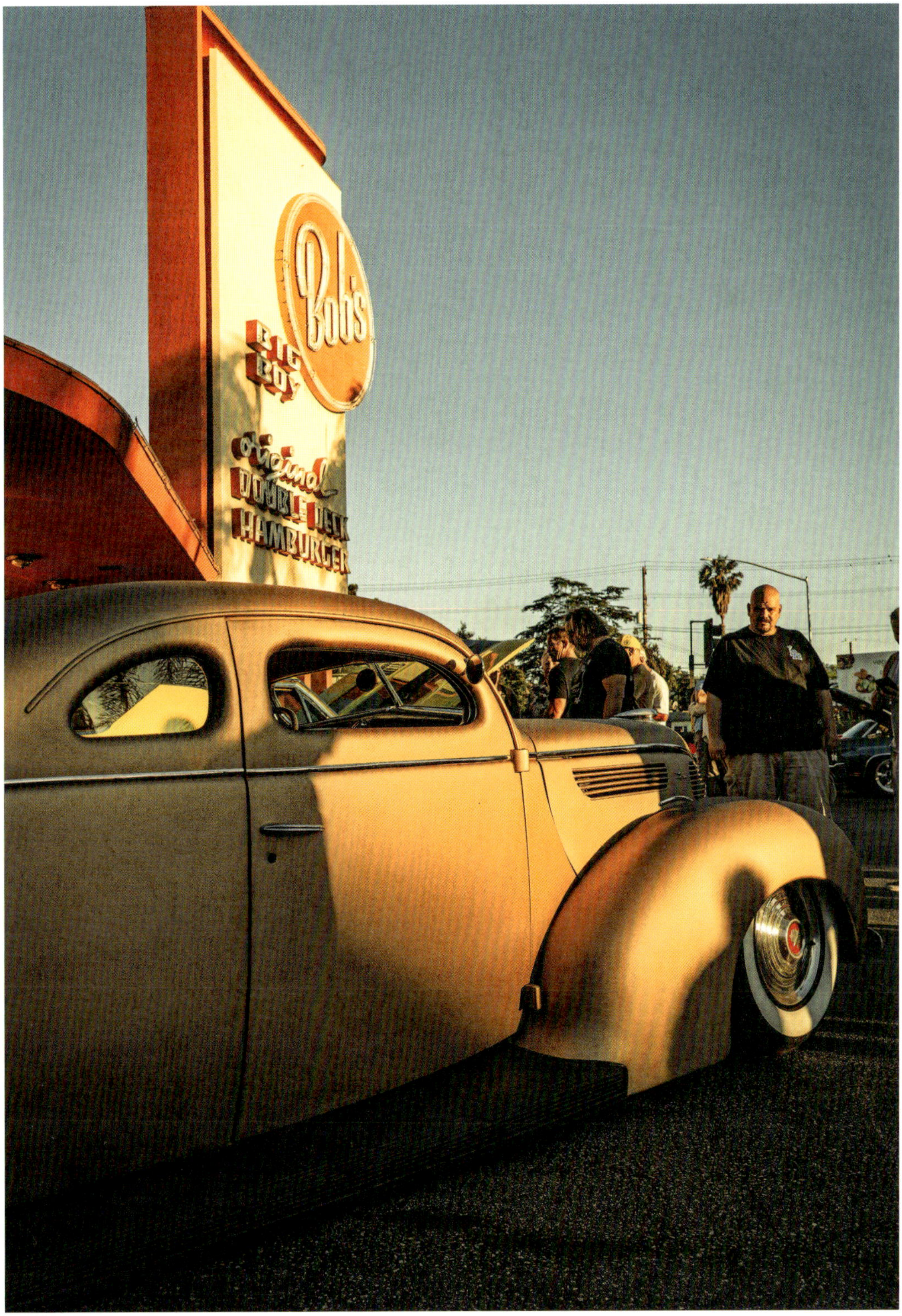

Friday evenings are the best time to go to Bob's—it's when aficionados of classic cars fight for space in the parking lot and raise the hoods for looks inside.

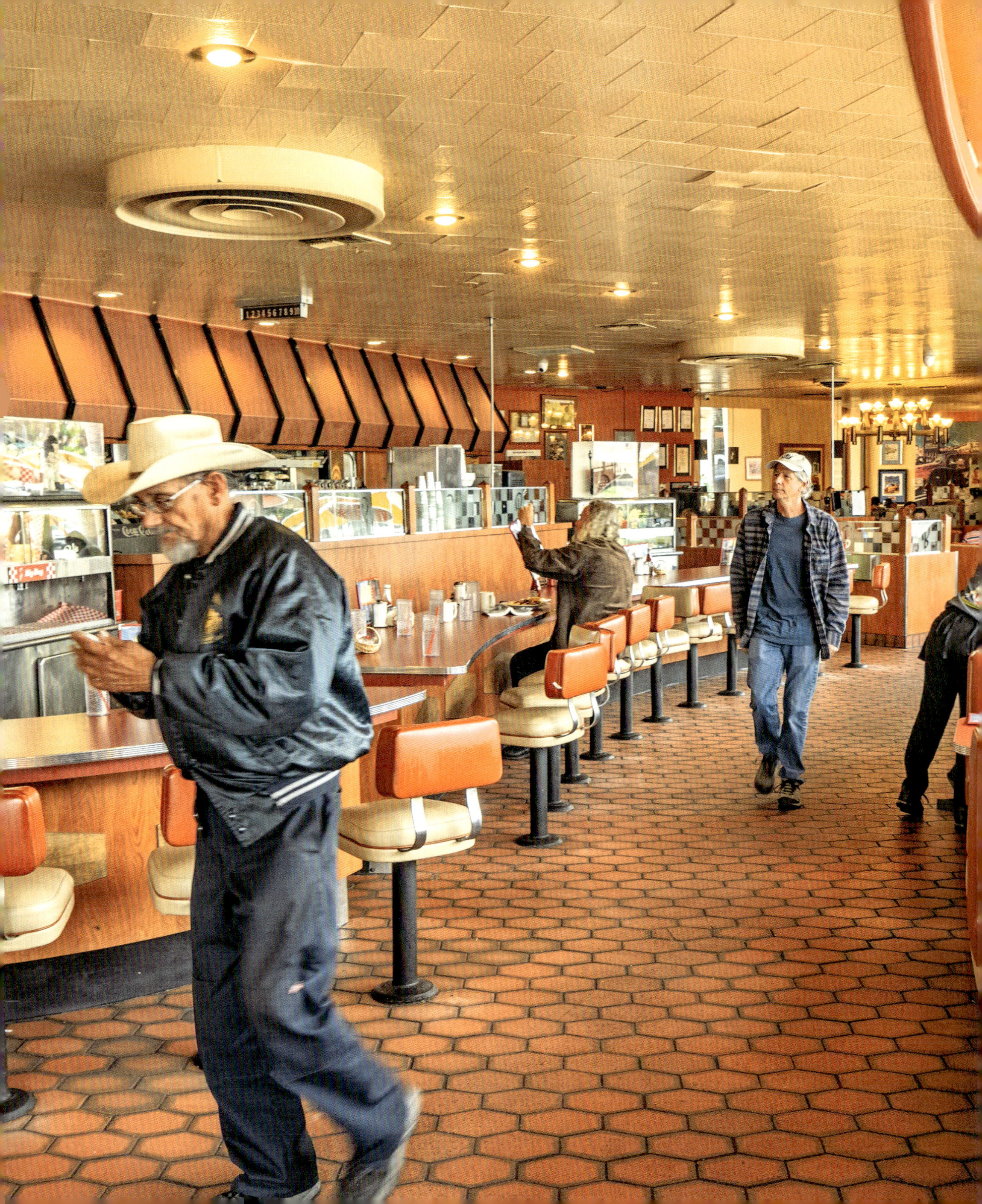

Along with all the regulars, stars dine at Bob's as well—the Beatles ate here in 1965, and people ask to sit in their booth.

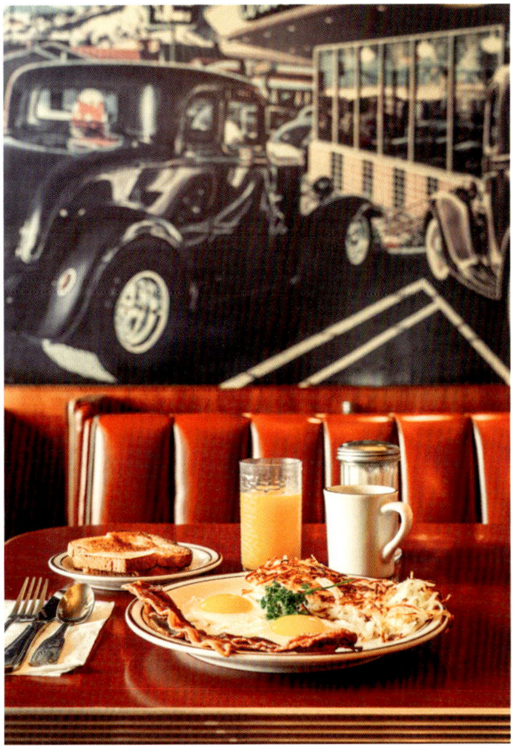

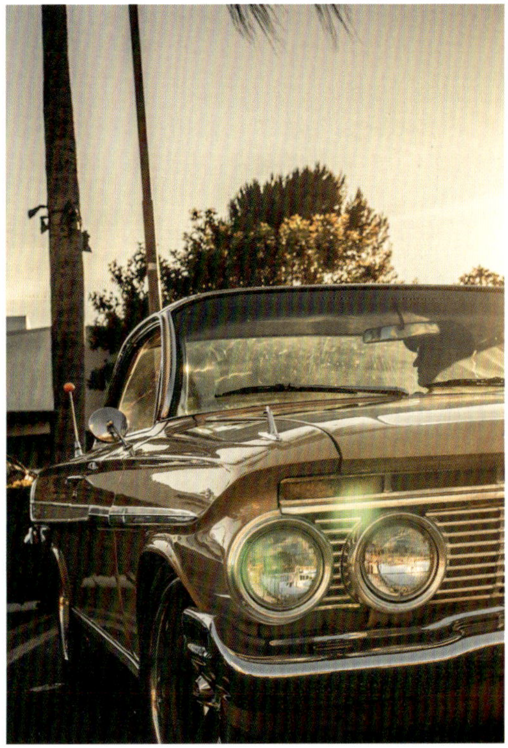

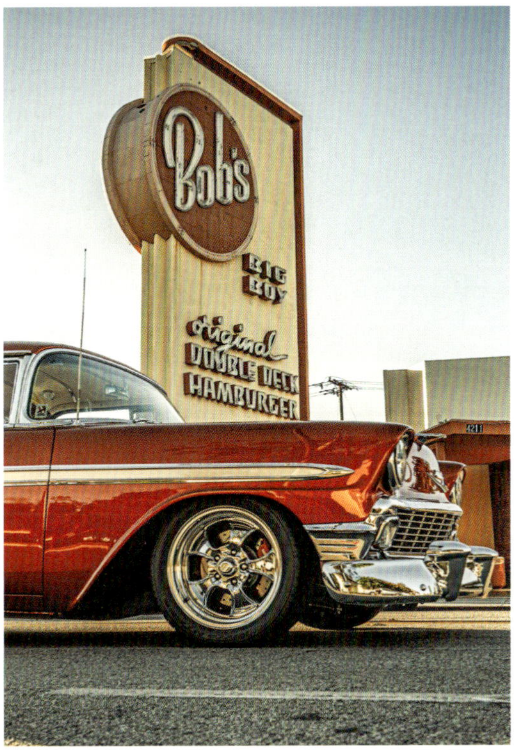

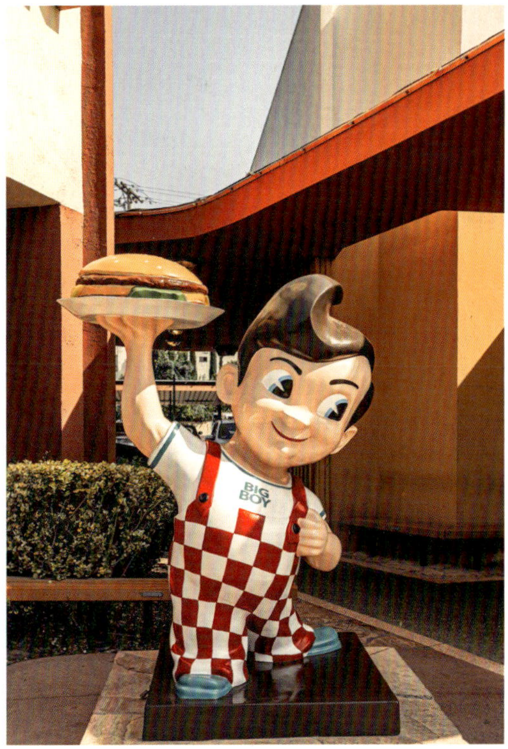

At Bob's, breakfast is served all day, as is the way at a classic American diner.

"Turkey sandwiches or tuna melts ... with Swiss cheese, golden brown French fries, and coffee," Lynch says. "Maybe a piece of cherry pie or blueberry pie for dessert. How does that sound to you?" —director David Lynch in the documentary *Don't Look at Me.*

The neon lights, streamlined architecture, and classic cars take patrons back in time.

The mascot of Bob's is the Big Boy character.

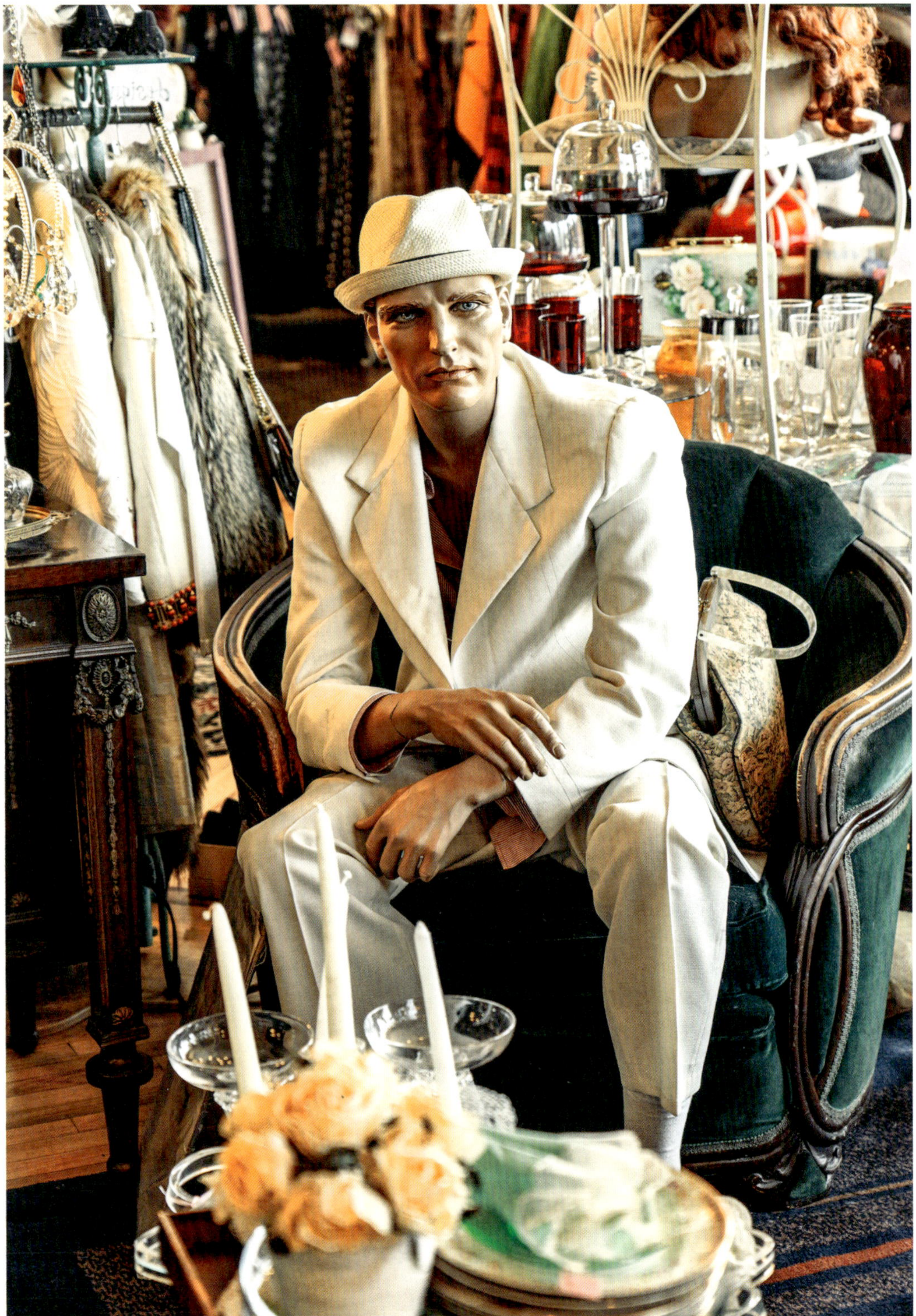

Playclothes, in Burbank, is rated LA's best vintage clothing store by *Los Angeles* magazine.

Playclothes Vintage

Timeless Style for Valley Adventures

Both Pasadena and the San Fernando Valley are known for being excellent places to shop for vintage clothes, from upscale boutiques to thrift stores and flea markets. Pasadena boasts two incredible monthly flea markets, the Rose Bowl Flea Market (the best flea market in the US), held the second Sunday of every month, and the less well-known Pasadena City College Flea Market, held on the first Sunday of the month.

But really, the best place to go for vintage is the San Fernando Valley, which seems to have a great shop on every corner. The best of these is Playclothes, located in Burbank's Antique Row in the Magnolia Park neighborhood. Playclothes is a temple of timeless style, a 4,500-square-foot vintage superstore that includes, as they say, "everything from Grandma's front porch glider to Grandpa's garters!"

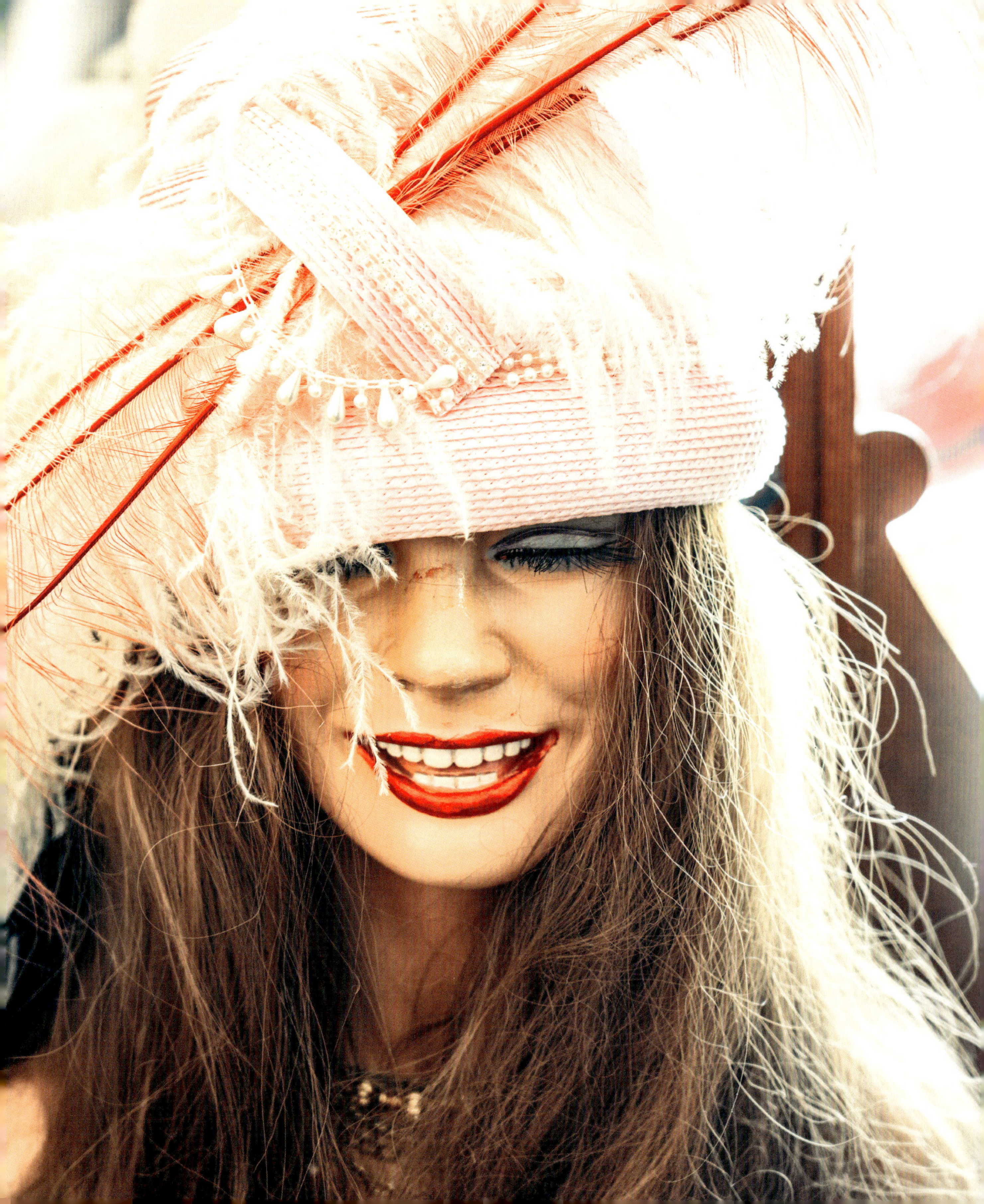

"Hollywood style means classic glamour. My reference is the 1940s through the 1960s." —designer Kelly Wearstler

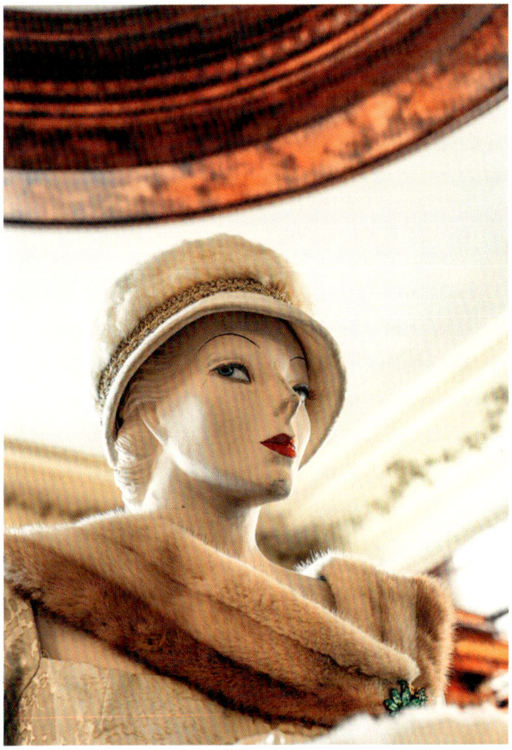

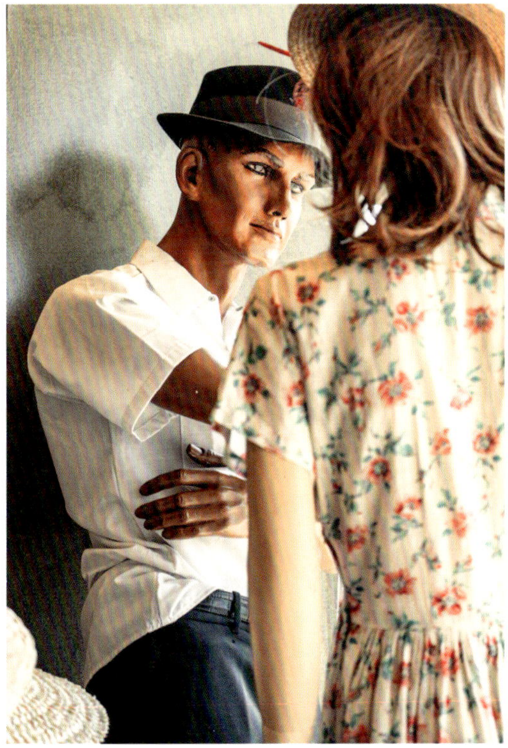

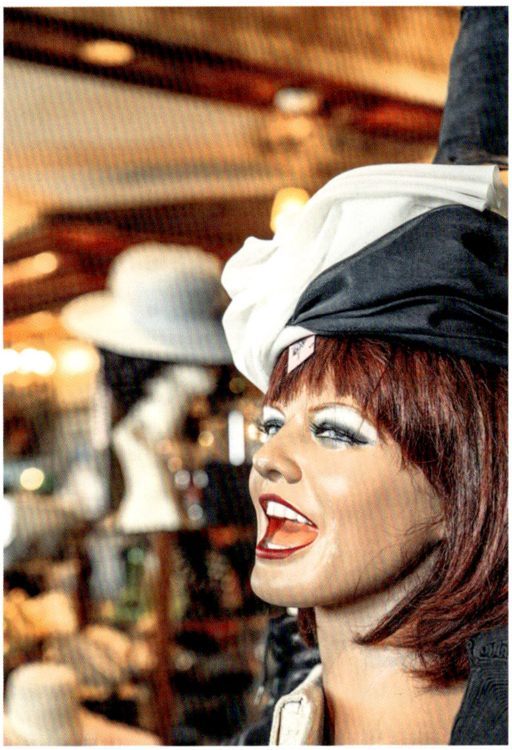

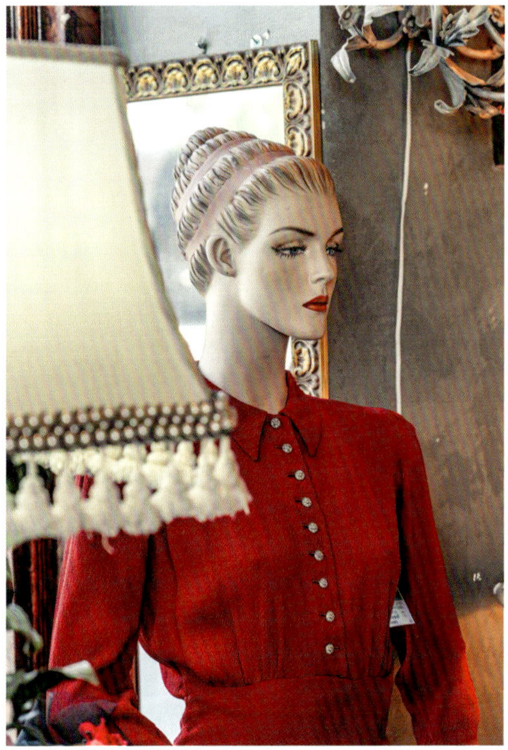

The shop features treasures like 1960s Pucci dresses and Rudi Gernreich pantsuits.

Gamble House

An Arts and Crafts Masterpiece in Pasadena

In the late nineteenth and early twentieth century, Pasadena served as a fashionable resort for wealthy Easterners, who would spend the winter season among the orange groves. Many of the prominent people who came to visit ended up building homes in the area, creating "Millionaire's Row" (Orange Grove Avenue), a street of impressive architectural mansions.
Designed in 1908 by the Pasadena-based firm of Greene & Greene, the Gamble House was the winter residence of David and Mary Gamble, who were part of the family that founded the Procter and Gamble company.
Considered to be the best example of early twentieth-century Craftsman architecture, the Gamble home is largely intact and unaltered from the Greenes' original vision, leading many to call it "the ultimate bungalow." Listed on the National Register of Historic Places, even the original furnishings, designed by the Greenes, remain to be appreciated.

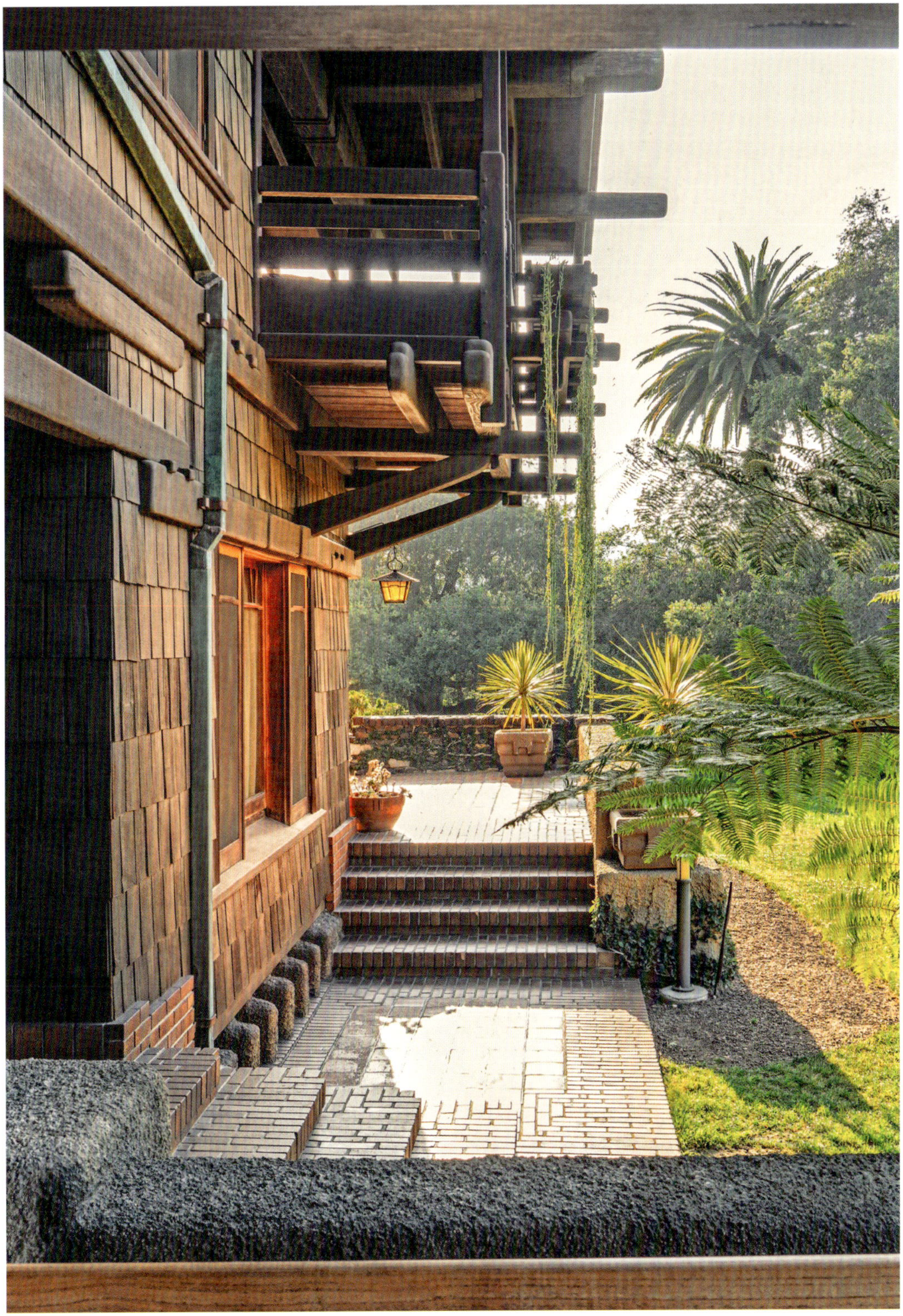

Tours of the Gamble House are available several days a week; check their website for times and dates.

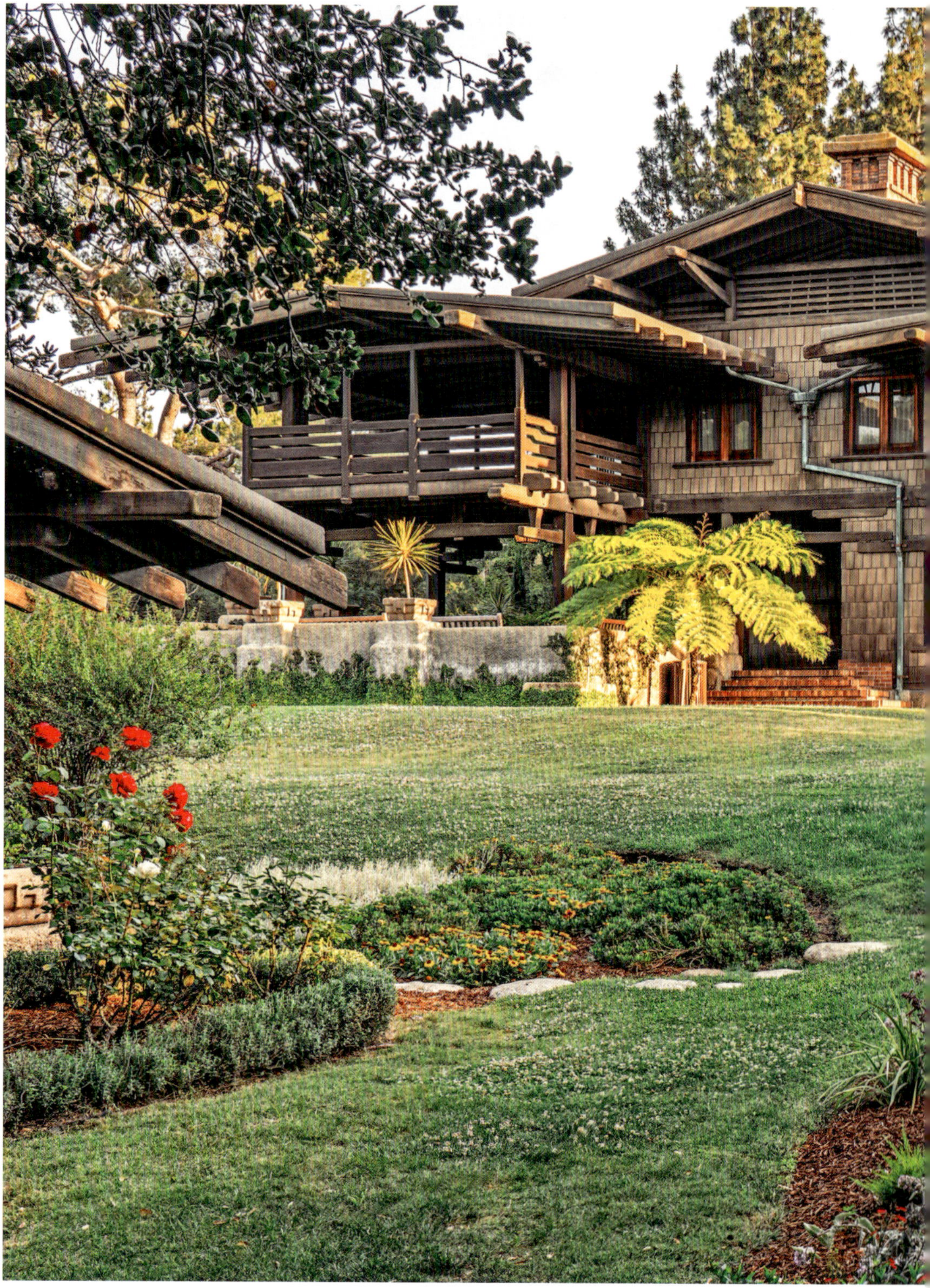

"The style of the house should be as far as possible determined by four conditions: first, climate; second, environment; third, kinds of materials available; fourth, habits and tastes—i.e., life of the owner."
—designer Charles Greene

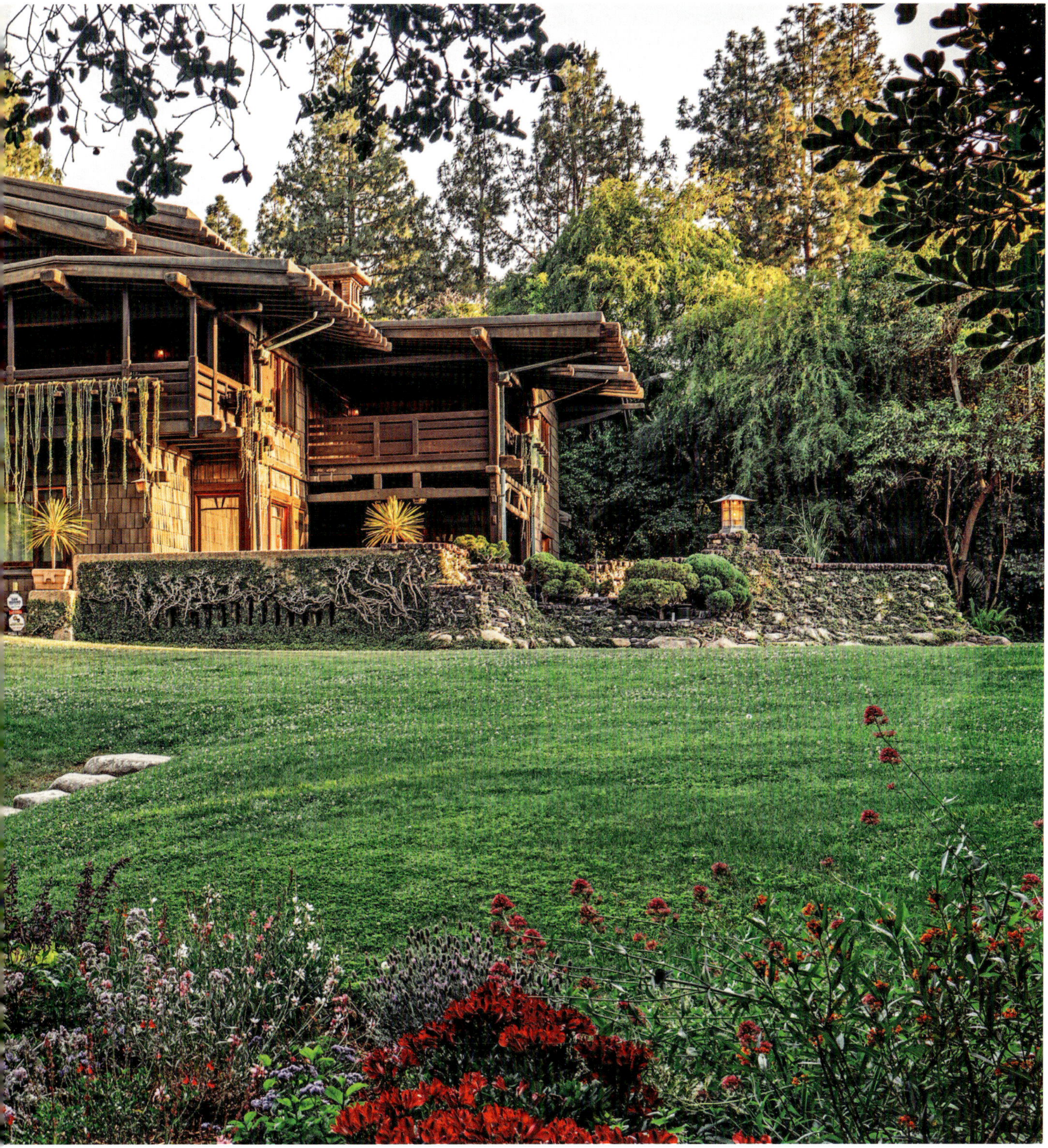

Index

South Los Angeles

The San Fernando Valley and Pasadena

(Page 270–271)
"I do love America. And LA is a very short commute to America—it's like half an hour on the plane."
— comedian Craig Ferguson

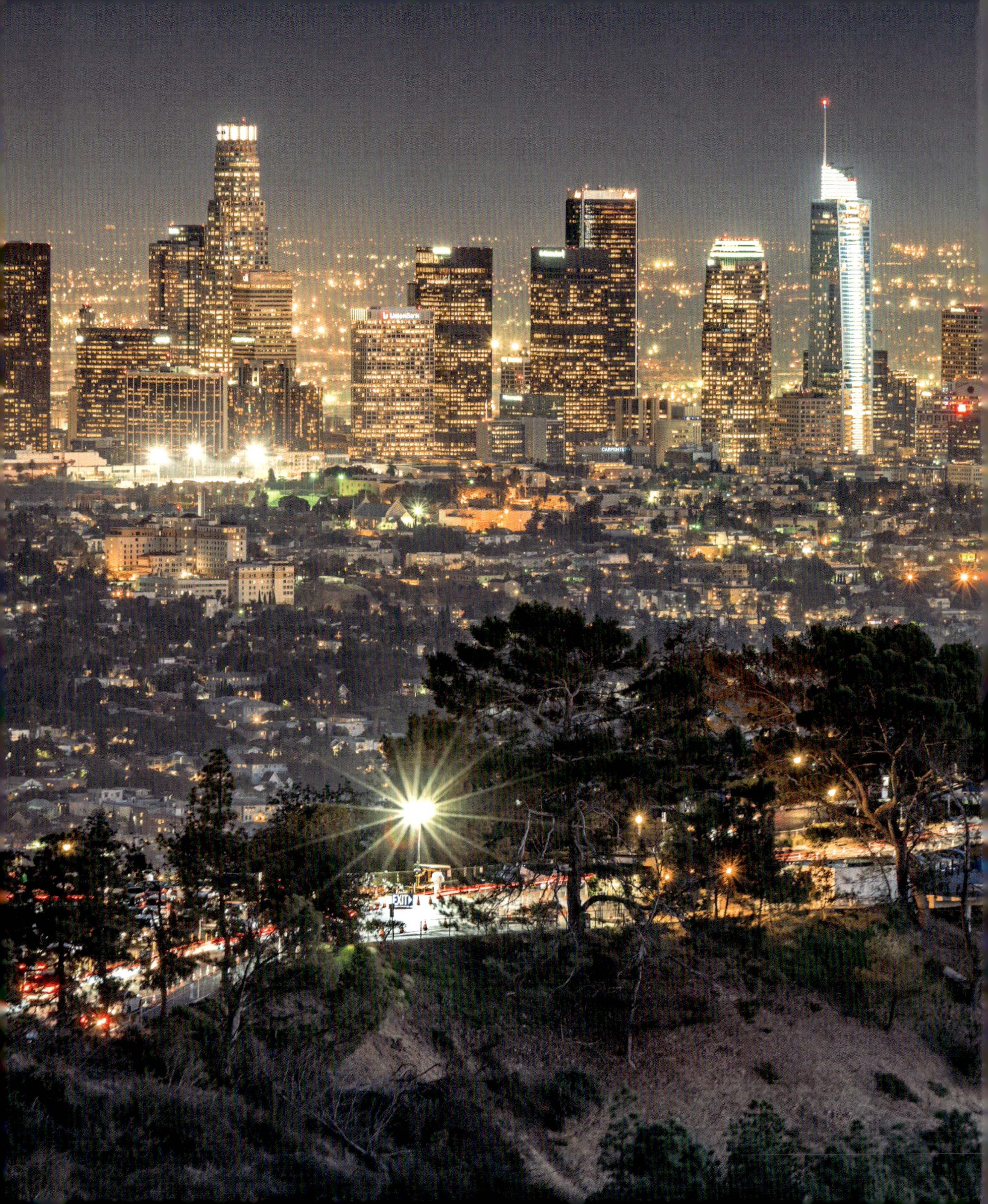
EXIT

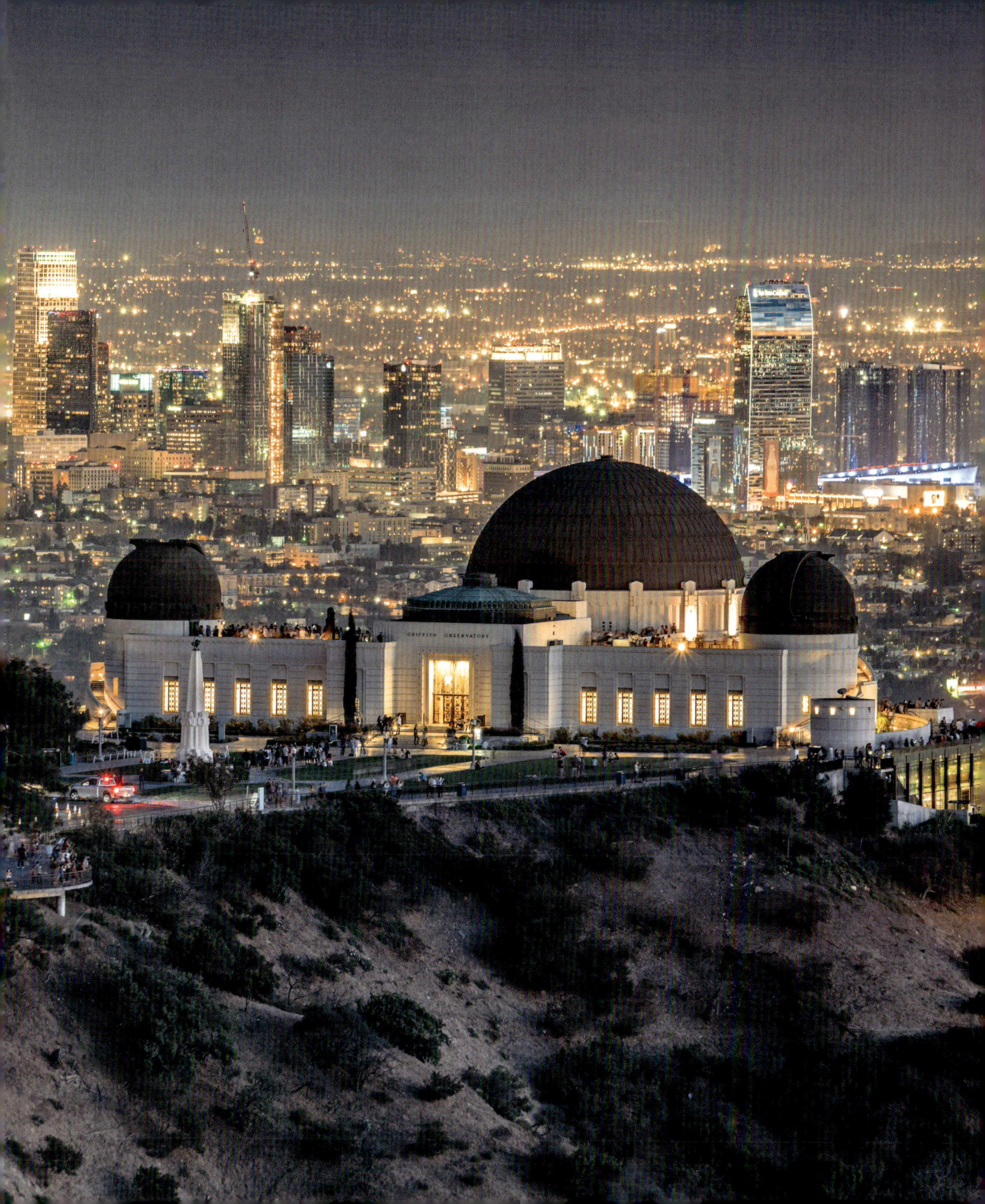
GRIFFITH OBSERVATORY

Original publisher
SIME S.r.l.

Co-published and distributed
in United States and Canada by
SUNSET & VENICE, LLC

Text Andrea Richards
Copy Edits Carlo Irek, Sara DeGonia
Design Italo Meneghini
Alice Tassan-Gurle
Prepress Fabio Mascanzoni
Photographers All images are by Giovanni Simeone, except:
Simon Burch p 2-3
Brook Mitchell p 59
Pietro Canali p 26-27
Andrea Alborno p 29

Most of the photos are available on www.simephoto.com

I Edition 2025
ISBN 978-88-31403-71-9

Distributed in Europe by
SIME BOOKS
www.simebooks.com

Distributed in United States and Canada by SUNSET & VENICE, LLC
www.sunsetandvenice.com

BE